T0334654

AMERICAN CHINESE RESTAURANTS

With case studies from the USA, Canada, Chile, and other countries in Latin America, *American Chinese Restaurants* examines the lived experiences of what it is like to work in a Chinese restaurant.

The book provides ethnographic insights on small family businesses, struggling immigrant parents, and kids working, living, and growing up in an American Chinese restaurant. This is the first book based on personal histories to document and analyze the American Chinese restaurant world. New narratives by various international and American contributors have presented Chinese restaurants as dynamic agencies that raise questions on identity, ethnicity, transnationalism, industrialization, (post) modernity, assimilation, public and civic spheres, and socioeconomic differences.

American Chinese Restaurants will be of interest to general readers, scholars, and college students from undergraduate to graduate level, who wish to know Chinese restaurant life and understand the relationship between food and society.

Jenny Banh is an Assistant Professor at California State University, Fresno in Anthropology and Asian American Studies. She received her BA from UCLA, her MA from Claremont Graduate University, and her PhD from the University of California, Riverside. Her research focuses on Asia/Asian American studies, cultural anthropology, and popular culture. Her current research is on restaurants, barriers/ bridges to minority college students, and a Hong Kong transnational corporation. She has previously published "Barack Obama or B Hussein" (2012) and "DACA Spaces" (2018), and co-edited *Anthropology of Los Angeles: Place and Agency in an Urban Setting* (2017).

Haiming Liu is a Professor of Ethnic and Women Studies at California Polytechnic University, Pomona, and received his doctorate from the University of California, Irvine. He is an expert on Chinese herbalists, food, restaurants, globalization, and migration. He has authored *From Canton Restaurant to Panda Express: A History of Chinese Food in the United States* (2015) and *The Transnational History of a Chinese Family: Immigrant Letters, Family Business* (2005), and numerous journal articles and book chapters on Chinese Americans.

AMERICAN CHINESE RESTAURANTS

Society, Culture and Consumption

Edited by
Jenny Banh and Haiming Liu

Routledge
Taylor & Francis Group
LONDON AND NEW YORK

First published 2020
by Routledge
2 Park Square, Milton Park, Abingdon, Oxon OX14 4RN

and by Routledge
52 Vanderbilt Avenue, New York, NY 10017

Routledge is an imprint of the Taylor & Francis Group, an informa business

British Library Cataloguing-in-Publication Data
A catalogue record for this book is available from the British Library

Library of Congress Cataloging-in-Publication Data
Names: Banh, Jenny, editor. | Liu, Haiming, 1953– editor.
Title: American Chinese restaurants : society, culture and consumption / edited by Jenny Banh
    and Haiming Liu.
Description: Abingdon, Oxon ; New York, NY : Routledge, 2019. | Includes bibliographical
    references and index.
Subjects: LCSH: Chinese restaurants—Social aspects—America. | Cooking, Chinese. |
    Chinese—America—Social life and customs.
Classification: LCC TX945.4 .A64 2019 | DDC 641.5951—dc23
LC record available at https://lccn.loc.gov/2019017390

ISBN: 978-1-138-59986-4 (hbk)
ISBN: 978-0-367-27316-3 (pbk)
ISBN: 978-0-429-48549-7 (ebk)

Typeset in Bembo
by Apex CoVantage, LLC

To my mother Nancy Banh (*née* Ngo) 吳佩珍, father Chuck Banh 彭灼才, sister Christina Banh 彭麗儀 and all global Chinese restaurant families.

CONTENTS

CONTRIBUTORS

E. N. Anderson is Professor of Anthropology, Emeritus, at the University of California, Riverside. He received his PhD in Anthropology from the University of California, Berkeley, in 1967. He has done research on ethnobiology, cultural ecology, political ecology, and medical anthropology, in several areas, especially Hong Kong, British Columbia, California, and the Yucatan Peninsula of Mexico. His books include *The Food of China* (Yale University Press, 1988), *Ecologies of the Heart* (Oxford University Press, 1996), *The Pursuit of Ecotopia* (Praeger, 2010), *Caring for Place* (2014), *Everyone Eats* (2014), *Food and Environment in Early and Medieval China* (2014), and, with Barbara A. Anderson, *Warning Signs of Genocide* (2012). He has five children and five grandchildren. He lives in Riverside, California, with his wife Barbara Anderson and three dogs.

Jenny Banh is an Assistant Professor in Asian American Studies and Anthropology at California State University, Fresno. She received her PhD in Anthropology from the University of California, Riverside, her MA in Cultural Studies from Claremont Graduate University, and her BA in anthropology from UCLA. Her research focuses on Asia/Asian American studies, cultural anthropology, and popular culture. Her current research is on restaurants, barriers/bridges to minority college students, and a Hong Kong transnational corporation. She is the author of *Barack Obama or B Hussien* (2012), *DACA Spaces* (2018), and was selected as the 2016 Concha Delgado Gaitan Council of Anthropology and Education Presidential Fellow. She previously has published in and co-edited *Anthropology of Los Angeles: Place and Agency in an Urban Setting* (Lexington, 2017).

Nicholas Bauch is a Master of Fine Arts candidate in the Department of Art at the University of Minnesota-Twin Cities. He holds a PhD in Geography from the University of California-Los Angeles, where he specialized in cultural and historical geography. He is author of *Enchanting the Desert* (2016, Stanford University Press) and *A Geography of Digestion* (2017, University of California Press). Prior to pursuing an M.F.A. degree, he was founding faculty director of the Experimental Geography Studio at the University of Oklahoma. In 2018 he was artist-in-residence at the Institute of Advanced Uncertainty in San Francisco, where he made a large-scale drawing called *This is Not a Map: Routes to Watering Places in the Mojave Desert*. www.nicholasbauch.com

Carol Chan is a postdoctoral fellow at the Interdisciplinary Program for Migration Studies (Programa Interdisciplinario de Estudios Migratorios/PRIEM), Universidad Alberto Hurtado. Her current research on the multi-nodal mobilities and experiences of the ethnic Chinese population in Santiago de Chile is sponsored by the Chilean National Foundation for Scientific and Technological Development (Fondo Nacional de Desarrollo Científico y Tecnológico/FONDECYT N° 3170051). She earned her PhD in Cultural Anthropology at the University of Pittsburgh, and is author of *In Sickness and in Wealth: Migration, Gendered Morality, and Central Java* (Indiana University Press, 2018).

Yong Chen received his BA from Renmin University of China in 1994 and his PhD in Religion from Vanderbilt University, USA, in 2005. Since 2009 he has been Research Professor at the Center for Asian and African Studies of El Colegio de México. His research focuses on Confucianism as religion and China-Latin America inter-cultural transformations. He has published three books: *Es Confucianismo una Religión* (Spanish), *Confucianism as Religion: Controversies and Consequences* (English), and *Yinni kongjiao 28 tian xingji* (Chinese).

Sidney C.H. Cheung is a Professor of Anthropology at The Chinese University of Hong Kong. He received his doctorate from Osaka University on the study of cultural relations between Ainu people and Japanese. His co-edited books include *Tourism, Anthropology and China* (White Lotus, 2001), *The Globalization of Chinese Food* (RoutledgeCurzon, 2002), *Food and Foodways in Asia: Resource, Tradition and Cooking* (Routledge, 2007), and *Rethinking Asian Food Heritage* (Foundation of Chinese Dietary Culture in Taipei, 2015). He is also General Editor of *Berkshire Encyclopedia of Chinese Cuisines, Vol. I–V* (Berkshire, forthcoming).

Lily Cho is an Associate Professor in the Department of English at York University. Her book, *Eating Chinese: Culture on the Menu in Small Town Canada* (2010), examines the relationship between Chinese restaurants and Canadian culture. Her SSHRC-funded project, *Mass Capture: Chinese Head Tax and the Making of Non-Citizens in Canada*, focusing on Chinese Canadian head tax certificates known as "C.I. 9's," explores the relationship between citizenship, photography, and anticipation as a mode of agency. Her essays on Asian Canadian literature and culture have appeared in *ARIEL, Canadian Literature, Canadian Journal of Law and Society, Citizenship Studies, Interventions, Postmodern Culture*, and *Studies in Canadian Literature*.

Erin M. Curtis is a Los Angeles-based historian and curator. She currently serves as the Senior Curator at LA Plaza de Cultura y Artes in Los Angeles, and has worked for the Skirball Cultural Center and the experience design firm Local Projects. Curtis was also a Smithsonian Institution predoctoral fellow at the National Museum of American History. She holds a PhD in American Studies and an MA in Public Humanities from Brown University. Curtis is the co-author of *¡Murales Rebeldes! L.A. Chicana/o Murals Under Siege* (Angel City Press, 2017) and was published in *Eating Asian America: A Food Studies Reader* (New York University Press, 2013).

Frances Huynh is a second-generation Teochew Chinese American with working-class family roots in Vietnam. She is based in San Gabriel Valley and devotes much of her time to grassroots organizing with the all-volunteer organization Chinatown Community for Equitable Development in Los Angeles Chinatown. Her passions lie in the intersection of Chinese Vietnamese foodways, working-class immigrant communities, anti-capitalist economic models, multimedia storytelling, community health, and urban planning. In 2018, she received her Master of Arts in Asian American Studies and Master of Public Health, in addition to a graduate certificate in Food Studies from University of California, Los Angeles. Her thesis was titled "From the Garden to the Streets: Working-Class Immigrant Foodways as Resistance in a Gentrifying Los Angeles Chinatown."

Samuel C. King is a PhD candidate in the History Department at the University of South Carolina. His research explores the historical relationship between Chinese restaurants and Chinese American immigration, as well as the shifting perception of China and Chinese culture among non-Chinese Americans. His dissertation, "Exclusive Dining: Immigration and Restaurants during the Era of Chinese Exclusion, 1882–1943," focuses on the historical development of Chinese restaurants in Chicago during the Exclusion period as sites of cultural exchange, interaction, and contest between Chinese immigrants and the native society. His research interrogates linkages between American imperialism, Orientalist discourse, and Chinese restaurants, as well as the relationship between restaurant spaces and the sociopolitical status of Chinese American immigrants.

Cheuk Kwan grew up in Singapore, Hong Kong, and Japan. After studying engineering in the United States, he immigrated to Canada in 1976 where he embarked upon a successful career in information technology. In 1978, Kwan co-founded *The Asianadian*, an influential quarterly dedicated to the promotion of Asian Canadian arts, culture, and politics. In 1979, Kwan helped lead a nationwide Anti-W5 Campaign to fight against the racist portrayal of Chinese Canadians in the media that led to the founding of the Chinese Canadian National Council. Kwan's diasporic upbringing and his love of travel, food, and culture inspired him to produce and direct the 15-part *Chinese Restaurants* documentary series.

Jacob R. Levin lives in Maryland and is a graduate student at American University in Washington, DC. He lives with his wife, Alicia Brands, who is an educator and graduate student in education. His previous publications explore the intersections between race, civil rights, religion, and professional sports. His primary research focus is on the relationship between African-Americans and Jewish Americans in Maryland.

Haiming Liu is a Professor of Ethnic and Women Studies at California Polytechnic University, Pomona. He received his doctorate from the University of California, Irvine. He is an expert in China and Chinese American herbalists, food, restaurants, globalization, and migration. He has authored *From Canton Restaurant to Panda Express: A History of Chinese Food in the United States* (Rutgers University Press, 2015) and *The Transnational History of a Chinese Family: Immigrant Letters, Family Business* (Rutgers University Press, 2005).

Anthony Miller is a Visiting Assistant Professor in the Department of Humanities and Creative Studies at Miami University. Dr. Miller teaches courses related to the Cold War and Modern Chinese History. Prior to working for Miami University, he worked for US universities in the People's Republic of China and Japan while continuing his research on the Cold War in East Asia. In 2017, Dr. Miller published the following article: "The Chinese Dream in Peril: Xi Jinping and the Korean Crisis," in *The Diplomat*, the premier international current-affairs magazine for the Asia-Pacific region. Currently, his research explores the historical impact of China on the US Midwest focusing the transnational links formed between the two in the areas of trade, diplomacy, education, immigration, and religion.

Rick Miller researches settlement and urbanization processes in Global South cities. He holds a PhD from UCLA Department of Geography, where he teaches courses in international development and urbanization. Since 2013 he has been a traveling faculty member of the School for International Training program Cities in the 21st Century.

Maria Montt Strabucchi is Assistant Professor at the Pontificia Universidad Católica de Chile, and member of the Asian Studies Center at the same university. She received her doctorate from the University of Manchester, UK in 2017. Her PhD examined the representation of China in contemporary Latin American novels. Her research focuses on China in Latin America, Chinese–Latin American relations, as well as representations of China in contemporary Latin American literature and cultural production.

Karl Orozco is an interdisciplinary artist and educator based in Queens, NY. Orozco uses narrative to challenge assumed notions of race, family, migration, and power. Orozco works to complicate ties between the hospitality industry and the Filipinx diaspora by highlighting quiet acts of home making. Orozco is the 2018

National Artist-in-Residence at the Neon Museum (Las Vegas, NV) where he leads *mahjong* workshops with local community groups and creates sculptures in reference to the museum's collection of neon signage and historical monuments. He has exhibited and taught throughout New York City, as well as Las Vegas, Los Angeles, Denver, and Albuquerque. You may view his portfolio and complete CV at www.karlorozco.com.

Patricia Palma is a postdoctoral fellow and instructor at the Pontificia Universidad Católica de Chile. She received her doctorate in Latin America History from University of California, Davis in 2017. Her research focuses on global health and migration, the influence of Chinese medicine in the Andes, and the Chinese diaspora in Peru and Chile. Her current project examines the Chinese diaspora in Peru and their local and transnational networks between 1900 and 1949.

José Ragas holds a PhD from University of California, Davis (2015). He is an Assistant Professor at the Pontificia Católica Universidad de Chile. Prior to his appointment in Chile, he was a Mellon Postdoctoral Fellow at the Department of Science & Technology Studies at Cornell University and Lecturer in the Program in the History of Science and Medicine at Yale. His research focuses on the circulation and appropriation of technologies in the Global South. Currently, he is studying the ice trade along the Pacific Rim during the transition from the end of the Little Ice Age to the early global warming between 1800 and 1900.

Christopher Sullivan is an Assistant Professor of Sociology at California State University, Fresno. He received his PhD in Sociology and Demography from the University of California, Berkeley in 2013. His research explores ethnicity and inequality in China from quantitative, ethnographic, and visual perspectives. He is also working on a project that examines the development of accountability mechanisms at international financial institutions.

Oliver Wang is a Professor of Sociology at California State University, Long Beach. He is the author of *Legions of Boom: Filipino American Mobile DJ Crews of the San Francisco Bay Area* (Duke, 2015). He writes on arts and culture for NPR, the Los Angeles Review of Books, Kore Asian Media and KCET's Artbound.

David Y. H. Wu, former Chair Professor of Anthropology, Chinese University of Hong Kong, is a long-term Senior Fellow at the East-West Center, Honolulu, and Affiliate Professor of the University of Hawaii. He has for 60 years conducted fieldwork in the South Pacific, Southeast Asia, China, Japan, and Taiwan, on the cultural politics of diaspora of Chinese, ethnic, and national identity among minority peoples, and the globalization of Chinese and Japanese cuisines. His many publications include books on *The Chinese in Papua New Guinea* (1982), *Chinese Culture and Mental Health* (1985), *Preschool in Three Cultures: Japan, China, and the U.S.* (1989), *Where is Home?* (2011), and edited books on *From Beijing to Port Moresby* (1998),

Changing Chinese Foodways in East Asia (2001), *Globalization of Chinese Food* (2002), and *Overseas March: How the Chinese Cuisine Spread?* (2011). He has served as an international Advisor to many journals of anthropology, and is Co-Chief Editor of the *Journal of Archeology and Anthropology*, Taipei.

Hongyan Yang is a PhD candidate in the Architecture in Buildings-Landscapes-Cultures program at the University of Wisconsin-Milwaukee. She holds a BS in Urban and Rural Planning & Resource Management, a BA in English, and an MS degree in Human Geography. Her undergraduate research and overseas studying and living experiences inspired her to look beyond the fundamental role of food to its significance in studying architectural history, ethnic culture, immigration history, and racial dynamics. Her interdisciplinary doctoral studies focus on how culinary practices translate into space, in particular how Asian immigrants' cooking traditions and cultural sensibilities invest new meanings to the built environments and cultural landscapes in the United States. She is the author of the chapter "Cooking in the Hmong Cultural Kitchen" in the *Routledge Handbook of Food in Asia* (2018).

FOREWORD

Sidney C.H. Cheung

I was honored to be asked by Jenny Banh and Liu Haiming to write the Foreword for their new book about Chinese restaurants in the Americas even though I have not visited enough to give reflections on this topic. Having said that, I co-edited a book on Chinese food in Asian countries drawing people's attention to how Chinese restaurants reflect the interactions between Chinese migrants and the host communities; in particular, we wanted to emphasize that Chinese cuisine is culturally constructed in various Asian countries in many different ways.[1] The project started in 1995 as part of a four-member research team in Hong Kong, and examined the relationship of culinary tradition, dietary rules, and consumption trends to the city's cultural identity in the years leading up to the handover in 1997, which made my food journey continue. Recently, several books on Chinese restaurants in North America have further revised our long-held understanding of Chinese restaurants in the context of diaspora and taken us to investigate it from the perspectives of multi-ethnic relations and global migrations,[2] and with no doubt, there are still many perspectives to the investigation of Chinese restaurants. In particular, this book is split into personal reflections, histories, interviews, and visual analysis, which in fact inspires me in many ways.

Here, I would like to share some personal experiences of eating at Japanese Chinese restaurants since the 1980s. Growing up in Hong Kong with Cantonese parents, Cantonese food was served at home most of the time, and it is quite common for most Hong Kong people to have traditional "simple" Cantonese food at home with some experiences of non-Cantonese regional cuisines through eating out. I went to Japan in 1984 when Japanese food was not widely known in Hong Kong, and probably the two most famous Japanese foods were *sushi-go-round* and *teppanyaki*, which were mentioned in a popular comedy movie in which the specific skills of a *teppanyaki* chef were turned into the farcical actions of a local chef directed and played by a famous comedian—Michael Hui. On the contrary, Chinese cuisine, as well as *chuka ryori* (中華料理) in Japan, was a bit boring compared with the unlimited colorful moving sushi and the lively (cowboy style) cooking shown in *teppanyaki*, especially since most of those Chinese restaurants did not have much choice on their menus. Fried rice, dumplings, stirred fried vegetables with meats, and ramen were probably the four major kind of dishes I found in most of the small Chinese restaurants all over Japan. Until, that is, I got the chance to visit some upscale types of Chinese restaurants where they served banquet food with dishes from various origins, such as Sichuan spicy tofu, Cantonese dim sum, Tianjin omelette, Shanghai dumplings, sweet and sour pork, chili shrimp, Beijing roasted duck, Yangzhou fried rice, almond tofu dissert, etc. For me, that was definitely a hybrid Chinese meal set; I realized that each dish was a well-known as well as a representative dish in that regional cuisine, but the way of having all of them together as Chinese cuisine was something I had never encountered before going to Japan.

Again, in the 1980s, the "China boom" in Japan made Chinatowns in Yokohama and Kobe popular tourist destinations among Japanese; with the tremendous increase in the numbers of Japanese working and traveling abroad for business and tourism came the idea of internationalization infiltrating into individual lifestyles and diets. Being able to appreciate foreign cuisine gave a person the reputation of being an international citizen. Nevertheless, the popularization of the distinctive and exotic Cantonese dim sum, starting from Yokohama Chinatown, serves as a good example of changing tastes and social values in the search for delicacies among Japanese consumers;[3] furthermore, in the 1990s, the influx of Chinese immigrants changed the food which used to be Cantonese-oriented to a wide range of variety of local cuisines from different parts of mainland China, such as Sichuan, Huaiyang, Northeastern, etc. Therefore, the changing dishes in Japanese Chinese restaurants reflected not only the patterns of Chinese migrants going to Japan, but also how and what Japanese might learn about China through eating different kinds of Chinese food. Coming back to this exciting volume, I can see there are far more varieties in terms of regional migrants and their foodways, together with how they made use of food to get themselves settled in the Americas, and I am sure the efforts of Jenny Banh and Liu Haiming will definitely broaden the horizon on the studies of Chinese diaspora and global migrations.

Notes

1 Wu, David and Sidney Cheung eds. (2002) *The Globalization of Chinese Food*, Surrey: Curzon Press, and Honolulu: University of Hawaii Press.
2 Cho, Lily (2010) *Eating Chinese: Culture on the Menu in Small Town Canada*. Toronto: University of Toronto Press; Liu, Haiming (2015) *From Canton Restaurant to Panda Express: A History of Chinese Food in the United States*. New Brunswick, New Jersey: Rutgers University Press; and Arnold, Bruce Makoto, Tanfer Emin Tunç, and Raymond Douglas Chong eds. (2018) *Choy Suey and Sushi from Sea to Shining Sea: Chinese and Japanese Restaurants in the United States*. Favetteville: The University of Arkansas Press.
3 Cheung, Sidney C. H. (2002) The Invention of Delicacy: Cantonese Food in Yokohama Chinatown. In *The Globalization of Chinese Food*, David Wu and Sidney Cheung eds. Surrey: RoutledgeCurzon Press, and Honolulu: University of Hawaii Press, pp. 170–182.

ACKNOWLEDGMENTS

Jenny Banh

First, I would like to thank my esteemed co-editor Haiming Liu who agreed to go on this food journey with me. The seed of this book was from my upbringing as a Chinese Restaurant kid and I just thought there are so many "hidden stories" of Chinese Restaurants that need to be told. So, I did an international call out and I am so grateful to each and every one of these chapter contributors who answered the call. It was like a Wong Kar Wai movie at times, getting these contributors involved. I would especially like to thank my extended family: Sharon Banh, Alex Pang, Louis Duong, and Sara Duong. Gene Anderson and Sidney Cheung were also so generous to agree to write the Afterword and Foreword. Ruth Anderson, Faye Leerink, Sarah Webb, and Egle Zigaite are wonderful Routledge editors who were very professional. I would to thank my research assistants: Madeline De Leon, Yunang Thao, Mai Julie Her, Kaylee Hinds, and *especially* Sanjay Soundarajan. I would like to thank my California State University Fresno State Anthropology colleagues, especially the faculty and staff from Anthropology and Asian American Studies. I would like to thank Christina Owens, Genevieve Beenen, and Dean Michelle Denbeste for their academic support. I would like to thank the National Center for Faculty Diversity, which enabled me to meet my supportive academic fellowship of assistant professors: Taneisha Means, Michael Bennett McNulty, and Kevin Jones. I could not survive as a person without my girlfriends, whom I met in 8th grade (Jennifer Chang, Lia Guntle), UCLA (Kim Tran, Ly Phan, Judy Liu, Ruby Chen), CGU (Herbert Ruffin II), and UCR (Sandra Xochipiltecatl, Silvia Ventura Luna, Jelena Radovic, Holly Okonkwo, Danessa Murdock, and Melissa King), and Chaffey (Allison Tripp). Thank you to Sean Slusser, Maxwell Slusser-Banh, and Alexandra Slusser-Banh for putting up with my writing deadlines. I want to thank my parents, Chuck and Nancy Banh (Pang), and sister Christina Banh (and brother-in-law David Yu), who came here are as Chinese diaspora from Vietnam and fought hard to make a new life for us. Lastly, I want to thank all Chinese restaurant families around the world.

INTRODUCTION

Jenny Banh and Haiming Liu

Dis-moi ce que tu manges, je te dirai ce que tu es, or, Tell me what you eat, and I will tell you what you are, Anthelme Brillat-Savarin wrote, in *Physiologie du Gout*, 1826.[1]

Jennifer 8. Lee asserts, "There are more Chinese restaurants in the United States than McDonald's, Burger King, Kentucky Fried Chicken and Wendy, combined,"[2] now around 50,000.[3]

Today's renewed interest in American Chinese restaurants and food has become apparent, as seen in two recent museum exhibits in New York City, designed specifically to explore "the impact of Chinese food on America's collective culinary culture, as well as its influence on the generations of Chinese Americans who have introduced, developed and served it up since the mid-19th century."[4] The Museum of Chinese in America's exhibition "Sour, Sweet, Bitter, Spicy" depicts 33 chef stories and 18 regional Chinese cuisines and how they intertwine with Chinese American life. The Museum of Food and Drink (MOFAD) exhibition, with the catchy title "CHOW," offers an interactive history of the poor treatment Chinese immigrants received upon their arrival to America and how they turned to opening restaurants for survival, which, in turn, has transformed American life.

Scholarly publications on Chinese food and restaurants in America has also been steadily growing. Andrew Coe's *Chop Suey*[5] is a fascinating historical narrative on the relationship between China and the United States and how Western perceptions of Chinese culture shaped the recipes for Chinese food in America. Yong Chen's *Chop Suey, USA*[6] provided an in-depth discussion on how chop suey became a popular food in America. He argued that Chinese restaurant operators actually created the concept of the open kitchen and home delivery service. They were pioneers in the American fast food business. Robert Ku's *Dubious Gastronomy*[7] pointed out that many Americans still viewed American Chinese food as exotic and foreign despite its long history in America. Haiming Liu's book, *From Canton Restaurant to Panda Express: A History of Chinese Food in the United States*,[8] illustrated how food and restaurant operations were an important part of Chinese American history. *American Chinese Restaurants: Society, Culture and Consumption* adds more hidden stories and facts about Chinese food and restaurant history. Different from the existing publications, this anthology covers Chinese restaurant operation not only in the United States but also in countries like Argentina, Mexico, Canada, Peru, and Chile. It presents Chinese food as a diaspora and global food.

Complementary Food Volumes

China is the cultural home of all Chinese restaurants overseas. There are other food volumes on Chinese culinary traditions discussing classic histories of Chinese food such as E. N. Anderson's *The Food of China*,[9] Thomas Höllmann's *The Land of the Five Flavors*,[10] and Hsiang Ju Lin's *Slippery Noodles: A Culinary History of China*.[11] This edited volume shares some similarity to *Eating Asian America* by Robert Ku and Martin Manalansan[12] in that we would like to highlight social and historical inequalities in American Chinese restaurants. Three Chinese food histories of note are *From Canton Restaurant to Panda Express* by Haiming Liu,[13] *Chop Suey, USA* by Yong Chen[14] and *Chop Suey: A Cultural History of Chinese Food in the United States* by Andrew Coe.[15] Andrew Coe and Yong Chen present fascinating stories of the interactions between China and the United States and how they shaped our food. Internationally focused volumes are *The Globalization of Chinese Food* by David Wu and Sidney Cheung.[16] Hidden gems like *Sweet and Sour: Life in Chinese Family Restaurants* by John Jung present a historical look at Chinese restaurants in the United States and served as an inspiration for this volume.[17]

Jennifer 8. Lee's *The Fortune Cookie Chronicles: Adventures in the World of Chinese Food*[18] was a best seller about the American made Fortune Cookie. There are interesting books about Asian foodways in general, such as *Chopsticks* by Edward Wang,[19] *Dubious Gastronomy: The Cultural Politics of Eating Asian in the USA* by Robert Ji-Song Ku,[20] and *Eating Asian American* edited by Robert Ji-Song Ku and Anita Mannur.[21] There are books that look at noodles, such as *Noodle Narratives: The Global Rise of an Industrial Food into the Twenty-First Century*,[22] George Solt's *The Untold History of Ramen*,[23] and Barak Kushner's *Slurp! A Social and Culinary History of Ramen*.[24] *American Chinese Restaurants: Society, Culture and Consumption* is anthropologically, historically, and sociologically oriented.

There are many academic writings about Chinese American restaurants, in the form of journal articles, chapters in thematic volumes as listed above, and singular books. However, none of them has put the spatial, labor, and personal narratives at the forefront. In this volume, we have not just a history of American Chinese restaurants but a diverse narrative collection of essays that highlight what goes on inside, out the front, and behind the restaurant. Our edited volume looks behind the Chinese American restaurant wok, with a thematic focus on social analysis, culinary histories, person-centered narratives, comics, and visual analysis.

Description of the Book

American Chinese Restaurants: Society, Culture and Consumption is intended to be consumed by everyone! It attempts to contribute to the literature of Asian, Asian American, Americas, Anthropology, and Food Studies. American Chinese restaurants from regional areas such as the Midwest, East and West coasts of the United States; and other "Americas" will be explored in new pieces focused on Mexico, Argentina, Canada, Peru, and Chile.

Many undergraduate and graduate classes will find this a helpful addition to their literary resources. Scholars in various fields (from Food Science, Anthropology, History, Americas, Asia, Asian American, Sociology to Ethnic Studies) will find useful information about *American Chinese Restaurants: Society, Culture and Consumption* in relation to theoretical concerns of the urban, visual, personal, and political. Theoretically, this book aims to draw on a social scientific tradition that recognizes urban spaces in relation to industrialization, (post)modernity, assimilation, public and civic spheres, particular paradigms of visuality, and the immediacy of vast socioeconomic differences. It also seeks to incorporate views that attend to contemporary experiences and discourses related to globalization and visual studies, as well as to personal narratives and interviews. *American Chinese Restaurants: Society, Culture and Consumption* hopes to present a snapshot of various authors' individual insights, analytical styles, urbanization, place-making, racial formation, or other relevant topics of expertise in order to address American Chinese restaurants as a diverse site.

Chapter Overview

This edited volume is divided into five parts: I. Social Analysis; II. Culinary Histories; III. Person-Centered Narratives; IV. Comics; and V. Visual Analysis. Part I has Carol Chan and Maria Montt Strabucchi addressing the topic of "Creating and Negotiating 'Chineseness' through Chinese Restaurants in Santiago, Chile" and is about how national identity is created through food.

Patricia Palma and José Ragas, in "Feeding Prejudices: Chinese *Fondas* and the Culinary Making of National Identity in Peru" show how Chinese restaurants were linked to prejudices and the national identity in Peru. Erin Curtis's, "Selling Donuts in the Fragmented Metropolis: Chinese Cambodian Donut Shops in Los Angeles and the Practices of Chinese Restaurants" and Francis Huynh's "From Chinese Donuts to Leek Cakes: Navigating Los Angeles Chinatown's Golden Waters" use Los Angeles as their backdrop. They both analyze Southeast Asian diasporic Chinese donut and restaurateurs' practices and how they navigate through difficult economic constraints. Anthony Miller's "Talk Doesn't Cook Rice: Chinese Restaurants and the Chinese (American) Dream in Ohio" adds to the conversation by observing older generations of Chinese American restaurants in Ohio that are facing interethnic competition from newer generations of newly arrived Mainland Chinese restaurateurs.

Part II is about culinary histories such as Yong Chen's "Surveying the Genealogy of Chinese Restaurant in Mexico: From High-End Franchises to Makeshift Stands," which looks at the four primary genres of Chinese Restaurants in Mexico. He reveals that a lot of the new restaurants are being opened by returned Mexican migrants who previously worked in Asian eateries in the United States. David Wu's "Under the Banner of Northern Chinese Cuisine: Invention of the Pan-China Cuisine in American Chinese Restaurants" traces the development of Pan-China Cuisine. Haiming Liu's "Chop Suey, P.F. Chang's, and Chinese Food History in America" adds to Chinese food history in America by illuminating the origins of the dining establishment, P.F. Chang's. Samuel King's "Oriental Palaces: Chin F. Foin and Chinese Fine Dining in Exclusion-Era Chicago" is a culinary history of a famous Chinese restaurateur and food establishment. Oliver Wang's "Live at the China Royal: A Funky Ode to Fall River's Chow Mein Sandwich" reveals where his three passions overlap: Asian American studies, music, and food. It is an in-depth look at the regional specific Chow Mein Sandwich in Fall Rivers, Massachusetts.

Part III presents person-centered narratives such as Jacob R. Levin's "Chinese Restaurants and Jewish American Culture," an endearing look at how his Jewish family and other Jewish Americans interact generationally with Chinese food. Cheuk Kwan's "Last Tango in Argentina" is another first-person magical narrative of Kwan's global Chinese restaurant trek landing him this time in Argentina.[25] He considers the history and familial life of one Chinese restaurateur, Foo-Ching Chiang. The last chapters in this Part consist of a discussion with members of my Chinese restaurant family, "Chinese Restaurant Kids Speak about Labor, Lifeways, and Legacies," and interviews with chefs Martin Yan and Ming Tsai in "Chinese American Chef Ming Tsai," and "Culinary Ambassador Chef Martin Yan Speaks."

Part IV, Comics, is a sequence of images in a panel that has a plot inside a Chinese restaurant of getting the "winning" number. "Prologue: What Number Did We Get?" is written by Isha Aran and illustrated by Karl Orozco. "#372 and #1 A Winning Combo" is written by Isha Aran, Daniel Tam-Claiborne, Sophia Park, and Julian Tucker, and illustrated by Karl Orozco and Sophia Park. "#249 Dim Sum Drama" is written and illustrated by Isha Aran. "#818 First in Our Hearts" is written and illustrated by Amelea Kim.

Part V includes visual analyses. Nicholas Bauch and Rick Miller's "A Visual Habitat Study for Chinese Restaurants in a California Conurbation" looks at the surrounding areas around the Chinese food mecca San Gabriel Valley, CA. Christopher Sullivan's "Redefining and Challenging the Boundaries of Chinese Cuisine: A Visually Based Exploration of Uyghur Restaurants in the United States" is historically one of the first pieces to visually analyze Chinese ethnic Uyghur restaurants in the United States. Lily Cho's "Diasporic Counterpublics: The Chinese Restaurant as Institution and Installation in Canada" examines a Canadian

Chinese restaurant exhibition in Canada. The last chapter, Hongyan Yang's "Toy's Chinese Restaurants: Exploring the Political Dimension of Race through the Built Environment," is a historical and pictorial analysis of Toy's restaurant in Milwaukee, Wisconsin. The chapters are bracketed with a Foreword and an Afterword by Chinese scholar powerhouses Sidney Cheung and E. N. Anderson, respectively.

Notes

1 Savarin, Brillat. 2008 [1825]. *Physiologie du goût*. Fairford: Echo Library.
2 Lee, Jennifer 8. 2008. *The Fortune Cookie Chronicles: Adventures in the World of Chinese Food*. New York: Twelve. See: Jennifer 8 Lee Tedtalk. www.ted.com/talks/jennifer_8_lee_looks_for_general_tso
3 See Ferdman, Roberto and Christopher Ingraham. We analyzed the names of almost every Chinese restaurant in America. This is what we learned. *Washington Post*. April 8, 2016. www.washingtonpost.com/news/wonk/wp/2016/04/08/we-analyzed-the-names-of-almost-every-chinese-restaurant-in-america-this-is-what-we-learned/
4 See www.nbcnews.com/news/asian-america/new-york-city-exhibits-explore-chinese-american-experience-culture-through-n696061
5 Coe, Andrew. 2009. *Chop Suey: A Cultural History of Chinese Food in the United States*. New York: Oxford University Press.
6 Chen, Yong. 2014. *Chop Suey, USA: The Story of Chinese Food in America. Arts and Traditions of the Table*. New York: Columbia University Press.
7 Ku, Robert Ji-Song. 2014. *Dubious Gastronomy: The Cultural Politics of Eating Asian in the USA (Food in Asia and the Pacific)*. Honolulu: University of Hawaii Press.
8 Liu, Haiming. 2015. *From Canton Restaurant to Panda Express: A History of Chinese Food in the United States*. New Brunswick: Rutgers University Press.
9 Anderson, E. N. 1988. *The Food of China*. New Haven: Yale University Press.
10 Höllmann, Thomas O., and Margolis, Karen (trans.). 2013. *The Land of the Five Flavors: A Cultural History of Chinese Cuisine*. New York: Columbia University Press.
11 Lin, Hsiang Ju. 2015. *Slippery Noodles: A Culinary History of China*. London: Prospect Books.
12 Ku, Robert Ji-Song; Manalansan, Martin F., and Mannur Anita. 2013. *Eating Asian America*. New York: NYU Press.
13 Anderson, E. N. 1988. *The Food of China*. New Haven: Yale University Press.
14 Höllmann, Thomas O., and Margolis, Karen (trans.). 2013. *The Land of the Five Flavors: A Cultural History of Chinese Cuisine*. New York: Columbia University Press.
15 Lin, Hsiang Ju. 2015. *Slippery Noodles: A Culinary History of China*. London: Prospect Books.
16 Wu, David Y.H., and Sidney C.H. Cheung. 2002. *The Globalization of Chinese Food*. Honolulu: University of Hawaii Press.
17 Jung, John. 2010. *Sweet and Sour: Life in Chinese Family Restaurants*. Yin and Yang Press.
18 Lee, Jennifer 8. 2008. *The Fortune Cookie Chronicles: Adventures in the World of Chinese Food*. New York: Twelve.
19 Wang, Edward Q. 2015. *Chopsticks: A Cultural and Culinary History*. Cambridge: Cambridge University Press.
20 Ku, Robert Ji-Song. 2014. *Dubious Gastronomy: The Cultural Politics of Eating Asian in the USA (Food in Asia and the Pacific)*. Honolulu: University of Hawaii Press.
21 Ku, Robert Ji-Song; Manalansan, Martin F., and Mannur Anita. 2013. *Eating Asian America*. New York: NYU Press.
22 Errington, Fredrick, Gewertz, Deborah, and Fujikura Tatsuro. 2013. *Noodle Narratives: The Global Rise of an Industrial Food into the Twenty-First Century*. Berkeley: University of California Press.

23 Solt, George. 2014. *The Untold History of Ramen: How Political Crisis in Japan Spawned a Global Food Craze.* Berkeley: University of California Press.

24 Kushner, Barak. 2014. *Slurp! A Social and Culinary History of Ramen: Japan's Favorite Noodle Soup.* Kent: Global Oriental.

25 See Cheuk Kwan's excellent 15-part documentary series in which he travels to 13 countries in 4 years to look at the emic stories of Chinese restaurants. www.chineserestau rants.tv

KEY TERMS

Adaptation	How cultural forms change in response to external forces or influences.
"Americanized" Chinese food	The modified dishes and flavors offered by most Chinese restaurants in the United States to cater to the palate of the general clientele.
Ashkenazi Jews	Jewish communities who lived in Central and Eastern Europe, making up the great majority of Jewish immigrants to the United States from 1880 to 1924.
Authentic	Of undisputed origin; genuine.
Built environment	Man-made structures, features, and facilities viewed collectively as an environment in which people live and work.
Canadianness	Having qualities that can be identified as Canadian.
Chifa	Term used to denote both Chinese food and Peruvian-Chinese *fondas*. As a meal, it refers to a set of dishes that combine Chinese and local ingredients, well liked among both popular sectors and elites. Originally known as "fondas" until the early twentieth-century, their expansion was accompanied with a change in their name, and "chifa" became the popular way to refer to them.
Chinese American restaurant	Most popular restaurant in the United States, numbering over 52,000, which is more than McDonald's, KFC, and Burger King combined.

Chinese exclusion	The desired prohibition on the immigration and/or entry of Chinese laborers and women into the United States, as well as the barring of Chinese Americans from enjoying the full rights and privileges of citizenship, based on racial animus.
Chinese food in America	A general term in the chapter including both Americanized Chinese food and more authentic Chinese food in America.
Chinese immigration in the US	From the nineteenth century to the present, Chinese immigrants have played an integral role in the development of the US as representatives of their culture and people but also as laborers, entrepreneurs, and citizens.
Chinese restaurant kids	Chinese children who were raised in a Chinese restaurant with their family members. They often worked at a very young age in the restaurant doing odd jobs such as answering the phone, taking orders, peeling shrimp, and cleanup.
Chinese Vietnamese	Chinese people who settled in Vietnam over many centuries. In the late 1970s their businesses were nationalized and many fled to various countries.
Chineseness	Having qualities that can be identified as Chinese.
Chop suey	An Americanized Chinese restaurant dish which contains chopped meat with stir-fried bean sprouts, bamboo shoots, and onions and served with rice.
Coolies	A derogatory term to name the first group of Chinese newcomers to Peru and the Americas. They arrived in 1849 in a moment of transition to a post-African slavery society. As such, they worked as peons in coastal plantations under harsh conditions until the end of their contracts. Once released of their duties, many of them moved to urban areas to work as cooks. This inhuman human trade was ended by the Peruvian government in 1874.
Counterpublic	A community that exists as a counter to a dominant or mainstream community.
Cultural diplomacy	The exchange of art, cuisine, religion, music, and aspects of material culture to promote cultural understanding and aid diplomacy between two or more countries.

Diaspora	Dispersion of a group of people from their original homeland.
Diasporic ethnography	Writing the personal experiences of Chinese people in their diasporic communities.
Dim sum	A style of Chinese cuisine that is usually served during breakfast and lunch and prepared as small bite-sized portion of food.
Emotional labor	The regulation and deployment of one's emotions to meet particular workplace demands.
Fondas chinas	Small Chinese restaurants in Peru where cooks adapted food and beverages to local culinary traditions and patron tastes. A significant number of Chinese immigrants became owners and managers of these establishments, gaining autonomy from their former status as workers in plantations. Fondas provided affordable meals among local populations, especially in moments of economic crises.
Food culture	The customs, practices, and attitudes towards the production, procurement, circulation, and consumption of food.
Foodie	Term used to describe a person with a strong interest in food. A "foodie" enjoys food for pleasure, or out of an interest or hobby, rather than simply out of hunger. A gourmet.
Gentrification	An unsustainable and inequitable form of neoliberal economic development facilitated by capitalist structures of power, gentrification is an intentional process of racial, spatial, and economic segregation. It physically and figuratively erase the livelihoods and narratives of working-class communities of color.
Globalization	Spreading from one cultural center to around the world of popular cultural symbols, new technologies, and national cuisines.
Halal	Meaning sanctioned by Islamic law. It involves preparing, serving, and selling food in accordance with Islamic law.
Hybridity	The incorporation of multiple forms into a new/novel form, or the synthesis of multiple forms (experiences, medias, world views, etc.) to create new ways of understanding conventional or traditional frameworks.
Imaginary	Existing in fantasy or the imagination; not rooted in empirical realities.

Improvisation	With new cooking skills and ingredients, migrants create versions of well-known food and cooking styles from home, and serve in restaurants claiming to provide authentic ethnic cuisine.
Informal economy	Forms of trade or exchange that are not regulated by state actors.
Kosher	The collection of dietary restrictions (laws) followed by observant Jewish people around the world. The most commonly known and followed of these rules bans the consumption of shellfish and pork products. It also forbids the combination of dairy and meat products in a single meal.
Le Cordon Bleu	Prestigious cooking school in Paris.
Liminality	A state of existence in between two recognizable phenomena, in which new properties tend to emerge that had beforehand not existed.
Mandarin cuisine	Reinvented dishes of various reginal home-style cooking of old China, served since the 1960s in Taiwan and in American Chinese restaurants that claim to be authentic Northern Chinese (but include Sichuan, Hunan, Shanghai, and Taiwanese dishes).
Material culture	The everyday mundane cultural artifacts that appear in buildings and landscapes. It is significant in revealing specific social mentalities and behaviors of groups in different cultures.
Mexican-owned Chinese restaurant	Chinese restaurant owned and managed by Mexicans who used to work in Chinese restaurants in the United States.
Migrant identities	Subjectivities of persons who live in countries where they are generally considered foreigners.
Orientalism	According to Edward Said, "a style of thought based upon an ontological and epistemological distinction made between 'the Orient' and (most of the time) 'the Occident.'"
Palate	A person's appreciation of taste and flavor, especially when sophisticated and discriminating.
P.F. Chang's China Bistro	A high end Chinese American restaurant chain that caters to mainstream or non-Chinese Americans that was developed by Paul Fleming and Philip Chiang.
Photographic research methods	A set of activities involving cameras and photographs through which questions are posed and knowledge is generated within the social sciences and humanities.

Pogrom	The persecution of a specific ethnic or religious group, often associated with state-sanctioned or condoned violence and murder against Jewish communities. Most commonly associated with Russia and other Eastern European destruction of Jewish communities, seizure of Jewish property, and mass murder of Jewish individuals.
Racial representation	The portrayal of certain races through various mediums.
Representation	The description or portrayal of someone or something in a particular way.
Social capital	An individual's combination of skills, education, experiences, and social relationships.
Steam table buffet	Fast food Chinese restaurants put their cooked food in stainless steel trays on the steam table for the diners to choose from. This way, they don't need to order food from the menu.
Suburban landscapes	These denote the conjoined natural and built environments—the land as altered by human activity—in urban areas that are less dense than traditional city centers.
Teochew	Teochew is both a people and their spoken word, a distinct variant of the Southern Min language (Minnan, also known as Hokkien). Teochew people hail from the Chaozhou district of the Guangdong province in China. There is a significant diasporic Teochew community.
Traditional	The transmission of customs or beliefs from generation to generation, or the fact of being passed on in this way.
Upscale	Relatively expensive and designed to cater and appeal to affluent and distinguished customers.
Uyghur	A Turkic Muslim ethnic minority group in China. The Uyghur predominantly live in China's northwestern Xinjiang province.
Xi Jinping and the Chinese Dream	A reference to Xi Jinping's ideological pursuit of Chinese global power, influence, and prosperity in the twenty-first century.

PART I
Social Analysis

1

CREATING AND NEGOTIATING "CHINESENESS" THROUGH CHINESE RESTAURANTS IN SANTIAGO, CHILE

Carol Chan and Maria Montt Strabucchi

Introduction

One of the oldest industries in which the Chinese have been involved and known for in Chile is the food industry. Indeed, as a relatively recent ethnic Chinese migrant to Chile, Carol was regularly asked by her Chilean kin, friends, and colleagues about the kinds of food she cooked or ate at home, in comparison with what was offered at local Chinese restaurants. Whenever she found herself in smaller towns in the country, local residents would assume and ask if she was the daughter of the Chinese family who ran a restaurant nearby. In some Chinese restaurants, waiters and restauranteurs would offer her "real tea" (*té de verdad*)—made from Chinese tea leaves—as opposed to the generic Jasmine teabag, and check if she wanted white rice (which the restauranteurs and Chinese customers often preferred) as opposed to *chaufan* (fried rice), which was more popular with Chilean clients. Where available, Carol would be offered a separate menu mainly reserved for Chinese clients. In contrast, whenever Chilean-born and raised Maria went to Chinese restaurants reputed to have two menus—one for Chinese persons and another for local Chileans—she would ask for and regularly be refused to be given the "Chinese menu." We begin this chapter with these brief anecdotes to reveal that Chinese restaurants are not simply commercial spaces. They also involve the subtle production, consumption, and negotiation of expected "cultural" tastes and behaviors between Chinese restauranteurs and their Chilean or Chinese clientele.

This chapter examines the dynamic ways in which "Chineseness" and contemporary Chinese identities are being articulated and contested in these Chinese restaurants, with dialogues with historic representations and perceptions of Chinese persons in Chile in cultural media. Although Chinese persons have been present in Chile for more than a century, the term "chino" is still used in everyday speech to mark certain foreignness. Colloquialisms such as to speak "chino"—incomprehensibly—or to "work like a Chinese" (*trabajar como chino*) must be contextualized within the historic and systematic exclusion of ethnic Chinese on the continent and decades of their forced labor after the abolition of slavery.[1]

By drawing on archival and qualitative research data, we look at how ethnic Chinese persons and their families in Chile reproduce and/or subvert enduring and changing representations of Chinese persons and businesses in Chile. Data are based on participant observation of Chinese restaurants in Santiago, semi-structured interviews, and follow-up informal conversations with 20 ethnic Chinese women, men, and youths working in these restaurants.[2] Research was conducted between October 2016 and April 2018, and participants vary according to age, place of origin, gender, class, nationality, migrant status, and length of time spent in the country.

We highlight the diverse experiences of the ethnic Chinese and their restaurants within the contemporary political and socio-cultural context, where their historical and current presence is marginalized in charged public discussions about migrants in Chile today. "Ethnic" restaurants in general and Chinese restaurants in particular constitute a key but underdeveloped theme in scholarship on diasporic identity.[3] Daniel Parker has argued, for example, that Chinese take-aways in Britain constitute "diaspora-space," where "multiple subject positions are juxtaposed, contested, proclaimed, or disavowed."[4] Studies of overseas Chinese restauranteurs highlight how they learn to present their food and culture as "foreign, but not too foreign."[5] Mu Li's research in Canada demonstrated how Chinese restauranteurs carefully negotiated the addition of Chinese decoration in their restaurants over the twentieth century, in response to the increasing social acceptability of Chinese persons and businesses.[6] In Chile, the framework for negotiating Chinese identities is, however, shifting in the new era of Trans-Pacific relations, marked by China's geopolitical growth. As Monica DeHart demonstrates, what it means to be Chinese is articulated by shifting global regimes of value, where the Chinese in Latin America may now be positioned as brokers of increasingly significant cross-cultural relations.[7]

Chinese restaurants, like Chinatowns, can create a restrictive delineation of space, associated with a narrowly conceived cultural tradition, evoking limited images of Chineseness.[8] Yet, Chinese restaurants can simultaneously challenge understandings of Chineseness by creatively repackaging "Chinese food" or aesthetics. Conversely, some well-known Chinese restaurants in Santiago are not evidently Chinese, with names such as *Danubio Azul* and *New York*. This chapter argues for the significant discursive role that restaurant aesthetics and cuisine play in engaging with multidimensional evocations of Chineseness.

Although we embrace a diasporic, anti-essentialist approach to Chineseness, we acknowledge the diverse ways some interviewees articulate and define "authentic" and "inauthentic" Chineseness, even as others seek to subvert the exclusiveness of such binary thinking. Additionally, we acknowledge that intra-ethnic divisions are rife, and our study is necessarily limited to Cantonese-Chinese persons, who are known for dominating the restaurant industry in Chile. Thus, we do not claim to represent a homogenous and bounded "Chinese" community in Chile, but agree that "quests for either an essence of 'Chineseness' or boundaries to it are bound to fail."[9] Instead, we take a discursive approach to Chineseness, which entails "a disruption of the ontological stability and certainty of Chinese identity," an approach which "does not, however, negate [the] operative power [of Chineseness] as a cultural principle in the social constitution of identities as Chinese."[10] Focusing on Chinese restaurants, their histories, and actors within them, we thus investigate how this Chineseness operates in practice, such as how self-identified ethnic Chinese persons articulate their subjectivities—such as through presenting food and talking about tastes—vis-à-vis other Chinese or Chilean persons. This chapter sheds light on the relevance of ethnicity, nationality, and cultural and financial capital in the power dynamics of reproducing or contesting meanings and practices associated with Chineseness or being "Chinese" in Chile.

In the following sections, we first contextualize the historical presence of Chinese persons and their restaurants in Chile, alongside a brief note on the changing and enduring representations of Chineseness in Chilean cultural productions. Drawing on interviews with Chinese restaurant owners and workers in Santiago, we then explore how they articulate "Chileanness," "Chineseness," and other indices to "foreignness" in dynamic ways, in order to adhere, negotiate, and contest their belonging to Chinese and Chilean communities. Finally, we briefly discuss how the social imaginaries of Chineseness are shaped by their (dis)connection with the local community and their histories, politics, social identities, and transnational networks.

Contextualizing Chinese Presence and Businesses in Chile

Chinese presence in Latin America should be contextualized in terms of Chinese vulnerability and resilience to racial discrimination and marginalization throughout the nineteenth and twentieth centuries. Jason Chang notably argued for viewing the hundreds of Chinese restaurants in Mexicali, Mexico as "symbols" of the historical eviction of naturalized Chinese citizens from their agricultural property and exclusion from national economic reforms.[11] In contrast to Chinese economic diversity in the early twentieth century, Chang argued that their current "isolation within the marginal niche market of ethnic food service" evidences how thoroughly "the Mexican state organized economic resources along racial lines" over decades.[12] While Chinese restaurants are ubiquitous in Chile, the Chinese in Chile arguably adopt more complex and diverse socioeconomic positions. Despite a growing presence and knowledge of the centrality of Chinese businesses and residence to Chile's cultural landscape and economic development, literature on the topic is scant, both in academic work,[13] and non-academic outlets.[14]

Significant Chinese presence in the Americas can be traced back to the years 1840–1900, when 2.5 million Chinese arrived in California to work in gold mines.

Many others—mainly from Guangdong—arrived in Peru and Cuba as "coolies" or contract labor.[15] "Coolies" worked primarily in sugar plantations, agriculture, and mining; historians have argued that their living and working conditions were akin to slavery in all but name.[16] Documented Chinese presence in Chile dates from the 1850s, possibly resulting from Chinese movement or escape from Cuba and Peru, and the establishment of a Chilean consul in Guangzhou in 1845. The latter intensified economic exchange between Chile and China, associated with the maritime traffic between both countries.[17] Attracted by the growing nitrate industry, some Chinese in Chile settled in the province of Tarapacá in northern Chile, after the end of the *War of the Pacific* (1879–1884). They worked both in manual labor and service industries related to the nitrate boom.[18]

These Chinese in northern Chile in the nineteenth century were mainly traders, although in census documents many were also identified as cooks (*cocineros*).[19] By the 1920s, some Chinese residents were street vendors; others established minimarkets (*almacenes*), butcheries, and bakeries.[20] Some also established coffeeshops (*cafés chinos),* which Diego Lin Chou described as "improper" businesses due to activities such as prostitution.[21] One of the early descriptions of Chinese restaurants in Chile is of *Cantón*, a hotel and dinner venue offering Cantonese food established in 1920 by Guillermo Wong. Another was *Chung Wha*, run by Roberto Chaisan, which also offered typical Chinese cuisine and hosted banquets.[22]

The dispersal of the Chinese to other parts of Chile—especially Santiago— began after many Chinese businesses closed in northern Chile, when nitrate production violently declined due to the invention of synthetic nitrate.[23] Shortly after the 1930s depression, Chinese attempts to establish food and meat businesses in the north led to conflicts with local (Chilean) businessmen.[24] Racialized and nationalistic discourses were employed against the Chinese, who were not only accused of "unfair competition," but associated with unsanitary living and working conditions. Local elites called to restrict their migration in order to not "weaken" the Chilean race.[25] During this time, the initially dominantly male Chinese community in Chile began to grow and diversify, partly due to the second generation.[26] Responding to persistent Sinophobia, some Chinese established networks of solidarity to defend their interests as a group, establish a formal presence in the country, and work on reducing racial violence against them.[27] The Chinese were a heterogeneous group: some nevertheless enjoyed great economic success despite anti-Chinese sentiments. The businessman Chau, for example, owned a building which included a restaurant, a brothel, two hairdressing saloons, and a cabaret with a big dancing area called *El Asia*, which was very popular in the 1940s.[28] That some big Chinese restaurants were successful, while other food-sellers were scorned and associated with immorality, grime, and unfair competition, is evidence of the long history of competing perceptions of these two broad kinds of Chineseness vis-à-vis their involvement in the food industry. We return to this theme later in discussions on the diversity of Chinese restaurants in Santiago today.

With the establishment of the People's Republic of China (PRC) in 1949, some Chinese restaurants in Chile were said to host activities for those sympathetic to Communist China.[29] Later, the 1980s economic liberalization of China saw the arrival of a new group of Chinese migrants to Chile, which changed the Chinese culinary landscape. Unlike the first elegant Chinese restaurants in Santiago, the new generation of Chinese restaurants tended to be modest and cheap.[30] According to the Chinese Club of Santiago, there were around 100 to 120 Chinese restaurants in the Metropolitan region in Chile in 2004, where many owners, cooks, and helpers were affiliated to the Chinese from the PRC, the majority from Guangdong.[31]

By the twenty-first century, Chinese restaurants were no longer associated with grand dining or dance halls, but evoked low socio-economic status in Chile and within other members of the Chinese population. Three comments by ethnic Chinese themselves on the state of Chinese restaurants in Chile evidence growing frictions amongst three intra-ethnic social groups that Lin Chou identifies: Chilean-Chinese, continental Chinese (PRC), and Taiwanese persons. A second-generation Chilean-Chinese remarked on the Cantonese-Chinese in Santiago that "The Chinese restaurants in Santiago have terrible reputations. They are of low class, not like those of Japan or other countries."[32] Another "first-generation Chinese descendant" declared that PRC Chinese migrants in the North of Chile were "persons of limited culture, without social grace, who do not know how to develop themselves, and whose lives only revolve around their restaurants."[33] In our own interviews with Taiwanese-affiliated and PRC-affiliated residents and restaurant owners, there was a diversity in terms of a perception of any "conflict" between these categories that Lin Chou identified. Generally, the few Taiwanese descendants or citizens who have recently established restaurants in Santiago have specifically sought to market their food as "comida Taiwanesa" (Taiwanese food), rather than "comida china," to prevent customers from expecting cheap food, as they have come to demand from Chinese restaurants. Taiwanese and PRC-affiliated businessmen expressed two broad perspectives that contradicted one another. While some remarked that there exists little conflict between the two groups in terms of businesses, since the conflicts are mainly political in nature, Taiwanese-affiliated persons expressed tensions between Taiwanese and PRC business owners. It was difficult for Taiwanese goods to compete with Chinese prices, and Taiwanese associates found it difficult to work with the Chinese in terms of different business styles and work ethics.

Despite the ubiquity of Chinese restaurants in Chile,[34] the presently approximately 50,000 Chinese population in Chile is relatively ignored and invisible, neither considered "locals" nor "migrants," while public discussions on migration are largely associated with migrants from Latin America and the Caribbean.[35] Overall mutual ignorance and distance between the Chinese population and the average Chilean are evident in the exoticization of Chinese restaurants and othering of Chinese persons in public discourses and representations. Carlos Reyes Medel, for example, describes the restaurants as "theatrical montages" and "millenary *bling bling*."[36]

Before discussing the role restauranteurs play in reproducing, creating, or negotiating notions of Chineseness vis-à-vis other socio-cultural categories, we briefly
note that representations of Chineseness and Chinese restaurants have varied
widely throughout Chilean history. While such variety may affirm the dynamic
nature of Chineseness, popular representations still tend to be essentialist and racist.[37] Nevertheless, specific notions of Chineseness have endured. Associations of
the Chinese with vice, grime, humor, or inarticulation co-exist alongside more
romantic ideas about the mysticism of the "Orient." Stereotypical representations
of Chinese people in Chile through characters in television series, movies, comics,
and advertisements not only reveal the nature of orientalism in the country but also
a conflation of China and Asia as a whole. They also reveal the assumed passivity
of the Chinese as objects—not subjects—of representation. In this context, we
now turn to analyze the ways in which Chinese owners and managers in Chinese
restaurants in Chile engage with the limitations and potentialities of discursive
Chineseness.

Hidden Stories of Chinese Restaurants in Contemporary Chile

Chinese restaurants play a key role in discourses of migration and representations
of the Chinese as exotic/incomprehensible Other in Chile, partly because Chinese
restaurants today in Santiago constitute a large proportion of the culinary landscape.[38] They are usually perceived as being "inexpensive" and "family-friendly,"
where the food is "abundant," as affirmed by Chilean user reviews on Google
Maps or TripAdvisor. The extensive influence of Chinese food in Chilean households is evident in that street vendors and markets in Santiago sell pre-chopped
vegetables for making "*chapsui.*" [39] Chilean-Chinese dishes like "*carne mongoliana*"
are sold in malls and canteens as part of Chilean menus.[40]

We trace the diversity among restaurants in terms of how they are marketed
as "Chinese" (in comparison with others as Japanese or pan-Asian), the type of
food they serve, and how their owners and workers talk about and value their
work, the businesses, and spaces. We discuss them in terms of four broad categories: Chilean-Chinese, "Authentic" Chinese, Pan-Asian, and Modern Chinese.
While most restaurants could arguably occupy more than one category, thinking in terms of categories illuminates the multiple types of Chinese food and
Chineseness that the restaurants themselves (explicitly or implicitly) evoke and
engage with.

Contextualizing the Production of Chilean-Chinese Menus

The visibility of Chinese restaurants in Santiago as Chileans know them today can
be traced back to the 1960s and 1970s. According to our interviewees with multi-
generational familial involvement in the industry in Santiago, there was an initial
increase in visibility in elegant Chinese restaurants selling Chinese food in Santiago
in the 1960s and 1970s,[41] including the restaurant *Tong Fang*, a place described as

having an "exotic" ambience (Figure 1.1).[42] Later, smaller and more diverse types of restaurants, such as *Los Chinos Pobres* and take-aways, appeared in different areas of the city from the 1980s.[43] Notably, three of these older establishments in the city—*Hao Hwa*, *Lung Fung*, and *Violeta de Persia*—are architecturally "traditional" in terms of externally using green tiles (*dougong*, a tiered bracketing system for roofs). These roofs and patterned ceilings are clearly for purely aesthetic rather than practical purposes, signifying their use as cultural symbols. The restaurants also use furniture directly imported from China, with classic motifs such as golden dragon symbols and large porcelain vases, and colors associated with good fortune such as gold and red. This generation of restaurants in Santiago clearly drew on self-exoticizing strategies, as the grand restaurants of the 1920s and 1940s did. However, the popularity of these elegant restaurants through time does not indicate the absence of racism against the Chinese. Set in its broader socio-political context of

FIGURE 1.1 Tong Fang restaurant in downtown Santiago.

Source: Photo by Hart Preston, 1941.

persistent marginalization of the community, these grand restaurants can instead be read as signs by their Chinese owners to actively construct spaces to counter prevalent representations of the Chinese as unsanitary and inferior. Such counter-representations nonetheless entailed "exotic" elements that were integral in creating value for these Chinese restaurants and food as cultural commodities.[44] As Li found in the case of Canada in the 1970s and 1980s, there was a strong link between a Chinese restaurant's explicit "Chinese" decoration and its popularity with local customers, where restaurants remade themselves over time—via menu and aesthetics—to meet the changing cultural expectations of American diners.[45]

Many Santiago residents today are familiar with a fairly standard menu in Chilean-Chinese restaurants, where key items are *chapsui, carne mongoliana*, and *wantán frito* (see Figure 1.2). Before we examine diverse Chinese restaurant aesthetics and menus in Santiago, it is important to outline familial histories of how these "standard" menus were developed. Their emergence reveals the processes of negotiating between "Chinese" and "Chilean" tastes, and how the pioneering restaurateurs sought to produce and sell Chinese food (*comida china*) in a then culinarily homogenous city.

According to an interview with John, a third-generation Chinese man, born in Chile to a family of Chinese restaurant owners, there are multiple factors explaining why Chilean-Chinese menus are so ubiquitous in Chile, how they come to exist, and why there are not more restaurants selling "real Chinese food." Recalling

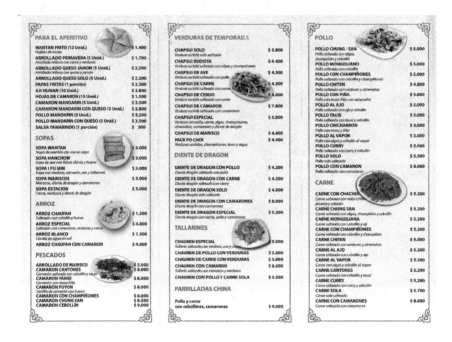

FIGURE 1.2 Typical dishes on a Chilean-Chinese restaurant menu.

stories about how his grandfather, father, and uncle established their first Chinese restaurant in the 1970s, he said:

> There wasn't even soy sauce when my grandpa came you know. So it was Chinese food, but it wasn't really. People liked it . . . *they see a Chinese guy doing it, you know.* [The Chilean-Chinese menu], it sells. We [restauranteurs] try to copy from the US. Some places tried to put real Chinese food on the table but they all closed down, wouldn't sell, you know why? Because all the Chinese people have their own restaurants, and when we [restaurant workers] go out to eat [at] 1 a.m., 2 a.m., and we go to the [Chinese] restaurants that sell that. [Those restaurants] don't even do so well. Everybody knows this is what you should do [adopt a Chilean-Chinese menu]. It sells, it's fast.

Framing the family's decision to sell mainly Chilean-Chinese food in terms of the "market" and consumer demand, John explained that there was a period when one of the family's restaurants tried to experiment with selling dishes that the family would eat at home. However, the clients did not like it and complained there was:

> too much garlic, too much ginger . . . So that's the main thing you know, you got to sell what sells. You can bring the best meal out, hire the best chef, but if it doesn't sell you're not going to make profit out of it. And the community, the people who actually like it [authentic Chinese food] . . . it is very small. It may be changing, but it's still not worth it [to change the menu].

John thus articulates what many other interviewees did in their discussion of "Chilean-Chinese" restaurant menus: that there are tastes and dishes meant for Chilean "locals," and other "real" or "authentic" Chinese food for Chinese consumers dishes (see Figure 1.3). Generally, Chinese restaurants, regardless of their focus on selling "authentic," "fusion," or "Chilean-Chinese" food, as we will elaborate below, all expressed the economic necessity to include the standard "Chilean-Chinese" food items. Catering to "local tastes," Lee, for example, who has run her Chinese restaurant in Santiago for more than ten years, spoke of, and criticized, how the Chileans "prefer their food rather bland and salty." Having worked previously in Peru, also in a Chinese restaurant, she admitted to preferring Peruvian-Chinese food better, not only because the Peruvians have "better tastes," but because Peru had better spices available in general. Thus, while John's narrative is representative of how much older multi-generational family restaurants may resist adaptations to "newer" types of consumers, relatively more recent Chinese migrants also learn to reproduce Chilean-Chinese menus and thus reproduce and meet—not exceed or subvert—locals' expectations of Chinese restaurants, food, and menus. Similarly, the owner of an elegant Chinese restaurant that seeks to elevate Chinese cuisine in the country—serving both "fusion" and "authentic"—insisted, almost in resignation, "Administratively, I can't exclude Chilean-Chinese food from the menu."

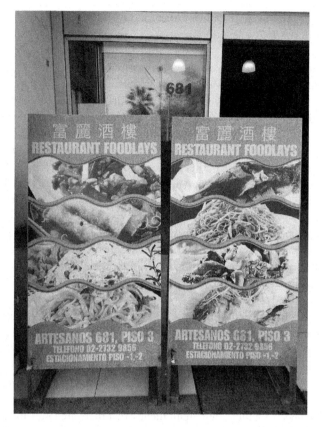

FIGURE 1.3 Two types of menu available in some Chinese restaurants in Santiago.
Source: Photo by Carol Chan.

The ubiquity of Chilean-Chinese cuisine thus can be attributed to pragmatic concerns; despite restauranteurs' varied views on the genre, it remains a central feature in Chinese restaurants in Santiago today. This recalls the observation that "the ubiquity of exoticism doesn't make it less exotic—but it does help to convey the illusion of cross-cultural *reciprocity*."[46] Thus, despite initial and ongoing attempts to diversify the types of Chinese food available in Santiago, the pragmatic necessity for restauranteurs to serve Chilean-Chinese menus contributes to maintaining an internal coherence between the restaurants as well as a superficial recognition of the "integration" of Chinese residents and their "culture" in the city-scape.[47]

Multi-generational Chilean-Chinese Restaurants

Family histories of multi-generational Chinese restaurant owners and workers can illuminate how and why newer Cantonese-Guangdong migrants are over-represented in the restaurant industry. The post-1980s Chinese migrants arrived in Chile on invitation from relatives or friends, usually Chinese restaurant owners.[48] After a period of working in these restaurants and saving money, many opened their own Chinese restaurants. Patrick, for example, arrived in Chile with his mother in the mid-2000s, when he was 14. By that time, the Chinese restaurant industry was already ubiquitous in Santiago, including the outskirts of the city. They had come to Chile with the sponsorship of Patrick's maternal relatives, who had been living in Santiago since the 1980s. Patrick recounted that upon arrival, both his mother and he helped out at relatives' Chinese take-away shops in poorer and more violent neighborhoods. He helped out at the shop after school, and, as he described,

> I felt a great responsibility as the oldest son. My mother told me at the very beginning, "You must learn to speak Spanish well. The future of our whole family depends on that." Generally, the Cantonese are highly conservative, especially in doing business. That works if they do not understand Spanish well, and because of that, they prefer to do things slowly and by the book. It is the nature of their industry . . . if they encounter problems, they will then find solutions, or ask for help from others, rather than pay for someone to help them solve a problem [referring to bribery or hiring a lawyer]. For the Cantonese, they just hope to get their own shop, a license, and their mentality is just to work a little harder, they have no problem with that. They earn money by each plate of rice sold . . . slowly. They're different this way from the Zhejiangnese and Fujianese. Those run the video arcades and wholesale retail shops. They make faster money . . . risky, but much more profitable. The Cantonese . . . follow business models of their relatives who came before them, and try to avoid trouble.

Such fear of risk that Patrick identifies as a specifically Cantonese trait is also affirmed by Patrick's parents' preference for him *not* go to university; insisting instead that he worked in the family's restaurant. According to Patrick, this was based on their observation of other Chinese families, where despite the hopes and financial investments of parents on their children's university education, the youth tend to return to work in the family business. Patrick, however, in describing the strong self-identification of Cantonese persons in Chile with the restaurant industry, is critical of this outlook. At 18, he left home and self-financed his part-time engineering degree while working for non-Cantonese Chinese employers.

John similarly describes his father's business conservatism and work ethic. Remarkably, even as a child of the restaurant owner, he was meticulously trained to learn every aspect of the single restaurant, and gradually took on more responsibilities. Growing up in the restaurant, John declared that the staff treated him as their adopted son, especially the Chilean cooks, due to how much time he had spent in the kitchen as a child. Corroborating this pattern was a Chilean woman in her fifties who had worked with the same family in another Chinese restaurant for

30 years. She had watched fortunes change in the shop and the family's lives. While more details are beyond the scope of this chapter, it suffices to note that Chinese restaurants are rarely spaces of limited Chineseness, but are instead spaces of intimate interactions and long-term negotiations between local non-Chinese cooks, waiters, and staff, and Chinese workers and restaurant owners.[49] Additionally, all interviewees said that apart from the remaining few long-term Chilean workers (as cooks or waiters), most of their staff are now Latin American migrants from Peru, Bolivia, and Venezuela. The impact of this diversity on Chinese restaurants' menu and self-presentations will be discussed later.

Aesthetically, the restaurants of multi-generational families, and those that fit into the "Chilean-Chinese" category are extremely diverse. However, it is important to point out the deliberate ways restaurant owners fashion the restaurants as "Chinese" for the guests' consumption, and the decisions they make for their own beliefs about necessary design and objects that may bring the business prosperity. It is worthwhile here to contrast Lee's large 15-year-old restaurant, and Cheng's rather small and modest 20-year-old business.

Lee brought with her from Peru an impressive, gigantic figure of the Chinese war deity, *Guan Gong*, including a large altar for him. Her restaurant is also furnished with wood-and-ivory chairs for customers to sit in while waiting for their take-away orders, a big fish-tank, an artificial pond, large Chinese-ink paintings, and porcelain vases.[50] Of these impressive items, Lee said that the Guan Gong is the most important, because she was told it was necessary in spaces of business for fortune and to ward off enemies. It would be difficult and expensive to get one in Chile now, and fortunately she managed to obtain it in Peru due to the large Chinese community there at the time. Behind the cash register counter, dozens of figures line the shelves. All of them evoke typical Chinese symbols: two figures of children dressed in Chinese garb, and figures of a fish and a horse. Lee explained that these smaller objects were new and purchased from Chile.

While Lee was not so explicit about their differences other than pointing to the significance of Guan Gong and highlighting that the others were bought rather cheaply from a wholesale district in Santiago, Cheng was blunt in responding to questions about similar decorative items in her shop. "The customers like this sort of thing," she said, gesturing to a Japanese cat of fortune and a false jade ingot. When asked about the lack of symbolically important objects—such as the almost ubiquitous *Guan Gong* or *Guan Yin* in older Chinese restaurants in the country—Cheng lowered her voice. She said, "You can't just place *those things* anywhere you like, they are sometimes too powerful." Her point was to be cautious about objects of cultural and spiritual value; "superficial" decorative items for the gaze of mainly Chilean clients were much safer than those meant for unseen spirits. Cheng's discussion—as someone more senior in age—reveals that issues of representation of culturally symbolic objects are not to be taken for granted, and that representations of Chineseness to non-Chinese persons are less important or impactful than concerns about what *should not* be represented or displayed inappropriately. Her position emphasizes that the terms of representation and visibility of Chinese identities and cultural symbols can sometimes undermine the alleged power of such representation.[51] Further questioning of the strategic presence or absence of "exotic" objects in Chinese restaurants can illuminate the ways that Chinese restauranteurs negotiate the tensions of visibility and invisibility of the Chinese population and their cultural symbols.

"Authentic" Chinese Menus

A handful of Chinese restaurants in Santiago offer a "Chinese menu" in Mandarin, for Chinese consumers, in addition to their regular menu for Chilean clients. Such restaurants include *Xing Shun* in the neighborhood La Florida (a neighborhood where many Guangdong migrants reside and work), *Foodlays, I-Ching, Sheng Xing,* and *Mr. Wu* in the city center, particularly in multicultural commercial neighborhoods where there are increasingly more diverse types of Chinese-run businesses and residents. Based on several of their own accounts, these restaurants started in the late 1980s and early 1990s, when there was a surge of "new" Cantonese-Chinese migrants in the city, along with their restaurants. This group of "authentic" restaurants had a common strategy: to cater during the day and the week to Chilean customers, and during the late nights to Chinese consumers. A restauranteur claiming to be among the first in Santiago to start selling real *dim sum* from the early 2000s explained, 'Some of my Chinese clients even run their own restaurants nearby [. . .] we offer a place for them to just be customers themselves, to eat good authentic food from home, to drink good tea and chat about their day.'

The aesthetics of these restaurants tend to be less ostentatious than the multigenerational restaurant owners who pioneered contemporary Chilean-Chinese cuisine in the country, but rather more minimalist, although with round tables, a Guan Gong figure, and high ceilings. Their "Chinese menus" typically include whole steamed or fried fish, *dim sum*, and a variety of braised meats, rice noodles, and Chinese vegetables such as *bakchoy* (See Figure 1.4).

By juxtaposing "Chinese" and "Chilean-Chinese" menus, these restaurants signal explicitly to their Chilean consumers that they are not consuming "real" Chinese food, but rather dishes modified for their specific tastes. Thus, the presumed "reciprocal" relationship in the institution of "multiculturalism" or Chinese "integration" is revealed to be unequal between producers and consumers.[52] It is an open question however, of how practical or subversive the inclusion of an "authentic" menu is. Recalling John's view before, that selling "authentic" food is ultimately not profitable since most clients are Chileans unaccustomed to condiments used in the cuisine, introducing "authentic" menus is arguably a business strategy catering to a niche clientele and/or an act of defiance in a ubiquitous landscape offering Chilean-Chinese cuisine. For example, comparing the two menus of *Foodlays* and of *Xing Shun*, in both cases, dishes on the "Chilean-Chinese" menu are cheaper, whereas a higher value is attached to the production of "authentic"

FIGURE 1.4 Sample page of an "authentic" menu given to ethnic Chinese clients.
Source: Photo by Carol Chan.

Chinese cuisine. While the Chinese menu includes professional photographs of the dishes, the Chilean menu is more modest and contains a fairly standard repertoire offered elsewhere. The subversiveness of these two-menu restaurants lies in the explicit resignification of Chilean-Chinese food as "inauthentic," even as restaurants produce and sell it.

Indeed, among ethnic Chinese clients and other self-proclaimed "foodies" in Santiago, the restaurant *I-Ching* is known for spatially segregating its clientele. Ethnic Chinese or Asian customers are ushered to the right, where they are attended to in Mandarin Chinese or Cantonese by Cantonese-Chinese staff. Non-Chinese customers are ushered to tables on the left-hand side of the restaurant, where they are attended to by Chilean staff in the Spanish language. A Cantonese-Chinese waiter interviewed explained that the left side of the restaurant serves "Chilean food," while the right side serves "Chinese food." Her distinctions highlight a strict definition of Chinese cuisine, where all adapted versions are considered "foreign"—in this case—Chilean cuisine.

Pan-Asian Restaurants and Non-Chinese Menus

In contrast to pre-1990s restaurants, which espouse ideas of "traditional" and imperial China, and others seeking to distinguish between "authentic" and "Chileanized" Chinese cuisine, a third category of restaurants demonstrate a desire to go beyond these categories of "Chinese" and "Chilean-Chinese," thereby expanding ideas of what "China" and Chinese restaurants as spaces can constitute. Described below are two examples of how transnational and transcultural ties of the Chinese shape their inclusion of typically "non-Chinese" cuisine and aesthetics in their restaurants, partly due to economic pragmatism. Nevertheless, their embrace of diverse cultural styles contrasts with those that define and represent their restaurants and by extension, "Chinese culture," in more exclusivist terms—"authentic" or "adapted."

The restaurant *Hao Hwa*, in a middle-class central neighborhood, is an example of such adaptations over time. The restaurant was founded in its current location in 1977 and was renovated in 2008. Reflecting on the renovations, a Chinese restaurant manager said that Chinese restaurants in Chile are either aesthetically "traditional" or "modern." *Hao Hwa*'s aesthetics clearly lean towards the former, with green Chinese-style roofs, and shelves of Chinese ornaments, Buddha figurines, and gold ingots lining the dining room. Its furniture was also imported from China. However, its impressive entrance is also lined with modern back-lit photographs of Thai and Japanese food. Despite its "Chinese" beginnings, it is now effectively a pan-Asian restaurant, with a neon sign outside advertising its sushi menu. According to the restaurant manager, this was serendipitous: the inclusion of both Japanese and later Thai food was due to the arrival of a Japanese cook and a Thai cook looking for work. The restaurant owners were keen to hire these chefs and to include non-Chinese food on their menu, partly based on projections that a more varied menu would appeal to changing clients' tastes and demography. Aware of how the new menu would change the cultural position of the restaurant, the manager said,

> [The other restaurant branch of this family] is more authentic, here, we cater more for foreigners. Here, there are many cultured clients, those who know more about the world and other cultures, the other [neighborhood] has more regular Chilean families.

The location of the restaurant, the diverse or "cosmopolitan" pool of potential clients, and the serendipitous availability of foreign chefs, thus all contributed to the restaurant's active reworking as a strictly "Chinese" space. The reworking of Chineseness here is evident: the restaurant boasts a sushi bar in a special corner of the restaurant, complete with cutlery and plates specifically to serve sushi and Japanese food (see Figure 1.5). Reviews of the restaurant on Google show the success of its strategy: clients praise the "authentic" Thai food and "good sushi," while referring to it mainly as a Chinese restaurant. While one could argue for the restaurant's

FIGURE 1.5 Sushi bar in *Hao Hwa* restaurant.
Source: Photo by Carol Chan.

"pan-Asian" characteristics, *Hao Hwa*'s exterior and interior design, in addition to its name, is better categorized as a restaurant that attempts to include other elements of Asia under the all-encompassing and flexible umbrella of "China."

Another restaurant that subsumes diversity under the guise of Chineseness is located in a multicultural lower middle-class commercial neighborhood. The restaurant is owned by Cai, a woman from Guangdong, who runs the place with a Peruvian waitress and Peruvian male cooks. While externally the restaurant is designed as a typical Chilean-Chinese restaurant, an additional colored poster and menu board on the sidewalk advertise two menus: Peruvian food and Chilean-Chinese food. According to Cai, she had decided to include Peruvian food on the menu for several reasons: there was a demand for it among Chilean clients, and there were also more Peruvian migrants seeking cheap cuisine in the neighborhood. Moreover, she had only been able to hire Peruvian cooks, as it was difficult to find any Chileans who wanted to do the job, and it was expensive to bring Chinese cooks from China. Observing that the Peruvian chefs were good cooks of their own cuisine (for their own consumption), she agreed to their suggestion of adding classic Peruvian dishes to the menu. She claimed that as many people order Peruvian as Chinese food. However, the restaurant did not mix the two cuisines in a way that could be termed "fusion," instead adopting the Peruvian staff's suggestions to serve bread to clients who ordered Peruvian food. When Chinese food is ordered, no bread is served, demonstrating a distinction not only in the food offered but certain culinary and cultural norms associated with each cuisine. The co-existence of both menus and cultural-culinary norms in a Chinese restaurant is notable, particularly since there are more Peruvian than Chinese restaurants in the city.[53]

In both examples, the restaurants not only expand ideas of what "Chinese" restaurants can contain, or what kinds of cuisines, practices, and persons can belong in these spaces. They simultaneously challenge the static notion of place as demarcated by singular identities such as "Peruvian" or "Japanese," and open the possibility for places to be thought about in terms of interaction. These restaurants as places of social and cultural interactions—of Peruvian and Chinese workers, or of Thai, Chinese, and Japanese chefs and Latin American waiters—are vibrant examples contradicting stereotypes of the Chinese as incomprehensible, "closed-minded persons," or their restaurants as "closed" spaces of their work and lives. Rather than reproducing a limited idea of Chineseness as a singular Other, such restaurants constitute and open the possibility of daily intercultural interactions, representations, and tensions, where social interactions are not motionless either, but change over time.

Modern Chinese

Nueva China is an example of its owners' attempts to draw on ideas about a modern China in their design of the business.[54] The restaurant's name (New China), and its website design and content, explicitly appeal to cosmopolitan consumers, while emphasizing its authenticity as serving Chinese food in a particular context. For example, this restaurant uses furniture with modern and minimalist design, as opposed to the restaurants described earlier, which emphasize "tradition" by using green, red, and gold motifs. Yet it maintains the basic elements that distinguish it from regular Chilean restaurants—its name references China, its logo is in the form of an old Chinese official seal, and many of its tables are round and thus suited for sharing dishes as is commonplace in this type of restaurant. A gallery of images of the restaurant's dishes includes not only Chilean-Chinese classics like *carne mongoliana*, but also sushi and Peruvian desserts. Its menu uniquely offers pan-Asian dishes its owners have called "teppan-xiu," which appear to be a mix of Japanese and Chinese cooking styles.

Despite these evidently fusion and pan-Asian elements to its design and menu, *Nueva China* actively engages in remaking existing ideas about Chilean-Chinese restaurants and pan-Asian restaurants, by subsuming elements of those two categories into one—a "new China." It uniquely insists on being a "Chinese" space, where the website proudly declares that its chefs are "directly from China," who bring to their guests "traditional gastronomy of the region, molded to the particular tastes of the *santiaguino* (a Santiago city-dweller)." Its menu does not substantially differ from other existing Chilean-Chinese restaurants and pan-Chinese restaurants, but what it does differently is outwardly declare a modern China that can engage with and contain the paradox that its "direct from China" chefs produce "traditional" food, which includes *carne mongoliana* and *sushi*. We can thus read this as a response to the idea that "anyone" can cook Chinese food, and that Chinese food is an empty signifier. What *Nueva China*'s restaurant owners and designers claim instead is that Chineseness is *embodied*, thus the presence of Chinese chefs and owners marks the production of spaces and food by default as authentic experiences of "China."

To emphasize this point, the webpage displays a photo of what is ostensibly the restaurant's team of Chinese chefs; an image notable because of popular knowledge and stereotype that the Chinese often employ migrant labor to do the cooking and cleaning instead (as discussed above), leaving the impression that the production of "Chinese food" and ambience involves relatively inexpensive and unskilled labor. It is also important to note that restaurants which espouse ideas such as a "new," "vanguard," or "millennial" China (direct quotes from other restaurants' marketing campaigns) are also generally more expensive than average Chilean-Chinese restaurants. In other words, practical and economic reasons, alongside cultural ones, co-exist in these attempts to reshape public valuation of "China," "Chinese food," and what it means to be a Chinese restaurant and cook. Despite claiming 16 years of existence, *Nueva China* has only renovated its shop with new furnishing in the past year. This timeline is suggestive of the influence on such materializations of "new China" of broader discussions about multiculturalism in Chile—in terms of the increased demand for "ethnic" cultural products and the commodification of "diversity"—as well as the greater economic dominance of China in the region.[55]

Conclusion

This chapter has outlined the dynamics between forms of self-exoticism and creative reworking of Chineseness in the restaurant industry in Santiago, which highlight the dynamic relations between migration, race, the restaurant industry, and national identity in Santiago. We have examined how the production and consumption of "Chinese" cuisine in Chile have changed alongside shifting socioeconomic relations between the Chinese restaurant workers, Chileans, and other migrants, influenced by local, national, regional, and global dynamics. We argue that these processes must be contextualized in the historical marginalization and racialized representations of Chinese populations in Chile and Latin America. In other words, what is at stake in these active representations of Chineseness by Chinese restauranteurs is, as Ang asserted, "the possibilities and responsibilities of these subjects to participate, as citizens of the world, in the ongoing political construction of world futures."[56] Nuanced and complex understandings of Chineseness can and do still rely on essentialist understandings of identity and stereotypes. Despite the apparent lack of reflexivity in popular cultural media representations of Chinese culture and persons, we argue that Chinese restaurants and menus can themselves constitute spaces for the possible interrogation of Chineseness in Chile.

This chapter thus offers new dimensions through which to study Chinese migration in Chile. Our focus on the negotiated identities of the ethnic Chinese illuminates identity discourses and ethnic representations that mutually constitute and interact with broader discourses on ethno-national identity and Chineseness in Santiago and Chile. Through examining the history and practices of Chinese restauranteurs in Santiago, we have interrogated the paradoxical nature of the "absent presence" or elusiveness of the ethnic Chinese in Chilean society and national imaginary. This paradox is evident from the unreflexive uses of the term "*chino*" in everyday conversation, and the ubiquity and popularity of Chinese restaurants and food in the city. Further examination of this paradox can contribute to advancing emerging conversations about race, multiculturalism, and migration not only in Chile, but in the Americas more broadly.

Acknowledgments

This research was supported by Fondo Nacional de Desarrollo Científico y Tecnológico (FONDECYT) Chile, Proyecto Postdoctorado Numero 3170051, 2017–2020. Special thanks to the Chinese restaurant owners, workers, and family members we spoke to for their time and patience; to Mao Cheng Li for his help with some interviews; and to Vivi Hsu for her transcription work.

Key Terms

> **Authenticity**: That which is considered original, true, and genuine.
> **Migrant identities**: Subjectivities of persons who live in countries where they are generally considered foreigners.
> **Representation**: The description or portrayal of someone or something in a particular way.

Discussion Questions

1. What are the various kinds of "Chineseness" present in Chinese restaurants in Santiago de Chile, and how are these ideas mediated through restaurants' spatial organization, aesthetics, publicity, and menus?
2. What historical, cultural, or pragmatic elements are attributed by restaurateurs to explain the kinds of dishes available in their restaurants?
3. This chapter contextualizes the role and public perceptions of Chinese restaurants and restaurant workers in a broader historical and political background of Chinese marginalization and discrimination in Chile. In what ways are representations of Chineseness and authenticity in the restaurants mutually shaped by these broader cultural discourses about Chinese food, Chinese migrants, and Chinese culture?

Notes

1 Lisa Yun, *The Coolie Speaks: Chinese Indentured Laborers and African Slaves in Cuba* (Philadelphia: Temple University Press, 2008).
2 All but one of the interviews were conducted by the first author in Mandarin, Spanish, or English, depending on the interviewees' preferences. The translation of the interview data into English is our own. Maria Elvira Ríos Peñafiel co-conducted some interviews and visits to Chinese restaurants, as well as post-research analysis. We acknowledge her contributions.
3 Martin F. Manalasan, "Beyond Authenticity: Rerouting the Filipino Culinary Diaspora," in *Eating Asia America*, ed. Robert Ji-Song Ky, Manalasan, Martin F., and Anita Mannur (New York: New York University Press, 2013), 288–302.
4 Brah 1996, in David Parker, "The Chinese Takeaway and the Diasporic Habitus: Space, Time and Power Geometries," in *Un/Settled Multiculturalisms: Diasporas, Entanglements, Transruptions*, ed. Barnor Hesse (London: Zed Books, 2000), 73.
5 Ching Lin Pang, "Business Opportunity or Food Pornography?: Chinese Restaurant Ventures in Antwerp," *International Journal of Entrepreneurial Behavior & Research* 8, no. 1/2 (February 1, 2002): 148–161.
6 Mu Li, "Chinese Restaurants' Interior Decor as Ethnographic Objects in Newfoundland 1," *Western Folklore* 75, no. 1 (2016): 33–75. Central to other similar work is the consensus that "Chineseness" is inherently an open and indeterminate signifier, whose meanings are constantly renegotiated in varied ways amongst the Chinese diaspora, as shaped by local circumstances. See Ien Ang, "Can One Say No to Chineseness? Pushing the Limits of the Diasporic Paradigm," *Boundary* 2 25, no. 3 (1998): 225; Lok Siu, "Diasporic Cultural Citizenship: Chineseness and Belonging in Central America," *Social Text* 19, no. 4 (December 1, 2001): 7–28; Lok Siu, "Chino Latino Restaurants: Converging Communities, Identities, and Cultures," *Afro-Hispanic Review* 27, no. 1 (2008): 161–171.
7 Monica DeHart, "Chino Tico Routes and Repertoires: Cultivating Chineseness and Entrepreneurism for a New Era of Trans-Pacific Relations," *The Journal of Latin American and Caribbean Anthropology*, 2018: 74–93.
8 Elena Barabantseva, "Seeing beyond an 'Ethnic Enclave': The Time/Space of Manchester Chinatown," *Identities* 23, no. 1 (2016): 2.
9 Anthony Reid, "Chineseness Unbound," *Asian Ethnicity* 10, no. 3 (October 2009): 199.
10 Ien Ang, "Can One Say No to Chineseness? Pushing the Limits of the Diasporic Paradigm," 227.
11 Jason Oliver Chang, "Racial Alterity in the Mestizo Nation," *Journal of Asian American Studies* 14, no. 3 (2011): 331–359.
12 Chang, 331.
13 Diego Lin Chou, *Chile y China: inmigración y relaciones bilaterales, 1845–1970* (Santiago: Pontificia Universidad Católica de Chile, Centro de Investigaciones Diego Barrios Arana, 2004); Alfonso Díaz Aguad, "Los consulados chilenos en Oriente y su participación en el proceso de inmigración china al norte de Chile," *Diálogo Andino* 27 (2006): 61–74; Alfonso Díaz Aguad, Alberto Díaz Araya, and Eugenio Sánchez Espinoza, "Comercio local y redes sociales de la población China en Arica y Tarapacá, Chile (1900–1930)," *Revista Interciencia* 39, no. 7 (2014): 476–482; Marcos Agustín Calle Recabarren, "Hijos del dragón: Inmigrantes chinos y su inserción socioeconómica en la provincia de Tarapacá, 1860–1940," *Revista de Ciencias Sociales* 32 (2014): 25–62; Patricia Palma and Maria Montt Strabucchi, "La diáspora china en Iquique y su rol en la política de ultramar durante la República y el inicio de la Guerra Fría (1911–1950)," *Diálogo Andino* 54 (2017): 143–152.
14 Carlos Reyes Medel, "Cuando China se hizo Chile," in *Viaje al sabor. Crónicas gastronómicas de un Chile que no conoces* (Santiago: Ediciones B, 2016), 49–62.
15 Yun, *The Coolie Speaks*.

16 Evelyn Hu-DeHart, "Inclusion and Exclusion. The Chinese in Multiracial Latin America and the Caribbean," in *Routledge Handbook of the Chinese Diaspora*, ed. Tan Chee-Beng (London: Routledge, 2013), 89–107; Yun, *The Coolie Speaks*.

17 Lin Chou, *Chile y China*, 155, 267.

18 Calle Recabarren, "Hijos del dragón: Inmigrantes chinos y su inserción socioeconómica en la provincia de Tarapacá, 1860–1940," 37.

19 Díaz Aguad, Díaz Araya, and Sánchez Espinoza, "Comercio local y redes sociales de la población China en Arica y Tarapacá, Chile (1900–1930)"; Calle Recabarren, "Hijos del dragón: Inmigrantes chinos y su inserción socioeconómica en la provincia de Tarapacá, 1860–1940."

20 Calle Recabarren, "Hijos del dragón: Inmigrantes chinos y su inserción socioeconómica en la provincia de Tarapacá, 1860–1940," 38; Lin Chou, *Chile y China*, 170–178, 234.

21 Lin Chou, *Chile y China*, 174–175.

22 Calle Recabarren, "Hijos del dragón: Inmigrantes chinos y su inserción socioeconómica en la provincia de Tarapacá, 1860–1940," 40.

23 Lin Chou, *Chile y China*, 227–229; Reyes Medel, "Cuando China se hizo Chile," 54.

24 Damir Galaz-Mandakovic Fernández, "El escenario de la migración en Tocopilla en el devenir del siglo XX. Tres colectivos alóctonos y la fuga autóctona," *Revista de Ciencias Sociales*, no. 29 (2012): 110.

25 Cristóbal Cornejo, "Damir Galaz-Mandakovic, historiador tocopillano: 'Desde niño vi que mis amigos tenían un desprecio por la ciudad en la cual vivían,'" *El Ciudadano*, 2013, www.elciudadano.cl/medio-ambiente/damir-galaz-mandakovic-historiador-toco pillano-desde-nino-vi-que-mis-amigos-tenian-un-desprecio-por-la-ciudad-en-la-cual-vivian/11/12/.

26 Lin Chou, *Chile y China*, 219; Bernardo Guerrero Jiménez, "Los chinos, su identidad y su lugar en la literatura nortina," *Estudios Atacameños*, no. 13 (1997): 97.

27 Palma and Montt Strabucchi, "La diáspora china en Iquique y su rol en la política de ultramar durante la República y el inicio de la Guerra Fría (1911–1950)."

28 Galaz-Mandakovic Fernández, "El escenario de la migración en Tocopilla en el devenir del siglo XX. Tres colectivos alóctonos y la fuga autóctona," 112.

29 Lin Chou, *Chile y China*, 359–360.

30 Reyes Medel, "Cuando China se hizo Chile," 56–57.

31 Lin Chou, *Chile y China*, 256.

32 Lin Chou, 263.

33 Lin Chou, 263.

34 María Valentina Ruiz Silva, "Identidad Gastronómica Chilena: ¿Cómo se construye el patrimonio culinario nacional?" (Universidad de Chile, 2015), 13–14.

35 The estimate of the Chinese demographic is according to the Chinese embassy in Chile; see Carlos Salazar, "Embajada China en Chile celebra la integración de sus inmigrantes," *La Nación*, August 1, 2014, http://lanacion.cl/2014/01/08/embajada-china-en-chile-celebra-la-integracion-de-sus-inmigrantes/.

36 Reyes Medel, "Cuando China se hizo Chile," 50.

37 See for example, Canal Claro Chile 2016, ¿Ya conoces la nueva Tarifa Duplica? www.youtube.com/watch?v=Be9GClEaRZg; and TVN, 2017, "La Colombiana."

38 Ruiz Silva, "Identidad Gastronómica Chilena."

39 Reyes Medel, "Cuando China se hizo Chile," 62.

40 Humberto Merino, "Los Top Chefs de la cocina chilena," *Revista Enfoque*, May 8, 2016, www.revistaenfoque.cl/los-top-chefs-de-la-cocina-chilena.

41 Eugenio Pereira Salas, *Apuntes para la historia de la cocina chilena* (Santiago: Editorial Universitaria, 1977), 96.

42 Manuel Peña Muñoz, *Los Cafés Literarios En Chile* (Santiago: RIL Editores, 2001), 131.

43 Reyes Medel, "Cuando China se hizo Chile," 56–57.

44 Graham Huggan, "The Postcolonial Exotic," *Transition*, no. 64 (1994): 22–29; our analysis is informed by Huggan's notion of "strategic exoticism," which refers to "the means by

which postcolonial writers/thinkers, working from within exoticist codes of representation, either manage to subvert those codes [. . .] or succeed in redeploying them for the purposes of uncovering differential relations of power" (32). Our discussion of Chinese restaurants in Chile thus engages with Huggan's observation that desire "can easily lend itself to various forms of exploitation and manipulation" (154) as we analyze how and to what extent Chinese restaurant owners and workers in Chile may be obliged to participate in the marketization of particular "Chinese" spaces for consumption.

45 Li, "Chinese Restaurants' Interior Decor as Ethnographic Objects in Newfoundland 1," 60.
46 Huggan, "The Postcolonial Exotic," 27, emphasis added.
47 Salazar, "Embajada China en Chile celebra la integración de sus inmigrantes."
48 Lin Chou, *Chile y China*, 257.
49 Barabantseva, "Seeing beyond an 'Ethnic Enclave.'"
50 Compare Li, "Chinese Restaurants' Interior Decor as Ethnographic Objects in Newfoundland 1."
51 Peggy Phelan, *Unmarked: The Politics of Performance* (London; New York: Routledge, 1993).
52 Li, "Chinese Restaurants' Interior Decor as Ethnographic Objects in Newfoundland 1"; Parker, "The Chinese Takeaway and the Diasporic Habitus: Space, Time and Power Geometries."
53 Ruiz Silva, "Identidad Gastronómica Chilena."
54 See www.nuevachina.cl.
55 On the increase of ethnic cultural products and images and diversity, see studies on Buenos Aires Ignacio Aguiló, "Tropical Buenos Aires: Representations of Race in Argentine Literature during the 2001 Crisis and Its Aftermath," in *Argentina since the 2001 Crisis. Recovering the Past, Reclaiming the Future*, ed. Cara Levey, Daniel Ozarow, and Christopher Wylde (New York: Palgrave Macmillan, 2014), 177–194; Chisu Teresa Ko, "From Whiteness to Diversity: Crossing the Racial Threshold in Bicentennial Argentina," *Ethnic and Racial Studies* 37, no. 14 (2014): 2529–2546.
56 Ang, "Can One Say No to Chineseness?," 242.

References

Aguiló, Ignacio. "Tropical Buenos Aires: Representations of Race in Argentine Literature during the 2001 Crisis and Its Aftermath." In *Argentina since the 2001 Crisis. Recovering the Past, Reclaiming the Future*, edited by Cara Levey, Daniel Ozarow, and Christopher Wylde, 177–194. New York: Palgrave Macmillan, 2014.

Ang, Ien. "Can One Say No to Chineseness? Pushing the Limits of the Diasporic Paradigm." *Boundary 2* 25, no. 3 (1998): 223–242.

Barabantseva, Elena. "Seeing beyond an 'Ethnic Enclave': The Time/Space of Manchester Chinatown." *Identities* 23, no. 1 (2016): 99–115.

Calle Recabarren, Marcos Agustín. "Hijos Del Dragón: Inmigrantes Chinos y Su Inserción Socioeconómica En La Provincia de Tarapacá, 1860–1940." *Revista de Ciencias Sociales* 32 (2014): 25–62.

Chang, Jason Oliver. "Racial Alterity in the Mestizo Nation." *Journal of Asian American Studies* 14, no. 3 (2011): 331–359.

Cornejo, Cristóbal. "Damir Galaz-Mandakovic, historiador tocopillano: 'Desde niño vi que mis amigos tenían un desprecio por la ciudad en la cual vivían.'" *El Ciudadano*, 2013. www.elciudadano.cl/medio-ambiente/damir-galaz-mandakovic-historiador-tocopil lano-desde-nino-vi-que-mis-amigos-tenian-un-desprecio-por-la-ciudad-en-la-cual-vivian/11/12/.

DeHart, Monica. "Chino Tico Routes and Repertoires: Cultivating Chineseness and Entrepreneurism for a New Era of Trans-Pacific Relations." *The Journal of Latin American and Caribbean Anthropology* (2018): 74–93.

Díaz Aguad, Alfonso. "Los consulados chilenos en Oriente y su participación en el proceso de inmigración china al norte de Chile." *Diálogo Andino* 27 (2006): 61–74.

Díaz Aguad, Alfonso, Alberto Díaz Araya, and Eugenio Sánchez Espinoza. "Comercio local y redes sociales de la población China en Arica y Tarapacá, Chile (1900–1930)." *Revista Interciencia* 39, no. 7 (2014): 476–482.

Galaz-Mandakovic Fernández, Damir. "El escenario de la migración en Tocopilla en el devenir del siglo XX. Tres colectivos alóctonos y la fuga autóctona." *Revista de Ciencias Sociales*, no. 29 (2012): 105–131.

Guerrero Jiménez, Bernardo. "Los chinos, su identidad y su lugar en la literatura nortina." *Estudios Atacameños*, no. 13 (1997): 95–103.

Hu-DeHart, Evelyn. "Inclusion and Exclusion. The Chinese in Multiracial Latin America and the Caribbean." In *Routledge Handbook of the Chinese Diaspora*, edited by Tan Chee-Beng, 89–107. London: Routledge, 2013.

Huggan, Graham. "The Postcolonial Exotic." *Transition*, no. 64 (1994): 22–29.

Ko, Chisu Teresa. "From Whiteness to Diversity: Crossing the Racial Threshold in Bicentennial Argentina." *Ethnic and Racial Studies* 37, no. 14 (2014): 2529–2546.

Li, Mu. "Chinese Restaurants' Interior Decor as Ethnographic Objects in Newfoundland 1." *Western Folklore* 75, no. 1 (2016): 33–75.

Lin Chou, Diego. *Chile y China: inmigración y relaciones bilaterales, 1845–1970*. Santiago: Pontificia Universidad Católica de Chile, Centro de Investigaciones Diego Barrios Arana, 2004.

Manalasan, Martin F. "Beyond Authenticity: Rerouting the Filipino Culinary Diaspora." In *Eating Asia America*, edited by Robert Ji-Song Ky, Manalasan, Martin F., and Anita Mannur, 288–302. New York: New York University Press, 2013.

Merino, Humberto. "Los Top Chefs de la cocina chilena." *Revista Enfoque*, May 8, 2016. www.revistaenfoque.cl/los-top-chefs-de-la-cocina-chilena.

Palma, Patricia, and Maria Montt Strabucchi. "La diáspora china en Iquique y su rol en la política de ultramar durante la República y el inicio de la Guerra Fría (1911–1950)." *Diálogo Andino* 54 (2017): 143–152.

Pang, Ching Lin. "Business Opportunity or Food Pornography?: Chinese Restaurant Ventures in Antwerp." *International Journal of Entrepreneurial Behavior & Research* 8, no. 1/2 (February 1, 2002): 148–161.

Parker, David. "The Chinese Takeaway and the Diasporic Habitus: Space, Time and Power Geometries." In *Un/Settled Multiculturalisms: Diasporas, Entanglements, Transruptions*, edited by Barnor Hesse, 73–95. London: Zed Books, 2000.

Peña Muñoz, Manuel. *Los Cafés Literarios En Chile*. Santiago: RIL Editores, 2001.

Pereira Salas, Eugenio. *Apuntes para la historia de la cocina chilena*. Santiago: Editorial Universitaria, 1977.

Phelan, Peggy. *Unmarked: The Politics of Performance*. London; New York: Routledge, 1993.

Reid, Anthony. "Chineseness Unbound." *Asian Ethnicity* 10, no. 3 (October 2009): 197–200.

Reyes Medel, Carlos. "Cuando China se hizo Chile." In *Viaje al sabor. Crónicas gastronómicas de un Chile que no conoces*, 49–62. Santiago: Ediciones B, 2016.

Ruiz Silva, María Valentina. "Identidad Gastronómica Chilena: ¿Cómo se construye el patrimonio culinario nacional?" Undergraduate thesis, Universidad de Chile, 2015.

Salazar, Carlos. "Embajada China en Chile celebra la integración de sus inmigrantes." *La Nación*. August 1, 2014. http://lanacion.cl/2014/01/08/embajada-china-en-chile-celebra-la-integracion-de-sus-inmigrantes/.

Yun, Lisa. *The Coolie Speaks: Chinese Indentured Laborers and African Slaves in Cuba*. Philadelphia: Temple University Press, 2008.

2

FROM CHINESE DONUTS TO LEEK CAKES

Navigating Los Angeles Chinatown's Golden Waters

Frances Huynh

In the wake of the Khmer Rouge genocide of the late 1970s, the ethnically Chinese Kim Chuy Tang fled Cambodia and found refuge in Thailand. His family, including his daughter and her son, soon joined him. After securing sponsorship for immigration, they left for the United States and established their lives in Los Angeles Chinatown. Soon, this historical immigrant ethnic enclave became a place that they, alongside many newly arriving Chinese and Southeast Asian refugees, could call home following displacement from war-torn homelands facilitated by complex histories of U.S. imperialism, socialist regimes, and social and economic turmoil. When he arrived in Chinatown, Tang brought with him his skills as a popular noodle maker in Cambodia. He would go on to make and sell *yóutiáo* (油條), long and crisp deep-fried Chinese donuts, door-to-door throughout Chinatown as a means of financially supporting his family. He became a business partnership at the local Mayflower Restaurant and, a few years later, in 1982, he opened Kim Chuy (金水), a Teochew-style restaurant located at the heart of the community's commercial district.

Given its existence as a longstanding, intergenerational family-owned restaurant in a gentrifying Chinatown, the importance of Kim Chuy is two-fold. First, Kim Chuy represents an archive of memory work that speaks to a diasporic Southeast Asian Chinese community's navigation of Teochew cultural and ethnic identity. The affective commodities produced in the space of the restaurant enable us to unpack how customers construct Teochew identity for themselves and how they conceptualize Teochew as a community. Pronounced Chaozhou in Mandarin and sometimes spelled Chiu Chow, Teochew describes both a people and their spoken word, a distinct variant of the Southern Min language (Minnan, also known as Hokkien). Teochew people hail from the Chaozhou district of the Guangdong province in China. However, generations separate many in the diaspora from this ancestral home. The history of Kim Chuy highlights how nuanced Teochew identity can be.

Second, Kim Chuy is a space, both physical and social, that provides a lens for analyzing and understanding the socioeconomic, cultural, and physical changes Chinatown faces because of increasing privatization and displacement. Analyzing dynamics of gender, race, ethnicity, and class surrounding Kim Chuy offers a rich insight into the ways this business and its current owner Matthew, Tang's grandson, navigate and negotiate identity and positionality in a rapidly gentrifying Chinatown. Foodways in relation to race, culture, and affect provide a framework of analysis that enables the possibility of the impossible. In the context of gentrification, this is the impossible notion of the continued existence of working-class residents and longstanding traditional small businesses. With the recent surge of capitalist real estate speculation and influx of commercial and residential development projects that cater to upwardly mobile and whiter professionals and creatives, spaces such as Kim Chuy are increasingly vulnerable to both physical and cultural erasure.

Both the name of the restaurant and the nickname of the late Tang, "Kim Chuy" symbolize the restaurant's rich historical and contemporary significance in Chinatown. In English, "Kim Chuy" literally translates from Teochew and other Chinese languages as the words "golden water." In Chinese culture, the combination of the words gold and water in the name of a business can be considered auspicious. Tang's navigation of the "golden waters" of a Chinatown shifting and growing to support a new influx of working-class immigrants during the 1970s to 1990s who came as a "boat person," one of thousands of poor individuals who left Vietnam, Cambodia, and Laos by boat following the American war in Vietnam. As Chinatown gentrifies, Kim Chuy the restaurant continues to navigate "golden waters" but perhaps in a new form—one that is now concentrated with the financial wealth of inequitable investment and development of the past few years: market-rate apartments, new wave eateries, high-end boutiques, art galleries, and real estate speculation.

A diasporic people

Teochew people have ancestral roots in the Chaoshan region of China's Guangdong province. Yet, they are significantly a diasporic people. It is estimated that 60 percent of 25 million of Teochew people live outside of China.[1] Generations separate many, given that Teochew people have emigrated overseas from China in various waves across history. As early as the seventeenth century, Teochew immigrants lived in Vietnam. According to Hannah Hoang, who cites the book *Folk Culture of Vietnamese in Southern Vietnam*, Teochew people were one of three groups of Ming royalists who left southern China for the Mekong provinces of Vietnam during the late 1960s.[2] Alongside the Teochew were other poor coastal residents from Fujian (or Hokkien), Guangdong, and Hainan. Between the nineteenth and mid-twentieth century, a large exodus migrated to Southeast Asian countries.[3] The Opium War of 1839 to 1842 drove many Chinese to Southeast Asia and elsewhere. The Japanese invasion of China in the 1930s again pushed many Southern Chinese to Vietnam, Laos, and Cambodia.[4]

While the migration of Teochew people was never properly documented or studied, port records have shown that three million passengers left the Shantou city in Chaoshan between 1904 and 1935.[5] Tens of thousands of letters written by Teochew migrants to send with remittances to their families back at home were also archived during this period. More recently, violent political and socioeconomic forces, such as the Vietnam War and Khmer Rouge, facilitated the emigration—and displacement—of Teochew people from Southeast Asia to countries such as the United States. The multilayered experiences of this ethnic community challenge conventional understandings of migration as linear and clear-cut and highlight how complicated meaningful geographical ties that diasporic Teochew have to China could be.

Kim Chuy as a site of identity formation

Amidst a gentrifying Chinatown, Kim Chuy remains open after 36 years of business (see Figure 2.1). This restaurant claims to be the first of its kind in the

FIGURE 2.1 Individuals standing outside Kim Chuy look at a large poster of the restaurant's Teochew dishes.

country. While it can be interpreted as symbolizing various things, one of Kim Chuy's key roles in history is its existence as a site of identity formation for the diasporic Teochew community in the United States, specifically Los Angeles. It is a space for many neighboring workers, residents, and visitors who identify as Teochew Cambodians, Vietnamese, and/or Chinese to negotiate and construct ethnic identity through food. Mark Padoongpatt argues that ethnic restaurants, alongside ethnic markets, are what Rick Bonus and Huping Ling would describe as important "locations" for forming "cultural communities" for geographically unbounded groups.[6] For a diasporic Teochew identity that oscillates between feeling geographically connected to Cambodia, Vietnam, China, and other countries, this restaurant fosters a space for grappling and affirming various aspects of Teochew culture—a culture that, while multidimensional, can be specific to those who live in the United States.

The creation and consumption of the commodities produced in the restaurant offer Teochew people, including the owners and some customers of Kim Chuy, a space to negotiate and construct their notions of Teochew identity. In the process of marketing itself, the restaurant creates and claims a distinct Teochew identity throughout its cuisine, menu, and signage. Through the site of the restaurant, Matthew, Tang's grandson and Kim Chuy's current owner, is constantly confronted with moments of identity negotiation and formation and must make decisions over the type of food they serve, the choice of words used to describe the dishes, and the kind of décor he wants to decorate the place with. Thus, he symbolically manipulates the dishes, menu, and signage to make intentional statements about his ethnic identity, using foodways as both a means for navigating and establishing self-identity and a demonstration of this identity to his customers.[7] This iterative process enables Matthew to "form, reform, and maintain"[8] his individual ethnic membership as Teochew.

Matthew continues to serve his late grandfather's original Teochew dishes but also experiments with his own variations of the recipes to, according to him, make them taste better. Fish balls (*heu-ī* or 鱼丸), grey orbits of seasoned fish paste that swim in many of the noodle soups, are one of the foods that continue to be served at Kim Chuy. They are made in-house like the staple ingredients of the restaurant's other dishes and are also available frozen for take-out. While these foods remain largely the same, Matthew has experimented with the recipes throughout the years. He (re)negotiates his Teochew identity through his alterations of Teochew cuisine, adjusting the dish without changing it to the point that it no longer has the characteristics that the restaurant would consider essential to Teochew-style food.

While Teochew food in the United States is a diasporic cuisine that has both Chinese and Southeast Asian influences, there are also elements that can be argued to be distinctly Teochew. One can even consider the ways the dishes have transformed to reflect the diverse histories of immigration and multiethnic identities of the community as the key defining aspect of Teochew cuisine in the United States. At Kim Chuy, more than half the appetizers, noodle soups, dry noodle, and rice dishes listed in their menu are described as being specifically Teochew while other dishes are not. Flavorful and filling, many of these Teochew-identified dishes, such as the Chiu Chow Wonton Soup, Chiu Chow Porridge, and Chiu Chow Beef Chow Mein/Chow Fun resonate familiarity to popular dishes found in Cantonese and other Southern Chinese restaurants. What sets apart Kim Chuy's wonton soup is the generous addition of ingredients such as fish cake, imitation crab, squid, and pork meatball. While traditional Cantonese-style wontons are filled with minced pork and shrimp, Kim Chuy adds imitation crab and onions into their Teochew-style wontons. What may seem like subtle differences set Teochew cuisine apart from their Southern Chinese counterparts, all the while speaking to the influence these geographic regions have on one another.

Another element that makes Kim Chuy's cuisine uniquely Teochew is the simple and plain style that makes Teochew food resonate as "commoner food."[9] A similar handful of ingredients, such as rice noodle or egg noodle, shrimp, thick cuts of poultry, or meatballs and hams made of fish, pork, or beef, are used to make various combinations of dishes at Kim Chuy. All the while, the superior broth, a single large pot of stock simmered overnight to achieve a rich umami flavor, creates the foundation for all of the restaurant's noodle soups and complements the addition of meat and seafood found in these dishes, according to Matthew. Pan-fried (or steamed) Teochew-style leek cakes (*gú chài guè* or 韭菜粿), fried rice cakes (*chài tạo guè* or 菜头粿), and Teochew noodle dishes (*gué diāo* or 粿条) are considered to be distinctly Teochew (see Figure 2.2). These dishes are what the restaurant is arguably known for.

At Kim Chuy, the options for *gué diāo* are seemingly endless, ranging from salted duck to beef variety to their house special seafood. In its various forms, *gué diāo* can come as a noodle soup or a dry noodle dish with soup on the side. Called hủ tiếu in Vietnamese and *kuy teav* in Cambodian, these Teochew noodle dishes are often served in Southeast Asian restaurants such as Vietnamese shops that specialize in phở, a Vietnamese soup dish made of broth, bánh phở rice noodles, herbs, bean sprouts, and chicken or beef. In Vietnam and other Southeast Asian countries, *gué diāo* can often be found at local shops and street-side vendors. The presence of these dishes speaks to the influence that the Teochew community has on Southeast Asian foodways, something that can be traced back to the history of Chinese immigrants and their families in these countries.[10] Significantly, these cultural influences also speak to the complexities of Teochew cuisine as a rich historical archive of the diaspora and the multiple migrations of its people from China to Southeast Asian countries to countries such as the United States, where Matthew's family settled.

The text and images Kim Chuy uses to brand itself reflect the nuances in navigating and performing identity. Throughout the restaurant, and online, Kim Chuy's menus, business cards, posters, and storefront signage display varying lines of English, Chinese, and Romanized Teochew text. While minimal, the English and Chinese are not always exact translations. Their subtle differences speak to the marketing strategies the restaurant employs for different groups of customers. On its menu, for example, Kim Chuy describes itself as simply a "Chinese

FIGURE 2.2 A bowl of dry seafood *guédiāo* from Kim Chuy.

restaurant" (see Figure 2.3). Only in Chinese is its description made more specific: "金水" (Kim Chuy) promotes itself as "正宗潮州金塔粿條 金水" (authentic Teochew noodle dishes). By doing this, Kim Chuy stakes claim to its Teochew identity. *Gué diāo*, or Teochew noodle dishes, is what sets it apart from other "Chinese restaurants." However, by simply reading these signs, only those with Chinese literacy would know that Kim Chuy specifically makes Teochew-style cuisine. Those with English literacy unfamiliar with Teochew cuisine must look to other places to know that this is not only a Chinese restaurant but a Teochew restaurant with roots in Cambodia: the names of menu items, restaurant reviews, interviews with Matthew and his family, and Kim Chuy's website. Next to the "KC" logo that hovers on the front page of its website, the restaurant has replaced the English text that read "Chinese restaurant" on its menu with the more specific words "Chiu Chow restaurant." A proud exclamation of historical significance follows: "Home of the first Teochew style restaurant in the United States!"

The restaurant, and more specifically Matthew, exercises agency when deciding when to explicitly insert Kim Chuy's unique Teochew identity. Scattered throughout

FIGURE 2.3 The front cover of Kim Chuy's menu in 2016. Several lines of text are stacked above one another. Towards the bottom is the phrase "WA CI GA GI NANG!" (I am Teochew!)

the shop, phrases written in Romanized Teochew affirm this collective and individual identity, while possibly teaching non-Teochew customers something new. These common phrases include "*hor chea*," which means delicious, and "*wa ci ga gi nang*," which literally translates as "I am my own people" but is understood as "I am Teochew." Sometimes, it may be enough for a new customer to know that Kim Chuy is a Chinese restaurant, especially in a Chinatown where longstanding, traditional, and family-owned small businesses are increasingly vulnerable with displacement. For returning customers, whether they identify as Teochew, Chinese, Cambodian, or not, Kim Chuy is simply the place to get authentic Teochew noodle dishes.

Personal Connections

Kim Chuy not only serves as a site of identity formation for Matthew and his family, it is also a space for customers to negotiate their constructions of Teochew identity and culture through the affect that is produced in their consumption of the restaurant's commodities. Similar to Purnima Mankekar's analysis of Indian grocery stores as sites for the diasporic community to produce and consume different constructions of India and Indian identity,[11] Kim Chuy produces commodities of "Teochew identity" that are consumed by first- and second-generation Teochew customers. The restaurant evokes a range of affect for its Teochew customers. As a second-generation Teochew American, my ethnic Chinese identity oftentimes felt geographically unbounded as I was growing up in the United States, despite being able to trace back multiple generations of family in Vietnam. Where was home? And was I Chinese or Vietnamese or both? These questions of ethnic identity were unsettling for me as a child who lacked a clear and nuanced understanding of the politics and cultures that shaped definitions of ethnicity. Teochew foodways have been integral in providing me an outlet to unpack what it personally and collectively means to be Teochew. Negotiating my ethnic identity has included a lifelong process of distancing, welcoming, and questioning Teochew food and how it helps me make sense of aspects of my multicultural identity.

When I visited Kim Chuy in 2014 for the first time since my parents took me as a child, I was overwhelmed with nostalgia from the familiarity of the space, not quite able to adequately put into words what the experience of eating the food again felt and meant to me. I had never eaten here without the guidance of my parents and the natural ease in which they spoke Teochew. Hesitantly, I asked the uncle serving me for seafood noodle soup. "*Háichi guédiāo,*" the words felt new and different in my mouth. At the time, it was one of the few moments that I could remember speaking Teochew outside of my home and to someone who was not family or a close family friend. I was nervous. Yet, at the same time, I felt an overwhelming sense of comfort in being able to speak my first language and to be understood.

In the past few years, my visits to Kim Chuy became more frequent as I moved back to Los Angeles and got involved in grassroots organizing in Chinatown. My short interactions with Matthew, the uncle, and other family and friends who work there are held mostly in Teochew; the feelings of uneasiness and embarrassment of pronunciation failures having long passed. The umami and doughy texture of the golden pan-fried leek cakes and fried rice cakes doused in a mix of red vinegar and fish sauce continue to evoke memories of home for me, ones that I associate with childhood memories in Chinatown. I recall a childhood I spent walking through the aisles of the now closed Wing Hop Fung next door, where I snuck pieces of ginseng in my mouth to savor. It was a childhood spent hearing my auntie haggle with business owners for better prices on the matching pajama sets abundant in the maze of swapmeet stalls in Saigon Plaza, and a childhood spent wondering whether I was Chinese or Vietnamese or both or neither.

The experience of eating at Kim Chuy arouses affective responses of nostalgia and unsettlement in me, enabling the production and consumption of particular narratives of my past. Consumption of the food, interactions, images, and text present in this space enmeshes with the notion of objectification. My consumption becomes a form in which I construct understandings of myself in the world.[12] Through the affect that it produces, my consumption provokes a process of negotiating my position in relation to Chinatown and my identity as Teochew. As I eat the foods demarcated as Teochew by Kim Chuy, I negotiate whether or not they are actually Teochew, comparing it with my interactions with the cuisine at home and at other restaurants. My questioning often leads to me to concede to the claims made by the restaurant; I negotiate and incorporate their construction of Teochew identity into my own.

However, this narrow focus on the authenticity of Kim Chuy's cuisine as Teochew begs the larger question: "Who gets to define what is authentic and when, where, why?"[13] Although I share a mother tongue with Matthew, his family, and other Teochew customers, our diasporic narratives, affective responses to foodways, and positions in Chinatown differ as much as they may intersect. My construction of Teochew identity is not generalizable to this diasporic community and their Asian American family members whose culture and ethnic identities are much more complex than my subjective notions of Teochew-ness. As a site of collaboration and tension, Kim Chuy exists as a social space where members of this diaspora are able to interact with other ethnic groups and *gaginang*—a common Teochew phrase for "our own people"—and process their understanding of an individual and collective Teochew identity through the affective responses the space and its commodities evoke. This process may not be conscious, positive, or universal for everyone, but Kim Chuy enables the potential for it to occur.

Gentrification

Facilitated by growing real estate speculation and a long history of the state's disinvestment from poor urban communities of color, gentrification is a multifaceted process of unfettered privatization of land that is inherently inequitable. It aims to restructure Chinatown so that it no longer serves its predominantly working-class immigrant population. The large community of elders, immigrants, and the poor in Chinatown demands resources such as quality affordable housing, community gathering spaces, and culturally competent services. However, they encounter a system that favors urban planning, which is driven by affluent individuals and corporations such as real estate developers, upper-class Chinese Americans who participate in both state and market processes that favor gentrification, and a demographic of upwardly mobile professionals, creatives, and consumers.

While it includes the dismantling of social networks, decentering of narratives, and physical displacement of tenants all in regards to the working-class, gentrification most visibly manifests as neoliberal economic development. With neoliberalism comes the defunding of social programs that serve poor people of color, the deregulation of market forces that enable elite interests and corporations to flourish, and the increased commodification of places and people. In Chinatown, neoliberal economic development looks like an influx of new residential and commercial projects that range from luxury market-rate apartment buildings to art galleries to aesthetically hip coffee shops and eateries. From Jia Apartments and Blossom Plaza apartments on Broadway to The Good Luck Gallery and The Public School on Chung King Road, these spaces all function together to drive and

FIGURE 2.4 Signage for Far East Plaza display: a mix of names for the old and new businesses.

sustain socioeconomic inequity. One of the most visible manifestations of gentrification in Chinatown is the commercial center, Far East Plaza: the nexus of the neighborhood's changing food scene (see Figure 2.4).

Far East Plaza: The Inequity Behind Chinatown's Rising Hip Culinary Food Scene

Oftentimes, the changes and displacement associated with gentrification are seen as inevitable, especially in order for a city to progress and grow. However, presenting gentrification as the "revitalization"[14] of a low-income neighborhood ignores how deeply unjust and unequal this process is. The social and economic forces that enable the recent wave of well-known chefs and entrepreneurs, a significant number of whom are Asian American men, to open their businesses in the neighborhood come in contrast with, and perhaps challenge, the forces that sustain Kim Chuy's existence in a gentrifying Chinatown. Alongside Fortune Gourmet

Kitchen and Thien Huong, Kim Chuy is one of the very few longstanding China-town restaurants in Far East Plaza that is accessible, both physically, financially, and culturally, to the working-class immigrant neighborhood and visitors.

This new wave of eateries presumably caters primarily to the younger, upwardly mobile demographic of professionals and creatives that downtown and interna-tional developers, such as Tom Gilmore, Izek Shomof, and Goodwin Gaw, market to and profit from. These are the commercial spaces that line developers' visions of trendy urban destinations and the people who they want to move into the market-rate apartments and hotels they are proposing. Built in 2014, Jia Apartments is a luxury mixed-use (retail and commercial) building in Chinatown with monthly market-rate rents that currently start at around $1,918 for a 571 square foot studio and $2,262 for a two-bedroom apartment.[15] Down the street, Blossom Apartments, which opened in 2016, has monthly market-rate rents that start at $2,255 for a 407 square foot studio and $2,036 for a one-bedroom apartment.[16] Spaces like these are ridiculously unaffordable and inaccessible for the majority of the neighborhood where the median household income is $18,657,[17] one of the lowest in the city.

These development projects are not built to house or serve the neighborhood's working-class residents, despite there being a nationwide affordable housing crisis and growing homeless community in the city. With their influx, the neighbor-hood's long-term small businesses and residents are increasingly threatened with the displacement that comes from legal and illegal rent increases for residential and retail spaces, evictions, and cash-for-keys, an illegal predatory tactic in which landlords pay residents to voluntarily vacate units in order to flip and sell properties or move in residents who are capable of paying higher rents.

Wealthy property owners and developers, such as Tom Gilmore, sit on the board of directors of the Chinatown Business Improvement District (BID), an entity that plays a disproportionately large role in driving the decision-making processes of the neighborhood's urban redevelopment. BID is far from represen-tative of or accountable to the needs of the neighborhood. Collaborating closely with local governments and private investors—such as the ones who sit on their boards—Business Improvement Districts are a tool of gentrification[18] and partici-pate directly in the increasing criminalization and privatization of urban cities. They work to make neighborhoods attractive for consumerism and investment, targeting those who stand in the way. In Chinatown, these "red shirts" have harassed informal street vendors, musicians, and homeless individuals who are inte-gral residents of the community. To "keep crime down in the neighborhood," George Yu, the executive director of BID, works closely with the Los Angeles Police Department.[19]

The chefs and entrepreneurs of the new wave of eateries garner attention from not only their celebrity and fan following but the support of key players who have disproportionate power in Chinatown such as George Yu. They often celebrate and credit Yu for bringing them into the neighborhood,[20] given that he is not only oversees BID but also serves as the vice president of Macco Investments Corp., the investment company that owns Far East Plaza. Considered to be "the man pulling the strings,"[21] Yu crafts his own vision for Chinatown by overseeing leasing at the commercial center. This vision grossly erases the existing working-class community and ultimately favors those who benefit from the inequity of gentrification.

In the spring of 2013, Korean American Roy Choi opened Chinatown's first celebrity-chef-driven restaurant, Chego, after meeting with George Yu.[22] Over the next few years, Chego's opening would bring an influx of similar "hot-ticket"[23] eateries and boutiques that catered to upwardly mobile professionals and creatives. According to Nguyen Tran of the former Starry Kitchen that opened in late 2013, Choi "shined a guiding light towards Chinatown"[24] and was "the catalyst that convinced us to consider [opening shop there]."[25] Others followed soon after, including Filipino American Alvin Cailan of the downtown Grand Central Market's Egg Slut fame, Taiwanese American Eddie Huang of New York's Bauhaus and autobiography turned TV-show *Fresh Off the Boat,* and Korean American David Chang of New York's Momofuku restaurant enterprise. The early 2018 opening of Chang's Majordomo in what one writer dismissively calls "north Downtown,"[26] a far side of Chinatown filled with industrial warehouses that another writer foresees becoming the next Arts District,[27] brought wide support from celebrity friends. This social capital easily translates to financial wealth that comes in the form of investments and recognition from powerful players who monopolize and unequally benefit from the redevelopment of working-class neighborhoods such as Chinatown.

In her critical analysis of David Chang's recent Netflix series *Ugly Delicious,* Rachel Kuo points to Brandon Jew of Mister Jiu's in San Francisco Chinatown to emphasize how second-generation and third-generation Asian American chefs can contribute to the gentrification of low-income Asian immigrant communities.[28] While she speaks of Chinese cuisine in this context, Kuo poses questions that should be directed to all of the Asian American restaurateurs in this new culinary wave:

> What happens when the Chinese food that people can feel pride in isn't affordable by working class immigrant populations? What happens when Chinese food is valued only when it caters to a more elite class of Asian Americans and other clientele who can afford the uptick in price?

Kuo goes on to say: "Jew, like Chang, is styled as 'ethnic haute' cuisine; both capitalize upon their 'ethnic expertise' as culinary ambassadors of non-white cuisines for white audiences." She cites food scholar Krishnendu Ray, arguing that "the ethnic cook is remade and promoted through proper skills, habits, and training to fit 'middle-class aspiration and upper-class consumption.'" As gentrification worsens an already widening income gap, health disparities, and socioeconomic inequities, it is imperative for people to question who in Chinatown can afford and feel welcomed in spaces that serve food such as $4 baos (BaoHaus) or $32 Cave Aged Butter & White Sturgeon Caviar (Majordomo).

The Chois, Huangs, Changs, and Cailans carry with them social and financial capital that the owners and cooks of many longstanding, family-run, and traditional restaurants, like the existing Kim Chuy and the recently shuttered *cha chaan teng* (茶餐廳)—a specific type of Hong-Kong style diner—J&K Hong Kong Cuisine in Far East Plaza, arguably do not. The restaurateurs of these newer eateries are often quoted as being empathetic toward and appreciative of the older generation of small businesses that continue to or used to exist in the neighborhood.[29] However, they lack—or at least fail to articulate publicly—a critical, nuanced understanding of Chinatown's changes as being rooted in a larger process of inequitable economic development, one that values them but will eventually displace the older businesses that they try to honor. Is it possible for these hip eateries to coexist with small businesses like Kim Chuy? Without self-critiquing the financial and social capital that enables them to open shop and exist in Chinatown, and without explicitly challenging inequitable development, these businesses are complicit in the neighborhood's gentrification. Their presence drives further inequitable development and enables the discourse that ignorantly frames Chinatown's gentrification as "a new commercial renaissance"[30] rather than working-class displacement.

Navigating Change

"The lines used to go out the door," Matthew tells me as we continue our conversation over the restaurant's history during a moderately slow Saturday evening in May 2016.[31] With fluctuations in the U.S. economy, such as the 2008 economic recession, and the migration of different ethnic groups throughout Los Angeles, he has found it imperative to adjust the restaurant to serve the changing demographics of customers, all the while staying true to his grandfather's recipes and vision of a Teochew-style restaurant. Business may not be as popular or stable as it was in its heyday for Matthew, but it continues to garner some attention from media platforms such as interviews from KCET.[32] More importantly, it continues to see loyal returning customers.

Over the years, Kim Chuy has adjusted its menu to cater to its growing Latinx and white clientele, in addition to its Asian American clientele whose taste preferences may differ from their first-generation parents' inclinations for food. Thus, beef with broccoli noodles and fried fish with steam rice, dishes that Matthew believes these ethnic groups enjoy more of compared with the traditional Teochew *guédiāo*, are offered. "You can't just have Teochew noodle [because] the Teochew noodle are basically for Teochew people only,"[33] a sentiment that is reflected in the Chinese text of Kim Chuy's logo.

Another response to the changing clientele is the first page of the restaurant's menu, which dawns large images of the many available options of noodles that customers can choose for their order. This "noodle choice" page, in addition to the newer dishes, represents the restaurant's negotiations over its menu to help customers unfamiliar with traditional Teochew cuisine better navigate the restaurant. To expand Kim Chuy's clientele base and maintain business, Matthew makes adjustments to the restaurant to cater to the diverse customers' taste preferences and needs, while maintaining the elements of the menu and dishes that make the restaurant distinctly Teochew-style.

While navigating the racial and ethnic dynamics of the restaurant's growing customer base, Kim Chuy has also had to adjust to accommodate the changing racial and ethnic dynamics of its employees. A large number of the restaurant's employees work in the back and front kitchen cooking the dishes. Over time, the cooks have transitioned from being only Cantonese, Vietnamese, and Teochew immigrants to consisting of a significant number of Latinx immigrants. Hiring workers has posed some difficulties over the years for Kim Chuy, particularly because of the strenuous physical labor that working in a restaurant demands, especially from its kitchen staff. Because of this, Matthew believes that "not even Asians want to work in a restaurant."[34] However, more Latinx immigrants have expressed interest in working at Kim Chuy. His sentiment speaks to the varying socioeconomic positions of different generations and waves of immigrants in the United States and in Los Angeles County in particular. Consisting of older and newer generations of immigrants, Chinatown's population has a concentration of 62 percent Asians.[35] Yet, Chinatown's existence as an ethnic enclave, made up of mostly Cantonese immigrants, has gradually transformed with the influx of Southeast Asians and Latinx over the years. Kim Chuy's immigrant workers have had to make individual and collective negotiations over what type of employment is accessible, available, and feasible for them to support their livelihoods.

To adjust to the changing racial and ethnic dynamics of the workers, Kim Chuy has developed various techniques to address language barriers and ensure clear communication among its multiethnic employees. After customer orders are taken by either Matthew or his family members, who play multiple roles of server and host, they are typed up and printed out in slips of English, Spanish, and Chinese before being given to the kitchen. When the Latinx kitchen staff first learn how to cook the food the restaurant serves, they work with Matthew to develop a code where they use shortened terms to easily communicate the ingredients and dishes to each other. This code, which is also reflected in the printed orders the kitchen receives, becomes a separate language that utilizes the employees' respective languages. It increases the accessibility of foodways in relation to language for the front staff and kitchen staff. Communication has been important in ensuring Kim Chuy's diverse workers can work together. Assuming that they both speak Spanish, Matthew believes that if the head chef is Latinx, then it is important that the sous chef, the one preparing the ingredients, is also Latinx, rather than Asian. This ensures clear communication between the two key players in the kitchen, which is key to maintaining the restaurant business.

While unpacking the racial and ethnic dynamics of Kim Chuy, it is also important to explore the gender and intergenerational dynamics of this family-owned restaurant. Matthew was a child when his grandfather Tang secured the financial means to open the restaurant in 1982. Since then, the restaurant continues to occupy the same corner location on the first floor of the Far East Plaza commercial space on North Broadway. Kim Chuy has been passed on generationally from his grandfather to his parents to Matthew and his siblings. While describing his family's years spent running and sustaining the restaurant, Matthew humbly says that they are merely trying to make enough to live day by day.[36] For him, this is what Teochew people do. It is a livelihood and responsibility that is intrinsic for this diasporic community in the United States, a significant number of whom are working-class refugees because of the Vietnam War and Khmer Rouge.

The recent passing of his father leaves Matthew as the owner as his siblings pursue other careers. As the owner, he makes decisions over marketing and menus, alongside financial and logistical matters. Yet his mother, one of many women who work at the restaurant, ultimately oversees Kim Chuy as the daughter of the first owner and founder, Tang. She, alongside Matthew, his biological aunties, a middle-aged man, and family friends he refers to as his uncle and aunties work in the front of the restaurant as both servers, hosts, and bussers, while the rest of the employees work solely in the kitchen or as bussers. In addition to the front staff, immigrant women also contribute significantly to the cooking done in the kitchen. The physical and emotional labor they invest in ensuring the restaurant operates speaks to the history of women's key role in Asian foodways. As Matthew balances multiple tasks during our conversation, the sound of Cantonese and Toisan can be heard slowly and loudly making its way out of the back kitchen. While he serves as the representative for the restaurant, answering interview inquiries such as mine, his decisions are greatly informed by his mother, leaving Kim Chuy to be a collectively run business rather than one run solely by him.

Matthew identifies the restaurant as a physically and mentally strenuous place to work in for both the front staff and kitchen staff, given the long business hours and obligations to meet customer demands for food. Because of this, he does not want his own children to work here. He believes that he will be the family's last generation at Kim Chuy. Throughout our conversations, he has reiterated multiple times that his family works at the restaurant as a necessary means to financially sustain themselves and keep themselves occupied. Compared with his own position as an immigrant whose parents and grandfather had fewer socioeconomic means, his children's positions as second-generation Cambodian Teochew American appear to provide them more flexibility and capacity to pursue various occupations. Working in the restaurant industry does not align with Matthew's notions of an "American Dream," something he wants his teenage sons to achieve.[37]

Looking at Kim Chuy in relation to foodways provides a site for deconstructing the complexities of the intersections of intergenerational expectations, class, race, culture, and space. Matthew's expectations for his children construct a perception of the restaurant industry that contrasts with the hip eateries that neighbor Kim Chuy in Far East Plaza. These newer restaurants signal a shift in the plaza's businesses and the neighborhood's demographic. From chef-driven restaurants, such as Chego and BaoHaus, to smaller eateries and cafes, such as Endorffeine, Lao Tao, and Scoops, the majority of these new shops are operated by relatively young entrepreneurs who presumably view the restaurant industry as a field they have the interest and socio-economic capacity to pursue. Aware of the age of the new restaurateurs, several of whom are second-generation Asian Americans like his children, and their relative success in the burgeoning food industry, Matthew still prefers his sons to pursue careers outside of his own. For him, the restaurant is a space of rigorous work. His desires and expectations for his children speak to his experiences of working multiple roles in a restaurant and understanding the labor that is demanded of its workers. His positionality as a first-generation immigrant with a working-class background influences his expectations for his own children, whose socioeconomic position and generational perceptions may well differ from his own.

The Wealth of Kim Chuy

In contrast to the restaurateurs of Far East Plaza's new eateries, Kim Chuy's social capital stems from the Teochew identity it represents and fosters with the cuisine it serves, the languages spoken by its customers and employees, the descriptions in its menu, and, ultimately, its history of existence in Chinatown. A wealth of cultural, historical, and contemporary knowledge has been fostered here. The social relationships that the space has built and maintained with residents and returning customers since Matthew's grandfather Tang opened it in 1982 help keeps its doors open for business. Matthew often makes humble remarks about work as a means to sustain life day to day. What he, alongside his family and the other workers, do to keep Kim Chuy running can be demanding work, but it is a testament to the deep compassion and care they create in the space of the restaurant. Sustaining Kim Chuy is an act of historical and cultural preservation, especially in the face of gentrification.

Amidst the unsettling political and socioeconomic forces of gentrification, foodways in relation to race, culture, and affect provide a framework of analysis that centers the narratives of Kim Chuy and its working-class workers and customers. By highlighting the historical and contemporary significance of this intergenerational family-owned restaurant, the ways in which the workers and customers navigate racial and ethnic identity, and the class and gender dynamics in foodways, there is greater possibility for Kim Chuy, alongside working-class residents and similar immigrant-run small businesses, to continue existing in the midst of a gentrifying Chinatown.

Key Terms

Diaspora: Dispersion of a group of people from their original homeland.

Gentrification: An unsustainable and inequitable form of neoliberal economic development facilitated by capitalist structures of power, gentrification is an intentional process of racial, spatial, and economic segregation. It physically and figuratively erases the livelihoods and narratives of working-class communities of color.

Teochew: Teochew is both a people and their spoken word, a distinct variant of the Southern Min language (Minnan, also known as Hokkien). Teochew people hail from the Chaozhou district of the Guangdong province in China. There is a significant diasporic Teochew community.

Discussion Questions

1. How does gentrification impact working-class communities of color such as Los Angeles Chinatown? What are the multiple aspects of gentrification?
2. What narratives, experiences, and issues can be communicated through food?
3. What is one dish in your life that holds cultural and/or political significance, and why?

Notes

1 Lee Hsien Loong, "Teochews Can Take Pride in Successes," YaleGlobal Online, Yale University, November 24, 2003, accessed July 14, 2018, https://yaleglobal.yale.edu/content/teochews-can-take-pride-successes.
2 Hannah Hoang, "Bánh Pía: The Dreamy Mooncake Alternative with a Side of Teochew History," *Saigoneer*, September 17, 2018, accessed October 1, 2018, https://saigoneer.com/eat-drink/eat-drink-categories/saigon-food-culture/14494-b%C3%A1nh-p%C3%ADa-the-dreamy-mooncake-alternative-with-a-side-of-teochew-history.
3 "Teochew Letters," accessed July 14, 2018, www.teochewletters.org/about.
4 Haiming Liu, *From Canton Restaurant to Panda Express: A History of Chinese Food in the United States* (Rutgers University Press, 2015), 123.
5 "Teochew Letters: The Story of A People, Penned by The People," The Teochew Store, October 30, 2016, accessed July 14, 2018, www.theteochewstore.org/blogs/latest/teochew-letters-the-story-of-a-people-penned-by-the-people.
6 Tanachai Mark Padoongpatt, "Too Hot to Handle: Food, Empire, and Race in Thai Los Angeles." *Radical History Review* (Duke University Press, 2011), 86–90.
7 Susan Kalcik, "Ethnic Foodways in America: Symbol and the Performance of Identity" (Ethnic and Regional Foodways, 1984), 46–55.
8 Ibid.
9 "Kim Chuy Cambodian Restaurant: The Lim Family," *KCET*, June 30, 2010, accessed June 5, 2016, www.kcet.org/shows/departures/kim-chuy-cambodian-restaurant-the-lim-family.
10 Huynh Cuong. "Hu Tieu Or Hủ Tiếu—Paying Respect to Pho's Cousin," *Lovingpho.com*, July 2009, accessed June 5, 2016, www.lovingpho.com/pho-opinion-editorial/hu-tieu-noodles-and-hu-tieu-soup-noodle-dish/.
11 Purnima Mankekar, "'India Shopping': Indian Grocery Stores and Transnational Configurations of Belonging" (*The Cultural Politics of Food and Eating*, 2005), 202–206.
12 Ibid.
13 Teochew Letters.
14 Farley Elliot, "Inside the 20-Year Effort to Turn Chinatown into a Thriving Cultural Center Once Again," *Eater*, March 7, 2017, https://la.eater.com/2017/3/7/14796842/morning-briefing-restaurant-news-los-angeles-chinatown-history.
15 "Jia Apartments," Equity Apartments, Equity Residential, October 22, 2018, accessed October 22, 2018, www.equityapartments.com/los-angeles/chinatown/jia-apartments##bedroom-type-section-0.
16 "Floor Plans." Blossom Plaza Apartments, October 22, 2018, accessed October 22, 2018, www.blossomplazala.com/floor-plans/.

17 Wendy Chung, "One Chinatown" (Los Angeles: University of Southern California, 2016), 18.

18 Max Rivlin-Nader, "Business Improvement Districts Ruin Neighborhoods," February 19, 2016, accessed September 1, 2018, https://newrepublic.com/article/130188/business-improvement-districts-ruin-neighborhoods.

19 Jean Trinh, "The Past, Present, and Future of Chinatown's Changing Culinary Landscape," February 28, 2017, accessed March 19, 2018, www.kcet.org/shows/the-migrant-kitchen/the-past-present-and-future-of-chinatowns-changing-culinary-landscape.

20 Kalcik, "Ethnic Foodways in America."

21 Farley Elliot, "Meet the Man Who Brought Chinatown's Far East Plaza Back to Life," March 28, 2016, accessed March 14, 2018, https://la.eater.com/2016/3/28/11318662/chinatown-far-east-plaza-george-yu.

22 Katherine Spiers, "Chinatown's Far East Plaza Is a Dining Destination Thanks to George Yu," LAWeekly.com, May 3, 2017, accessed November 3, 2017, www.laweekly.com/restaurants/george-yu-turned-chinatowns-far-east-plaza-into-a-culinary-hotspot-8174773.

23 Ibid.

24 Nguyen Tran, "How to Run an Illegal Restaurant," munchies.com, September 27, 2017, accessed March 14, 2018, https://munchies.vice.com/en_us/article/pgxvxv/how-to-run-an-illegal-restaurant.

25 Lesley Balla, "Starry Kitchen Begins Serving in Chinatown This Weekend," zagat.com, July 12, 2013, accessed March 14, 2018, www.zagat.com/b/los-angeles/starry-kitchen-begins-serving-in-chinatown-this-weekend.

26 Matthew Kang, "David Chang's Majordomo Opens Tonight: Here's What to Expect," LA.Eater.com, Eater Los Angeles, January 23, 2018, accessed April 22, 2018, https://la.eater.com/2018/1/23/16923818/majordomo-david-chang-momofuku-los-angeles-opening-food.

27 Farley Elliot, "Is Majordomo Already Changing Real Estate Fortunes in Far Chinatown?" LA.Eater.com, Eater Los Angeles, April 19, 2018, accessed April 22, 2018, https://la.eater.com/2018/4/19/17246950/morning-briefing-restaurant-news-los-angeles-chinatown-real-estate.

28 Rachel Kuo, "Digging into the Racial Politics of 'Ugly Delicious,'" Reappropriate.co, May 16, 2018, accessed July 10, 2018, http://reappropriate.co/2018/05/digging-into-the-racial-politics-of-ugly-delicious/.

29 Eddie Kim, "How an Aging Chinatown Mall Became a Hipster Food Haven," ladowntownnews.com, March 28, 2016, accessed September 1, 2017, www.ladowntownnews.com/news/how-an-aging-chinatown-mall-became-a-hipster-food-haven/article_b407e372-f2c3-11e5-a794-e70f2ee0afe3.html.

30 Elliot, "Is Majordomo Already Changing Real Estate Fortunes in Far Chinatown?"

31 "Matthew Lim." Personal interview, May 15, 2016.

32 Kalcik, "Ethnic Foodways in America."

33 "Matthew Lim." Personal interview, May 15, 2016.

34 Ibid.

35 Randy Mai and Bonnie Chen, "The State of Los Angeles Chinatown" (Los Angeles: University of California, Los Angeles, 2013), 8.

36 "Matthew Lim." Personal interview, May 15, 2016.

37 Ibid.

3

FEEDING PREJUDICES

Chinese *Fondas* and the Culinary Making of National Identity in Peru

Patricia Palma and José Ragas

> The current gastronomy, known as Peruvian cuisine, would not certainly exist as such without the Chinese influence that carries on it.
>
> Jaime Bedoya, "Cebiche de Wong."

Introduction

Between 1849 and 1874, nearly 100,000 Chinese moved from Canton to the Peruvian coast to replace the declining African slavery in the country. Since then, Chinese have shaped Peruvian history in numerous and unexpected ways: from the labor system with *coolie* workers to the Shining Path's Maoist ideological influence. Their presence as one of the most ubiquitous immigrant communities in the country—and the second largest Chinese community in the Pacific Rim, only after California—challenged the ideological foundations of a national identity envisioned by the local elite as European-oriented, reserving the place of second-class citizens to Chinese newcomers and other future immigrants (i.e. Japanese and Andean migrants). In recent times, Peruvian nationalist discourse has struggled to reconcile a more inclusive narrative with a legacy of derogatory treatment toward immigrants, embracing certain elements of the Chinese immigration to the nation.

Peruvian-Chinese food, also known as *chifa*, constitutes a crucial yet problematic legacy of the Chinese presence in the country, with ramifications that traverse beyond the space of kitchens and dining rooms. The massive migration of Chinese to Lima, the capital city, and other cities modified the food culture of all social groups in Peru. This chapter situates the early development of Chinese food in the country, between the arrival of the first coolie workers and the Great Depression, to highlight the convoluted trajectory of *chifas* (Peruvian-Chinese restaurants) and *fondas* (small restaurants) before they were embraced by the nationalist discourse.

Drawing from classical and recent scholarship, as well as from a varied body of sources including travel logs, cartoons, commercial statistics, songs, and others, we argue that Chinese food offers a window onto everyday social practices between Chinese and Peruvians. Furthermore, we consider that food provides an original analytical approach to examine the role of Chinese food in the development of the cultural identity in the Peruvian Andes.

Cuisine prestige is a sensitive topic in Peru; a country whose national identity has been built on its fierce defense of its alleged contributions to the global palate, such as potatoes and quinoa. By studying the trajectory of Chinese food in Peru, we aim to challenge the Peruvian culinary narrative by highlighting and situating *chifas*, *fondas*, and Chinese cooks' contributions within the Peruvian national identity. In recent years, the Peruvian gastronomic boom has tried to revert this situation by incorporating *chifa* as part of national dishes yet presenting it as an elite cuisine and separating it from its popular roots. This chapter aims to rescue that history by introducing an overview of how Chinese food reached a prominent position among national citizens, because it was an affordable and varied cuisine option. *Fonda* owners, farmers, cooks, merchants, patrons, authorities, chroniclers, and journalists were responsible for turning Chinese cuisine into the most important immigrant gastronomy in the country, which transformed Peruvians' palates and culinary habits.

From Haciendas to Early *Fondas*

The origin of the Chinese colony in Peru can be traced back to the massive importation of coolie workers who arrived in 1849 to work in the guano deposits and coastal agriculture.[1] The coolie trade contributed significantly to the expansion of the Peruvian economy by mining guano, building railroads, and working on cotton and sugarcane plantations.[2] The magnitude of the arrival of Chinese workers in Peru is only comparable to Cuba and California during the second half of the nineteenth century. This trade brought more than 100,000 Chinese men to Peru and lasted until 1874, the year the Treaty of Friendship, Commerce and Navigation at Tianjin was signed, and it ended the coolie trade after several international commissions denounced the coolies' inhumane living and working conditions in Peruvian haciendas.[3]

Newcomers' culinary skills and preferences were not interrupted during their tenures as rural laborers in Peru. On the contrary, rural estates became early gastronomic laboratories where Chinese struggled to maintain their habits by adapting local condiments while obtaining some native ingredients in small shops that imported items from Asia. Chinese turned haciendas into their first *fondas* by establishing small shops, obtaining utensils by credit from the *hacienda*, and introducing Asian dishes to other rural workers. Chinese laborers were also allowed to grow their own vegetables in certain parts of the plantations. Given that by contract *hacendados* had the obligation to feed their contracted workers, the selection of products delivered by owners consolidated the Chinese diet. Many *haciendas* provided their

Chinese workers with rice and pork, but the most important item—that characterized Chinese food and coastal dishes in the ensuing years—was rice. On average, the standard ration in the *haciendas* was one-half pound of rice for a day's work.[4] Humberto Rodríguez Pastor has estimated the amount of rice distributed alongside the *haciendas* in the country, and he has calculated that 840 and 1,050 tons of rice were consumed on a monthly basis amongst the 40,000 and 50,000 Chinese laborers who consumed 61,000 to 77,000 pounds of rice on a daily basis.[5]

Once released from their onerous contracts in plantations, many Chinese laborers maintained their skills as cooks in their new destinations, whether opening their own establishments or working as independent cooks in households. As an article in the newspaper *El Comercio*—the most important newspaper in the country—noted in October 1873: "Nearly all settlers who have finished their contracts are in Chinatown and work as cooks, which is really what they like to do."[6] From their position as servants and cooks, and especially as owners of small restaurants (or *fondas*), Chinese laborers decisively influenced the food market. Chinese laborers who moved to urban areas could also enter the labor system as cooks in households. Middle- and upper-class families, who needed help after slavery was ended, hired Chinese workers to take care of their meals and to do other domestic errands. Most of the travelers who visited Peru in the second half of the nineteenth century noted the large presence of Chinese people in the city. During his visit to Lima (1853–1888), the German doctor Ernst Middendorf pointed out that the majority of the Chinese who moved to Lima after their contracts expired had learned different trades and become craftsmen, shoemakers, or wood carvers, and those who lacked manual skills worked as domestic servants and cooks.[7] Although Chinese laborers earned a degree of autonomy as cooks that they did not have as contract workers, they were not necessarily treated better. As contemporary ads show, they were treated like property and chased by their masters if they decided to escape from their abusive households. In an analysis of runaway Chinese workers between 1852 and 1872, Rodríguez Pastor found that 38 percent of them were employed as maids and cooks.[8]

In just a few years, the Chinese positioned themselves formidably in the small restaurant business of the capital. According to Evelyn Hu, the Chinese restaurants in Lima in 1869 were dedicated to *fondas* (19 establishments or 37 percent).[9] The ubiquitous presence of Chinese cooks and *fondas* inadvertently responded to the eating habits of Limeños. In 1891 Theodore Child, an American writer and journalist who visited Spanish America in the 1880s, informed his readers: "In Lima the Chinese are very numerous; some of them sell water-ices and others fruits, which they carry in Oriental style in baskets suspended from a long bamboo pole balanced on their shoulders; they also do all work as porters and servants, but their specialty is keeping cheap restaurants."[10] The writer noted that most of the people in Lima did not cook at home, and instead they went to the nearest *fonda* to buy a meal.[11] This turned *fondas* into an important source of independence and a safe investment for other Asian immigrants. Many Chinese cooks working in the domestic service aimed to save money and establish their own businesses, which were most likely going to be small *fondas* around the market of La Concepción, located at the heart of downtown Lima and just a few blocks away from the Palace of Government (Figure 3.1). Since 1854, many free Chinese laborers settled around this market establishing their more important firms, associations, and guilds, transforming this area in the Peruvian Chinatown.[12]

This pattern was replicated in others parts of the country. Trujillo, a city in northwestern Peru, acted as an urban magnet for those who wanted to leave behind rural work and settle in the city. Surrounded by myriad rural estates, Trujillo rapidly became the second largest place in the coastal area to host Chinese immigrants. In a recent thesis, Cesilia Sánchez has estimated that during the early twentieth century, one in ten Chinese immigrants had a *fonda* in the city ("fonderos"). Although *fonderos* captured the 10 percent of the businesses run by the Chinese community, they were outnumbered by butchers (20 percent) and pulperos (55 percent).[13] *Fondas* also provided additional services. Given the lack of proper accommodation in Trujillo, American adventurer George Squier was advised to stay in a Chinese *fonda* during one of his archaeological expeditions in the country. The *fonda* took care of Squier's necessities: not only by having a room for him but also by delivering his breakfast and meals to his expedition along with ice, which

CELESTIALS IN PERU.

FIGURE 3.1   A Chinese cook in Lima. Our artist is seen here resisting the tempting offer of a bowl of what appears to be buzzed soup, in front of one of the Chinese cook-shops that abound in the neighborhood of the market at Lima.

Source: Geo Carleton. *Our Artist in Peru* (New York, 1866), 19.

was a necessary item due to the high temperatures of the region.[14] Squier's only complaint was that the bill was written in Chinese characters, making it impossible for him to review the expenses and dispute any unsolicited service.

Chinese *fondas* shared many aspects of other working-class restaurants, such as being simple places while maintaining an "Oriental" flavor by including Chinese characters and chopsticks.[15] Carlos Paz Soldán, a renowned physician, visited Chinatown in 1916, and noted the presence of some "Oriental" aspects in *fondas*, similar to other Chinese business such as herbal shops and opium dens. He also acknowledged that *fondas* attracted a large number of the local population, and this was largely due to Chinese cooks having adapted food and beverages to Chinese and Peruvian cooking traditions. While Chinese people drank tea regularly and ate unsalted rice in chinaware with chopsticks, local customers requested cutlery and asked the cook to add some salt to their portions.[16] Décor was another aspect distinctive of Chinese *fondas* that captured the attention of observers. Child remembered that in Chinatown some of the small restaurants were decorated with vertical inscriptions written on black or orange-red paper.[17] These descriptions correspond with accounts provided by travelers in other Chinatowns across the Americas.[18]

Writers praised the contribution of these restaurants to the Peruvian society and food culture. The well-known poet and writer Juan de Arona, a rare and solitary voice amidst a looming anti-Chinese sentiment among Peruvian nationals, praised the commitment and cleanliness of these restaurants.[19] Arona highlighted the contribution of these *fondas* to Peruvian manners, since "[The Chinese] have habituated our plebeians to eating with tablecloths, and using silverware and glasses."[20] Other writers expressed their admiration of these restaurants for the quality of their service. Abelardo Gamarra wrote a lot of praise for *fondas* in a story entitled "La Fondita Criolla" (the local *fonda*). In this story, Gamarra expressed the frustration of diners in local Peruvian eateries over their poor service, long waiting time, limited availability of food, and the idleness of local patrons. Gamarra contrasted these establishments with Chinese *fondas* by saying, in a derogatory way,

> a single Chinese person serves two hundred patrons and from a whole street away one can hear his beckoning call, rice on its own, meat with rice, steak, pudding. One can see the throng people coming and going, hardly sitting down presented [to the customer]: the menu, the bread, the tea, all is presented as if moved by a spring.[21]

Chinese *fondas* played an important role in the social landscape of the city, serving as privileged scenarios to narrate the misadventures of people from lower classes and inspiring local writers and composers. For instance, in 1872, readers of *El Correo* learned the story of "Panchito," a fictitious character portraying an Indigenous migrant who arrived in the capital for the very first time. Excited to be in the city, Panchito woke up early in the morning determined to see Lima himself.

Having had lunch in a "*fonda* in Chinatown," he soon realized he had no money to pay the bill, so he left his fiancé's ring while another person accompanied him to the hotel to get the money.[22] Local music (or *música criolla*) reproduced the prevailing segregationist attitudes shared by Limeños toward the Asian population.[23] In general, lyrics portrayed *fondas* as places where Chinese offered bad food ("La fonda de la Inquisición") or as scenarios of comic scenes and misadventures ("Pleito en una fonda de chinos").[24] A possible exception is a song composed by local musician Filomeno Ormeño ("Fonda china"), in which the lyrics depict *fondas* in a more positive light by praising them for the variety of food that patrons may find.

Attacks

As the historian Paulo Drinot states, the food in Peru in the early twentieth century was at the center of a number of conflicts shaped by race, class, and gender. The price, quality, and availability of food played a role in the politicization of the urban working class.[25] As a consequence of the economic recession of 1907, industrial activity decreased and severance became a serious problem, especially in the popular classes. This phenomenon coincided with the influx of Chinese migration in 1909.[26] In a climate of shortage and increased food prices—especially of meat—the press played a key role in placing particular blame on Chinese stores for the rise in the price of food products. Popular reactions to Chinese restaurants—which included attacks in the press and direct action—were common in the first decades of the twentieth century, and these did not differ significantly from acts of violence in other parts of the Americas, such as Mexico and Cuba in the 1920s and 1930s. According to Haiming Liu, it is clear that Peruvian food was used as a tool in racial ideology where every element of Chinese culture was distorted and stereotyped as negative for Peruvian tradition and harmful to local population.[27]

The medical discourse—conveniently disseminated through the media—portrayed the Chinese community as the dirtiest in the country.[28] Magazines and newspapers like *Fray K. Bezón* and *Variedades* devoted much of their space to a systematic series of stories characterizing the Chinese community—and particularly its food and *fondas*—in unhygienic terms, as a major menace to the health of the workers. "Harmful piggery" and "repugnant stores" became commonplace adjectives used to describe Chinese businesses, although many small stores did not differ significantly in term of hygiene from other establishments owned by Peruvians.[29] As expected, the association between the Chinese and dirtiness exacerbated in moments of racial conflicts. In 1909, Lima's working-class hatred of the Chinese reached a peak in the riots of May of that year, which also impacted the attacks in the press against food culture. As the late Adam McKeown demonstrates, this particular year the standard of cleanliness in small Chinese restaurants was a common target of criticism in newspapers, which often accused the Chinese of eating and serving rats.[30]

The image of Chinese eating rats or using them as ingredients for their dishes was part of the stereotypical image of Chinese food.[31] The rat-eating representation of Chinese food surfaced at about the same time that Chinese cooks opened the firsts *fondas* in Lima in the 1860s. For instance, in 1863 the newspaper *El Comercio* informed their readers that the basis of Chinese gastronomy was rats.[32] Since by those years *fondas* were primarily frequented by the Chinese community, this information was just another disgusting anecdote about the newcomers' culinary habits. However, decades later, when Chinese food gained a broader presence in the capital, news items like these were viewed under a distinct light by readers and authorities. Although there was no proof to back up the information, the rumor about the use of rats in *fondas* was perceived as a threat to national public health, especially so soon after the epidemic of bubonic plague that affected the coastal area in 1903.[33] The anti-Chinese climate of 1909 only exacerbated the stereotypes about Chinese culinary habits. In April of that year, *Variedades* lodged a complaint against "[a] son of the Celestial Empire" who aroused customers' distrust of what they were consuming in *fondas*, arguing that the *macacos* (racial slur for Chinese immigrants) had discovered that the meat of disgusting animals was more nutritional and profitable for their business than acceptable forms of meat. The magazine also denounced an anonymous "individual from the lower class" who bought a *mimpao* [baozi 包子] in the Callejon Otaiza—a conglomerate of buildings in Chinatown—and found "some suspicious traces" on it. After analysis, the Hygienic Institute concluded that "it was a roll seasoned with rat's meat."[34] Thus, health authorities, who had previously authorized fondas, reversed their opinion and joined the critics of the press and public opinion amid an anti-Chinese climate.

It is interesting to note that even ardent advocates of the Chinese community like Dora Mayer de Zulen never denied that rats were part of the Chinese diet. Mayer de Zulen was a prolific journalist and writer who published regularly in Lima's major newspapers and magazines, and actively took up the cause of defending the Chinese community in Peru.[35] In 1924, she penned *La China Silenciosa y Elocuente*, a book commissioned by the Chinese Benevolent Association to portray a respectable image of the community. In the book, Mayer concluded that the consumption of rats would unite the cultural aspects and experiences between the Chinese community and the indigenous people in Peru.[36] Mayer pointed out that some tribes in the mountain region of Peru ate *pericotes* (large rodents), insect larvae, and frogs for their nutrition, and she argued that it was problematic to generalize the food habits of a whole nation only because one group consumed it.[37]

Undoubtedly, the most extreme racist attack against Chinese food was the accusation that *fondas* used human flesh. The medicinal use of mummified parts of the human body was not unknown in Chinese medical tradition, but cannibalism was not a regular practice.[38] Despite the accusations against Chinese food and rumors of the consumption of human flesh, residents in the capital conveniently ignored the fact that cannibalism was practiced in some parts of Peru. As the doctor Hermilio

Valdizán informed in his book *Peruvian Popular Medicine* published in 1922, some groups in the Peruvian Amazon were cannibals, who enjoyed digesting human flesh both for its taste as well as for medical reasons.[39] The malicious spread of rumors against the consumption of human flesh stressed their alleged lacking of any moral or scruple by Chinese cooks. In 1872, *El Comercio* retracted a piece that contained false information about the sale of human flesh in a Chinese shop in Lima. The information falsely accused a Chinese cook of using chili and human flesh in his dishes.[40]

Not only was Chinese food the target of critics and prejudices, but *fondas* were also vulnerable sites exposed to attacks in the media or by mobs during periods of social upheaval. The negative image that portrayed *fondas* as unhealthy places along with the diatribes against the community fueled the attacks against these sites and their owners. From the 1860s onward the press reported acts against *fondas* and their owners.[41] In January 1868, amid one of the worst epidemics of yellow fever in the country, looters sacked and destroyed numerous *fondas* in Lima.[42] These episodes ceased until the 1940s, when a new wave of anti-Asian sentiment—this time against the Peruvian Japanese—targeted *fondas* along with other establishments associated with Chinese immigrants. In the past, Chinese owners had employed several strategies to counter the rage of the populace in moments of turmoil. Some of them, for instance, married Peruvian women, co-managing food businesses as part of a family venture while raising multi-ethnic offspring. It is most likely that interracial marriages gave *fondas* and their owners more access to and acceptance by a diverse clientele that would provide some protection against xenophobic campaigns.[43] Furthermore, Chinese owners passively resisted by leaving groceries and other items outside of their establishments, so that the mob would take them instead of destroying their stores. During the riots against the Japanese in the early 1940s, Chinese store owners sought to avoid being confused with Japanese immigrants by posting a Chinese flag outside their restaurants and exclaiming "I am Chinese! I am Chinese!" when a mob approached.[44]

Popularity and Expansion

The continuous hostility toward the Chinese community and its businesses—particularly restaurants—did not impede the silent but steady expansion of its dishes and new flavors in the capital city and other regions. How was this possible? In his study on the history of chop suey in America, Andrew Coe points out that the most important factor in the success of Chinese food was its low price.[45] This was what occurred in Peru, as evidenced by the vast clientele that was attracted to Chinese cuisine as an affordable alternative, especially among working-class sectors. This explains why, despite the growing animosity toward the newcomers, various actors and groups raised their voices to defend the existence of *fondas* and its role in containing poverty and hunger among the urban poor, the nascent working class, and the fragile urban middle class. Not without resignation, doctor and traveler Ernst Middendorf accepted that Chinese restaurants in Peru offered affordable meals, and that "if someday Chinese were forced to leave the country, like it is happening nowadays in California, they will be missed by the most impoverished."[46] Like him, many others tolerated *fondas* and *chifa* as the lesser of two evils.

In order to maintain its food as affordable and accepted by local customers, Chinese restaurateurs developed a robust infrastructure and supply network to import ingredients from their hometown to combine them with local Peruvian products. Dozens of items crossed the Pacific Ocean from China to Callao to feed the Chinese community and the voracious local clientele. The transfer of products from the mainland to the new communities abroad began at a personal level, when in preparation for their transoceanic journey, coolie workers packed some provisions that included: rice, dried seafood, sausages, and condiments. These provisions, however, ran out very quickly upon their arrival in the Americas.[47] As a result, European ships transported products from Asia to Peru that included rice, cinnamon, or dried food as early as 1848; all of which were requested in coastal plantations full of coolies. Isabelle Lausent-Herrera has demonstrated that by the mid-nineteenth century, Chinese companies were becoming more specialized in food items, covering Lima and other cities and ports with a significant Chinese population (Cañete, Chancay, or Supe in Ancash). These commercial houses cemented a transpacific trade with other establishments in China and California, increasing the volume and diversity of the items originally introduced in Peru, especially canned and dried food products.[48]

By the turn of the century, Peru was the most important destination for Chinese products in Latin America. According to the 1913 International Chinese Business Directory, Peru hosted 554 businesses, professional agents, and institutions, with half of them located in Lima. Groceries constituted the most important segment of the whole commerce with 43 percent, but this percentage rises to over 50 percent if we add "beans and rice" (8.5 percent) and "dry goods" (0.7 percent). In a distant second place, with nearly half of that percentage, is general merchandising with 22.6 percent (Figure 3.2).

The Directory is also a helpful source to determine the scope of Chinese businesses beyond the capital city. Through this list, it is possible to observe the presence of Chinese commercial companies in 44 Peruvians cities and towns. As the map shows (Figure 3.3), Chinese food establishments or consumers had a robust presence along the coast, even in regions that were not originally the destination of coolie workers, like the Central Valley or Arequipa. The presence of *fondas* in those areas may suggest that former rural workers moved to the interior rather than to urban areas like the bulk of their fellow nationals, or that non-Chinese groups were beginning to open their own establishments and compete side-by-side with those managed by Chinese owners. The map also reveals a trend that continued in the following decades: the penetration of Chinese food in the highlands and the Amazon, even in areas where Chinese communities were small. Enrique Ramírez Angulo explains that in Arequipa by the 1940s, two of the six establishments listed

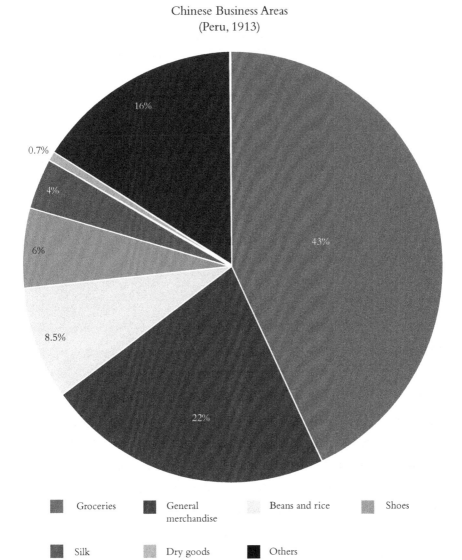

Chinese Business Areas
(Peru, 1913)

43%

22%

8.5%

6%

4%

0.7%

16%

| ■ | Groceries | ■ | General merchandise | ▨ | Beans and rice | ▨ | Shoes |
| ■ | Silk | ▨ | Dry goods | ■ | Others |

FIGURE 3.2 Chinese business areas (Peru 1913).

Source: Wong Kin (comp.) *International Chinese Business Directory of the World* (San Francisco: International Chinese Business Directory Co, 1913). Designed by the authors.

as "Bars and restaurants" were Chinese *fondas*; they were named "Restaurant Chifa Man Shang" and "Gran Chifa Restaurant de Kuong Tong y Cia," both of which were located in Mercaderes Street, the most important avenue in the city.[49] Simultaneously, other emergent urban centers like Iquitos in the Amazon hosted an energetic group of Chinese restaurateurs who sought to obtain their municipal licenses and open *fondas* for the first time in the region.

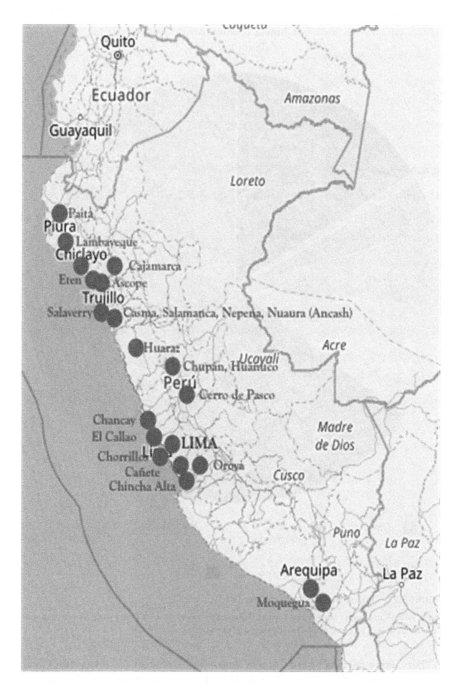

FIGURE 3.3 *Fondas* and food establishments in Peru, *c.* 1913.

Source: Wong Kin (comp.) *International Chinese Business Directory of the World.* (San Francisco, 1913). Designed by the authors.

The commerce of Chinese products was a lucrative business that fostered the emergence of a prosperous economic and social elite within the Chinese-Peruvian community. Yet not all the participants in this activity benefited from it. Owning and managing a restaurant was not exactly a prestigious business, and its owners did not belong to the Chinese upper-class in the country. If Chinese Peruvians sought to leave behind their rural origins and attain a better employment while preserving their recently obtained social privilege, they had to turn themselves into notorious businessmen and open an import firm of Chinese items, a drugstore, a bodega, but not a *fonda*. Based on the close examination of the fees paid by Chinese businesses in the nineteenth century in Lima, Wilma Derpich found that *fondas* were ranked in a very low position. In 1869 each *fonda* owner paid 4 soles to the local treasury whereas other establishment owners paid 5 soles, and bakeries 22 soles.[50] In a recent study of the Chinese community in Lima, Benjamín Narváez highlights the case of some restaurant owners who were drowning in debts and had delayed payments to other Chinese creditors. José Leon, for instance, owed 600 pesos and since he could not pay the debt, he had no choice but to flee the capital.[51]

While *fondas* owners were condemned to anonymity and a precarious existence, their fellow Chinese merchants or herbalists enjoyed social capital due to their professional status by competing with local professional counterparts and enjoying being portrayed in prestigious magazines such as *Variedades* and local newspapers.[52] The low esteem in which cooks and small restaurateurs were held by other members of the Chinese colony can further be seen in the publication of the *Album de la Colonia China en el Perú* in 1924. The *Album* had been commissioned to coincide with the end of the celebrations for the Centennial of the Peruvian Independence and was an astute strategy engineered by the Chinese community to integrate itself into the national discourse through the presentation of its most prominent members. As Ana María Candela states, the *Album* represents a careful strategy of the Chinese Legation to craft an image of the community as "progressive and commercial prosperous."[53] The *Album* presented photographs of the most successful Chinese merchants, and it deliberately excluded those who worked in other businesses, like restaurateurs. In seeking to build their own social capital, the new generation of Chinese-Peruvians was determined to create a distance between the first generation of coolie workers and their social spaces.

Confining the analysis of social prestige to the immigrant elite obscures the participation of *fonda* owners in an inter-ethnic milieu. Restaurateurs may not have been portrayed in fancy clothes in famous publications, but their prestige and social capital came from the management of a venue that served as a public space of eating and sociability in a cosmopolitan and multicultural environment. Fonda owners were key actors in the daily experience of poor and middle-class Chinese and Peruvian dwellers, and they were known and highly respected in those circles. The *fonda* run by ex-coolie José Cruz was a meeting center, and Cruz himself assisted his fellow countrymen when times were difficult, by providing shelter and food to those who were in need. Cruz's role among coolies did not go unnoticed, it turned him into a prominent leader in the community and he was granted the title of "representante de todos los Chinos."[54] During his stay in the country, Irish adventurer Theodore Child met one of these owners, who managed a joint in Concepción Market in downtown Lima. Child simply could not resist documenting a Chinese person's appeal, calling him "the exclusive restaurateur of the poor, of the working class, and of the market people."[55]

Epilogue

The Chinese community has endured harsh treatment in Peru since the arrival of the first Chinese in the mid-nineteenth century. Its members have absorbed local habits and merged with non-Asian populations. The dissemination of Chinese food through *fondas* and *chifa* was crucial in the fusion of both Peruvian and Chinese cuisines and societies, and its integration into the national identity in the past century and a half. In the years after the Great Depression, Chinese food witnessed an extraordinary nationwide expansion. Further research may prove this hypothesis, but some testimonies suggest that *chifas* were not always the exclusive domain of Chinese cooks. As an article appeared in a local newspaper in Lima in 1975 expressed: "Chinese cooks now are Peruvians. They are as good as their Chinese counterparts."[56] It is most likely that a new wave of immigrants, coming from the highlands, embraced *chifa* from their Asian counterparts and further contributed to its dissemination. In a testimony collected from residents of Barrios Altos in Lima, one of them recalled seeing "many serranos" serving *chifa* in the streets, "cholos con su chifa al paso."[57]

Most recently, *chifa* has made its own way into global Peruvian Gastronomy thanks to cuisine guru Gastón Acurio. In April 2011, he opened "Madame Tusan," a franchise of his chain of restaurants devoted to Peruvian *chifa*. The name of the establishment had been carefully chosen, evoking—perhaps inadvertently—the elitist *chifas* of the 1950s that appeared as an alternative to already existing popular *fondas*.[58] The "Peruvian *chifa* for the world," as the motto of the restaurant claims, sought to offer a stylized version of Peruvian-Chinese gastronomy by unconsciously erasing the convoluted and problematic narrative of *fondas* and the little known history of the triumph of Chinese taste in a hostile environment.

Acknowledgments

We would like to thank to Jenny Banh and Haiming Liu for their invitation to submit a chapter to this volume. We would also like to show our gratitude to Juan Carlos Chávez, Adrián Lerner, Jorge Lossio, and Enrique Ramírez Angulo for their generosity in providing invaluable information about *chifas* in various parts of Peru. Kenia Munguia did a splendid job in revising a previous version of this paper.

Key Terms

Chifa: Term used to denote both Chinese food and Peruvian-Chinese *fondas*. As a meal, it refers to a set of dishes that combines Chinese and local ingredients, well liked among both popular sectors and elites. Originally known as "fondas" until the early twentieth century, their expansion was accompanied with a change in their name, and "chifa" became the popular way to refer to them.

Coolies: A derogatory term to name the first group of Chinese newcomers to Peru and the Americas. They arrived in 1849 at a time of transition to a post-African slavery society. As such, they worked as peons in coastal plantations under harsh conditions until the end of their contracts. Once relieved of their duties, many of them moved to urban areas to work as cooks. This inhumane trade was ended by the Peruvian government in 1874.

Fondas chinas: Small Chinese restaurants in Peru where cooks adapted food and beverages to local culinary traditions and patron tastes. A significant number of Chinese immigrants became owners and managers of these establishments, gaining autonomy from their former status as workers in plantations. *Fondas* provided affordable meals among local populations, especially in moments of economic crises.

Discussion Questions

1. How did Chinese immigrants influence Peruvian society and food habits?
2. What were the main arguments deployed to attack Chinese *fondas* and Chinese food in the first decades of the twentieth century?
3. How did Chinese *fondas* and their owners manage to expand nationwide?

Notes

1 The bibliography about Chinese migration in Peru during the nineteenth century is extensive. For some examples, see Watt Stewart, *Chinese Bondage in Peru* (Durham: Duke University Press, 1951), Humberto Rodríguez Pastor, *Hijos del Celeste Imperio en el Perú (1850–1900): Migración, Agricultura, Mentalidad y Explotación* (Lima: Sur Casa de Estudios del Socialismo, 1989), and Evelyn Hu-DeHart, "Opium and Social Control: Coolies and Plantations of Peru and Cuba." *Journal of Chinese Overseas* 1, no. 2 (2005), among others. On gastronomic habits in post-colonial Peru see Vincent Peloso, "Succulence and Substance: Region, Class and Diet in Nineteenth-Century Peru," in John C. Supper and Thomas C. Wright, eds. *Food, Politics and Society in Latin America* (Lincoln: University of Nebraska Press, 1985), 45–64.
2 Gonzales, Michael J. "Chinese Plantation Workers and Social Conflict in Peru in the Late Nineteenth Century." *Journal of Latin American Studies* 21, no. 3 (1989): 386.
3 Isabelle Lausent-Herrera, "Chinatown in Peru and the Changing Peruvian Chinese Community(ies)." *Journal of Chinese Overseas* 7 (2011), 70, and Ignacio López Calvo, *Dragons in the Land of the Condor: Writing Tusán in Peru* (Tucson: The University of Arizona Press, 2014), 24.
4 Gonzales, "Chinese Plantation," 99.

5 Humberto Rodríguez Pastor, "Del Kon Hei Fat Choy al Chifa Peruano," in *Cultura, Identidad y Cocina en el Perú*, Rosario Olivas ed. (Lima: Universidad San Martín de Porres, 1996), 192.

6 Mariella Balbi, *Los Chifas en Perú: historias y recetas* (Lima: Universidad San Martín de Porres, 1999), 49. *El Comercio,* October 19, 1873.

7 Ernst Middendorf, *Perú. Observaciones y estudios del país y sus habitantes durante una permanencia de 25 Años vol. 1,* trans. Ernesto More (Lima: Universidad Nacional Mayor de San Marcos, Dirección Universitaria de Biblioteca, 1973), 173.

8 Humberto Rodríguez Pastor, "Chinos cimarrones en Lima: rostros, facciones, edades, apelativos, ropaje y otros pormenores." *Investigaciones Sociales* 3 (1999):13.

9 Evelyn Hu-DeHart, "Chinos comerciantes en el Perú: Breve y preliminar bosquejo histórico," in *Actas del Primer Seminario sobre Poblaciones Inmigrantes* (Lima: Consejo Nacional de la Ciencia y la Tecnología, 1988), 133.

10 Theodore Child, *The Spanish-American Republics* (New York: Harper & Brothers, Franklin Square, 1891), 196–197.

11 Unfortunately, we lack information regarding the list of dishes offered in Chinese *fondas*. However, Mariella Balbi has compiled a list of ingredients used by Chinese cooks, such as: rice, eggs, potato flour, various sauces, noodles, mushrooms, pickled products, dry vegetables, and fruits. Balbi, *Los Chifas en Perú*, 34.

12 Lausent-Herrera, "Chinatown in Peru," 71.

13 Juan Carlos Chávez, La inmigración china en el Departamento de La Libertad," http://truxillo.pe/4415/inmigracion-china-departamento-la-libertad/, accessed December 1, 2017.

14 George Squier, *Peru. Incidents of Travel and Exploration in the Land of the Incas* (New York: Harper & Brothers, Publishers, 1877), 112, 115, 135.

15 Balbi, *Los Chifas en Perú*, 62.

16 Carlos Paz Soldán, "El 'Chinatown' Limeño," *El Comercio*, September 29, 1916.

17 Child, *The Spanish-American*, 197.

18 For instance, J.W. Ames, "A Day in Chinatown." *Lippincott's Magazine of Popular Literature and Science* 16 (1875): 497.

19 Juan de Arona, *La inmigración en el Perú* (Lima: Imprenta del Universo de Carlos Prince, 1891).

20 Arona, *La inmigración*, 53.

21 Abelardo Gamarra, *Lima, unos cuantos barrios y unos cuantos tipos: al comenzar el siglo XX* (Lima: P. Berrio, 1907), 43–44 cited by Paulo Drinot, *The Allure of Labor: Workers, Race and the Making of the Peruvian State* (Durham: Duke University Press, 2011), 166.

22 "Panchito a Pancho. Cartas de un joven trasandino. Carta segunda," *El Correo del Perú*, May 4, 1872, 139.

23 Luis Gómez, "Música criolla. Cultural Practices and National Issues in Modern Peru. The Case of Lima (1920–1960)" (Ph.D diss., Stony Brook University, 2010), 149.

24 Gómez, "Música criolla," 118 and 149.

25 Drinot, *The Allure of Labor*, 163.

26 Augusto Ruiz, "Los motines de mayo de 1909. Inmigrantes y nativos en el mercado laboral de Lima a comienzos del siglo XX," *Boletín del Instituto Francés de Estudios Andinos* 29, no. 2 (2000): 175–176.

27 Haiming Liu, *From Canton Restaurant to Panda Express: A History of Chinese Food in the United States* (New Brunswick: Rutgers University Press, 2015), 2.

28 Patricia Palma and José Ragas, "Enclaves sanitarios: Higiene, epidemias y salud en el Barrio chino de Lima, 1880–1910," *Anuario Colombiano de Historia Social y de la Cultura* 45, no. 1 (2018): 159–190.

29 *El Bien Público,* January 13, 1866, 1. "Higiene. Tiendas de los chinos. (. . .) Se distinguen por su repugnante desaseo." *El Comercio*, December 1, 1866, 3.

30 Adam McKeown, *Chinese Migrant Networks and Cultural Change: Peru, Chicago, Hawaii, 1900–1936* (Chicago: University of Chicago Press, 2001), 151.

31 Liu, *From Canton Restaurant*, 38.
32 *El Comercio*, September 12, 1863, 3.
33 Palma and Ragas, "Enclaves sanitarios," 174–179.
34 "De jueves a jueves. Chinerías." *Variedades* 4, no. 60 (1909): 174–175.
35 Ana María Candela, "Nation, Migration and Governance: Cantonese Migrants to Peru and the Making of Overseas Chinese Nationalism, 1849–2013" (Ph.D. Diss., University of California, Santa Cruz, 2013), 173.
36 López Calvo, *Dragons*, 33.
37 Dora Mayer de Zulen, *La China silenciosa y elocuente. Homenaje de la Colonia China al Perú* (Lima: Editorial Renovación. 1924), 110. It is also interesting to note the absence of any reference to *cuyes* (guinea pigs) since they are part of the culinary tradition in the Peruvian highlands.
38 Mary Roach, *Stiff: The Curious Lives of Human Cadavers* (New York: W.W. Norton, 2003), 237.
39 Hermilio Valdizán, *La medicina popular peruana tomo* I (Lima: Torres Aguirre, 1922), 210–211.
40 *El Comercio*, May 15, 1872.
41 *El Comercio*, January 8, 1868.
42 "Excesos." *El Comercio* 9593 (January 8, 1868).
43 *El Comercio*, May 15, 1872. Benjamín Narváez, "Becoming Sino-Peruvian: Post-Indenture Chinese in Nineteenth-Century Peru." *Asian Journal of Latin American Studies* 29.3 (2016): 17, 19–20; Squier, *Peru*, 115.
44 Organización de Estados Iberoamericanos para la Educación, la Ciencia y la Cultura. *Barrios Altos, tradiciones orales* (Lima: Municipalidad Metropolitana de Lima, 1998), 80.
45 Andrew Coe, *Chop Suey: A Cultural History of Chinese food in the United States* (New York: Oxford University Press, 2009), 110.
46 Middendorf, *Perú. Observaciones y estudios*, 173.
47 Coe, *Chop Suey*, 118.
48 Lausent-Herrera, "Chinatown in Peru," 72.
49 Enrique Ramírez Angulo. "Ofertas gastronómicas en el Cuatricentenario de Arequipa." *Adegopa* 1 (December 2011): 4–5.
50 Derpich, *El otro lado azul*, 98.
51 Narváez, "Becoming Sino-Peruvian," 10.
52 Patricia Palma, "'Science Can't Save Me": Public Health, Professional Medicine, and Medical Pluralism in Peru (1856–1935)" (Ph.D. Diss., University of California, Davis, 2017).
53 Candela, "Nation, Migration," 136.
54 Narváez, Becoming Sino-Peruvian, 14–15.
55 Child, *The Spanish-American Republics*, 197.
56 *La Imagen* 37, (November 16, 1975): 10–11.
57 "Monólogo del sastre," in *Habla la ciudad*, ed., Universidad Nacional Mayor de San Marcos (Lima: Municipalidad de Lima Metropolitana, 1986), 118.
58 "Nosotros," Madam Tusan Restaurant, accessed December 1, 2017: www.madamtusan.pe/nosotros/#nosotros-historia

Bibliography

Primary sources

Álbum de la Colonia China. Lima: Libreria e imprenta GIL, 1924.
Ames, J.W. "A Day in Chinatown." *Lippincott's Magazine of Popular Literature and Science* 16 (1875): 495–502.
Arona, Juan de. *La inmigración en el Perú*. Lima: Imprenta del Universo, 1891.

Carleton, Geo. *Our Artist in Peru*. New York: Carleton, 1866.

Child, Theodore. *The Spanish-American Republics*. New York: Harper & Brothers, Franklin Square, 1891.

Kin, Wong, comp., *International Chinese Business Directory of the World*. San Francisco: International Chinese Business Directory Co., 1913.

Mayer de Zulen, Dora. *La China silenciosa y elocuente. Homenaje de la Colonia China al Perú*. Lima: Editorial Renovación. 1924.

Middendorf, Ernst. *Perú. Observaciones y estudios del país y sus habitantes durante una permanencia de 25 Años vol. 1*. Translated by Ernesto More. Lima: Universidad Nacional Mayor de San Marcos, Dirección Universitaria de Biblioteca, 1973.

Squier, George. *Peru. Incidents of Travel and Exploration in the Land of the Incas*. New York: Harper & Brothers, Publishers, 1877.

Valdizán, Hermilio. *La medicina popular peruana tomo I*. Lima: Torres Aguirre, 1922.

Secondary sources

Balbi, Mariella. *Los chifas en el Perú: historia y recetas*. Lima: Universidad San Martín de Porres, 1999.

Candela, Ana María. "Nation, Migration and Governance: Cantonese Migrants to Peru and the Making of Overseas Chinese Nationalism, 1849–2013." Ph.D. Diss., University of California, Santa Cruz, 2013.

Chávez, Juan Carlos. "La inmigración china en el Departamento de La Libertad," *Truxillo.pe*. Accessed December 1, 2017. http://truxillo.pe/4415/inmigracion-china-departamento-la-libertad/

Coe, Andrew. *Chop suey: A Cultural History of Chinese Food in the United States*. New York: Oxford University Press, 2009.

Derpich, Wilma. *El otro lado azul. Empresarios chinos en el Perú, 1890–1930*. Lima: Fondo Editorial del Congreso del Perú, 1999.

Drinot, Paulo. *The Allure of Labor. Workers, Race, and the Making of the Peruvian State*. Durham: Duke University Press, 2011.

Gómez, Luis. "Música criolla. Cultural Practices and National Issues in Modern Peru. The case of Lima (1920–1960)." Ph.D diss., Stony Brook University, 2010.

Gonzáles, Michael. "Chinese Plantation Workers and Social Conflict in Peru in the late Nineteenth Century." *Journal of Latin American Studies* 21, no.3 (1989): 385–424.

Hu-DeHart, Evelyn. "Chinos comerciantes en el Perú: Breve y preliminar bosquejo histórico." In *Actas del Primer Seminario sobre Poblaciones Inmigrantes*, 127–135. Lima: Consejo Nacional de la Ciencia y la Tecnología, 1988.

Hu-DeHart, Evelyn. "Opium and Social Control: Coolies and Plantations of Peru and Cuba." *Journal of Chinese Overseas* 1, no 2 (2005): 169–183.

Laussent-Herrera, Isabelle. "The Chinatown in Peru and the Changing Peruvian Chinese Community(ies)." *Journal of Chinese Overseas* 7 (2011): 69–113.

Liu, Haiming. *From Canton Restaurant to Panda Express: A History of Chinese Food in the United States*. New Brunswick: Rutgers University Press, 2015.

López Calvo, Ignacio. *Dragons in the Land of the Condor: Writing Tusán in Peru*. Tucson: The University of Arizona Press, 2014.

McKeown, Adam. *Chinese Migrant Networks and Cultural Change. Peru, Chicago and Hawaii 1900–1936*. Chicago and London: The University of Chicago Press, 2001.

Narváez, Benjamín N. "Becoming Sino-Peruvian: Post-Indenture Chinese in Nineteenth-Century Peru." *Asian Journal of Latin American Studies* 29, no. 3 (2016): 1–27.

Organización de Estados Iberoamericanos para la Educación, la Ciencia y la Cultura. *Barrios Altos, tradiciones orales*. Lima: Municipalidad de Lima, 1998.

Palma, Patricia. "Science Can't Save Me". Public Health, Professional Medicine, and Medical Pluralism in Peru (1856–1935)." Ph.D. Diss., University of California, Davis, 2017.

Palma, Patricia and José Ragas. "Enclaves sanitarios: Higiene, epidemias y salud en el Barrio chino de Lima, 1880–1910." *Anuario Colombiano de Historia Social y de la Cultura* 45, no. 1 (2018): 159–190.

Peloso, Vincent. "Succulence and Substance: Region, Class and Diet in Nineteenth-Century Peru," in Supper, John C. & Thomas C. Wright, eds. *Food, Politics and Society in Latin America* (Lincoln: University of Nebraska Press, 1985), 45–64.

Ramírez Angulo, Enrique. "Ofertas gastronómicas en el Cuatricentenario de Arequipa." *Adegopa* 1 (December 2011): 4–5.

Roach, Mary. *Stiff: The Curious Lives of Human Cadavers*. New York: W.W. Norton, 2003.

Rodríguez Pastor, Humberto. *Hijos del Celeste Imperio en el Perú (1850–1900): Migración, Agricultura, Mentalidad y Explotación*. Lima: Sur Casa de Estudios del Socialismo, 1989.

Rodríguez Pastor, Humberto. "Del Kon Hei Fat Choy al Chifa Peruano." In *Cultura, Identidad y Cocina en el Perú*, edited by Rosario Olivas, 189–238. Lima: Universidad San Martín de Porres, 1996.

Rodríguez Pastor, Humberto. "Chinos cimarrones en Lima: rostros, facciones, edades, apelativos, ropaje y otros pormenores." *Investigaciones Sociales* 3 (1999): 9–26.

Rodríguez Pastor, Humberto. "La pasión por el chifa." *Nueva Sociedad* 203 (2006): 79–88.

Ruiz, Augusto. "Los motines de mayo de 1909. Inmigrantes y nativos en el mercado laboral de Lima a comienzos del siglo XX." *Boletín del Instituto Francés de Estudios Andinos* 29, no. 2 (2000): 173–188.

Stewart, Watt. *Chinese Bondage in Peru. A History of the Chinese Coolie in Peru, 1849–1874*. Durham: Duke University Press, 1951.

Universidad Nacional Mayor de San Marcos, ed. *Habla la ciudad*. Lima: Municipalidad de Lima Metropolitana, 1986.

4

SELLING DONUTS IN THE FRAGMENTED METROPOLIS

Chinese Cambodian Donut Shops in Los Angeles and the Practices of Chinese Restaurants

Erin M. Curtis

Sunrise Donuts

Sunrise Donuts[1] occupies a small storefront in a typical Southern California strip mall—a long and low one-story building with a peeling coat of white paint and a roof of clay tiles. The shop sits on a busy, wide thoroughfare that runs through Rosemead, a city in the predominantly Asian and Latino San Gabriel Valley. When I arrived to interview donut shop owner Susan Chhu, two men were playing a game of checkers outside the shop's front door.

I sat at a formica-topped table with our mutual contact, Namoch Sokhom, who immediately pointed out that the clean but faded decor likely had not changed since the store opened.[2] Chhu, a Chinese Cambodian who arrived in the United States in 1985, talked with us for an hour. She broke away frequently to help customers who arrived alone or in pairs. Her patrons spanned a wide range of ages and ethnicities, but all had friendly, familiar relationships with Chhu. She carried on lively conversations in several different languages, including Spanish, Vietnamese, Cantonese, and Mandarin. (Sokhom told me that Cantonese is the preferred language of Chinese Cambodians like Chhu; she later added that her command of Mandarin came from the middle-class education she had received at a Chinese school in Cambodia.)[3]

Chhu's husband wakes early in the morning to bake donuts, using ingredients and equipment purchased from bakery wholesaler Bakemark USA, located just south of the shop in the city of Pico Rivera. Chhu spends the rest of the day selling donuts and beverages, working for as long as 12 hours each day, 6 or 7 days per week. At first they hired no one to help them, relying on the assistance of their brother-in-law, their three children, and friends who also own donut shops. Currently, they "hire part time,"[4] employing Chinese Cambodian or Latino workers.

Chhu's store is a typical example of how Cambodian owners of donut shops run their business. She uses the advantages of her Chinese Cambodian upbringing and education, and depends on family labor, to begin and sustain her business. She also contracts Cambodian and Latino workers, and sources ingredients from large wholesale suppliers on a daily basis. This chapter delves into these practices, and examines the daily operation of Cambodian donut shops in Southern California. I will focus on the deployment of social capital, the conscription of labor from family members as well as hired hands, the relationship between shop owners and wholesale bakery suppliers, the daily minutiae of producing, displaying, and selling donuts, the risks and insecurities that donut shop owners must confront, and the financial tactics that have made donut shops profitable for many owners.

I document these tactics to demonstrate how Chinese Cambodians came to dominate the Southern California donut market, owning and operating an estimated 80 to 90 percent of the area's donut shops.[5] At the same time, I explore the close resemblance between Chinese Cambodian donut shops in Los Angeles and Chinese restaurants in the United States and United Kingdom. An estimated two-thirds of Los Angeles Cambodian donut shop owners hail from Cambodia's Chinese ethnic minority. I contend that this background offers particular advantages for the owners and operators of small businesses such as donut shops. Furthermore, I argue that the business practices of Chinese Cambodian donut shop owners resemble strategies historically deployed by Chinese restaurant owners. I also examine the recent rise of Cambodian donut shops that sell Americanized Chinese food, and conclude by discussing whether the Chinese Cambodian donut shops of Los Angeles can expand accepted notions of what constitutes a Chinese restaurant.

Social Capital

Sucheng Chan asserts that social capital, or each individual's unique combination of "language competence, education, occupational skills, and transferrable work experiences,"[6] directly influenced the socioeconomic outcome of every Cambodian refugee in the United States. Cambodian donut shop owners leveraged two forms of social capital to start and to run their businesses. First, they arrived in America earlier than other Cambodians did as elite or wealthy people, which meant they had escaped the worst atrocities of the Khmer Rouge. Second, they were Chinese Cambodians. Their cultural background provided business skills, language fluency, access to global networks, and experience operating as a minority group. This chapter concentrates on the advantages that Chinese Cambodian heritage conferred to many donut shop owners, but it is important to note that these two sources of social capital frequently intersected.

"Among the Cambodian refugees," Aihwa Ong writes, Chinese Cambodians were "perhaps the best able to take advantage of the American economic scene."[7] Before the rise of the Khmer Rouge, Cambodians of Chinese and partially Chinese descent formed the largest ethnic minority in Cambodia. They "composed one-third of the population of Phnom Penh, and were also found in Battambang and Kampot."[8] Like Susan Chhu, "most Sino-Khmer children in Cambodia, especially males, were sent by their parents to Chinese school to study Mandarin for at least a short time."[9] They were often involved in business and politics[10] and frequently were wealthy, acting as cultural brokers and forming elaborate networks and institutions that reached across Cambodia and beyond.

While they maintained a comfortable financial and political status in Cambodia, Chinese Cambodians frequently experienced class resentment and cultural discrimination. Maltreatment of the group intensified under the Khmer Rouge, who disrupted their trading activities and persecuted them due to their class status.[11] Yet they continued to engage in trading, taking their business underground. After escaping the Khmer Rouge, many Chinese Cambodians applied their accumulated wealth, acquired business knowledge, experience as cultural resource brokers, and ability to marshal local and overseas networks to available opportunities within the United States.[12] They largely succeeded: approximately "two-thirds of Cambodian businesses in Southern California are owned by Chinese Cambodians."[13]

The Cambodian donut trade in the Los Angeles area is no exception. Marshaling their financial resources and professional ties, and aided on a daily basis by their language proficiency and business acumen, Chinese Cambodians have opened donut shops in Los Angeles in high numbers. Both Chan and Ong point out that Ted Ngoy, who founded a large chain of Los Angeles-area donut shops called Christy's and arguably began the Cambodian donut business in Los Angeles by inspiring and helping others to start their own shops, is a Chinese Cambodian.[14] Many other Chinese Cambodians followed his lead, quickly taking over the donut business. However, Chinese Cambodians' economic success has come at a cost. While Chinese Cambodians and other members of the Cambodian American middle class are "determined to be financially independent and are very proud of that fact" and "show a great deal of concern for other Cambodians, they "are not always able to satisfy all the wants of so many needy compatriots . . . [and] in some instances reap opprobrium instead of appreciation."[15]

Researchers have observed similar patterns of business ownership and labor conscription in Chinese restaurants. Heather R. Lee describes the recruitment of "paper sons," Chinese immigrants who deflected restrictive immigration policies by posing as the children of Chinese already residing in the United States, for work in restaurants serving Americanized Chinese food.[16] Haiming Liu also notes that shared "lifestyles, social values, and kinship networks bonded the Chinese together"[17] in ethnic businesses, including Chinese restaurants.

Labor

Labor patterns in Cambodian donut shops evince two key characteristics. First, the work necessitates long, hard hours. Donut shop owners and workers must rise early to make fresh donuts for workers before business hours commence, sell donuts throughout the work day and well into the evening to maximize sales and remain competitive, and clean their shops at night—only to begin the process once again the next morning. Second, Cambodian donut shop owners exploit their own labor as well as that of their families, Cambodian apprentices or workers, and other groups within the multiethnic neighborhoods of Los Angeles. Low-cost labor is essential to keeping donut shops running.

Donut shop owners have long regarded working extended hours as a necessity, one which intensified as the Southern California market became increasingly saturated with donut shops. Most shop owners and workers report laboring at least 12 hours per day, if not longer, and often to the detriment of their health and well-being. Shop owner Cecilia Van Noup estimates that her work day is 14 hours long: "I get to the shop at 5:00 in the morning to open for breakfast, and I usually leave around 7:00 p.m. I work behind the counter, serving customers, and do the cleaning and sweeping. I work all by myself most of the time."[18] The nature of the work in a donut shop demands long hours: shop owners and workers must complete certain tasks such as baking and cleaning at specific, set times throughout the day. Donut shop owners also work long shifts to maximize sales and remain competitive in a crowded market. Many shops stay open late into the night or even 24 hours per day to attract extra customers. As shop owner Bunna Men notes, "I brought the experience with me, how to work hard. How to work no shift, no first shift, no second shift, and no third shift. Anything that we can work, and we can get from what we work, we have to do it."[19]

Sokhom points to another key aspect of labor in Cambodian donut shops: in addition to keeping long, difficult hours, Cambodian donut shop owners attempt to employ as few laborers as possible in order to keep the cost of labor down and maximize profits. They most consistently—and almost unanimously—rely upon their own labor before that of anyone else. Both Van Noup and shop owner Leng Hing report frequently working alone.[20] Husband and wife teams who run a donut shop will also leave a single representative in charge for long stretches of time.[21]

The next most likely labor pool is immediate family members of donut shop owners. Although it only takes two or three people to run a donut shop,[22] shops depend upon "unpaid or underpaid family labor"[23] to keep from going out of business. Like the operators of Chinese take-out restaurants in Great Britain that Miri Song examines, Cambodian families "engage in self-exploitation as a strategy to stay competitive."[24] Chan declares, "Were it not for the unpaid family labor that sustains these small eateries . . . many would have gone under."[25] Labor provided by families in donut shops can extend across generations: while Helen Chin worked in a relative's Long Beach donut shop, her daughter Christina Nhek assisted her: "I'd mop and things like that. I never sold the actual donuts, it was always . . . cleaning things, and I used to fold the donut boxes."[26] Heather Lee notes that Chinese restaurants in early twentieth-century New York City were also "small, family-run businesses that turned a profit only because the owners paid themselves and their relatives very little."[27]

Family members help out in donut shops for many reasons, but largely because they understand that their labor benefits their families in the short term and themselves in the long run. Cambodian children are acutely aware that their family's economic survival depends in part on their help, and like the subjects in Song's study of Chinese restaurants, they believe that their labor "has enabled their families to have a much better standard of living and more economic security than they would otherwise have achieved through waged work."[28] They also benefit directly from helping out—wages or profits from a donut shop often go toward their education. All three of Susan Chhu's children worked at Sunrise Donuts when they were younger; all have since moved on to white collar careers.[29] After working alongside her mother as a child, Christina Nhek became a librarian.[30] Overall, Chinese Cambodian families regard donut shops as collective ventures which ensure immediate survival and afford upward mobility to future generations, much as many Chinese families have perceived Chinese restaurants.

Women's labor as both owners and workers is also critical to the success of many donut shops. Many women took up the work to support themselves after losing spouses to the Khmer Rouge or because their surviving spouses are unable to do so.[31] Others work to supplement their family's income. This phenomenon is due in part to donut shops' reliance on emotional labor (the regulation and deployment of one's emotions to meet particular workplace demands)[32] in order to ensure stellar customer service and thereby increase sales. Gendered forms of labor necessary for the survival of donut shops happen outside of shops as well as within them. As Karen Quintiliani notes, "Cambodian families rely upon the contributions of both the older and younger generation to enable social and economic well-being of the entire family."[33] While working or helping out in shops is common, childcare, housecleaning, and other tasks performed by family members (usually women) at home are also crucial to the success of a shop, as they enable owners to remain at work for long stretches of time.[34]

Yet Cambodian donut shops frequently seek additional labor that family members cannot provide. They generally find it in two forms: Cambodian apprentices (which may or may not include extended family members) and hired Chinese Cambodian, Cambodian, or Latino help. It can be difficult to distinguish between the family labor described above and the labor that Cambodian apprentices provide. Apprentices are often extended family members or family friends aiming to learn the business, earn money, and eventually open their own donut shops. The former is more likely the goal, because, as Ong notes, apprentices frequently work for free: "These family businesses did not need to bother with union rules, and apprentices were trained for up to a year without pay, often working at night."[35] Donut shop owners and workers regularly hire other Cambodians or work for other Cambodians, but the nature of these arrangements varies. For example, Helen Chin's and Christina Nhek's work in a family donut shop fell somewhere in between helping out, apprenticeship, and labor. Chhu and Dul had hired other Cambodians to work, but also mentioned friends who provided help in their shops, suggesting that these arrangements were informal and perhaps even interchangeable.[36] Whether or not an apprentice earns money, apprenticeships in donut shops offer many of the initial advantages of the donut business as a whole, including working alongside other Cambodians, entering a field that does not require extensive training or prior knowledge, and being able to work while learning English.[37] Ultimately, apprentices gain firsthand experience, forge connections with shop owners, help out in a fashion that may be repaid in the future, and perhaps even save money to open their own donut shops. It is important to remember, however, that donut shop owners depend on these kinds of free labor in order to remain profitable.

Latino workers also frequently provide labor for Cambodian donut shops. Many areas of Los Angeles with significant numbers of Cambodians, including Long Beach and the San Gabriel Valley, have also historically been home to large, mixed Latino and Asian populations. As such, Cambodians look to Latinos to fill low-wage positions when they cannot rely upon family members or hire apprentices. Susan Chhu spoke of hiring Latino workers, and Ong writes that the practice is common among donut shop owners, who often recruit "pseudo-kin"[38] from other ethnic minorities. Chinese restaurants as well as other ethnic business enclaves in Southern California engage in similar practices; Marta López-Garza asserts that Latino labor is vital to the informal economy of Los Angeles as a whole.[39]

Supplies

Decades of innovation in donut-making machinery and baking technology have dramatically streamlined and eased the process of donut preparation, allowing Cambodian refugees to quickly master its necessary techniques. As a result, a donut shop requires little more than "premixed ingredients and some basic machinery"[40] to operate successfully. Cambodian donut shop owners purchase both machinery and ingredients—as well as additional equipment, utensils, packaging, and even coffee beans and coffee makers—from local bakery suppliers or national wholesalers. They most frequently visit the latter, citing BakeMark (which describes itself as a national "confederation of leading bakery ingredient manufacturers and distributers in North America operating under the finest names")[41] or Costco as their sources for donut shop supplies.[42] Having absorbed numerous trademarks, Bake-Mark currently offers almost 60 donut mixes, including special varieties designed to produce Southern California favorites such as blueberry cake donuts. Its wide selection and fairly central location in Pico Rivera make it a particularly convenient source of supplies for Cambodian donut shops.

Local suppliers, many of them operated by Cambodian refugees with donut shop experience looking to run larger businesses and offer a community service, have also played an important role in outfitting Cambodian donut shops and facilitating the entry of many Cambodians into the donut business. Cambodian refugee Bun H. Tao, nephew of Ted Ngoy and founder of B & H Distributors in Santa Ana, is among the earliest and most prominent of the California bakery wholesalers. Like his uncle, Tao helped many Cambodians open their own donut shops: in addition to offering machinery, mixes, and other supplies, B & H provided credit to new donut shop owners with limited funds. The *Los Angeles Times* reported that Tao "loaned 300 coffee machines to stores that buy coffee from him," and even interceded for inexperienced shop owners in rent disputes.[43]

Golden Bake Foods, another independent donut supply wholesaler, did brisk business in Cerritos and Anaheim for decades, advertising each year in the *Cambodian American Yellow Pages*, a publication of the Cambodian American Chamber of Commerce in Long Beach designed to promote Cambodian businesses and target Cambodian consumers.[44] Golden Bake courted new donut shop owners, emphasizing the autonomy and security independent business ownership could potentially offer while equating that security with their merchandise. In 2015, the supplier merged with BakeMark.

Daily Work

Bakers begin the work of making donuts as early as 3:30 a.m., using a combination of hand preparation and mechanical production via a few basic pieces of equipment: a mixer, a cutter, a fryer, and a glazer. They combine prefabricated mixes with wet ingredients to form dough, which they either cut and form by hand or drop into the fryer through a cutter that creates ring or bar shapes. They turn the donuts in the oil with long chopsticks before removing the donuts to draining and cooling racks. Glazes and icings are prepared from prefabricated mixes. Bakers glaze the donuts by sweeping a glazer, which distributes even sheets of icing, back and forth over the donuts by hand; they also manually apply flavored frostings and toppings. Cambodian donut shops generally produce a standard selection of donuts found in West Coast grocery stores, bakeries, and donut shops since the mid-twentieth century: raised, cake, and old-fashioned donuts with a variety of toppings and fillings in various combinations, including glazes, icings, custards, jellies, sugar, cinnamon, crumb coatings, coconut flakes, nuts, and sprinkles. They frequently offer other baked goods such as croissants, cookies, and muffins. Workers prepare fresh coffee before customers arrive and replenish it throughout the day. A drip coffee maker with a coffee pot is a staple in most Cambodian donut shops, although specialty coffees, usually premixed and dispensed automatically from specialized machines, are gaining traction as well.[45] Additional beverages are also generally available.

Sales begin as customers arrive during their morning commutes, usually around 5:30 a.m. Just as the earliest American Chinese restaurants courted working-class customers such as railroad workers and miners,[46] Cambodian donut shops primarily serve workers in nearby industries; for example, donut shop owners in the Rosemead area cited the local Southern California Edison power company as a frequent source of business.[47] Sokhom points out that many donut shops provide a refuge for unemployed or low-income customers with no other place to go; for the price of a donut, they frequently remain in a shop throughout the day.[48] Chhu added that her customers were African American, Asian, and Latino, while Dul noted a wide range of ages in his patrons.[49]

Sales continue late into the evening or even through the night. At the end of the day, shop owners take home, throw out, or donate leftover baked goods. Then cleaning commences: the entire shop, including floors, cases, and machines, must be prepared for the next day. Chhu maintains that donut shops are smaller and generally easier to clean than restaurants, but the work is still arduous.[50] As Chin noted, "I clean all machine, clean *everything*."[51]

Finances

Like many American Chinese restaurants, Cambodian donut shops survive and even profit by keeping overhead costs—including rent, equipment, supplies, and labor—as low as possible while maintaining steady sales by selling a cheap yet calorically rich food and diversifying their menus. Additionally, they maintain financial stability and flexibility by circumventing the trappings of the U.S. financial system. Opening a small store in the 1990s required an initial investment of about $80,000, and recent arrivals used various means to accumulate the necessary capital relatively quickly. Many refugees worked low-wage jobs until they could combine their savings with loans obtained through informal credit arrangements.[52] These include apprenticeships as described above, loans from family and friends, and *tong tines*, informal lending clubs that allow immigrants to pool their money.[53] Many shops are cash only in order to avoid credit card transaction fees. Cambodian donut shops also find legal ways to rarely or never pay banking fees, interest fees on business loans, and sales tax.[54] In order to maximize their profits, many shop owners follow the example of Ted Ngoy and recruit other Cambodians to run donut shops, creating informal chains.

Risks and Insecurities

While there are many insecurities inherent to small business ownership, two major risks attend the operation of donut shops in particular: their dependence upon broader trends in the U.S. economy for their economic survival, and the difficulty of selling donuts during warm seasons and for meals other than breakfast. Cambodian donut shop owners have used various strategies to mitigate these risks.

The fortunes of Chinese Cambodian donut shops are closely tied to the health of the U.S. economy. Although the donut is a "recession-resistant"[55] foodstuff, a cheap food purchased consistently and frequently across classes in a variety of economic climates, other costs associated with donut production can fluctuate. These include rent (which has become increasingly prohibitive for donut shop owners in the highly competitive real estate market of Los Angeles) and supplies. Sokhom estimates that rents have doubled for donut shop owners since the 1990s.[56] Supply costs fluctuate seasonally, and have risen overall during recent decades. It is difficult, however, for shop owners to raise prices accordingly. Cambodian donut shop owners and workers struggle to effectively combat these issues, and frequently resort to working longer hours to cover increasing costs.

Decreases in donut sales during warm seasons have existed since the earliest days of donut manufacturing. Daily temporal issues plague Cambodian donut shop owners as well: donuts are not popular past morning hours due to their short shelf life and general consumer preferences. The most frequent response of Cambodian donut shop owners to these concerns is diversification of the donut shop menu. In addition to selling other baked goods as noted above, many shops sell other foods entirely. It is not unusual to see a donut shop touting sandwiches for afternoon and evening consumption or ice cream for warm weather; in fact, the practice is so common that donut shop signs often list additional offerings as well.

Some Cambodian donut shops have mitigated these risks by transforming into hybridized Chinese restaurants, selling Chinese food alongside donuts. The combination arose out of shop owners' attempts to stand out in a crowded market and to have food available for sale all day long in any season. The availability of low-cost, pre-made Chinese food from restaurant wholesalers may also have contributed to the development of these restaurants, along with the ubiquitous presence of fryers and oil (both needed to produce Americanized Chinese food) at Cambodian donut shops. Selling Chinese food alongside donuts does not, however, appear connected to the Chinese Cambodian heritage of donut shop owners, as the offerings are standard Americanized Chinese dishes.

Local Adaptation

Liu documents the growth of the Chinese restaurant business in the San Gabriel Valley after the Immigration and Nationality Act of 1965 brought a new wave of Chinese immigrants to Los Angeles, noting the "thousands of Chinese restaurants, food stores, and groceries"[57] in the area. A decade after this reform, Chinese Cambodian refugees came to Southern California and soon began opening donut shops. Although they arrived under different circumstances, they too marshaled social capital, labor, supplies, and production and sales strategies to build a business model that has achieved great success in Los Angeles. While these practices are tied to their experiences as refugees, they also resemble techniques long used within ethnic business niches—Chinese restaurants in particular, as demonstrated above.

Perhaps the most remarkable strategy deployed by Chinese restauranteurs since the earliest days of the industry has been the adaptation of Chinese restaurants to local populations and tastes. Cambodian donut shop owners have replicated this practice in Los Angeles. They draw upon local supply chains, and have even entered the supply business. Their recruitment of Asian and Latino labor reflects the unique demographics of the neighborhoods in which they reside as well as Los Angeles as a whole, which boasted a majority Latino, Asian, and African American population in 2015.[58] They have also dealt with risks and insecurities unique to California, including seasonal sales reductions due to the area's warm climate, potential increases in rent as real estate costs soar throughout the area, and, most recently, potential supply insecurities posed by the specter of long-term drought.

Cambodian donut shops even reflect the highly individualized nature of Southern Californian cities and neighborhoods. Rather than buying into a franchise, which imposes a uniform product and experience across vast areas, Cambodian donut shop owners have taken over territory without entirely standardizing shop names, décor, or menus, opening or acquiring shops in neighborhoods and cities throughout Southern California. They operate them according to the general strategies outlined above while incorporating practices that reflect the individual character and population of each place. A shop's décor, for example, will frequently include Cambodian art or Buddhist shrines, but can differ widely based on the socioeconomic status of the area in which it is located. While most donut shop owners adhere to standard recipes, some produce popular specialty donuts. Other shops emerge as local favorites based on one particularly stellar offering, such as Gladstone's Donuts, which serves an African-American neighborhood of Pasadena and receives attention for its buttermilk bars. A shop's labor pool can also vary from neighborhood to neighborhood.

In the course of adapting their businesses to the greater Los Angeles area, Cambodian refugees irrevocably shaped the local donut industry. They bested traditional donut chains by combining the uniformity of a franchise with the necessary specialization that a sprawling, fragmented metropolis demands. Their businesses reflect conscious processes through which Chinese Cambodian donut shop owners have negotiated not only social capital, labor, finances, risks, and insecurities, but also place. I believe that this capacity for local adaptation, together with similarities to other practices of Chinese eating places, compels us to view the Chinese Cambodian donut shops of Los Angeles as a kind of Chinese restaurant. Donut shops can expand our definition of Chinese restaurants beyond cuisine, incorporating ownership and business practices. I have demonstrated that the tactics of Chinese Cambodian donut entrepreneurs place their enterprises within the lineage of Chinese restaurants in the United States and United Kingdom. The recent emergence of hybridized Cambodian donut shops and Chinese restaurants only serves to concretize the relationship between these two ethnic business niches.

Key Terms

Emotional labor: The regulation and deployment of one's emotions to meet particular workplace demands.

Informal economy: Forms of trade or exchange that are not regulated by state actors.

Social capital: An individual's combination of skills, education, experiences, and social relationships.

Discussion Questions

1. How do you define a Chinese restaurant? Does a Chinese restaurant have to serve Chinese cuisine, be owned or operated by Chinese people, or participate in certain kinds of business practices?
2. What other kinds of immigrant businesses use strategies similar to those of Cambodian donut shops? How have they adapted their businesses to their specific locations?
3. What roles do race and gender play in the development and deployment of immigrant business practices?

Notes

1 While "doughnut" is the traditional spelling of the word, I use "donut" to reflect the spelling most frequently deployed by Cambodian donut shops in Los Angeles and to link their products to the mass-production and mass-marketing of donuts that emerged in the United States during the twentieth century.
2 Namoch Sokhom and Susan Chhu, interviews held in Rosemead, California, December 2011.
3 *Ibid.*
4 Chhu.
5 Seth Mydans, "Long Beach Journal; From Cambodia to Doughnut Shops." *The New York Times*, May 26, 1995, A10.
6 Sucheng Chan, *Survivors: Cambodian Refugees in the United States* (Urbana: University of Illinois Press, 2004), 129. Min Zhou makes similar arguments with regard to urban Chinese enclaves. See Min Zhou, *Chinatown: The Socioeconomic Potential of an Urban Enclave* (Philadelphia: Temple University Press, 1992).
7 Aihwa Ong, *Buddha Is Hiding: Refugees, Citizenship, the New America* (Berkeley: University of California Press, 2003), 241.
8 Ibid.
9 Nancy J. Smith-Hefner, "The Culture of Entrepreneurship Among Khmer Refugees," in Marilyn Halter, ed., *New Migrants in the Marketplace: Boston's Ethnic Entrepreneurs* (Amherst: University of Massachusetts Press, 1995), 148.
10 Sokhom.
11 See Pal Nyiri and Igor Saveliev, eds., *Globalizing Chinese Migration: Trends in Europe and Asia* (Farnham: Ashgate Publishing Limited, 2002).
12 See Adam McKeown, *Chinese Migrant Networks and Cultural Change: Peru, Chicago, and Hawaii 1900–1936* (Chicago: University of Chicago Press, 2001).
13 Chan, *Survivors*, 149.
14 Ong, *Buddha is Hiding*, 241. Also see Chan, *Survivors*, 147.
15 Chan, *Survivors*, 150–151.
16 Heather R. Lee, "A Life Cooking for Others: The Work and Migration Experiences of a Chinese Restaurant Worker in New York City, 1920–1946," in *Eating Asian America: A Food Studies Reader*, eds. Robert Ji-Song Ku, Martin F. Manalansan IV, and Anita Mannur (New York: New York University Press, 2013), 53–77.
17 Haiming Liu, *From Canton Restaurant to Panda Express: A History of Chinese Food in the United States* (New Brunswick: Rutgers University Press, 2015), 46.
18 Chan, *Survivors*, 148.
19 *Cambodian Doughnut Dreams*, DVD, directed by Chuck Davis (1989; Boulder: Throughline Productions, 2005).
20 Davis, *Cambodian Doughnut Dreams*; Chan, *Survivors*, 148.
21 Chhu; Belinda Chhem, interview held in Rosemead, California, December 2011.

22 Chhu; Helen Chin, interview held in Long Beach, California, December 2011; Allen Dul, interview held in Rosemead, California, December 2011.

23 Ong, *Buddha is Hiding*, 242. Also see Chan, *Survivors*, 148.

24 Miri Song, *Helping Out: Children's Labor in Ethnic Businesses* (Philadelphia: Temple University Press, 1999), 10.

25 Chan, *Survivors*, 148.

26 Christina Nhek, interview held in Long Beach, California, December 2011.

27 Lee, "A Life Cooking For Others," 55.

28 Song, *Helping Out*, 42.

29 Chhu.

30 Nhek.

31 Davis, *Cambodian Doughnut Dreams*; Chan, *Survivors*, 148.

32 See Arlie Russel Hochschild, *The Managed Heart: Commercialization of Human Feeling* (Berkeley: University of California Press, 1983).

33 Karen Quintiliani, "Cambodian Refugee Families in the Shadows of Welfare Reform," *Journal of Immigrant & Refugee Studies* 7, no. 2 (2009), 153.

34 Chin.

35 Ong, *Buddha is Hiding*, 242.

36 Chhu; Dul.

37 Paul Mullins, *Glazed America: A History of the Doughnut* (Gainesville: University Press of Florida, 2008), 89.

38 Ong, *Buddha is Hiding*. 243.

39 See Nancy Abelmann and John Lie, *Blue Dreams: Korean Americans and the Los Angeles Riots* (Cambridge: Harvard University Press, 1997); Amelia Pang, "Who's in the Kitchen at Chinese Restaurants?" Truthdig, November 2, 2016, www.truthdig.com/articles/whos-in-the-kitchen-at-chinese-restaurants-an-investigative-report-part-1/; Marta C. López-Garza and David R. Diaz, eds., *Asian and Latino Immigrants in a Restructuring Economy: The Metamorphosis of Southern California* (Palo Alto: Stanford University Press, 2001).

40 Mullins, *Glazed America*, 88.

41 "About Us," BakeMark USA, accessed July 9, 2015, www.yourbakemark.com/careers/about-us.html.

42 Chhu, Dul.

43 Daniel Akst, "Cruller Fates: Cambodians Find Slim Profit in Doughnuts," *Los Angeles Times*, March 9, 1993, http://articles.latimes.com/1993-03-09/business/fi-1073_1_dough nut-shop.

44 *Cambodian American Yellow Pages* (Long Beach: Cambodian American Chamber of Commerce, 2004), Cambodian Community History and Archive Project, Historical Society of Long Beach.

45 Sokhom.

46 See Liu, *From Canton Restaurant to Panda Express,* 22.

47 Chhu, Chhem.

48 Sokhom.

49 Chhu, Dul.

50 Chhu.

51 Chin.

52 Hak Lonh, interview held in Los Angeles, California, March 2011.

53 See Claudia Kolker, "Dipping in the Money Pool," *Houston Press*, March 30, 1995. Derived from the Italian term *tontine*, these informal, rotating credit associations are common among immigrant entrepreneur. The Vietnamese term for such an arrangement is *hui*, while the Ethiopian term is *ekub*. Nancy Abelmann and John Lie, for example, cite the use of rotating credit associations among Korean Americans, although they warn that many observers overemphasize the importance of these arrangements. Nancy Abelmann and John Lie, *Blue Dreams: Korean Americans and the Los Angeles Riots* (Cambridge: Harvard University Press, 1997), 134.

54 Ong, *Buddha is Hiding*, 245.
55 Sokhom.
56 *Ibid*.
57 Liu, *From Canton Restaurant to Panda Express*, 107.
58 Javier Panzar, "It's Official: Latinos Now Outnumber Whites in California," *Los Angeles Times*, July 8, 2015, www.latimes.com/local/california/la-me-census-latinos-20150708-story.html.

5

TALK DOESN'T COOK RICE

Chinese Restaurants and the Chinese (American) Dream in Ohio

Anthony Miller

In 2017, *The Cincinnati Enquirer* celebrated the retirement of Mike Wong, owner of Oriental Wok, as "a poster child for the immigrant American dream." The newspaper called Wong the latest in "a long tradition of well-known Chinese restaurant hosts in Cincinnati, genial men who act as a bridge between cultures and friend to their customers: impresarios of Chinese food." He was more than just a commercial and social success, and his career showed that "a restaurant is about much more than just food." Rather, Wong reveled in the role he played as a cultural ambassador for both Chinese-Americans and China.[1]

In the early twentieth century, southern Ohio was home to a number of Chinese restaurant owners such as Charlie Yee, who overcame racism and discrimination to gain the acceptance of the wider community. Known as the "Mayor of Chinatown" in Cincinnati in the 1940s and 1950s, Yee translated friendships with city officials and the popularity of chop suey's cheap exoticism into a powerful tool for cultural diplomacy. While running his restaurants, he raised thousands of dollars for China during the Second World War and promoted the rights of Chinese migrants living in Ohio. Like Wong's, Yee's retirement in 1961 was greeted by the *Cincinnati Enquirer* as proof that "The American Way is Better For Charlie Yee, His Children," his success seen as symbolic of the larger Chinese-American experience in U.S. history.[2]

But in reality the historical contexts surrounding Wong and Yee were vastly different as was the type of Chinese cuisine their restaurants served to Ohioans. Wong believed that he arrived in Cincinnati at a fortuitous moment: "Nixon had just gone to China, and people were interested in Chinese food, excited about it."[3] Indeed, from the 1970s onward newer generations of Chinese restaurant owners turned American curiosity for authentic Chinese cuisine into roles as cultural emissaries, urban taste makers, and the means for fulfilling their own American Dream. By introducing regional cuisines like Sichuan and Hunan, Wong's Oriental Wok succeeded in using the cultural diplomacy of food to create a more positive image of Chinese-Americans and their cultural heritage. And within a historical context of growing trade and immigration connecting Ohio to Taiwan and the People's Republic of China (PRC), eating authentic Chinese food came to symbolize a desire to embrace a more multicultural and racially diverse Midwest.

Over the past few years, however, the cultural dynamics and politics underlying immigration, US–China relations, and Chinese cuisine in Ohio have changed dramatically. Owners and employees of Chinese restaurants, many of them recent immigrants, operate their businesses in a state where President Trump's message of "American First" resonated powerfully with voters in the 2016 election. Fears of Chinese economic power cross party lines and have a longer history than just the Trump campaign. Ohio Senators Rob Portman (Republican) and Sherrod Brown (Democratic) have for the last few years railed against the PRC as a threat to the American economy, with Brown claiming that trade with China "has meant shuttered factories, lost jobs, and devastated communities across America."[4] Conversely, economists and farmers from the Buckeye State worry that President Trump's trade war with Beijing will make the state's pork and soybean producers, whose exports to China account for millions of dollars annually, the first casualties.[5]

Along with rising economic anxieties, the focal point of Chinese immigration in Ohio has shifted away from Chinatowns in metropolitan areas toward suburbs or colleges that are home to thousands of international faculty and students hailing from China. There, Chinese-owned establishments such as Tang Dynasty in college towns like Oxford, Ohio cater largely to a Chinese customer base. These owners still believe in Chinese food as a form of cultural diplomacy and as a platform to success in America. Many exhibit the mentality expressed by China House owner Xiaohui "Joey" Yang, as "光说不能做米饭," an old Chinese adage translated as "talk doesn't cook rice."[6] The phrase in many ways encapsulates the historic role played by Chinese restaurant owners to actively shape impressions of China and the Chinese-American on a daily basis for Ohioans.

But unlike Wong and his generation, many of the newer restaurant managers such as Zeng Xue of Tang Dynasty see Chinese food as part of their pursuit of the Chinese Dream, a reference to the quest of Xi Jinping for national rejuvenation and the export of Chinese influence globally.[7] Restaurants such as Tang Dynasty use authentic Chinese food like hot pot to demonstrate the prestige and power of their culinary heritage and home country. This chapter explores the meanings associated with authentic Chinese food in Ohio from the era of Mike Wong and Sino-American Rapprochement in Cincinnati to Tang Dynasty and the Chinese Dream in Oxford, Ohio. I look at how Chinese restaurant owners find themselves in the position of trying to gently introduce Ohioans to authentic Chinese food while pursuing their own dreams of prosperity and societal influence in mainstream America. Within a context of deepening trade and relations with the PRC, I argue that authentic Chinese food has come to have a dual meaning for Ohioans: signifying both the embrace of deepening trade and relations with the PRC, immigration, and multi-culturalism, but also fears about China's rising global dominance, its economic might, and the place of immigrants in the United States.

Sino-American Rapprochement and Oriental Wok

In the spring of 1979, Governor Jim Rhodes (Republican) of Ohio took part in one of the first trade missions to the PRC. On his trip, the enthusiastic governor extolled the potential benefits of trade with Ohio, offering Vice Prime Minister Yu Qiuli American aid and the know-how for projects such as the building of Disneyland-style amusement parks at the Great Wall and golf resorts next to Beijing's airport. In return, Rhodes was excited about the prospect of the PRC as a massive market to revitalize a struggling state economy suffering from de-industrialization and a sagging agricultural industry.[8]

However, the governor's appetite for authentic Chinese cuisine was not as robust as his hunger for business ventures. As noted by his biographers in *James A. Rhodes: Ohio Colossus*, the Republican stalwart managed to avoid any and all spicy dishes and fish at his daily luncheons and banquets. Rather, he survived by eating steamed rice and the lunch meats, cheese, and crackers he had brought from home.[9] The International Trade Division's report on the trip "Ohio Goes to China" labeled it a promising start to establishing commercial and cultural relations with the PRC. In the section entitled "Getting Used to China" the state agency also used food to symbolize the difficulty Ohio faced in learning to appreciate authentic Chinese culture and customs. The report explained to constituents in Ohio:

> Food served in China often bears little resemblance to that served in Chinese restaurants in the U.S. Twelve course meals were served with strange-sounding and tasting concoctions as duck brain, bird's nest, and shark's fin. On the beverage side there was the ever present tea, plus beer, warm orange soda and a high-powered drink.[10]

Like the governor, most of the Ohio staff that accompanied him ate little of the food prepared by their Chinese hosts, consuming instead care packages from home of sausages, cheese, bread, and candy bars.

While Rhodes and his staff never developed an appreciation for Chinese cuisine, the governor's delegation played a part in the more general revival of curiosity in Ohio and across the United States about newer, more authentic variants of Chinese food. In the 1980s and 1990s, Rhodes' trip was followed by a steady exchange of mayors, congressmen, Chinese delegations, travelers, and tourists, which sustained interest in Chinese dishes, aromas, and tastes that were deemed "authentic." Simultaneously, comments from politicians like Rhodes and the coverage devoted in U.S. media to Chinese banquets perpetuated the view that American-Chinese food wasn't "real" Chinese food.[11] This nascent understanding stimulated a curiosity for new, unfamiliar tastes and aromas and also a cultural impulse to unlearn what Americans thought they had always known about China.

Adding momentum to the demand for authentic Chinese food was the increasing number of Chinese immigrants coming to the United States and settling in Ohio after 1965. Since the Immigration and Nationality Act of 1965, hundreds of thousands of Chinese from Taiwan, Hong Kong, and, later the PRC, have migrated to the United States. As a result, the size of the Chinese-American community in Ohio has steadily grown from a few thousand to a population of over 172,000. This continuing influx of immigrants has created a considerable demand for more genuinely authentic Chinese food, met by restaurants offering regional cuisines such as Hunan, Sichuan, Shandong, and Shanghai.[12] By the early 2000s, the number of Chinese restaurants in Ohio and the United States had grown dramatically, with over 40,000 nationwide.[13]

The career of Mike Wong and his restaurant Oriental Wok perfectly exemplified the new patterns in immigration and Chinese cuisine in this era. Leaving mainland China as a teenager, Wong moved to Hong Kong to study for an engineering degree before arriving in California in the late 1960s. From there he worked his way across the country through a network of friends and relatives by gaining employment in the kitchens of restaurants like the Dragon Inn in Ohio. Once Wong's residency was established he, like thousands of Chinese-Americans at the time, reunited with his family through chain migration by "pulling" his wife and daughters to the United States. After opening his own restaurant, the first Oriental Work, in northern Kentucky in the 1970s, Wong and his daughters later opened a second one in Hyde Park of Cincinnati.[14]

Beyond Oriental Wok, Cincinnati in the 1970s and 1980s became home to a new generation of Chinese restaurants such as Yum Yum and China Gourmet that promised to deliver "real" Chinese food. Yum Yum's owners were Thomas Li, a chemist by training from mainland China, and his wife Mei, originally from Taiwan. The duo aggressively advertised their commitment to forgoing "American-Chinese" food in favor of Hunan and Sichuan dishes with Mrs. Li positioned as the guardian of its authenticity via her formal education as a cook and supervisor of all food preparation.[15] Reviews celebrated Yum Yum for bringing to the Queen City the popular dishes that were all the rave in New York's Chinatown. Similarly, the newly opened China Gourmet, owned by Bing Moy who was originally born in Canton in 1937, was praised for bringing the sorts of tastes and dishes to the area that one might encounter on a tour of Hong Kong or San Francisco.[16]

Creating and sustaining a market for authentic cuisine that appealed to Ohioans, however, was also a matter of relentless cultural diplomacy. Yum Yum, Oriental Wok, and China Gourmet were credited with creating from scratch a clientele for regional Hunan cuisines. Rather than accommodating American tastes, these businesses offered guided introductions to their menus to ease Ohioans into the unfamiliar delights of Sichuan string beans and black bean sauce. Helping patrons select dishes and explore new tastes, the *Cincinnati Enquirer* described the work of men like Moy as that of "businessman, a cook, a maitre'd, an artist, an educator."[17] In their efforts at cultural diplomacy this generation of Chinese-American emissaries benefited from partnerships with Organizations such as the Chinese American

Association of Cincinnati (CAAC), founded in 1971. Since its inception, the CAAC has played an integral role in hosting events such as the Chinese New Year and hosting speakers, artists, and exhibits related to Chinese culture in the area with the help of many of the area's restaurants. Wong was especially active in educating the public by offering cooking classes and demonstrations throughout the tri-state area (Ohio, Indiana, Kentucky) in the 1980s and 1990s.

Equally important though was the role that these restaurants and their owners played in strengthening ties with the PRC. From the late 1980s to the present, Oriental Wok has served as the "unofficial restaurant" of Cincinnati's Sister Cities Program with Liuzhou, hosting visitors and delegations from the PRC. Additionally, Oriental Wok participated in an exchange of chefs encouraging Americans to try the Chinese city's specialty *luosifen* (snail soup). Simultaneously, Wong and his generation of restaurant owners helped build organizations such as the Greater Cincinnati Chinese Chamber of Commerce and Cincinnati Chinese Culture Learning Association involved in charitable work and the exchange of artists, students, exhibits, and intellectuals with the PRC.[18]

As a result, Oriental Work, Yum Yum, and China Gourmet have been celebrated for the ways in which their food has enhanced Ohio's multiculturalism. The introduction of regional cuisines such as Sichuan was praised for not only enriching the Midwestern diet but also for revealing a diversity and depth to Chinese culture previously unknown to most non-Chinese in the United States. According to one Cincinnati food critic, prior to the influx of newer, regional-based Chinese restaurants, many in American had begun to think that all Chinese dishes tasted and looked the same. Reviews of China Gourmet thanked the proprietor for showing the city the diversity and creativity of Chinese cuisine, writing that the Chinese "like the French" knew how to accentuate the flavor of every ingredient.[19] In this sense these restaurants offered food that also satisfied a consumer appetite for a truer, deeper understanding of Chinese culture that strengthened Sino-American relations. Indeed, for most Ohioans their primary means of engaging with Chinese culture still came in the form of food and interactions with Chinese-Americans and new immigrants in restaurants. In seeking out authentic Chinese food, Ohioans expressed their desire to strengthen ties between the United States and China as well as their acceptance of a broader definition of multiculturalism in the Midwest.

The meanings of Chinese food in Ohio during this period, however, go beyond merely culture and diplomacy and reflect ideas about the economy. Since the 1970s Governors from Jim Rhodes to John Kasich have worked with organizations like the CAAC to deepen relations with the PRC as a means to rescue the state's slumping agricultural and industrial centers. As a result, the PRC has become the state's third largest export market for goods such as grains, navigational and aerospace technologies, and automobiles, worth $3.5 billion in trade in 2016. It is also the third largest market for Ohio's services primarily in education, travel, equipment, and trademarks worth another $1.1 billion.[20]

Eating authentic Chinese food has become a symbol of that relationship, representing an implicit bargain that Ohio's political leaders have promised their constituents. In embracing larger waves of Chinese immigrants, supporting immigrant-run businesses and the Chinese-American community, and learning to appreciate authentic Chinese culture, Ohioans have expected that deepening ties with China will strengthen the state's economy. Wong's retirement in 2017 then represented the fulfillment of that bargain. Ohioans helped him to achieve the American Dream as an immigrant business owner, and Oriental Wok had delivered a deeper appreciation for authentic Chinese culture and stronger ties to the PRC.

Tang Dynasty in Oxford, Ohio

Nowhere are the changing dynamics of immigration, Chinese food, and diplomacy better illustrated in Ohio than in the small city of Oxford. Less than an hour outside of Cincinnati and home to Miami University, Oxford is a small city of just over 21,000 people. Like many college-towns Oxford has seen its population of international students hailing from the PRC explode from just a few hundred in the early 2000s to over 1400 in 2014. Like Ohio State and the University of Cincinnati, Miami University has devoted considerable resources to increasing international student enrollment as a solution to declining state funding and domestic enrollment.

This sudden influx of Chinese students has resulted in a burst of businesses catering almost exclusively to Chinese students. Over ten new Chinese-owned enterprises have opened since 2012. Most of them are located just off campus on High Street—restaurants such as Tang Dynasty, Yum Yum, and Chunxi Kitchen. Across Oxford, though, there have also emerged new Chinese-owned groceries, clubs, housing, bakeries, and soon a fitness center.[21] Throughout the year, Oxford's city officials field three to four requests a month for retail space from Chinese entrepreneurs and companies, and the city of Oxford has looked very favorably upon the investment and contributions of these businesses to the local economy.

Tang Dynasty, China House, Yum Yum, and Chunxi Kitchen all primarily specialize in Sichuan cuisine, but also offer staples of Northern China cuisine such as hot pot, mala tang, and fu qi fei pian. Hoping to capitalize on the student demand for the comfort food of home, each restaurant employs mostly green card holders recruited from Sichuan as its staff and chefs to guarantee the cuisine's quality and identity.[22] Tang Dynasty, for example, secured its chef with the aid of the Chinese Consulate in Chicago by headhunting its cook from the kitchen of the city's famous Lao Sze Chuan.[23]

The owners and managers of these businesses also have remarkably different backgrounds. For example, Xianwei "Rico" Ren, the manager of Chunxi Kitchen, which opened in 2017, is originally from Daqing. In his early twenties, he is majoring in Small Business at Miami University while running the restaurant.[24] Zeng Xue, the manager of Tang Dynasty, is also his twenties and attending Miami University, but was born in Amoy and went to high school in Utah in the United States.[25] And Xiaohui "Joey" Yang, the owner of China House, is in his fifties; his family originally came from Sichuan but he grew up in northwest China and went to university in Beijing and later Singapore. Since the late 1990s he has worked in the United States as a researcher and professor in the field of Chemistry and Biochemistry, including at Miami University, where he decided to capitalize on the growing Chinese student population's need for home-cooked food by opening his own restaurant in 2014.[26]

Those businessmen see their role as a cultural emissary in much the same terms, trying to meet the demand not only for food but also for a sense of community for the Chinese students. The majority of each restaurant's daily customers are of Chinese descent, and each hosts parties to celebrate the Moon and Spring Festivals for the community and students. Zeng asserts that this is because Tang Dynasty provides Chinese students with food and a feeling of home that they could otherwise only get by driving an hour away to Cincinnati or other metropolitan areas like Indianapolis. Uncompromising in their authenticity, both Tang Dynasty and Chunxi Kitchen also proudly refuse to serve "American" Chinese food like egg rolls. Says Zeng, speaking for Oxford's newest batch of Chinese restaurant owners, "We want them (locals) to accept and taste our traditional food as it is." The modification of dishes to cater to American tastes is seen as a violation of their integrity.[27] More than ever before, these Chinese businesses feel less pressure, socially or economically, to accommodate to Americans. Rather, Zeng and Xianwei appear confident that their establishment's economic clout and the cultural prestige of their food makes them less inclined to cater to Americans, much like China today. Further, through their food and their presence in Oxford, these restaurants project an image of contemporary "Chineseness" as defined by affluence and global power.

Each is also eager to introduce locals and non-Chinese customers to the variety of authentic Chinese foods and flavors it provides. Indeed, Xianwei delights in guiding locals through "traditional" foods by encouraging them to try dishes with liver and cow stomach. When Xiaohui first opened China House, locals often walked in looking for General Tso's and left disappointed without ordering anything. He has learned to win them over by starting with dishes like hand-pulled noodles and hot pot, nothing too spicy, before encouraging them to order live fish or meats with lots of cartilage. Having built up his local clientele over the past few years, Xiaohui believes that China House has impressed upon many around Oxford that authentic Chinese food, in his words, should never be "sweet, sour, fried," but should have diverse tastes and aromas with many regional variations. He also hopes Oxford is gaining an appreciation for Chinese food's sophistication. By this he means that authentic Chinese food isn't meant to be fast food or made from pre-prepared sauces and ingredients by student laborers; rather, it requires a professional cook with culinary training and experience working with fresh produce.[28]

However, the introduction of so many new international students and Chinese-owned businesses in such a short period of time in such a small area has produced a number of tensions and controversies. University faculty and staff have raised academic concerns about the need for greater advising and institutional resources to aid the international students, but there was also a more sinister anonymous faculty letter to the student newspaper that called the Chinese students "dead weight" in the classrooms. This misperception persists in spite of the fact these international students are heavily recruited by universities like Miami, Ohio State, the University of Cincinnati, and nationally, where their tuition helps to lower costs for domestic students and sustain higher education in the United States.[29] Discontent among many American students ranges from casual racist complaints about the "smell" of Chinese food to annoyance that the language barrier at the new Chinese restaurants has made them feel unwelcome and unwanted in these establishments.[30]

More than just the prevalence of Chinese characters on signs and menus, these businesses have completely changed the look of the small college town's social landscape. Tang Dynasty moved into a building that housed a Quiznos; Chunxi Kitchen took the place of what was formerly an American-style breakfast diner; Chef Lin's Asian Restaurant and Sushi replaced a Kentucky Fried Chicken; Yum Yum Authentic Chinese resides where an Indian restaurant once was; and the HuaQi Salon moved into a storefront that used to be a Great Clips. As new businesses such as an Asian-style karaoke have opened, a few locals have taken to social media sites like Facebook or Twitter to voice their displeasure, circulating rumors that the businesses refuse to serve non-Chinese. Others are frustrated with the rhythms of these businesses, since many close for long periods in the summer as their clientele return home, something that city officials and other business owners feel is a "bad look" for the town's most visible shopping district.

Other complaints focus on the conspicuous consumption of the Chinese patrons of these establishments. Like those at other American colleges and universities, the current generation of international students on the Oxford campus often come from wealthy families. Chinese students parking luxury sports cars such as Lamborghinis and Maserati's on High Street have become common, adding a dimension of class conflict to the tensions stemming from the influx of Chinese businesses.[31]

On the Chinese side, there has been disappointment at what is seen as a cool reception to their investment in the community. Many owners have remained patient despite their difficulties finding new retail spaces or their inability to lease existing storefronts to launch new ventures, citing language and cultural barriers as part of the basis for their frustration. In other cases, some have felt discriminated against and rejected by Oxford and its residents, perceiving an actual effort to limit the presence and visibility of Chinese in the community.

Additionally, the claims these newer businesses have made to serving authentic food primarily for Chinese students have created tensions with mainstays in the Oxford community such as Phan Shin, the oldest Chinese restaurant in the town. Phan Shin opened in the 1980s, and is currently owned by Juan "Yvonne" Lin and her husband John, popular faces in the local community. Born to a construction worker and factory worker in China before migrating first to Canada and the US, Lin and her husband bought Phan Shin in 2008, and enjoyed considerable local support as one of the town's two Chinese restaurants at the time serving a variety of Cantonese, Sichuan, and "American" Chinese dishes.[32] On High Street, it was once in a prime location to draw the growing Chinese student population on campus, even going so far as to order specially made moon cakes from a vendor in New York City each year for the Full Moon Festival.

The sudden arrival of Tang Dynasty, Wild Asian Bistro, Yum Yum Authentic Chinese, Chunxi Kitchen, and others has left Phan Shin surrounded on High Street by competitors that simultaneously undermine Phan Shin's appeal to the Chinese students and its claims to authenticity in the larger community. In terms of cultural diplomacy, the social identity of these new restaurants risks elevating fears about competition and imbalance in trade and relations with China. Within this context, university officials, civic leaders, and the owners and managers themselves have done a great job to alleviate these fears. Much of the community—locals, city officials, campus faculty and students—looks positively on the transformation of the town as an expression of its diversity and economic vibrancy. Local patronage of the new arrivals like Tang Dynasty represents an embrace of Ohio's integration into the global economy, multiculturalism, and stronger relations with China. But it also means acceptance of a world in which Chinese immigrants are powerful, rich, and enjoy considerable power and clout in the United States as citizens, students, investors, businessmen, and consumers.

Conclusion: Kung Pao Chicken and America First

Since the early twentieth century, restaurants like Charlie Yee's Shanghai Inn have played a formative role in sustaining a sense of Chinese community and culture in the US Midwest despite racism and anti-immigration sentiment. Carrying on that tradition, restaurants like Mike Wong's Oriental Wok formed transnational networks invested in US–China relations that have built an appreciation for authentic Chinese cuisine and the contributions of American-born Chinese and immigrants to Ohio. These businesses were seen as enriching the social and cultural landscape of the Greater Cincinnati Area with new foods, aromas, tastes, and aesthetic styles. They also opened avenues between Ohio and the PRC that facilitated economic relations to strengthen the state's economy.

Today, however, many non-Chinese Ohioans still prefer to see Chinese food, culture, and people assimilated to mainstream America. This abiding preference might explain why Phan Shin in Oxford enjoys a much broader base of customers amongst the general population than its newer, more authentic competitors. Many locals say they prefer Phan Shin out of loyalty or because they like the taste of American-Chinese dishes like General Tso's over mala tang. More conservative voices see the insistence of Tang Dynasty and the other restaurants on authentic food, their priority in catering to Chinese clients, and their visible Chinese social identity in the community as not just ethnic pride but outright defiance and flouting of American influence and values.

In sum, authentic Chinese food in Midwestern states like Ohio has carried a dual meaning since the 1970s: it represents both a desire to deepen trade and relations with the PRC by embracing multiculturalism and Chinese immigration, but also a nervousness about China's global power and the affluence of Chinese immigrants in American society. It remains to be seen if this newest generation of Chinese restaurant owners can accomplish all they want by following Xi Jinping in pursuing the Chinese Dream by serving customers in Kung Pao Chicken without making Ohioans nervous about America remaining first in the world.

Key Terms

Xi Jinping and the Chinese Dream: A reference to Xi Jinping's ideological pursuit of Chinese global power, influence, and prosperity in the twenty-first century.

Cultural diplomacy: The exchange of art, cuisine, religion, music, and aspects of material culture to promote cultural understanding and aid diplomacy between two or more countries.

Chinese immigration in the US: From the nineteenth century to the present, Chinese immigrants have played an integral role in the development of the US as representatives of their culture and people but also as laborers, entrepreneurs, and citizens.

Discussion Questions

1. Why have Chinese restaurants and food played such a prominent role in the cultural diplomacy between the United States and China?
2. How does "authentic" food symbolize ideas about the status of Chinese immigrants and China's influence in the US Midwest?
3. Compare and contrast the aspirations and careers of restaurant owners and managers Charlie Yee, Mike Wong, and Zeng Xue. What aspects of these Chinese food and restaurants have remained the same and what has changed over time?

Notes

1 Polly Campbell, "Chinese Cuisine: Mike Wong," *The Cincinnati Enquirer*, September 24, 2017, p. E2.
2 "The American Way is Better—For Charlie Yee, His Children," *The Cincinnati Enquirer*, November 18, 1961, p. 11.
3 Polly Campbell, "Chinese Cuisine: Mike Wong," *The Cincinnati Enquirer*, September 24, 2017, p. E2.
4 Sherrod Brown, "For Our China Trade Emergency, Dial Section 301," *New York Times*, October 17, 2010.
5 Chris Mosby, "China Retaliates in Trade War, Midwest Will Get Hit: Experts," *The Cleveland Patch*, April 3, 2018.
6 Oral History of Xiaohui Yang. Interview of Xiaohui Yang by Anthony Miller. Oxford, Ohio, November 10, 2017.
7 Robert Lawrence Kuhn, "Xi Jinping's Chinese Dream," *New York Times*, June 4, 2013.

8 Tom Diemer, Lee Leonard, and Richard Zimmerman, *James A. Rhodes: Ohio Colossus* (Kent, OH: Kent State University Press, 2014); Bob Brumfeld, "Rhodes' Road Show Proposes a Fantasy," *The Cincinnati Enquirer*, July 11, 1979, p. 11.

9 Tom Diemer, Lee Leonard, and Richard Zimmerman, *James A. Rhodes: Ohio Colossus* (Kent, OH: Kent State University Press, 2014).

10 Ohio International Trade Division, "Report: Ohio Goes to China," (1979), pp. 7–9.

11 Sherry Smart, "Secret of Ancient Culture Bound by Centuries of Internal Conflicts," *Marion Star*, September 22, 1985. p. 17.

12 Haiming Liu, "General Tso's Chicken Made in Taiwan," in *From Canton Restaurant to Panda Express* (New Brunswick, NJ: Rutgers University Press, 2015), pp. 86–106.

13 "Fact Sheet: Immigrants in Ohio," *American Council on Immigration*, October 4, 2017; "Chinese Ohioans," Ohio History Central, 2017, www.ohiohistorycentral.org/w/ Chinese_Ohioans, accessed January 24, 2018.

14 Polly Campbell, "Chinese Cuisine: Mike Wong," *The Cincinnati Enquirer*, September 24, 2017, p. E2.

15 "Mother's Day is The Opening for Yum Yum," *The Cincinnati Enquirer,* May 8, 1976, p. 5.

16 David Hunter, "Combinations Are Bizarre, Tastes Great," *The Cincinnati Enquirer,* January 5, 1978, p. 47.

17 "Yum Yum," *The Cincinnati Enquirer*, September 1, 1979, p. 7; "City's Finest Restaurants," The Cincinnati Enquirer, November 16, 1978, p. 86.

18 Polly Campbell, "Oriental Wok Offers Menu from Chinese Sister City," *The Cincinnati Enquirer*, November 18, 2015.

19 David Hunter, "Combinations Are Bizarre, Tastes Great," *The Cincinnati Enquirer*, January 5, 1978, p. 47.

20 The US-China Business Council, "State Reports: Ohio's Exports to China," 2016.

21 Jim DeBrosse, "Waiting for the Great Leap Forward," *Cincinnati Magazine*, May 2017.

22 Oral History of Xianwei Ren. Interview of Xianwei Ren by Anthony Miller. Oxford, Ohio, October 13, 2017.

23 Oral History of Zeng Xue. Interview of Zeng Xue by Anthony Miller. Oxford, Ohio, October 13, 2017.

24 Oral History of Xianwei Ren. Interview of Xianwei Ren by Anthony Miller. Oxford, Ohio, October 13, 2017.

25 Oral History of Zeng Xue. Interview of Zeng Xue by Anthony Miller. Oxford, Ohio, October 13, 2017.

26 Oral History of Xiaohui Yang. Interview of Xiaohui Yang by Anthony Miller. Oxford, Ohio, November 10, 2017.

27 Oral History of Zeng Xue. Interview of Zeng Xue by Anthony Miller. Oxford, Ohio. October 13, 2017.

28 Oral History of Xiaohui Yang. Interview of Xiaohui Yang by Anthony Miller. Oxford, Ohio, November 10, 2017.

29 Tanza Loudenback, "International Students Are Now 'Subsidizing' Public American Universities to the Tune of $9 Billion a Year," *Business Insider*, September 16, 2016.

30 Jim DeBrosse, "Waiting for the Great Leap Forward," *Cincinnati Magazine*, May 2017.

31 Jim DeBrosse, "Waiting for the Great Leap Forward," *Cincinnati Magazine*, May 2017.

32 "Humans of Oxford: An Owner Glad to Sweep," *The Miami Student*, October 23, 2015.

PART II

Culinary Histories

6

SURVEYING THE GENEALOGY OF CHINESE RESTAURANTS IN MEXICO

From High-End Franchises to Makeshift Stands

Yong Chen

Introduction

It is difficult to know the exact number of Chinese restaurants in Mexico, as there has been no serious research on this topic, nor is there an umbrella organization such as The United Chinese Restaurant Association of America who can at least give an estimate by its membership.[1] The even bigger challenge in Mexico is that the category of Chinese restaurant is becoming increasingly ambiguous since more and more Mexicans who used to work in Chinese restaurants in the United States have returned to their native land and opened up their own "Chinese restaurants." Do we count them as such as well? This is certainly an interesting question that merits serious discussion.

My answer to this puzzling question, though, is to adopt an inclusive approach. I count the Mexican-owned "Chinese restaurants" as equally belonging to the general category, and I am not concerned with the question of what is "authentic" Chinese food and what is not. My survey of Chinese restaurants in Mexico is based on my research and on my personal experiences. During my nine years of residence in Mexico, I have visited numerous Chinese restaurants in Mexico City and adjacent states in the central part of the country. My first-hand experiences are not research-driven and my generalization draws from my casual observations and retrospective reflections, as well as my research based on information of both printed and online sources.

I have tentatively divided the Chinese restaurants in Mexico into four sub-categories: the restaurant chains hailing from the United States, the flavor-sensitive restaurants catering to the Chinese palate, the restaurants with steam table buffet targeting the more general clientele, and the restaurants owned by Mexicans who used to work in Chinese restaurants in the United States. In any case, the division is just an expedient strategy for the assortment of the massive number of Chinese restaurants that dot the landscape of Mexico, from small villages to metropolitans and from poverty-stricken slums to high-end commercial districts. The ordering of the four types of Chinese restaurants in this chapter is not by their importance or number but rather by the convenience of writing structure. If anything, there is indeed a numerical difference between the first two sub-categories and the latter two, because the restaurants with steam table buffet and the Mexican-owned restaurants are the foot soldiers that make up the bulk of Chinese restaurants in Mexico.

Chinese Restaurant Chains Hailing from the United States

The first type of Chinese restaurants refers to those that operate with a big sum of investments and multiple partnership, with P.F. Chang's China Bistro and Panda Express as primary examples. So far, there are only a small number of these restaurant chains with their foot in Mexico, mostly in Mexico City and its metropolitan area, but they usually occupy strategical locations in busy commercial districts. Occasionally scoffed at as "fake" Chinese restaurants, they are rapidly expanding their territories with a successful marketing strategy and are happy to offer "Americanized" Chinese food to a receptive clientele who are more concerned with dining environment, convenience, and style.

Founded 26 years ago in Arizona, today P.F. Chang's boasts of having 220 franchises present in 21 countries.[2] The first overseas franchise of P.F. Chang's opened in 2009 in a business district of Mexico City,[3] and in 2017 there were 25 franchises in Mexico, with the majority of them concentrated in the Mexican capital.[4] In fact, Mexico has become the second most important market for P.F. Chang's, and this joint venture of the restaurant chain plans to open at least 30 franchises by 2022.

The strategy of globalization of P.F. Chang's is best manifested in its menu, where the ten main courses are exactly the same all over the world, with the exception of some areas such as the Middle East, where people do not eat certain types of meat and do not consume alcohol. According to its co-founder, Philip Chiang, Mexico is a good choice for internationalization because it has a large base of clients.

> It's a key market, and yes, it was a potentially great market for us, because many of our clients in the United States come from Mexico, especially in Miami, Houston, Dallas, Los Angeles, San Diego and other border states. We knew in a certain way that there was great potential in the country.[5]

Like P.F. Chang's, Panda Express also identified Mexico as its first target for internationalization. Founded in 1973, this Chinese restaurant chain had more than 1,400 franchises in 2011 in the U.S. mainland, Hawaii, and Puerto Rico, and the number has expanded to more than 2,000 as of 2018.[6] Today there are 19 franchises in Mexico City and a few more in other states, but the long-term plan is to open as many as 300 franchises in the whole country.

FIGURE 6.1 A franchise of P.F. Chang's in Mexico City.

Similar to the marketing strategy of P.F. Chang's, Panda Express also seeks to open its franchises in commercial districts of Mexico City, including Lomas Verdes, Planco, Reforma, Insurgentes Sur, World Trade Center, and other places that have a high concentration of white-collar workers and a massive flow of commuters. Unlike P.F. Chang's, which is specifically targeting the high-end clientele, the customer base of Panda Express is more oriented toward the lower end of middle class and, as a result, it seems to have expanded more rapidly than P.F. Chang's. The motto of Panda Express, "fast/casual,"[7] is an accurate summary of its fast-food orientation.

The difference of marketing strategy between P.F. Chang's and Panda Express is also discernable in their respective menus. P.F. Chang's ostensibly claims: "Our food is served family style for the purpose of sharing. We use completely natural meat and responsibly caught seafood. In addition we offer you vegetables grown 100% naturally."[8] Besides the usual options of "Americanized" Chinese food, the exploratory client can find something special: Chang's Famous Chicken Lettuce Wraps, Dynamite Shrimp, Asian Caesar Salad, Asian Angus NY Strip, and other fancy dishes that cater to the hippies or even the "foodies" of the consumer base. In contrast, the menu of Panda Express only offers the typical options of "Americanized" Chinese food, including Orange Chicken, Sweet and Sour Chicken, Kung Pao Chicken, Broccoli Beef, Chow Mein, Fried Rice, Spring Rolls, and a handful of other dishes that can be found in almost every fast food Chinese restaurant in the United States.[9]

Flavor-sensitive Chinese Restaurants Catering to the Chinese Palate

The second type of Chinese restaurant is typically owned by new immigrants from all over China since the 1980s, although Guangdong Province is still the primary source of immigration. Many of these restaurants depend on a talented cook and special recipes to consolidate their place in the dining market. The representatives of this type of restaurant include Bei Dou Xing, Xin Tian, Yi Pin Ju, Meng Hua Ju, among others. They offer various kinds of regional dishes of China and their customers are mainly Chinese immigrants or visitors who are on the lookout for "authentic" Chinese food. They are usually located in the Chinatown (Barrio Chino) of metropolitans because that is where the Chinese population is often concentrated. Correspondingly, only in big cities like

FIGURE 6.2 A Cantonese restaurant specializing in dim sum, Mexico City.

Mexico City, Tijuana, and Mexicali can the diners find the flavor-sensitive Chinese restaurants.

A fascinating story about this type of restaurant is the case of Bei Dou Xing, a family-run restaurant that lived out its glory for a short period during the second decade of the twenty-first century. It was located on the corner of out-of-the-way streets and only had space for four small tables. The owner/cook, Ren Hongyu, was from Hebei Province but the restaurant was famous among Chinese for its specialization in Sichuan and Shandong dishes.[10] From the outside, there was not even a visible signage because it did not want to attract excessive customers. The wife of Ren Hongyu served as a kitchen assistant and waited on the tables at the same time, and their college-attending son lent his help during the weekends. Most of the time, the restaurant was so busy that the diners had to make a reservation several days ahead. Unfortunately, Bei Dou Xing closed its door after several years of business due to the shortage of labor, the cost of ingredients, and a host of other reasons. Out of desperation, the hungry customers tried very hard to find a

FIGURE 6.3　The menu of Meng Hua Ju, Viaducto, Mexico City.

substitute, and in a sense, Meng Hua Ju and Yi Pin Ju emerged partially because of the vacancy that Bei Dou Xing had left behind.

Meng Hua Ju (Perfecto Antojitos) is located in the so-called new Chinatown of Mexico City, which is a residential neighborhood east of the city's central artery, Calzada de Tlalpan, and south of Viaducto Aleman. It has a high concentration of new Chinese immigrants, mostly from economically distressed regions of Guang-dong Province, the Taishan region in particular. Dotting the streets are small and unmarked groceries, petite bakeries, herbal clinics, and barbershops, but the pre-dominant establishments are restaurants of Guangdong style. Only a few restaurants specialize in regional dishes from other parts of China, with Meng Hua Ju being the most recognized one. Although the bad service has deterred a potentially large customer base, a relatively stable flow of diners guarantees its daily business. In fact, Meng Hua Ju has become the favorite restaurant of my family after the closure of Bei Dou Xing, partially due to the dishes we are familiar with and partially due to its easy-to-access location. Most of the time, we order "chopped cucumber satu-rated in garlic sauce," "soy-sauce flavored beef," "dumplings stuffed with pork and

FIGURE 6.4 The arch of Chinatown, Mexico City.

chives," and "fried rice noodles with beef." The menu of Meng Hua Ju is far from exhaustive and sophisticated, but the clients find a wide array of regional dishes to choose from.

Yi Pin Ju is located in the Zona Rosa district of Mexico City, which is packed with bars, restaurants, and Korean grocery stores. It is not particularly known for Chinese food, but customers can easily name a handful of Chinese restaurants amid other international sensations. In spite of its short history, Yi Pin Ju is the first Chinese restaurant in Mexico City that has been widely acclaimed as an "authentic" Sichuan restaurant, though its menu offers dishes from both Sichuan and Shaanxi provinces. The appreciative diners are greatly pleased when they find "spicy and numbing chicken," "double-cooked pork," "sour and spicy rice noodle," "oven roasted duck," and other special dishes that are not readily offered in other places in Mexico City. An international gourmet has generously praised Yi Pin Ju as such:

> Yi Pin Ju is already the favorite of chefs and aficionados of the picante. The mainstay of its menu comes from the southwest provinces of Szechuan and Shaanxi to its north where the balance of ma-la—spicy and numbing— is the goal. Szechuan pepper is omnipresent as are chiles, dry and fresh. A number of dishes are labeled "estilo Sichuan" which implies a red, oily sauce that attempts to numb and stimulate at the same time, kind of a gustatory martini/valium cocktail.[11]

Fast Food Chinese Restaurants with Steam Table Buffet

Given the history of Chinese immigrants in Mexico, it is not surprising that the bulk of Chinese restaurants were originally opened by the older generations of Cantonese at the turn of the twentieth century and that many of them are still maintained by family members or relatives as a kind of family business. It is also true that many Chinese Mexicans depend on this type of business for a living. The old Chinatown of Mexico City and a stretch of the Revolution Avenue are packed with this kind of traditional Chinese restaurant.

Beyond the confinement of the Chinatowns and beyond the pockets of concentrated Chinese population, there is the greater open space for Chinese restaurants to take root and blossom. The anti-Chinese movements from the 1910s to the 1930s had traumatized and expelled the Chinese population as a whole and, decades later, through the repatriation policy of the Mexican government, many Chinese returned and relocated to other places.[12] The bulk of Chinese restaurants, owned by them and also latecomers, tells the very story of survival, adaptation, and acculturation. This type of Chinese restaurant is usually invested with moderate funds, family run, risk-taking, and connected with kinship or regional networks. Although they can be visible in busy streets, sizable cities or towns, and tourist sites, they almost never seek to boast of special dishes or "authentic" flavors. Instead, they most often opt for fast food as content and steam table buffet

FIGURE 6.5 A fast food Chinese restaurant, Tehuantepec, Oaxaca.

as form. Their marketing strategy is very simple: to standardize the food supply to feed the Mexican appetite with a Chinese signature. As Scarlett Lindeman has succinctly described it:

> Understated and resoundingly regular, Chinese steam table buffets are woven into the tapestry of Mexico City so seamlessly it's not until you start noticing them—like weed dispensaries in Los Angeles or a prolific New York City graffiti tag—that you realize they're all over the place. It is a standard model, with as many as one restaurant for every half-dozen blocks: nondescript cafeteria halls, decorated in red and gold colors, with Formica tables and long steam tables running through their centers, an all-you-can-eat prix fixe for around 70 to 100 pesos (or roughly $3.80 to $5.50 USD).[13]

I have personally encountered these types of Chinese restaurants in many unlikely places and on many unlikely occasions. They can be found in shopping malls, on roadsides, or on street corners of small towns, and their structures range from a grand dining compound to a humble counter or stand in a food court. In Mexico City, these types of Chinese restaurant have marched far beyond the few districts with high concentrations of Chinese population. Personally speaking, I have seen them in the center of Coyoacan and Tlalpan, in the crowded streets of Copilco, on the roadsides of Division de Norte and Picacho Ajusco, in the low-end shopping mall of Chedraui Ajusco, in the middle-to-high-end shopping mall of Plaza Loreto, amongst others.

FIGURE 6.6   The menu of a fast food Chinese restaurant, Puebla City.

My trips to various places in the adjacent states have also led me to acknowledge the almost ubiquitous existence of fast food Chinese restaurants in Mexico. In Oaxaca City in the state of Oaxaca, I saw at least three Chinese restaurants in passing, two in the historic center and one on the outskirt. In the remote town Tehuantepec on the Tehuantepec Isthmus, I encountered one such Chinese restaurant run by a family from Taishan of Guangdong Province. In the adjacent city Juchitan, also on the Tehuantepec Isthmus, I witnessed at least two Chinese restaurants jammed on busy streets. In one store of the supermarket Soriana in Puebla City, in the state of Puebla, there is one Chinese restaurant no bigger than a living room; the same restaurant (probably its franchise) is present in the main street of Atlixco, a small city in the state of Puebla. I even encountered a Chinese restaurant as small as a counter in the food court annexed to the aquarium of the port city Veracruz; and the list can go on and on.

The fast food Chinese restaurants usually lay out their food in stainless steel trays on the steam table buffet so the Mexican customers unfamiliar with Chinese dishes can visualize their choices. The options always include, but are not limited to, Chop Suey, Spring Rolls, Fried Rice, Lo Mein, Kung Pao Chicken, Sweet and Sour Chicken, Broccoli Beef, Wonton Soup, and so on and so forth. Small sized Chinese restaurants or food counters tend to offer packages with a range of prices. For example, the restaurant Mei Siem that I encountered in the Soriana supermarket of Puebla and in the small city of Atlixco has four packages for clients to choose from: rice or noodles and one main dish, 40 pesos; rice or noodles, one main dish, one egg roll, 50 pesos; rice or noodles, two main dishes, one egg roll, 62 pesos; rice or noodles, three main dishes, one egg roll, 72 pesos.

Chinese Restaurants Owned by Mexicans Returning from the United States

The fourth type of Chinese restaurant is run and owned by Mexicans who used to work in Chinese restaurants and other Asian restaurants in the United States and who have returned to their native land to open their own business with their newly learned cooking skills and management technics. This is, in my understanding, gastronomically less noticeable but culturally more significant in the genealogy of Chinese restaurant in Mexico. The popular saying that "wherever there are Chinese, there are Chinese restaurants" might have to be upgraded to a newer version: "Where there are no Chinese, there still can be Chinese restaurants."

My First Encounter with a Mexican-Owned Chinese Restaurant

On September 16, 2010, my friends and I went to visit a remote town to the south of Mexico City. The purpose of our visit was to experience the local celebration of Independence Day, which was packed with unique customs, tradition, history, food, music, dance, and a lot more. The town is called Ixtlilco el Grande, in the state of Morelos, about three hours' drive from the capital of Mexico. It is located in a small valley in the southern mountains outside of the central volcanic chain, about 1,000 meters above sea level and with a population of about 3,000. This agricultural town is famous for its production of tomato, onion, corn, peanut, rice, and for its history and scenic landscape.

The colorful celebration of Independence Day in Ixtlilco el Grande has a history of over 100 years. The most exciting part of my trip was the discovery of the unexpected connection of the small town with Chinese culinary culture. To my great surprise, about 1,000 young people from the town had migrated to Minnesota and almost all of them were working for a Chinese restaurant chain none other than Panda Express. It is estimated that there are more than 50,000 Chinese restaurants in the United States[14] and most of them hire Mexican workers in the kitchen. Many of these workers later return to their hometown in Mexico and open their own "Chinese" restaurants.

In Ixtlilco el Grande, there is one such example. When my friends and I first arrived at the town, a young woman was putting up a poster for her family

FIGURE 6.7   A Mexican-owned Chinese restaurant, Ixtlilco el Grande, Morelos.

restaurant—yes, a "Chinese" restaurant. The poster was utterly ostensible and overlooking the two main streets that crisscross the whole town. Out of sheer curiosity and on a whim to poke fun, I asked the woman in awkward Spanish: "Is it really a Chinese restaurant?" Probably because she had never seen an Asian face in the town before, she hurriedly nodded her head in panic. I decided to push the joke a little further, adding: "Just as much Chinese as I am (*Chino como yo*)?" The woman panicked even more and blushed. In a flash, we drove away from the scene of the crime, giggling.

During the parade, which was the most important part of the celebration, we met many hospitable people from the town and several of them were eager to show off their Chinese even though they could speak no more than a few words. I thus got to know Gerardo, a man in his mid-forties, who turned out to be the leader of the youngsters who were working for the franchised Chinese restaurant in Minnesota. He was extremely amiable and accompanied us throughout most of our stay.

The "Chinese" restaurant that we had seen in the town was owned by a returned worker from Minnesota. As a newly established business, the restaurant did not yet have a name and the poster was painted with "Chinese Food" (Comida China) in its central space. Under the letters of "Chinese Food", there was a line promoting the restaurant: "The Chinese Mexican" (El Chino Mexicano). The poster had a typical Chinese pavilion on the left side of the frame and a Mexican cook (with slight Chinese physical features such as the eyes, curiously) on the right side, and snow-capped mountains in the background. At the bottom was the indication of business hours. Under the main poster, there was a smaller, yellow paper poster, merely stating in large letters: "Chinese Rice" (Arroz Chino), which was obviously meant to suggest the specialty of the "Chinese" restaurant.

After the parade was over, we stepped over to the "Chinese" restaurant to have a late lunch since there was no other option in the whole town. It was already packed with people and two young men were happily enjoying their food while gulping down cold beer. In front of each of them was a plate piled with fried rice, broccoli, and other vegetables, and several egg rolls were laid on top. On the table there were several beer bottles and two different kinds of chile sauce, one an Asian brand and the other being Tabasco. When the two young diners saw us, obviously a bunch of Asian faces, they warmly greeted us and proudly showed us their food. I looked around and did not see any Chinese looking cook or waiter/waitress or customer. It is highly unlikely that a Chinese would ever show up in such a remote place, for whatever reason.

My Second Encounter with a Mexican-Owned Chinese Restaurant

My second encounter with a Mexican-owned Chinese restaurant was also fascinating and unexpected. It happened in the spring of 2013 when my family was traveling from Xalapa, the capital of the state Veracruz, to Cordoba, a major city in the central part of the state. The route is called the "Route of Mist" (Ruta de la Niebla), and it lies on the eastern slope of the Perote Mountain. The appearance of Restaurant EDDA in the middle of nowhere took us by great surprise. Well, it is actually located in a small town called Tlaltetela, in the central part, and mountainous region, of the state of Veracruz. The name EDDA is painted in the very center on the front of the restaurant, and on each side is written "Food Chinese" and "Comida China," in English and Spanish, respectively. One may not fail to notice that the phrase in English is reversely written as "Food Chinese" instead of "Chinese Food," which is obviously a Spanish rendering of English expression.

The owner and cook, Esteban Hernández Ruiz, worked in a Korean restaurant in North Carolina between 1999 and 2003. Later he returned to his hometown Tlaltetela and opened his own Chinese restaurant. Several photos of him posing with the Korean employers are on display and a plaque on the wall says: "Diana, Mr. Yoon, and Mrs. Masson, also known as Kiki, with them I had the fortune and luck to learn all about oriental food and now my dishes have a special touch, a Mexican touch."

Although Esteban's restaurant promotes Chinese food as its signature dish, the decoration and the signage are of a mixed "oriental" style. The Chinese name of the restaurant reads Han Gong in pinyin, but its name in letters is spelled as EDDA, a Japanese pronunciation that does not correspond to Han Gong phonetically. In addition, the two wall paintings each feature a young woman in traditional dress,

FIGURE 6.8 The author with the owner of Restaurant EDDA, Tlaltetela, Veracruz.

one playing zither and another holding two fans, and they are more like crossovers between Chinese courtier and Japanese geisha. Inadvertently, Restaurant EDDA has integrated the Chinese, Korean, Japanese, and Mexican flavors into a coherent mixture. To have a real Chinese customer in such a place was certainly something beyond the expectation of its owner. Esteban was tremendously pleased upon seeing me and wasted no time in asking me for an autograph in Chinese on the wall to promote his business. In return, he gave me a tourist handbook called "The Route of Mist."

The display board of EDDA features 18 main dishes, mostly Chinese, and several of their own creation. The signature dishes include Chicken Broccoli, Beef Broccoli, Pepper Steak, Chop Suey, House Lo Mein, House Fried Rice, etc. They are typical dishes that one may find in any "Americanized" Chinese restaurant in the United States. The interesting thing is that, while the names of the dishes are written in English, the ingredients under each dish are written in Spanish. At the time, we were the only customers in the restaurant and only two or three other diners entered when we were about to leave. One week ago, I called Restaurant EDDA to confirm the name of the owner and happily found that it is still in business. This suggests that a Mexican-owned Chinese restaurant in a remote mountainous town is enough to support a family, or, that it is at least profitable to the extent that it has remained in business for the past five years.

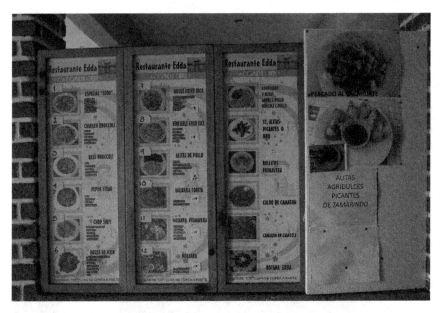

FIGURE 6.9 The menu of Restaurant EDDA.

My Third Encounter with a Mexican-Owned Chinese Restaurant

My third encounter with a Mexican Chinese restaurant happened in the state of Oaxaca when I was traveling with my family in 2015. We drove off the main road in the Oaxaca Valley just to check out what was interesting in smaller places. Santa Ana del Valle happened to be our random pick. One of the immediate surprises was the discovery of a Chinese restaurant in this small town with a population of no more than 2,000. This is probably the most humble "Chinese" restaurant I have ever seen. The place was just an ordinary residential house on the street and it had no formal decoration or signage.

The only thing for the establishment to identify itself as a "Chinese" restaurant was a chalkboard installed on top of the gate, on which was written "Comida China" (Chinese Food), and a phone number was provided at the bottom of the board. The funny thing was that the word "China" was erroneously spelled as "Cihina." Further down the street and around the corner, another paper announcement was pinned to the wall, and in this case, the word "China" as in "Comida China" was correctly written.

We wanted to check out what kind of Chinese food the restaurant might offer, as this had become our ritual while traveling in remote and isolated places. The gate was half shut and there was nobody inside. A passer-by told us that the restaurant was open but the owner had gone to get some supplies and advised us to come back later. We did go back a short while later but the owner had not yet

FIGURE 6.10 A humble Chinese restaurant in Atlixco, Puebla.

returned. We eventually gave up on the adventure and took several photos as a testimony of the discovery.

Key Terms

"Americanized" Chinese food: The modified dishes and flavors offered by most Chinese restaurants in the United States to cater to the palate of the general clientele.

Steam table buffet: Fast food Chinese restaurants put their cooked food in stainless steel trays on the steam table for the diners to choose from. This way, they don't need to order food from the menu.

Mexican-owned Chinese restaurant: Chinese restaurant owned and managed by Mexicans who used to work in Chinese restaurants in the United States.

Discussion Questions

1. Why are franchised Chinese restaurants such as P.F. Chang's and Panda Express expanding rapidly in Mexico? What are their marketing strategies?
2. Where do Chinese immigrants or visitors go if they want to east Chinese regional dishes that cater to their palate?
3. Why there are so many fast food Chinese restaurants, including Mexican-owned Chinese restaurants, in Mexico?

Notes

1 The Association estimates that there are over 38,000 Chinese-owned restaurants in the United States: www.ucraa.org/. According to the Chinese Embassy in Mexico, the number of Chinese restaurants in Mexico is in the hundreds, but I think it is highly underestimated since in the state of Jalisco alone there were 150 Chinese restaurants by 2015. See Patricia Romo, "Restaurantes chinos pierden 80% de clientes," in *El Economista*, May 10, 2015. www.eleconomista.com.mx/estados/Restaurantes-chinos-pierden-80-de-clientes-20150510-0094.html.

2 Sheila Sanchez Fermin, "Fundador de PF Chang's: 'México fue el lugar correcto para internacionalizarnos,'" in *Expansion*, October 26, 2017. https://expansion.mx/empre sas/2017/10/25/fundador-de-pf-changs-mexico-fue-el-lugar-correcto-para-internac ionalizarnos.

3 "Meishi zhongcan dajin moxige." *Yangcheng wanbao*, January 10, 2010. http://news.sina. com.cn/o/2010-01-02/154516869540s.shtml.

4 Sheila Sanchez Fermin, "Fundador de PF Chang's: 'México fue el lugar correcto para internacionalizarnos,'" in *Expansion*, October 26, 2017. https://expansion.mx/empre sas/2017/10/25/fundador-de-pf-changs-mexico-fue-el-lugar-correcto-para-internac ionalizarnos.

5 Ibid.

6 Paul Lara, "Llega a México Panda Express, el 'gigante' de la comida china", in *Excelsior*, August 15, 2011. www.excelsior.com.mx/2011/08/15/dinero/761022#view-1; Mark Abadi, "Conoce a la pareja de multimillonarios detrás de Panda Express," in *Business Insider*, May 22, 2018. www.msn.com/es-mx/dinero/finanzas-personales/%C2%BFpor-qu% C3%A9-no-puedes-pagar-en-efectivo-ciertas-transmisiones-de-bienes/conoce-a-la-pareja-de-multimillonarios-detr%C3%A1s-de-panda-express-%E2%80%94-poseen-cerca-de-2000-restaurantes-y-venden-m%C3%A1s-de-90-millones-de-libras-al-a% C3%B1o-de-pollo-a-la-naranja/ss-AAvZ37u.

7 Paul Lara, "Llega a México Panda Express, el 'gigante' de la comida china", in *Excelsior*, August 15, 2011. www.excelsior.com.mx/2011/08/15/dinero/761022#view-1.

8 The web page of P.F. Chang Mexico. www.pfchangsmexico.com.mx/menu.

9 The web page of Panda Express Mexico. www.pandaexpress.com.mx/menu.

10 Zou Zhipeng, "Zhongcan zhengfu moxigeren de wei." *People's Daily*, March 13, 2012. http://news.ifeng.com/gundong/detail_2012_03/13/13146304_0.shtml.

11 Nicholas Gilman, "Yi Pin Ju: Szechuan at Last and It's Hot," in "Good Food Mexico." www.goodfoodmexico.com/home/yi-pin-ju-szechuan-at-last-and-its-hot.

12 Schiavone Camacho and Julia Maria, "Crossing Boundaries, Claiming a Homeland: The Mexican Chinese Transpacific Journey to Becoming Mexican, 1930s–1960s." In *Pacific Historical Review*, Berkeley, November 2009, 78 (4): 546. doi:10.1525/phr.2009.78.4.545.

13 Scarlett Lindeman, "How Chinese Food Became a Mexico City Staple," in *Eater*, May 23, 2016. www.eater.com/2016/5/23/11739484/mexico-city-chinese-food.

14 There is no consistency in estimating the number of Chinese restaurants in the United States, but it normally falls between around 40,000 to slightly more than 50,000. A recent number from a mainstream media is close to 50,000. See Charles Passy, "Meet the Pilot Who Doubles as Block Island's Chinese-Food Delivery Guy," in *The Wall Street Journal*, August 27, 2015. www.wsj.com/articles/meet-the-pilot-who-doubles-as-block-islands-chinese-food-delivery-guy-1440636389.

7

LIVE AT THE CHINA ROYAL

A Funky Ode to Fall River's Chow Mein Sandwich

Oliver Wang

Introduction: The "Chow Mein Sandwich" on a Platter

In June of 1974, a group of Pacific Islander musicians took up residence as the in-house entertainment at China Royal Imperial Palace, a venerable and popular Chinese restaurant in Fall River, MA.[1] The band, calling themselves Alika and the Happy Samoans, turned out to be an instant success, as their show, which included both music and Polynesian dancing, resulted in "packing [crowds] in at Fall River's most opulent restaurant," according to one news story.[2]

China Royal's managers decided to capitalize on the act's burgeoning popularity by bankrolling a custom album that they could sell to restaurant customers.[3] Alika and the Happy Samoans drove an hour north to Boston's Brighton neighborhood to record at Hub Studios in July of 1974.[4] The session resulted in *At the China Royal*, a 12-song LP filled with covers of everything from Hoagy Carmichael's standard, "The Nearness of You," to Elvis Presley's tear-jerker, "Can't Help Falling in Love" (Figure 7.1). The album's minor hit at the time was "Portuguese Sailor," a cover of Don Ho's hit "Macao," in which a sailor jumps ship to see a girl, except in the Happy Samoans' rendition, it's not Macao but Fall River where this fateful decision was made. Within weeks of the album's release, local radio DJs began playing "Portuguese Sailor" and there were thoughts to issue it as a 45 rpm single.[5] However, the album's most enduring track, one that would span the decades, opened the B-side, the group's funky ode to one of the restaurant's—and Fall River's—most iconic dishes: "Chow Mein Sandwich (China Royal Special)."[6]

Anchored by a snappy breakbeat and strong rhythmic interplay between guitar and bass, most of the song features group leader Alika Armitage singing, "chow mein . . . chow mein sandwich" over and over.[7] He does take time to shout out both his bandmates ("Maif never gets fat on chow mein") and other China Royal menu items ("we've got wonton soup and some sub gum too") but the hook is straight to the point: "well, you like chow mein sandwich, I like chow mein sandwich."

FIGURE 7.1 Alika and the Happy Samoans album cover.

The chow mein sandwich was what people today might describe as a culinary "mash-up," i.e. combining two, seemingly incongruous dishes together. It is also, however, deeply American. The sandwich form is, of course, ubiquitous in American culture but chow mein, which translates as "fried noodles," is no less Americanized. The version that many Americans became familiar with over the course of the twentieth century bore little resemblance to the beige, wiggly noodles found in traditional Chinese preparations. The Fall River version is deep-fried into crunchy, dark brown, twig-like tangles. To create the sandwich, a slosh of gravy is placed atop and then everything is served between hamburger buns, either open face or wrapped in wax paper to allow the gravy to soften both the noodles and bun. For historian Imogene Lim, the chow mein sandwich represents the ultimate kind of culinary hybridization, i.e. "a perfect food amalgam—identified as Chinese yet basically an American invention . . . as American as apple pie."[8]

For all its relative exoticness, the chow mein sandwich has maintained a critical mass of loyal fans that spans generations. Chef/restauranteur Emeril Lagasse, a Fall River's native son, has recorded television segments on how to make it and has written how eating the sandwich at Fall River eateries like China Royal was "one of my favorite food memories growing up."[9] It is no surprise then that a house band, ensconced at the China Royal, might write a tune in tribute especially.

I've joked with peers that my fascination with the song owes to how it lands squarely within overlapping Venn diagram circles of personal interest: "Asian Pacific Islander (API) culinary hybridity" on one side, "obscure API funk songs" on the other. However, even if "Chow Mein Sandwich" is an obscure novelty song about a hyper-regional novelty dish, none of this undermines its worth as an object of critical inquiry. To explain how the song ever came to be requires tracing various socio-cultural pathways through decades of history. These include the stories behind both the chow mein sandwich and the China Royal restaurant, both of which owe much to the role of Chinese immigrant food entrepreneurs in the Fall River area. It also requires an explanation of how a group of Pacific Islander entertainers would end up in an Atlantic Ocean port city and this, in turn, requires an exploration of how Polynesian "tiki" culture has long intersected with the history of Chinese food and eateries in America. "Chow Mein Sandwich" is a simple song but within it is contained multitudes.

"The Better Chinese Restaurants of Southeastern Massachusetts": The Chow Mein Sandwich in Fall River

Every significant history of Chinese food in America makes the same, vital point: for the first 100 years of Chinese American cuisine, dishes tended to "reflect more Chinese adaptation to America than what Chinese eat in China," to quote Haiming Liu.[10] Like its close kin, chop suey, chow mein has long foresworn any claims to being "authentically" Chinese.[11] Rather, dishes like egg foo young, chop suey, and chow mein function as shorthand, a signal to patrons that this establishment caters to (non-Asian) American palates. In fact, one of the first mass producers of chow mein for the home market, La Choy, used to advertise itself as making "Chinese foods swing American."[12]

The chow mein sandwich takes things even further by adopting half its form from one of the most American of all food items: the sandwich. Imogene Lim notes that the chow mein sandwich bears resemblance to such popular sandwich incarnations as the open-faced turkey sandwich and sloppy joe.[13] In particular she suggests, "think about the popularity of fast food establishments and the standard menu offering of hamburger and french fries: moist/soft, crisp, portable. This essentially American combination of textures is found in the Chow Mein sandwich as well."[14] Lim also notes that mid-century, middlebrow American tastes held that "blandness was considered healthful" and, therefore, the relative blandness of the chow mein sandwich only helps to accentuate its American-ness.[15]

However, though these factors suggest that the sandwich could have had national, mass appeal, its associations have mostly been hyper-local; call it "Mass. appeal." Even in a globalized era today where dishes figuratively and literally travel everywhere, the chow mein sandwich remains a distinct regional specialty. It caters to clients almost exclusively in southeastern Massachusetts and nearby parts of Rhode Island, including Fall River, New Bedford, and Providence.[16] Yet, despite the fact that the dish is difficult to find anywhere outside of this region, it has continually drawn the curiosity of epicureans over the years. It is far easier to find articles about the chow mein sandwich than to find the dish itself. This fascination has made the sandwich a perpetually rediscovered dish, especially in recent times.[17]

Few famous dishes would intentionally document their history. The origin of the chow mein sandwich in the Fall River area is largely a story based on anecdotes rather than documented history. Even though Lim asserts that it is a "northeastern regional speciality centered in Fall River," she deliberately stops short from claiming it *originated* there.[18] She notes, for example, that the chop suey sandwich, associated with Salem's Willow Park (northeast of Boston), is at least 20 years older than the earliest documented mentions of the chow mein sandwich.[19] However, no one has claimed that the chop suey sandwich of northeastern MA directly gave rise to the chow mein sandwich of southeastern MA, least of all explained how it would have traveled 70 miles—completely skipping Boston in the process—and propagated itself in the Fall River region.[20]

Regina Mark, who runs Fall River's Mee Sum, now the city's oldest surviving Chinese restaurant, related one story of how the dish started in an unnamed New Bedford eatery:

> Long ago, a customer came in and ordered chow mein . . . but he wasn't feeling too well, so he asked for bread to go with it. The chef had no bread, so he gave the customer some hamburger buns. The customer returned the next day, feeling well, and happy to say that the buns and the chow mein had made an excellent sandwich.[21]

It's not an implausible origin story but the vagueness of the details—what restaurant and when?—makes it feel apocryphal.[22]

However, even if we don't know who was the first to offer a chow mein sandwich in Fall River, we do know the reason why it became so centralized there: the Oriental Chow Mein Company, started in 1938 by Frederick Wong, a Cantonese immigrant. Wong had come to the city in the 1920s to work at Hong Kong Restaurant, a downtown eatery run by his uncle,[23] not far from where the original China Royal itself was started. In branching off to start up the Oriental Chow Mein Co., Wong initially supplied noodles to local restaurants but soon expanded into the home consumer market with his Hoo-Mee Chow Mein Mix.[24] The brand became the common base for chow mein dishes (including sandwiches) in the region and it's still in production today, allowing curious cooks to create chow mein sandwiches at home.[25] Hoo-Mee is well aware of its regional legacy; on the side of the signature yellow box, the mix boasts you can use it to "make a delicious meal of chow mein, of the type generally served in the better Chinese restaurants of southeastern Massachusetts."[26]

"The Polynesian Show": Tiki-Pop and Chinese Restaurants in Massachusetts

In the same era that Frederick Wong came to Fall River, so did another immigrant from Canton: Chung Gong Wong (no relation). Wong first started his sojourn to the United States in California but a job offer brought him out to Connecticut and then another one took him to Fall River by the 1930s. He initially worked at Mark You, then one of the city's older Chinese establishments. He remained there until 1949 when Wong decided to start up his own restaurant: China Royal.[27]

Its original location was downtown, next door to the Durfee Theater on North Main Street, the words "Chow Mein" prominently centered on its marquee. It stayed there for nearly 25 years until 1973, when the property owners that Wong was leasing from wanted to expand, forcing the restaurant to find a new location. China Royal ended up moving less than a mile away, to 534 Pleasant St., south of Bedford, near Plymouth.[28]

The new China Royal was a much bigger space than its downtown predecessor, hence the new "Imperial Palace" suffix that Wong added to its name. The most spectacular part of the new facade was a 1.5 story jade green pagoda that anchored one of the corners while patrons could enter through doors flanked by glass-encased stone lions. The lobby was no less ornately furnished, with an intricate, wood-cut wall divider, smiling Buddha statues, and a pagoda-like awning over a pair of pay phones. The restaurant boasted a special banquet room and two large dining rooms, one of which featured lantern-like lighting. The side of one room featured a full-wall painting in the style of classic Chinese landscape art. Yet another part of the building held China Royal's wooden booths, inlaid with red cushioned backs and seating.

All this space meant there were more seats that needed to be filled. Wong's daughter, Betty Chang, explained that the restaurant's manager at the time, Kee Ying, proposed booking a "Polynesian show" to help draw in patrons. Chang recalled Ying saying, "that was something that in this area most people haven't seen." "The Polynesian show" refers to a form of popular live entertainment that belongs to what author Sven Kirsten terms "tiki pop," i.e. forms of pop culture rooted in quasi-Pacific Islander traditions.[29]

"Polynesia," in this case, doesn't refer to a geographically bounded region of island societies in the Pacific. Instead, this is the Polynesia of exotic, Western fantasy, what film scholar Jeffrey Geiger summarizes as "connoting solitude, release from cares . . . and renewal from urbanized modern life."[30] This fantasy of Polynesia has its roots as far back as the European Age of Discovery, when colonial explorers began sighting and landing on the likes of Tahiti and Fiji and their exploits, in turn, fueled eighteenth-century Enlightenment philosophers to developed the trope of the "noble savage," e.g. Pacific Islanders "released from the burdens of education, progress . . . privileged to live in a world of complete moral authenticity."[31]

The appeal of tiki-pop proved particularly popular in the United States, beginning in the nineteenth-century era of American imperialism with the annexations of Hawaii and other Pacific territories. For example, Hawaiian music, itself a hybridization of indigenous musical practices with Westernized instrumentation (such as the ukulele), first became popular in the United States in the 1910s, abetted by sheet music illustrations that depicted exotic paradises of beaches, palm trees, and grass-skirted women.[32] This, in turn, accelerated with the growth of the early recording and radio industries, both of which helped bring Hawaiian music to the mainland where it found audiences eager for the sound of tropical fantasy.[33] A related phenomenon came in the 1950s and 1960s, with the boom in so-called "exotica" records, i.e. easy-listening instrumental music, often with caricatured Pacific Islander, Asian, or African musical motifs and art work.[34] The term "tiki-pop" is meant to represent various forms of popular culture but, just in the musical realm itself, you might say that "tiki-pop pop" is its own genre.

However, tiki-pop was hardly limited to pop music or Hawaii. As early as the late 1910s, various novels and films found success by using "Polynesian" backdrops for their romances and dramas. These included Frederick O'Brien's hit 1919 novel, *White Shadows in the South Seas*, set in the French Polynesian Marquesas Islands, later turned into an MGM film of the same name in 1928. According to Geiger, O'Brien's book was partially meant to provide readers with a "chance to leave behind traumatic memories of World War I and escape to the palm-fringed beaches of solitary islands."[35] This link, between Polynesia and the specter of war would reach heretofore unseen heights once millions of American G.I.s became stationed throughout Pacific Islands during World War II and their homecomings helped throw fuel onto the fire of the Polynesian fantasy. One only need look at the decade-plus success of author James Michener's best-selling short story compendium, *Tales of the South Pacific* from 1946 that was turned into a popular Rodgers and Hammerstein musical, *South Pacific*, in 1949, and that later became both a hit movie and soundtrack of the same name in 1958.

Concurrent to this was the rise of the "Aloha/Hawaiian shirt," which helped to redefine casual and leisure wear in the American fashion industry, beginning in the 1930s.[36] Japanese Hawaiian entrepreneurs first created the style, using both indigenous Hawaiian and imported Japanese printed fabrics, and the shirts proved popular with American tourists, and later G.I.s, who brought the shirts back to the mainland, helping launch different waves of fashion trends in which the Aloha shirt has gone from "kitsch to chic" over its 80-plus year history. As with other forms of tiki-pop, the Aloha shirt's appeal is largely rooted in how the shirt serves as "a form of folk art [and] icon of a romanticized period in Hawai'i's past."[37]

In short, throughout the twentieth century, the conditions have constantly been ripe for a caricature of "Polynesian" society, as a pre-modern paradise of easy-living and sexual freedom, to reproduce within the United States. The appeal of all these entertainment forms lies in how they promised "a dose of excitement and glamour into [Americans'] normal, regulated everyday world: a touch of Hollywood fantasy to offset one's own humdrum routine."[38]

One direct result of these forces was the rise of a performance circuit for Pacific Islander entertainers, particularly musicians and dancers. Historian Adria Imada traces this circuit back to the nineteenth century, when the royal Hawaiian court in Honolulu would treat foreign visitors and dignitaries to hula dancing.[39] Its popularity, partially fueled through the sexualization of the dancers, spawned what Imada calls a "hula circuit," between Hawaii and the mainland, contributing to what she describes as an "imagined intimacy" between American spectators and Pacific Islander performers, which, in turn, became integral in how "commodified Hawaiian culture . . . [became] part of the American vernacular and everyday life."[40]

A group like Alika and the Happy Samoans were part of a larger wave of what Kirsten describes as "Hawaiian bands [who] toured the States as ambassadors of musical escapism, matching the tropical environs of supper clubs and bamboo bars across the country."[41] Throughout the twentieth century, this tiki-pop circuit allowed performers to travel between American cities, big and small, playing various lounges, restaurants, performance halls, community centers, etc.

The popularity of tiki pop also became deeply intertwined with both Chinese food and Chinese restaurants in the United States, beginning in the 1930s. The end of Prohibition helped spark the first wave of cocktail bars with tiki/"South Seas" themes, especially out West, with Ernest Gantt's Beachcomber in Southern California and Vic Bergeron's Trader Vic's in the Bay Area. From the very beginning, both these foundational tiki bars based their menus around Americanized Chinese food.[42] Much like how tiki pop conflates different Pacific Islander societies into a flattened mono-culture, the inclusion of quasi-Chinese cuisine — pineapple fried rice or crab Rangoon—on the same menu as boozy mai tais and zombies had mostly to do with an American conception of the exotic that reduced East Asia and Polynesia into one large, Orientalized East. Chinese food became the *cuisine de jour* at tiki bars because it was different enough to accentuate the exotic feel that bar owners wanted but still familiar enough to patrons to avoid scaring people off.

The association between Chinese food and tiki pop became so strong that, within a few years, it was Chinese restaurants that turned around and incorporated Polynesian themes into their menu and interior design. This phenomenon, which became known as "tiki-Chinese" began as early as the 1940s. Historian John Jung echoes some of Kirsten and Imada's themes in describing how the craze offered "South Shore décor with flaming torches and tiki Gods to promote the fantasy of an escape from a stressful industrial society to dine in a carefree paradise."[43]

This was especially true in suburban Massachusetts where food writer Garrett Snyder asserts "nowhere was this Sino-Polynesian alliance more impervious to change."[44] My own introduction to the tiki-Chinese phenomenon came in the mid-1970s at Yangtze River Restaurant in the Boston suburb of Lexington. The eatery was owned by family friends and while their decor wasn't full-on Polynesian, I distinctly recall that they served their cocktails in tiki glasses—with a paper umbrella, of course—and their menu included classic tiki bar items including the king of psuedo-Polynesian dishes: a *pupu* platter of mostly fried appetizers. Other notable Massachusetts tiki-Chinese restaurants included Bob Lee's Islander in Chinatown and the Polynesian Village at the Hotel Somerset, and one of the last surviving examples is also one of the grandest: the 1,200-seat Kowloon in Saugus, off of Route 1.[45]

According to foodways scholar Mark Padoongpatt, these examples of tiki-Chinese restaurants located in predominantly white suburbs were no coincidence: "this is where [middle class Whites are] allowed to encounter Asians, and the idea of Asia and the Pacific . . . This is a safe way for them to interact with an 'exotic' culture."[46] In a sense, the suburban tiki-Chinese eateries were an update of an older tradition: Chinatown bars, lounges, and restaurants, often built with kitschy, quasi-Asian architecture intentionally designed to lure in tourists to spend money in otherwise impoverished neighborhoods.[47] As filmmaker Arthur Dong has documented, these spaces offered up all manner of musical, dance, and other entertainment, often also self-Orientalizing, for the sake of those same tourist dollars. The tiki-Chinese craze was, through this lens, an off-shoot that exploited a similar form of Western fantasy that shifted from the Far East to an equally imaginary South Pacific. To be clear, tiki-Chinese establishments could be found throughout urban Chinatowns as well but their suburban cousins created more convenient outposts for suburbanites who wanted a taste of the exotic but with a closer commute and better parking. This is the larger context within which to understand how a group of Pacific Islander musicians and dancers would take up residence at the China Royal for nearly half a decade in the 1970s.

In the early 1970s, Alika Armitage was an upcoming Hawaiian musician within the Polynesian performance circuit. He had gigged successfully in Las Vegas, even opening for Sonny and Cher.[48] By 1974, he was on tour in Rochester NY where he met his future wife, Diane "Kelani" Armitage, a poi ball dancer, originally from Southern California. The two of them were invited to join with Evalani and South Sea Islanders, one of the larger Polynesian touring groups of the era. According to Diane, she and Alika ended up at the China Royal because the restaurant initially booked Evalani and the South Sea Islanders for a two-week stint. After it ended, restaurant manager Kee Ying liked Alika so much that he made him a proposition: "If I put a group together, would you be willing to come back and start up a group here?" Diane recalls Ying asking. "And [Alika] said 'yeah.'"[49]

The Happy Samoan musicians—drummer and bassist Jake Uili, guitarist Maif Poueu, and vocalist Deric Cadenet—were recruited via word of mouth within the Polynesian performance circuit. Alika's daughter, Shawna Dunn, remembers the band first doing rehearsal gigs in Las Vegas before leaving to take up residence at the China Royal.[50] Diane, alongside Alika's sisters Kekai and Sandy, were the main dancers and they were eventually billed on marketing material as the "Diamond Head '76 Revue" (Figure 7.2).[51] Like many tiki pop performers, Alika and the Happy Samoans mixed a variety of Polynesian dances and songs. "We had

FIGURE 7.2   Alika and the Happy Samoans at the China Royal.

Tahitian, Samoan numbers, we did Hawaiian numbers, we had a routine to [the musical] *Bali Hai*. It was a conglomerate of all kinds of things," says Diane.[52] They also hired fire dancers and comedians to help fill out their sets, with the group playing both week days and double shows on the weekends, starting in 1974 through 1979, an impressively long stint for any restaurant band.[53]

As noted earlier, the unexpected success of the group spurred the restaurant to produce an album in order to sell it to patrons. Initially, 2,000 units were pressed and, within months, hundreds of copies had been sold there.[54] "Chow Mein Sandwich" began as a rehearsal joke between the bandmates. "They were goofing around, eating, and they started coming up with 'Chow Mein Sandwich,'" Dunn shared. "The owner heard them and prodded them to develop the song because he got the biggest kick out of it."

After their long engagement at the China Royal ended in 1979, Alika and Diane moved back west, to Oregon. Jake eventually settled in Texas, Maif in California and Deric moved back to Samoa. China Royal continued in their same location on Pleasant St. until 2001, when they were unable to negotiate new lease terms and owners Betty and Walter Chang decided to close the restaurant, bringing an end to the eatery's 50-plus year history in Fall River. The space they occupied is now a CVS pharmacy but the restaurant's old booths ended up installed at Quang's Restaurant in Fall River where it occupies the old Mark You space.[55] They still have several different kinds of chow mein sandwich on their menu, all priced under $5.[56]

There was a spell when "Chow Mein Sandwich" had faded from Alika's memory until his son-in-law transferred the original vinyl onto CD in the late 1990s.[57] Once he was able to listen to the song more easily, he began performing it again, including at the Pac Island Grill, outside of Tacoma, WA. "That [song] was one their favorites," his daughter Dunn said. "He just had to play 'Chow Mein Sandwich,' even though nobody knew what it was about, they just loved the song."

Alika passed away in early spring 2015 and at the "celebration of life" party held in his memory, the family made chow mein sandwiches as part of the festivities. Dunn told me, "he was really proud of the song, especially as he got older, it was a big deal for him." Dunn hadn't tried the dish before but her aunt Sandy (Armitage's sister) made sure they did it correctly; she mailed them yellow boxes of Hoo-Mee Chow Mein Mix.[58]

Conclusion: In Pursuit of Novelty

My interest in "Chow Mein Sandwich," both the song and dish, is rooted in its qualities as a novelty precisely because it highlights new and novel avenues for cultural investigation. The chow mein sandwich, which is about as authentically inauthentic as any dish imaginable, opens us up to think about the important history of "fusion" cuisine within Asian Pacific Islander communities. Culinary examples of invention and hybridity are not the exceptions within API food history; they have long been the proverbial rule. The chow mein sandwich is merely one dish along a grand spectrum, with early twentieth-century chop suey on one end and early twenty-first century Korean BBQ tacos and poke pizzas on the other. Rather than perceiving these dishes as "dilutions" of an imagined authentic source, it may be worth reframing them to think of *adaptation* as an inherent part of *tradition*. To put it another way, the chow mein sandwich did not necessarily change the course of Chinese American foodways but it is a notable example of change *within* the history of Chinese American foodways. It is only by studying the former that we are able to flesh out the latter.

Along similar lines, the "Chow Mein Sandwich" song and its creators also compel us to do more to explore the role of Polynesian fantasy within American pop culture. Like Chinese American food, this is a tradition that goes far back into the nineteenth century but it remains curiously and conspicuously absent within the scholarly record. In *Aloha America*, Imada bemoans the very point that "the bodies of hula performers present a curious problem: they are hyper visible in popular culture while leaving only the faintest traces in archives."[59] Instead, most of the best documentation—and thus narrative building—around Polynesian pop has come from tiki culture enthusiasts who are overwhelmingly from outside of both academic and Pacific Islander communities.[60] Their documentation is important but they're less well-equipped to trace the necessary linkages between tiki bars, Polynesian pop, and the specter of the American empire in the Pacific or the legacies of European exploration and colonization. The "Chow Mein Sandwich" song may not ostensibly address any of these broader histories but, as I've attempted to show, its very existence is owed to all these intersecting pasts.

Meanwhile, stars like Don Ho, to say nothing of countless, forgotten Polynesian circuit acts like Alika and the Happy Samoans, played an outsized role in shaping the American imagination of Pacific Islanders through their music. However, I suspect that because their songs lacked an overt identity politics, these entertainers are almost never discussed within larger discourses around API music. "Chow Mein Sandwich" may not merit the same kind of consideration as a deliberately pan-ethnic anthem such as A Grain of Sand's 1973 song, "We Are the Children," but both, in their own way, serve as artifacts for the same moment in the mid-1970s when understandings of API identity and community were in flux.[61]

Lastly, to bring this back to the China Royal, Chinese restaurants have long been nexus points for all these currents; their sheer, staggering popularity over the last 100-plus years makes them essential sites of cultural contact and exchange, contestation, and contradiction. China Royal was not extraordinary in this sense (though *At the China Royal* was an exceptional case of a physical artifact that documented a moment) but simply one node in a sprawling, informal network of tens of thousands of similar restaurants, bars, food stands, etc. I noted a moment ago that much of the research on tiki-Chinese restaurants, for example, has come from amateur enthusiasts who've written entire books dedicated to single restaurants. Their example should be a challenge to our ranks of cultural historians and theorists to do similar work (such as the anthology you're holding now) and re/uncover similar sites of inquiry and exploration.

Key Terms

> **Hybridity**: The incorporation of multiple forms into a new/novel form.
> **Adaptation**: How cultural forms change in response to external forces or influences.
> **Imaginary**: Existing in fantasy or the imagination; not rooted in empirical realities.

Discussion Questions

1. The chow mein sandwich is one example of how different culinary forms combine to create a new form that finds appeal within the marketplace. What other examples can you think of? What makes those examples similar to or different from the chow mein sandwich?
2. Tiki-Chinese restaurants succeeded partially because they relied on two overlapping American imaginaries: the fantasy of the South Pacific and Far East. Are there other examples in which cultural imaginaries have found popularity in material forms?
3. On first glance, it may seem that a group of Pacific Islander musicians ending up in southeastern Massachusetts seems unusual but once you realize the historical context behind it, there is a clear, rational set of explanations for how this came to be. What other examples come to mind of cultural phenomena that initially may seem unexpected but turn out to have rational explanations?

Notes

1 Kerr, 1974.
2 Ibid.
3 A custom album, also known as private or vanity pressings, are manufactured by specialty companies, upon request by a client, similar to a custom/self-published novel. Custom pressed lounge albums were quite common from the 1950s through 1980s as they were sold to tourists or used as promotional materials. For more information on custom albums, see *Enjoy the Experience*, edited by Johan Kugelberg, Michael Daley and Paul Major (Sinecure, 2012).
4 Kerr, 1974.
5 Ibid. Far as I can tell, there was no single ever released.
6 Alika and the Happy Samoans, 1974. "Chow Mein Sandwich" has been uploaded to YouTube on several different occasions but if people are unable to locate a copy online to listen to, please just contact me directly (oliver.wang@csulb.edu).
7 Armitage's daughter, Shawna Dunn (2017) explained that "Chow Mein Sandwich" was a funk song because, as the album's sole original composition, it reflected Armitage's tastes, and as a musician originally trained as a drummer he wanted the song to have a funky percussive element.
8 Lim, 1993.
9 Lagasse, n.d.
10 Liu, 2015: 1.
11 Anne Mendelson (2016: 120), in her own history of early Chinese food in the United States, does an excellent job in tracing chow mein's (d)evolution in the American imagination to become associated with "a bed of uniformly crunchy noodles" that bears little resemblance to whatever Cantonese dishes originally inspired its creation.
12 Gazel, 1990: 54.
13 Lim, 1994: 134.
14 Ibid: 135.
15 Lim, 1993: 4.
16 This is purely anecdotal but as someone who grew up in and around Chinese restaurants in the Boston area in the 1970s, I had never heard of the dish until I stumbled across the Alika and the Happy Samoans album. I also asked my uncle Tien-Ho Wang about it as he worked in and ran Chinese restaurants in Massachusetts and Maine for over 30 years and he was also unfamiliar with it.

17 Just in 2017 for example, at least three pieces about the sandwich appeared. See Doyle, 2017, Harris and Lyon, 2017, and Landrigan, 2017b.

18 Lim, 1993: 4.

19 Lim, 1994 and Landrigan, 2017a.

20 One of my favorite examples of a chow mein-inspired invention is the Tuckee/Takee Cup, created by Tuck Yee Lee in the 1950s for sale at Tuck's, a food stand along the Rockaway Boardwalk. The Tuckee/Takee Cup created a small bowl out of pressed, deep fried noodles in which chow mein noodles were served (Young, n.d.). Though the chow mein sandwich has been described (Doyle, 2017) as the "original ramen burger" (a far more recent mash-up which uses pressed ramen noodles to replace a hamburger bun), the Tuckee/Takee Cup would seem to have a far stronger case.

21 Stern, n.d.

22 Journalist Corbo Eng relays a different theory of sorts that comes via Alfred Wong, son of Oriental Chow Mein Company founder, Frederick Wong. The younger Wong doesn't explain where the sandwich emerged from but does note that the large Catholic Portuguese population in the area helped to fuel the overall popularity of chow mein as a meatless version that could easily be served on Fridays for those observing religious food restrictions on that day. Eng writes, "because they received their paychecks on Thursdays, Wong notes, there was always a spike in chow mein sales on Friday" (2015: 20).

23 Cabral, 2011.

24 Landrigan, 2017b.

25 Behymer, 2015.

26 Original Chow Mein Co., n.d. By "better," I assume the box marketing copy is using it as a synonym for "finer" as in "served in the finer Chinese restaurants." However, it may also be a subtle form of authenticity claim that there is a style of Chinese cuisine specific to the Southeastern MA region which is unlike Chinese food in other parts of New England. Lim and John Eng-Wong (1994: 430) share an interviewee testimonial about how "Boston did not like this [Hoo-Mee] noodle" as the Fall River chow mein tends to be just the noodle whereas Boston chow mein has more ingredients, especially vegetables. As such, the two authors conclude "not surprisingly, the chow mein sandwich does not appear to have existed in Boston."

27 Chang, 2017. It should be noted: Fall River had a reputation for its density of Chinese restaurants. One unsubstantiated boast was that "Fall River may have claimed more Chinese restaurants per capita than any other place in Massachusetts" (Conforti, 2013: 86). Even if the author didn't provide empirical data to support the claim, the mere fact that one would even put it forward suggests that Chinese eateries loomed large within people's imagination of the city.

28 Chang, 2017.

29 Kirsten, 2014.

30 Geiger, 2007: 1.

31 Landsdown, 2006: 70.

32 Brown, 2004: 253–254.

33 Ibid: 254.

34 For more on exotica albums, see: Toop, David. *Exotica: Fabricated Soundscapes in a Real World*. Serpent's Tail, 1999. To be clear, *At the China Royal* was not an exotica album in either sound or marketing. It belongs more formally within the genre of lounge albums and/or Hawaiian easy-listening albums (e.g. Don Ho and the Aliis).

35 Geiger, 2002: 98.

36 Trufelman, 2018.

37 Margado, 2003: 86.

38 Kirsten, 2014: 55–57.

39 Imada, 2012: 25.

40 Ibid: 5, 11.

41 Ibid: 57.

42 Snyder, 2017.
43 Jung, 2010: 275.
44 Snyder, 2017.
45 O'Connell, 2016: 194.
46 Gershenson, 2017.
47 See Tsui, 2009: chapter 1.
48 Dunn, 2017.
49 D. Armitage, 2017.
50 Dunn, 2017.
51 T. Armitage, 2017.
52 D. Armitage, 2017.
53 Ibid.
54 Kerr, 1974.
55 Dion, 2012.
56 Quang's Kitchen, n.d.
57 Dunn, 2017.
58 Ibid.
59 Imada, 2012: 21.
60 See: Cate, Martin, and Rebecca Cate. *Smugglers Cove: Exotic Cocktails, Rum, and the Cult of Tiki*. Ten Speed Press, 2016. Glazner, Tim. *Mai-Kai: History and Mystery of the Iconic Tiki Restaurant*. Schiffer Publishing Ltd, 2016. Meyers, David, Elise Meyers Walker, Jeff Chenault, and Doug Motz. *Kahiki Supper Club: A Polynesian Paradise in Columbus*. Arcadia Publishing, 2014.
61 See Wang, Oliver. "Between the Notes: Finding Asian America in Popular Music." *American Music* 19, no. 4 (Winter 2001): 439–465. To make it clear, in that essay, I certainly failed to consider the role of API touring entertainers in my conception of "Asian American music" at the time.

References

Alika and the Happy Samoans. *At the China Royal*. Recorded July 1974. Vinyl recording.

"Armitage, Diane." Telephone interview by author. July 11, 2017.

"Armitage, Tanya." Personal interviews with author. 2017.

Behymer, Jim. "Cultural Assimilation and the Chow Mein Sandwich." *Sandwich Tribunal*. July 25, 2015. www.sandwichtribunal.com/2015/07/cultural-assimilation-and-the-chow-mein-sandwich/

Brown, DeSoto. "Beautiful, Romantic Hawaii: How the Fantasy Image Came to Be." *Journal of Decorative and Propaganda Arts* 20 (1994): 252–271.

Cabral, Lisa. "That's Using Your Noodle." *South Coast Today*. January 11, 2011. www.southcoasttoday.com/article/19980802/NEWS/308029997

"Chang, Betty." Telephone interview by author. July 27, 2017.

Conforti, Joseph. *Another City Upon a Hill: A New England Memoir*. UPNE, 2013.

Devitt, Phil. "Back in Business: Oriental Chow Mein Company Returns after Devastating Fire." *South Coast Today*. December 24, 2009. www.southcoasttoday.com/article/20091224/PUB03/912240416

Digregorio, Sarah. "Strange Snacks of the World—Noodle Sandwich." *Village Voice*. December 23, 2008. www.villagevoice.com/2008/12/23/strange-snacks-of-the-world-noodle-sandwich

Dion, Marc Munroe. "New Owners Take Over Fall River's Landmark Chinese Restaurant, Mixing Tradition with Fresh Ideas." *The Herald News*. June 27, 2012. www.heraldnews.com/article/20120626/NEWS/306269505

Doyle, Terrence. "The Chow Mein Sandwich Is the Original Ramen Burger." *Munchies.* April 29, 2017. https://munchies.vice.com/en_us/article/wn3jb9/the-chow-mein-sandwich-is-the-original-ramen burger

"Dunn, Shawna." Telephone interview by author. December 29, 2017.

Eng, Corbo. "Mein Roads." *The Cleaver Quarter* 6 (Autumn 2015): 15–25.

Freedman, Paul. *Ten Restaurants That Changed America.* Liveright Publishing, 2016.

Gazel, Neil. *Beatrice: From Buildup Through Breakup.* University of Illinois Press, 1990.

Geiger, Jeffrey. "Imagined Islands: *White Shadows in the South Seas* and Cultural Ambivalence." *Cinema Journal* 41, 3 (Spring 2002): 98–121.

Geiger, Jeffrey. *Facing the Pacific: Polynesia and the U.S. Imperial Imagination.* University of Hawaii Press, 2007.

Gershenson, Gabriella. "Tiki Drinks, Pupu Platters, and a Side of Bread: How Chinese Restaurants Came to Embrace Polynesian Kitsch." *Boston Globe.* January 24, 2017. www.bostonglobe.com/lifestyle/food-dining/2017/01/23/tiki-drinks-pupu-platters-and-side-bread-how-chinese-restaurants-came-embrace-polynesian-kitsch/K2uqZiaCt05TTsTvpTH4UI/story.html

Harris, Patricia and David Lyon. "Fork in the Road: Rich Sandwich Tradition Gives Fall River Diners a Lot to Hold Onto," *Boston Globe.* May 5, 2017. www.bostonglobe.com/lifestyle/travel/2017/05/04/fork-road-rich-sandwich-tradition-gives-fall-river-diners-lot-hold-onto/a7yH2NYsTMxN0PTuGQPAwJ/story.html

Imada, Adria. *Aloha America: Hula Circuits Through the U.S. Empire.* Duke University Press, 2012.

Jung, John. *Sweet and Sour: Life in Chinese Family Restaurants.* Yin and Yang Press, 2010.

Kirsten, Sven. *Tiki Pop. America Imagines Its Own Polynesian Paradise.* Taschen, 2014.

Lagasse, Emeril. "Fall River Chow Mein." *The Splendid Table.* www.splendidtable.org/recipes/fall-river-chow-mein

Landsdown, Richard. *Strangers in the South Seas: The Idea of the Pacific in Western Thought.* University of Hawaii Press, 2006.

Landrigan, Leslie. "Salem Chop Suey Sandwiches, A Sign of Summer." *New England Historical Society.* March 1, 2017. www.newenglandhistoricalsociety.com/salem-chop-suey-sandwiches-sign-summer

Landrigan, Leslie. "Fall River's Famous Chow Mein Sandwich." *New England Historical Society.* May 13, 2017. www.newenglandhistoricalsociety.com/fall-rivers-famous-chow-mein-sandwich

Lim, Imogene. "The Chow Mein Sandwich: American as Apple Pie." *Radcliffe Culinary Times* 3, 2 (October 1993): 4–5.

Lim, Imogene. "Chinese Cuisine Meets The American Palate: The Chow Mein Sandwich." *Chinese Cuisine American Palate: An Anthology*, edited by Jacqueline Newman and Roberta Halporn, Center for Thanatology Research & Eduction, 2004, pp. 130–139.

Liu, Haiming. *From Canton Restaurant to Panda Express: A History of Chinese Food in the United States.* Rutgers University Press, 2015.

Margado, Marcia. "From Kitsch to Chic: The Transformation of Hawaiian Shirt Aesthetics." *Clothing and Textiles Research Journal* 21, 2 (2003): 75–88.

Mendelson, Anne. *Chow Chop Suey: Food and the Chinese American Journey.* Columbia University Press, 2016.

O'Connell, James. *Dining Out in Boston: A Culinary History.* University Press of New England, 2016.

Oriental Chow Mein Co. "Original Hoo-Mee Chow Mein Mix." n.d. Fall River, MA.

Quang's Kitchen. "Menu." n.d. Fall River, MA. www.quangskitchen.com/menu.html

Snyder, Garrett. "How Did Tiki Become a Chinese Restaurant Staple?" *Punch.* January 5, 2017. https://punchdrink.com/articles/a-match-made-in-paradise-history-of-chinese-restaurants-and-tiki-cocktails

Stern, Michael. "Mee Sum Restaurant and Lounge." *Roadfood*, n.d. https://roadfood.com/restaurants/mee-sum-restaurant-and-lounge

Trufelman, Avery. "Hawaiian Shirts: Articles of Interest." *99% Invisible.* Podcast audio, October 5, 2018. https://99percentinvisible.org/episode/hawaiian-shirts-articles-of-interest-4/transcript

Tsui, Bonnie. *American Chinatown: A People's History of Five Neighborhoods.* Simon and Schuster, 2009.

Young, Richard. "Tuck's On the Boardwalk." *Far Rockaway* (web log). www.farrockaway.com/tucksontheboardwalk.html

8

UNDER THE BANNER OF NORTHERN CHINESE CUISINE

Invention of the Pan-China Cuisine in American Chinese Restaurants

David Y. H. Wu

Introduction

Being an anthropologist who has conducted research around the world on the issues of ethnic, cultural, and national identities, I have more recently focused my study on the globalization of Chinese cuisine. To satisfy the readers' curiosity of how I started to get into the anthropology of delicious food, I wish to say a few words about my humble self. In the early 1990s, after teaching in Hawaii for 20 years, I moved to Hong Kong to work, at the world capital of gourmet Chinese and international food. I was fortunate enough to initiate my new career as a gastronomic anthropologist by teaching new courses at the university and involving colleagues and students engaging in research on food and cuisine in East Asia. I initially managed to secure a huge and multi-year research grant from the Hong Kong University Grant Council to support a research project entitled "Cooking Up Hong Kong Identities," for which several colleagues and students from two major universities participated. Also, at the Chinese University of Hong Kong, I invited the pioneering senior American anthropologist of globalization of food, the late Professor Sidney Mintz, to join me in teaching the very first course in East and Southeast Asia on "the Anthropology of Food." It was my old friend, Professor James Watson, who not only introduced me to Professor Mintz but also involved me in his interesting cross-country study of the McDonald's in East Asia; whereas I was able to visit my Taiwan hometown on weekends to study the sociopolitical meanings of the McDonald's in Taipei. I am proud to say, such teaching, research, and publication on the anthropology of food has becoming a major academic tradition in Hong Kong that continues to this day.[1]

To me, American Chinese restaurants have been a fascinating subject of anthropological study. I have discovered that the "Chinese restaurant" in the United States is arguably the best arena for people to observe (or ignore), understand (or become confused), and learn (or never learn) about the contested meanings of ethnicity, ethnic boundaries, and ethnic relations (or, for many English-speaking people, the scientifically and politically incorrect term of "race relations"). In this chapter, I wish to tell the stories of one type of Chinese restaurant and restaurant food that sets the United States apart from Chinese restaurants and Chinese cuisines elsewhere. For two reasons I am prompted to tell these stories: to document my more than half a century of eating experience in American Chinese restaurants, and to tell both Chinese and non-Chinese customers how the Chinese can be so divided ethnically, culturally, and in terms of restaurant food taste.

We already have a well-documented history in the United States, via popular media reports and academic publications, of Chinese restaurant food in the making, in particular "chop suey" and "the imagined authentic Chinese cuisine," as scholars Haiming Liu and Yong Chen put it, that had dominated Chinese restaurant food in the United States from the end of the nineteenth century until the 1960s.[2] We can also find numerous popular writings in mass media discussing how Americans accepted Chinese restaurants and why the Jewish people adopted Chinese "chop suey" restaurant food, especially during Christmas.[3] However, as I have pointed out before, a huge page of American gastronomic history has not been well researched or documented—that is, the emergence and popularization across the United States, from the 1960s to the 1980s, of a new style of Chinese restaurant food, often claimed by restaurant owners to be "Northern Chinese cuisine" or "Mandarin cuisine." Thereafter, especially by the end of the twentieth century, and continuing to the present day, most of the Chinese restaurants in the United States, including the original "chop suey" restaurants that have converted, developed a new menu that demonstrates a combination of the so called "Northern Chinese" dishes as well as some of the long-term favorite "chop suey" dishes.

Both the names of these new style restaurants that emerged in the 1970s, and the dishes they served, reflect major regional Chinese cuisines, which were not part of the "chop suey" cuisine invented in the United States by early Cantonese immigrants. Some readers, long-term Chinese restaurant customers included, may be confused by "Northern Chinese" cuisine, which has been served in restaurants with a diversity of names, referring to many different regions of China. Many are even geographically in South China, although Chinese immigrants who opened restaurants in the United States would usually think "Northern Chinese cuisine" means "Peking cuisine." I myself encountered in the 1970s many new restaurants in Hawaii and major cities along the U.S. West Coast that named themselves "Peking" (meaning Beijing) or "Yen King" (meaning Yanjing, the ancient name of Beijing), "King-Tsing" (Beijing and Tianjin), "Shanghai," "Shi-Chuan" (Sichuan), "Hunan," "Hakka" (Kejia), and "Taiwan (this restaurant was right outside of the UC Berkeley campus)." At that time, the curious spellings of these terms (before *pinyin* came into widespread use) were the popular English spellings of the actual Chinese place-names, the new restaurant names, or the new dishes that became familiar to both the overseas Chinese and non-Chinese customers, while these terms often also appeared in the food sections of local newspaper advertisements. In other words, these restaurants served a collection of dishes that were not known or served in American restaurants established earlier by Cantonese immigrants. Such dishes originated in many parts of China and were first transplanted to Taiwan by mainland Chinese refugees, who in the late 1940s and 1950s fled China when the Chinese Communists defeated the Nationalist (Kuo-Ming-Tang or Guomindang) army and took control of the entire country, except Taiwan. By the 1980s and thereafter, when American customers ate at any of the "Northern Chinese" restaurants, they would discover a rather standardized menu, in which the selected dishes were imagined, improvised, and reinvented Chinese regional dishes, adapted from local home cooking (not the banquet dishes of Chinese high cuisine) to be found in pre-Communist China, which was transplanted and redeveloped for two decades (1950 to 1970) in all major cities on Taiwan (for this period of the restaurant history in Taiwan, see Wu (1995)). One must pay attention to bigger, global, socio-political factors behind the emergence of the new Chinese diasporic food business, just as Liu (2009, 2015) and Chen (2014) remind us about the coming of age of American "chop suey." By the late 1960s when thousands of young students and immigrants from Taiwan were coming to the United States every year, a new market for what I call the "Standardized Pan-China Cuisine" emerged to satisfy the new diasporic community's craving for "home" food. And, in addition, it helped many immigrant families to rely on their new restaurants and innovative dishes of nostalgia to earn a living.

Several participants I interviewed agreed with me that the most popular dishes that have appeared in American Northern Chinese restaurants since the late twentieth century include *mapodoufu* (麻婆豆腐), *rosidougan* (肉丝豆干), *gongbaojiding* (宫保鸡丁) or *lazijiding* (辣子鸡丁), *zhangchaya* (樟茶鸭), *yuxiangqiezi* (鱼香茄子), *muxurou* (木须肉), *hongshaotibang* (红烧蹄膀), *suanlatang* (酸辣汤), *chunjuan* (春卷), *guotie* (锅贴), *babaofan* (八宝饭), *tangyuan* (汤圆), *shaobing youtiao* (烧饼油条), and *doujiang* (豆浆 soy bean milk). All these dishes added to the common "chop suey" dishes, such as "chowfan" (fried rice), "chowmin" (fried noodle), *gulaorou* (咕老肉 sweet and sour pork), and *houyao* or *haoyou* (蚝油 oyster sauce) beef, chicken, and vegetables. Since the 1970s they have become standard and popular dishes featured in the menus of two typical "Northern Chinese" restaurants in my following accounts.

It is important to point out that owners of such "Northern Chinese" restaurants are a new breed of young, non-Cantonese migrants who mostly came from Taiwan from the 1960s onward, originally for the purpose of seeking graduate education at the universities of the United States. Many of these well-educated young men started a "North Chinese restaurant" in the United States due to global political circumstances, particularly the interplay among China, Taiwan, and the United States. Most of them came from displaced or exiled families in Taiwan, of "Mainland Chinese" parents, not the local Taiwanese (descendants of earlier Fujian and Guangdong migrants since the sixteenth century as well as Formosan aborigines). The United States became a new haven for these Chinese young men and their families, following President Nixon's visit to China in 1972, when the United

States abandoned the Republic of China on Taiwan and officially recognized the People's Republic of China, while the United Nations also voted (Communist) China in, making Taiwan leave the world organization. Some of these "desperate" Chinese students from Taiwan, with the sense of "no home to return to," chose to take up a restaurant business that would enable them and their families to survive. Most importantly, they would be eligible for a desirable U.S. immigration status of permanent resident, and eventually would become American citizens. According to available government statistics of the ROC Ministry of Overseas Affairs, between 1950 and 1980, more than 100,000 Taiwan students went to the United States to study at universities; however, fewer than 8,000 of them returned to Taiwan. I also discovered after many years of research that these students-turned-restauranteurs are predominantly children of Chinese urban elites in old China of high socio-economic standing prior to their escaping the Communists and arriving in Taiwan in the 1950s. The owners of these new "Northern Chinese restaurants" in the United States are different from earlier working-class Chinese migrants who mostly came in the late nineteenth and early twentieth centuries from rural South China. Without the catastrophic political interruption of their life courses, the young and highly educated Chinese students from Taiwan would have stayed in China and become elite scholars or officials of the ruling class (perhaps the very target of the Chinese communist revolution). Their life careers should not have been as restaurant helpers or owners, which in traditional Chinese culture, under thousands of years of Confucian male-chauvinist teaching, would be regarded as low-class and degrading. In a sense, we may regard these "Northern Chinese" restaurant owners as "accidental restaurateurs" of the late twentieth-century United States. One can draw parallels with the successful South Asian ethnic restauranteurs in the United States, as explained in terms of the diaspora of Indian food by Professor Krishnendu Ray in New York,[4] in the sense that South Asian gentlemen never cooked at home, yet arrived in the United States to become famed chefs of "Indian restaurants."

I can now tell the stories from the point of view of an experienced Chinese customer at Chinese restaurants in the United State for more than 50 years.[5] Being an anthropologist of food and cuisine, I also managed over many years to interview a good number of owners of Chinese restaurants, their family members and close friends, and business investors as well.[6] In this chapter I shall offer two previously untold stories about two successful "Northern Chinese" restaurants. One is in Honolulu, which I shall refer to as Autumn Leaves (a pseudonym, as it has been in business from 1976 to the present). The other one, Foo Yuan (meaning Lucky Garden in Mandarin), was in New Orleans (1979–2000). While the former in Honolulu initially catered to new Chinese immigrants from Taiwan, the latter in New Orleans served mainly non-Chinese Americans. I knew the owner of the Honolulu restaurant from its opening in the 1970s. (He passed away around 2010, but the restaurant continues in operation under his new partner-owner, a new Chinese immigrant from Guangdong, China.) The owner of the Lucky Garden in New Orleans is an old friend from Taiwan, who went to the same high school as

I did in the 1950s. I consider these two restaurants representative for our purpose of reconstructing a brief history of the late twentieth-century "Northern Chinese" cuisine, how it appeared, and how it subsequently became incorporated into a standardized "Pan-China Cuisine" in most of the Chinese restaurants across the vastness of America.

The Autumn Leaves in Honolulu

The Autumn Leaves, which has been at the same location for more than four decades,[7] is perhaps the best known "Northern Chinese" restaurant in Honolulu since it opened in the mid-1970s. It sits about a mile away from the University of Hawaii main campus, which since the late 1960s has seen an influx of "Taiwanese" migrants to Hawaii, including many university teaching staff and graduate students (the author of the present chapter himself included). Today, the two-story wooden building of the restaurant—with its renovated and remodeled interior, which was originally fashioned after the American-style diners of the 1950s—is still standing behind the same tall "University branch office" of a major bank in Hawaii. The restaurant has operated under its original name since it opened around 1975 to 1976, after an old bowling alley, in the heart of the old ethnic Japanese residential neighborhood of Mo'ili'ili, was torn down in 1973, giving way to a new commercial development along half a street block.[8]

In 2017 I interviewed two key persons in Honolulu, both friends for 40 years of the original owner, Mr. R, and both confirmed a similar version of the restaurant's history. It all started in 1970 to 1971, with the arrival in Honolulu from Taiwan of the young Mr. R, who had not long before graduated from a two-year college in Taipei. Mr. R intended to complete a second college education in Honolulu and to obtain a university degree in the "practical" field of engineering technology (at a time when engineering, medicine, and business were the most desirable fields of study for young Chinese immigrants). He first entered the Honolulu Community College in 1974 and later managed to transfer to the University of Hawaii, where eventually in 1979 he earned a bachelor's degree in engineering. While pursuing his degree as a student, Mr. R also at the same time held down two part-time jobs: as a taxi driver and as a waiter at a new Chinese restaurant. The restaurant he worked at was the very first "Shanghainese" or "Northern Chinese" restaurant started in the early 1970s at the new Kahala Mall shopping center, sited in the most expensive residential neighborhood of Honolulu, which used to be known as exclusively "for Whites only" before World War II.[9] Mr. R owned the taxi cab, which he operated in three shifts a day with another two or three drivers; all were university students from Taiwan. According to one of the taxi partners (whom I interviewed several times), Mr. R's family (in Taiwan) was wealthy enough to buy him a new car for him to run the taxi business, which altogether lasted for about five years.

The second informant I have interviewed many times in recent years was Mr. R's instructor of engineering at the Honolulu Community College during 1974–1975;

the teacher later became an investor in Mr. R's new restaurant. In 1975 or 1976, together with the other three taxi partners, Mr. R opened the Autumn Leaves, but he alone assumed (signed the lease of) the business ownership. All of the share-holders worked in the restaurant as cooks and waiting staff, as they had worked as waiters at the "Shanghainese" restaurant in Kahala Mall. At the time in Hawaii, there were already more than 100 Chinese restaurants, in the name of "such-and-such Chop Suey House," serving the old-style invented Cantonese "chop suey" dishes that were familiar to the local customers of Asian origin (and for all other American customers who were familiar with Chinatown restaurants anywhere in the United States). It is worth mentioning that, since the late 1960s, located within a stone's throw from the new Autumn Leaves were two of Honolulu's most popular "chop suey" houses, appropriately named the McCully Chop Suey (An eatery popular among University of Hawaii hard-working graduate students for late-night snacks such as a bowl of hot *chock* (粥) or Cantonese rice porridge. I once interviewed its former owner, a local third-generation Chinese, during the 1980s) and the Mo'ili'ili Chop Suey. The McCully Chop Suey closed in 2007 (thereafter no other restaurant was given the name of "chop suey"). The Mo'ili'ili Chop Suey by the mid-1970s had converted to a "Northern Chinese" restaurant, having been taken over by a new (wealthy) Cantonese immigrant family from Hong Kong. This Hong Kong style "Northern Chinese" restaurant did not go out of business until 2017. My late wife from Taiwan and I dined several times at both old chop suey places during the 1960s and 1970s, before the Autumn Leaves started in business. Although, interestingly enough, during those early days of the late 1960s and early 1970s, several other student immigrants from Taiwan, who all had connections one way or another with the University of Hawaii, opened small "Northern Chinese restaurants," but I shall skip the full stories about them. However, for the interest of our readers, I shall in the conclusion of this chapter offer a few notes about the amazing social-political backgrounds of these "failed" restaurant owners.

Allow me now to return to my story of the Autumn Leaves restaurant that started in the mid-1970s. After its opening, the business at Mr. R's new "Northern China" or "Mandarin" restaurant turned out to be slow in the initial two or three years. One can imagine why. Not only were Mr. R and his partners not profes-sional cooks or restaurant operators, but it seems their "Northern Chinese" dishes, reinvented by these "university students from Taiwan," were new, unfamiliar, and even strange to local Hawaiian Asian palates. (That would include in particular the second or third generation Chinese who came predominantly from Zhongshan County of Guangdong Province, which is the famed hometown of Dr. Sun Yat-sen, founding father of the Republic of China in 1912.) The "new" dishes at the Autumn Leaves, on the other hands, were familiar dishes of "old" home cooking or nostalgic "comfort" foods to the new (since the 1960s) "Taiwanese" commu-nity in Honolulu. In terms of language, foodways, and other cultural backgrounds, they were quite segregated from the old local Chinese communities (mainly the Zhongshanese and the Hakkas (*Kejiaren* or "客家人") from the nineteenth-century

Guangdong Province. However welcome it may have been to the ethnic "Taiwanese" community, such a small population could not sustain a restaurant as large as the Autumn Leaves, which could seat 50 customers or more at the same time.

It was Mr. R's good fortune that in 1978 (or 1979) his former teacher, the engineering instructor at the Honolulu Community College, a third-generation Japanese, born and raised on the rural Big (Hawaii) Island but educated on the U.S. mainland, came to his rescue. Mr. R's teacher and his wife often came to his restaurant to dine. (They happened to become close friends of mine in the late 1970s.) And by then this teacher had left his teaching job at the college to work for a private firm of civil engineers, where the owner and Director of the Board was a local "Korean" businessman of considerable means and influence. This Korean boss, for instance, at that time also served on the Board of Regent of the University of Hawaii. After learning about Mr. R's problem, his former teacher decided to help him. He was kind enough to first loan Mr. R $5,000 to buy out all the other shareholders of the restaurant, mainly Mr. R's friends who earlier were his fellow students at the University of Hawaii as well as his taxi partners. The Japanese teacher then introduced his Korean boss to Mr. R at a lunch banquet, hosted by Mr. R at his restaurant, to talk business. The Korean boss apparently liked the food and considered the new restaurant a good investment for his firm. (One may conjecture that this Korean businessman found the "Northern Chinese" food, with a lot of garlic and hot pepper, familiar and to his liking.[10]) He decided to buy out the lease from Mr. R while keeping him on to continue working at the restaurant as its manager. Thereafter, the new restaurant owner, the Korean businessman, often held parties at the restaurant to entertain his clients and guests. Other employees of the engineering firm, their families, and their friends did likewise. By then Mr. R had hired a professional chef from Taiwan to work in the kitchen. With the business changes and many new customers, the restaurant picked up enormously. It popularized "Northern Chinese food" in Honolulu even among the "local Hawaiian Asian" customers, whereas the "Taiwanese" continued to patronize the restaurant and still do so.

According to my Japanese friend and informant, the former engineering instructor at the community college of the University of Hawaii, he remembered some of his favorite dishes at Mr. R's restaurant in the late 1970s—which he could describe to me, although he never remembered the proper names of the dishes, either in English or Chinese. The dishes included "hot and sour eggplant," "*chawmin* (which in English refers to fried noodles, but not the same fried noodles prepared at the "Chop Suey Houses." I figured that it must be what is usually known as "Shanghai style thick noodles," which look and taste similar to the Japanese *udong* dish," "hot and sour soup," a deep fried pancake with sweet red bean filling (which sounds like a new dessert dish of pancake called *dousha-guobing* (豆沙锅饼), in Mandarin meaning "pancake with red bean filling," a popular dessert served at up-scale Northern Chinese restaurants in Taipei during the 1970s). My Japanese friend remembered another dish with the name "Pearl Dumpling" in English. He described it as a sweet dessert soup dish made of small sticky rice balls (*omochi* as known to the Japanese in Hawaii), filled with sugar and ground black sesame. I remember it being what Shanghainese or Taiwanese call *tangyuan* (汤圆 "soup balls") in Mandarin Chinese. This last item of Pearl Dumpling, as the former college instructor and investor told me, was a special dish Mr. R learned to cook from his own mother. It is interesting to note that my (Japanese) friend never remembered or ordered two dishes that were what I considered Autumn Leaves' signature attractions added to the menu in the late 1980s. One is a duck dish named "smoked Tea Duck" or *zhangchaya* (樟茶鸭), which in the United States has become an ethnic marker of "Northern Chinese," not served in Cantonese Chinese restaurants. This dish is supposed to have originated in the Province of Sichuan, considered by Chinese from China or Taiwan as located in South China. The other dish I also remember was a Northern Chinese breakfast dish mostly favored by the "Taiwanese" customers, served only on Sunday mornings: "*shaobing* and *youtiao* (烧饼油条)" (baked Chinese sesame bread and deep fried Chinese donuts, served with hot soy milk, either sweet or salty). Some informants from Taiwan I interviewed told me that Mr. R's aunt used to bake such bread at home and sold it to Mr. R to serve in the restaurant. Incidentally, some informants also mentioned that Mr. R's father came from Taiwan to join the restaurant as a staff member. But the old man was soon after fired by his son.

A few years later, once business was booming, Mr. R accumulated enough money to buy back the restaurant lease/ownership from the "Korean engineering firm." As the story goes, he got married to one of his Chinese waitresses at the restaurant, and they had a baby daughter. After many years, as the restaurant continued to prosper, Mr. R sent his daughter to one of the two elite private high schools in Hawaii (either Iolani or Punahou, which President Obama attended). And, eventually Mr. R's daughter studied at the Massachusetts Institute of Technology in Boston and gained a degree in engineering.

According to Mr. R's close friends in the old days, the success of his restaurant can be attributed to his personality and unexpected positive media exposure. Mr. R was described as a very intelligent and sociable person with a good memory. He gave repeat customers excellent service and would usually offer them free desserts. Some of the old Chinese professors from the university, especially those who helped Mr. R in the earlier days, would receive honorable treatment free of charge. In the 1980s he was lucky enough to have the local media praise his place as the "best" Chinese restaurant in Hawaii—which happened following the patronage a couple of times by the visiting Hollywood superstar, Sylvester Stallone. Thereafter the photo of smiling Mr. R taken with the Hollywood star as well as the raving newspaper review became important and permanent wall decorations in the restaurant.

Furthermore, as I have observed, since the 1990s a large banquet room at the back of his restaurant, where occasionally wedding parties were held, became the venue for a "China Seminar at Lunch" that was organized at first by a history professor of the University of Hawaii and currently by the East-West Center. At the seminar, held once every few months, known China expert scholars or journalists gave talks on current China affairs for a paying audience, numbering at least a few dozen to around 80. The seminar not only boosted the reputation of the restaurant of "Mandarin cuisine," it also attracted more customers who then came to dine on ordinary days. The restaurant continued to host the seminars, even after Mr. R passed away and the ownership changed. However, about 10 years ago, this restaurant joined other "cheap eats" Chinese restaurants in town by offering an inexpensive buffet at lunch time (Wu, 2008).

For comparison it would be good for me to tell a second story that I learned elsewhere and not in Hawaii. I also believe that if I tell another story about the emergence of "Northern Chinese" restaurants on the U.S. mainland, especially down in the heartland of America in the southern states of Texas and Louisiana, my readers would be more convinced of what happened in the 1970s across the country.

Foo Yuan (Lucky Garden) in New Orleans

The second story is about a 30-year-old Northern Chinese restaurant started in the late 1970s in New Orleans. It involves a senior high school friend of mine, Mr. Du, who immigrated to the United States in 1978 from Taiwan.[11] He took early retirement from his job as a college instructor and administrator in Taipei, and, with his life savings, brought his entire family to California to join his younger brother, who sponsored their immigration. I suspect the fund he brought to the United States included an inheritance from his father, a retired Professor and Air Force Colonel, who (during the 1950s and 1960s) was the Head of an Air Force Engineering Corp in Taichung City, Taiwan. The family of five included his wife, a middle-school teacher who was Mr. Du's high-school sweetheart, and their three children (the oldest having just graduated from a junior middle school in Taipei). Mr. Du's younger brother was my middle-school classmate and a life-long good friend, who came to the United States in the early 1970s to pursue graduate studies in industrial chemistry. After obtaining a graduate degree and securing a good job with an international company, he successfully applied for the U.S. immigration status of permanent residency, and, later American citizenship.

Once settled in the United States, the immediate and practical concern for the Du couple was to find jobs to support their family, and, more importantly, a sustainable income for the future. Like many of the new emigrants from Taiwan since the 1960s, they looked for jobs at Chinese restaurants. They both found jobs in a Sichuan restaurant, where Mr. Du worked as a waiter and his wife as a helper in the kitchen. They told me that they did not take their jobs as a temporary measure for earning income, but with the serious aim of learning all the tricks of restaurant cooking and operations. Therefore, Mr. Du at the restaurant also diligently learned and mastered the art of being a bartender. Mrs. Du told me how she had not known how to cook back at home in Taiwan (where they had had a maid servant ever since they both were young), but she worked very hard in the restaurant kitchen. Every day she would closely observe the restaurant chef in action, while secretly learning the tricks of preparation and cooking Sichuan and other Chinese dishes (but pretending not to be interested in cooking and never asking any questions).

After only six months of working at this "Sichuan" restaurant in California, an opportunity arose for the Du couple to move and for them to open a new Chinese restaurant in New Orleans. Mr. Du told me that he had made friends with the chef and learned that he had a friend who had recently made a lot of money in a new "Sichuan" restaurant he operated in New Orleans, Louisiana. The chef told them that it would be a good idea to open a Chinese restaurant in the American southern states of Texas and Louisiana, where many Americans had struck it rich in the oil business. Du decided to accept the chef's offer to move with him and become a partner in New Orleans of a new restaurant: Foo Yuan (Lucky Garden).

I can guess the reasons why and how Mr. Du could so soon establish a good rapport with the Sichuan restaurant chef. I knew that Mr. Du spoke the Sichuan dialect, which he had learned in childhood in Sichuan during World War II under the Japanese invasion. During the 1950s in Taiwan, in the elementary schools that were sponsored by the military (especially the Air Force) or in elite schools attended predominantly by Mainland Chinese children, the Sichuan dialect became their common language of communication when they were not in the classroom, where the official language was Mandarin.[12]

The new restaurant made good profits in no time. But after four years, the chef decided to move on again, leaving the Du couple to continue running Foo Yuan as sole owners. Mr. Du put himself in charge of the front as waiter, bartender, and cashier, while Mrs. Du attended to the kitchen and cooking. All three children, by this time in high school and middle school, came to the restaurant after school to help. According to Mr. Du, the most profitable part of the restaurant was the bar, as Americans like to drink. Mr. Du told the story of how one of his important jobs at the restaurant became educating American customers about Chinese food. He explained to them dish by dish (remember, he was a university lecturer in Taiwan) what "Northern Chinese cuisine" was and how it was authentically Chinese, much superior to the old Chinese food (Cantonese invented chop suey) that the customers were used to. He attracted new customers and kept the restaurant successful.

After another couple of years, as the restaurant business continued to prosper, the Du couple realized that their children were growing up, and two had already gone to college. They did not forget that their main purpose in immigrating to the United States, their hard work and sacrifices (giving up their comfortable lives as a professor and a high school teacher in Taiwan), were to provide a brighter future for their children, not just for their own survival.

After two or three more years running the Foo Yuan, when their first son had already entered university, their second child, a daughter, was admitted to medical school in Shreveport, another city in Louisiana. The Du couple as parents decided to give full support to their daughter's success in medical school by selling Foo Yuan in New Orleans and moving to Shreveport to open a new restaurant. Their third child, the second son, by this time a high-school student, also moved with his parents. After another six or seven years, the daughter finished her medical studies and internship, while the two sons also graduated from universities—the second son becoming an engineer with an oil company in Texas. All three children moved out of the family home, found good jobs in other part of the United States (two in New York and one in Monroe, California), and got married and started their own families. This is not yet the end of my story of my old friend of some 60 years.

To cut a long story short, the Du couple sold their restaurant and bought a 10-acre tract of land by the "lake" (as Mr. Du's younger brother told me recently) on which they built a large new home for retirement. My friend Mr. Du, in his younger brother's words, subsequently spent most of his time doing nothing but fishing and hunting birds (delicious wild ducks, I suspect). The Du couple often traveled to visit their children, while also taking long trips to Taiwan to visit their old friends. Thereafter, as their Northern Chinese restaurant ended, "they lived happily ever after." They told me in person about their story of restaurant life in the United States, when I by chance in 2010 met them in Taiwan during their nostalgic long trip "home."

Concluding Remarks

In this chapter, I told the untold stories of the history and broader social, cultural, economic, and political environments of two successful "Northern Chinese restaurants." These two exemplary restaurants and the stories of their owners help us to understand the emergence and expansion during the 1970s of a new generation of Chinese restaurants that served the "Pan-China Cuisines," which succeeded the earlier "Chop Suey Chinese Cuisine" in the United States. I hope that readers will be convinced by my stories to join the imagination of the evolution of American Chinese cuisine during the latter half of the twentieth century. What I would like to emphasize in the conclusion of my stories is the fact that these "restaurants and accidental owners" help us to learn about the amazing and unprecedented diasporic movement of a new breed of Chinese and Taiwanese immigrants to the United States.

As I promised earlier, at the beginning of this chapter, I would like now to offer some more amazing notes about those pioneering but "unsuccessful" restaurant owners of this new era of Chinese cuisine in the United States. For instance, one is a tiny "*jiaoziguan* (饺子馆 "dumpling place" or "Gyoza Place," in a globally familiar English term that was adopted from Japanese) operated in the late 1960s by a lone old lady (originally from Shandong Province via Taiwan), who was a professor's wife, and her son was a Civil Engineer Professor at the University of Hawaii from the late 1960s to the late 1990s. Another small "Northern Chinese" restaurant, also in the late 1960s, neighboring a small automobile repair shop (where I often sent my breaking down antique British car for repair) was operated by a Lecturer of Chinese Language and Literature Department at the University of Hawaii (a White American man who had studied Chinese in Taiwan) and his Taiwanese wife, serving Gyoza and soup noodles "Taiwanese style" (by the way, one of his senior professors at the same Chinese Department once complained to me about this colleague's behavior of often excusing himself during office hours to go to "help his wife in the restaurant"). There were another two University of Hawaii graduate students from Taiwan, each of whom started a small restaurant to serve their improvised "Shanghai" dishes, and which lasted only for a couple of years. One of the owners' mother was a famed Professor of English at the leading university in Taipei, while another owner studied linguistics at the University of Hawaii Graduate School toward a Ph.D. degree. In addition, a most gossiped about (in the Taiwanese academic community in Honolulu) "Hunan" restaurant was opened during the early 1970s in Wisconsin (bankrupted and closed within a few years) by a former Lecturer of Chinese Language and Literature at the same University of Hawaii. The Hunan restaurant owner is a close friend of mine, who had worked as my supervisor at the same academic institution in Taipei, before coming to the United States for graduate studies. In the early 1970s he quit his teaching job in Hawaii to pursue a Ph.D. degree in Anthropology on the U.S. mainland while running the restaurant. Eventually he received the degree in the late 1970s and became a tenured professor of Anthropology at the State University of California. Among the courses he offered at the university, the most popular one that attracted the highest enrollments, as I was told, was on Chinese cooking. One would be amazed at his family background (originally from Hunan Province of China) of extremely high socio-political standing in both Taiwan and China. This anthropology professor had one uncle and one aunt who both served (from the 1950s to the 1970s) as Senators (representing Hunan Province of China in the Legislative Yuan of the Republic of China) in Taiwan, while at the same time one of his paternal uncles was a senior member of the Chinese Communist Party in the new People's Republic of China.

My readers will be entertained, I hope, and agree with me that I have managed to offer some interesting and untold stories about Chinese restaurant and cuisine that belong to an important part of American gastronomic history of the late twentieth and early twenty-first centuries.

Key Terms

Mandarin cuisine: Reinvented dishes of various reginal home-style cooking of old China, served since the 1960s in Taiwan and in American Chinese restaurants that claim to be authentic Northern Chinese (but include Sichuan, Hunan, Shanghai, and Taiwanese dishes).

Globalization: Spreading from one cultural center to around the world of popular cultural symbols, new technologies, and national cuisines.

Improvisation: With new cooking skills and ingredients, migrants create versions of well-known food and cooking styles from home, and serve in restaurants claiming to provide authentic ethnic cuisine.

Discussion Questions

1. What did President Richard Nixon do in global Cold War Politics of the 1970s that helped to speed up the popularization of "Northern Chinese cuisine" in new American Chinese restaurants?
2. What are some of the new dishes in Mandarin restaurants that have become ethnic markers to represent different regional Chinese food and cooking styles?
3. Why and how have thousands of university graduate students from Taiwan become involved in the emergence and evolution of a "Pan-China Cuisine" in American Chinese restaurants, which has replaced the old "Chop Suey Houses"? What are the reasons or untold stories behind the popular Chinese restaurant dish of "Kung Pao Chicken (or *gongbao jiding* 宫保鸡丁) and the Jewish "Kung Pao Comedy" during the Holiday Season in San Francisco?

Notes

1 The research resulted in many books and journal articles, such as the following: Wu, Yen-ho "Cantonese Cuisine in Taiwan, Taiwanese Cuisine in Hong Kong: Food Culture and Ethnicity (in Chinese). In Lin, Ching-gu, Ed., *The 4th Symposium on Chinese Dietary Culture.* Taipei, pp. 5–21. 1995; Wu, D.Y.H. "McDonald's in Taipei: Hamburgers, Betel Nuts, and National Identity." In James L. Watson, Ed., *Golden Arches East: McDonald's in East Asia.* Stanford, CA: Stanford University Press, pp. 110–135. 1997; Wu, D.Y.H. "All You Can Eat Buffet: The Evolution of Chinese Cuisine in Hawaii," *Journal of Chinese Dietary Culture* 4 (1): 1–24. 2008; Wu, D.Y.H. and Chee-Beng Tan, Eds. *Changing Chinese Foodways in Asia.* Hong Kong: The Chinese University Press. 2000; Wu, D.Y.H. and Sidney C.H. Cheung, Eds., *The Globalization of Chinese Food.* Surrey, UK: Curzon Press. 2002; Wu, D.Y.H. "Global Encounter of Diasporic Chinese Restaurant Food." In Chee-Beng Tan, Ed., *Chinese Food and Foodways in Southeast Asia and Beyond.* Singapore: NUS Press, pp. 75–103. 2011; Wu, D.Y. H. *Where Is Home?* Taipei: Institute of Ethnology, Academia Sinica. 2011.
2 Liu, Haiming "Chop Suey as Imagined Authentic Chinese Food," *Journal of Transnational American Studies* 1 (1): Article 12. 2009; *From Canton Restaurant to Panda Express.* New Brunswick, NJ: Rutgers University Press. 2015; Chen, Yong *Chop Suey USA: The Story of Chinese Food in America.* New York: Columbia University Press. 2014.
3 Hamlin, Jesse "Kung Pao Kosher Comedy Marks 25 Years of Laughs During the Holidays," *San Francisco Chronicles, Arts and Entertainment.* December 21, 2017 (internet download on March 14, 2018); Tuchman, Geye and Harry Levine, "Chop Suey: An American Classic" *New York Times* (2017 online access at https://www.smithsonianmag.com/ 1993).
4 Ray, K. "Ethnic Succession and the New American Restaurant Cuisine," in David Beriss and David Sutton, Eds., *The Restaurants Book: Ethnographies of Where We Eat.* Oxford: Berg Publishers. 2007; *The Ethnic Restaurateur.* New York: Bloomsbury. 2016. Since the early years of the twenty-first century, when walking into a "Chinese restaurant" almost anywhere in the United States, one has found a standardized menu, created first by Chinese students from Taiwan during the 1970s. I have in my earlier work named such restaurant food the "Standardized Pan-China Cuisine" (see Wu 2008, 2011). Also, writers of a new academic book, *Chop Suey and Sushi from Sea to Shining Sea: Chinese and Japanese Restaurants in the United States* (Arnold et al., Eds., University of Arkansas Press. 2018) provide strong evidence in support of my earlier claim.
5 My credentials go beyond gastronomic ethnological observation (see Wu, D.Y.H., Ed., *Overseas March: How the Chinese Cuisine Spread.* Taipei: Foundation for Chinese Dietary Culture. 2012). As portrayed in my personal memoir (Wu, David Y.H. and Midori Hino, *Furusato, Huirudo, Ressha (Hometown, Fieldwork, The Train: Half Life of a Taiwanese Anthropologist).* Tokyo: Hukyosha. 2012 (First published in Chinese in Taipei by China Times Press.

2006), I built up an exceptional taste and a keen sense of food varieties at home (spoiled by professional cooks and nannies) since my early childhood in a distinguished diaspora Taiwanese family that sojourned and traveled through north and south China. Also, during my adult life as an anthropologist over the past 60 years, field research took me to many parts of China and to diaspora Chinese communities in East and Southeast Asia, the South Pacific islands, Australia, and Europe.

6 During the past three years I have interviewed the owners, former partners, close friends, and family members of these restaurant owners, in addition to long term customers (since the 1970s). Both the owners and Chinese customers came from families that originally lived in mainland China. These mainland Chinese immigrants to the United States grew up in Taiwan and came to America for higher education during the 1960s and 1970s. I also talked to many people on the U.S. mainland who patronized "Northern Chinese" restaurants that operated between the 1970s and the early 2000s. Special thanks are due to many who told me versions of inside stories about these two restaurants. I am particularly indebted to the following friends who kindly allowed me to bother them so many times to beg for stories: They include Charlie Yamamoto, Francis Tu, Guang-tou Chao, and Mary Wu. I wish also to thank Dr. Midori Hino and, especially, my friend Dr. Kennon Breazeale, for kindly proofreading my earlier chapter draft.

7 The original owners all are college graduates from Taiwan who came to study as graduate students at the University of Hawaii in the early 1970s. The restaurant name must be adopted from the first and most well-known up-scale "Hong Kong style Cantonese restaurant" of the early 1970s in Taipei: Fung Lum ("Maple Woods" in Cantonese) or *Fenglin Xiaoguan* ("Little Maple Restaurant" in Mandarin). It started in Hong Kong and was publicized for serving Hakka cuisine in a new five-story building in north Taipei City, in a booming new commercial neighborhood of tourism (the main target of tourists in those days were Japanese). Incidentally, since the 1970s I have known the original owner and his extended Hakka family in Hong Kong (they were Hakka or *kejiaren* (客家人) refugees who came in the late 1950s from Guangdong Province), and I visited their branches of luxury restaurants under the same name in San Jose and Los Angeles (at Universal Studios). All these Fung Lum (*Fenglin*) restaurants have long since closed, although many Chinese restaurants around the world today still use the famous name for their restaurants. I happened to visit Australia in 2017 and met some of their second and third generation family members in Sydney and Brisbane. A very long story about the original "Fung Lum" and its global expansion is still waiting to be told.

8 The old Honolulu during the late nineteenth century until the 1960s was a clearly segregated city divided into ethnic residential neighborhoods (see Glick, Clarence E., *Sojourners and Settlers: Chinese Migrants in Hawaii*. Honolulu: University of Hawaii Press 1980; and Wu, David Y.H. and Weilan Wang, *Xiaweiyi de Huayi Yimin (Chinese Immigrants in Hawaii)*. Taipei: Zhengzhong Book Publishers. 1985). I remember that, when I and my late wife first arrived in Honolulu in the late 1960s, looking for a house to rent, we experienced refusal of renting in Mo'ili'ili, because we were not Japanese. At an old two-story apartment building along University Avenue, we saw on the wall a sign advertising units available for rent. When we talked to the building owner/manager, an old man who was a first-generation ethnic Japanese, he politely and apologetically explained to us that they preferred to rent only to Japanese. His reasoning was that all the tenants in that building were real Japanese who were comfortable to communicate with their neighbors only in Japanese. Being fresh off-the-boat foreign students (from Taiwan, when people were used to authoritative government treatment or discrimination, with no regard to law and justice), we just accepted his explanation as justified and left.

9 This Shanghai restaurant, Winter Garden, where Mr. R worked part time and learned the tricks of cooking and restaurant operation, later changed its name to Yen King (meaning Yanjing, the ancient name of Peking). Yen King was eventually closed in 2006, but one of the Yen King partners, a more recent immigrant from Guangdong Province, joined Mr. R's business. Today the newer and repainted external restaurant sign of the Autumn Leaves still lists both restaurant names in English—Autumn Leaves and Yen King—while underneath the sign, printed in smaller characters, is another line: "Mandarin Cuisine."

10 Characterized by my Hawaiian local informants as hot and spicy (which is not what traditional Northern Chinese food in China is supposed to be, as Chinese in China would say). Also, I visited Seoul, South Korea, several times during the late 1970s, where I discovered many popular "Northern Chinese Restaurants" operated by Chinese immigrants from Shandong Province of China, adjacent to the Korean Peninsula. Shandong cuisine has been one of the core methods of cooking for traditional Beijing cuisine since the Qing Dynasty.

11 It so happened that I have another friend whose name is also Du. This Mr. Du (my late wife's elementary school classmate in Taipei) is the owner of a chain of Chinese restaurants, six in all, in Virginia with the name "Peking," that also started in the 1970s. That would be another long untold story of "Peking cuisine" in North American Chinese restaurants.

12 These students shared the same experience, or ethnic identity, of being born and spending their early childhood in Southwest China, where the Sichuan dialect was the de facto lingua-franca. From a linguistic point of view, as I have studied, the Southwest (sub-) dialects spoken by residents in Sichuan, Yunnan, Guizhou, and part of Guangxi, are all classified under mutually intelligible branches of the "Official Northern Chinese" or Mandarin. Even their classmates not born in Sichuan or other Southwest Provinces would often learn to imitate a Pidgin-style Sichuan dialect in order to make friends at school.

References

Chen, Yong. *Chop Suey USA: The Story of Chinese Food in America*. New York: Columbia University Press. 2014.

Liu, Haiming. "Chop Suey as Imagined Authentic Chinese Food," *Journal of Transnational American Studies* 1 (1): Article 12. 2009.

Liu, Haiming. *From Canton Restaurant to Panda Express*. New Brunswick, NJ: Rutgers University Press. 2015.

Wu, Yen-ho. "Cantonese Cuisine in Taiwan, Taiwanese Cuisine in Hong Kong: Food Culture and Ethnicity" (in Chinese). In Lin, Ching-gu, Ed., *The 4th Symposium on Chinese Dietary Culture*. Taipei, pp. 5–21. 1995.

Wu, D.Y.H. "All You Can Eat Buffet: The Evolution of Chinese Cuisine in Hawaii," *Journal of Chinese Dietary Culture* 4 (1): 1–24. 2008.

Wu, D.Y.H. *Where is Home?* Taipei: Institute of Ethnology, Academia Sinica. 2011.

9

ORIENTAL PALACES

Chin F. Foin and Chinese Fine Dining in Exclusion-Era Chicago

Samuel King

In 1911, the Mandarin Inn Café opened its doors to the Chicago public. Located in the downtown Loop, it was one of the most elaborate and celebrated Chinese restaurants in the city to date. In contrast to most other Chinese eateries of the era, its offerings were catered to the city's middle- and upper-class elite, rather than to the slummers, "riffraff," and victims of racial discrimination who had frequented Chinatown in the nineteenth century. Patrons of the multi-story restaurant sat down to their meals of chop suey, chow mein, or Euro-American cuisine, in an atmosphere marked by luxurious Asian and Western décor and ambience, including elaborate tableware and cutlery, an impressive fountain and chandelier above the main dining room, and Chinese musicians performing in the background. The Mandarin Inn blended "Oriental" and "Occidental" offerings in an upscale dining environment, creating a restaurant space that was simultaneously exotic yet familiar, entertaining yet respectable for middle-class patronage.

The next year, the proprietor of the Mandarin Inn, Chin Foin, moved his family into a Victorian style mansion in an exclusive, predominantly white, neighborhood in the city's South Side. At the time of the move, which coincided with the relocation of the Chicago Chinatown from its original site in the Loop to its current location in Armour Square, Chin was well known among Chicagoans as a particularly wealthy and Americanized Chinese immigrant of high class and distinction. Importantly, he was also widely renowned for the upscale Chinese restaurants, which one reporter dubbed "Oriental palaces," that he helped to pioneer in the city. At a time when Chinese immigrants to the United States were considered inherently alien and inassimilable, as well as an economic threat to the livelihoods of white American workers, Chin's association with luxury Chinese dining helped the restaurateur achieve a level of upward social mobility otherwise denied to most Chinese Americans during the Exclusion era. By crafting restaurant spaces that appealed to American Orientalist desires to consume Chinese culture, as well as the middle and upper classes' appetite for respectable luxury entertainment, Chin amassed a sizable fortune and demonstrated to white Chicagoans his membership in the "better element" of Chinese Americans, thereby rendering himself a more acceptable Chinese immigrant and winning a space for himself and his family in white America. In the midst of Chinese exclusion, Chin Foin took advantage of the burgeoning popularity of Chinese restaurants to accomplish a remarkable feat of upward social mobility for a member of an otherwise marginalized and ostracized immigrant population.

Chin F. Foin was born in the winter of 1876 in Guangdong Province in South China, an area from which the bulk of imperial China's emigrants originated. Like many other Chinese immigrants who made their way to Chicago during the Exclusion era, Chin was Taishanese, a native of Xinning County, or what is today recognized as the county-level city of Taishan, in Guangdong. When exactly Chin first arrived in the United States is not entirely clear. In a 1906 application to re-enter the United States after traveling to China, Chin described himself as having resided in the United States since 1892. However, in a 1924 application, his stated arrival in this country was listed as 1890. In any case, by 1895 a teenaged Chin had traveled east from San Francisco and taken up residence in the burgeoning Chinese enclave of the city of Chicago.[1]

Chin enjoyed significant social and economic support from the Chinese American community in the Windy City. By the time he arrived in Chicago, the city's Chinese inhabitants numbered more than 500 (with some reports calculating the number to be as high as 2,000), part of a foreign-born population that amounted to more than 40 percent of Chicago's 1.1 million residents.[2] In Chinatown, the Chin clan was one of the more powerful Chinese families at the turn of the twentieth century, standing as rivals to the dominant Moy clan, whose progenitors originally established the city's Chinese enclave in the 1870s. Chin Foin's first job in Chicago was working as an assistant manager of Wing Chong Hai, a Chinese grocery store located at 281 Clark Street in the Chinese enclave. By 1900, he graduated to full manager, and had invested $2,500 in the company by 1906.[3] Wing Chong Hai was a Chin family business: Chin Foin's brother, Chin Yun Quay, managed the grocery, which also employed several other members of the Chin clan full-time, including Chin Hee, Chin Wing, Chin Fung Kee, Chin Ning, and Chin Der Bow.[4] Hiring multiple family members was a common practice among Chinese businesses during the Exclusion era. Not only did such hiring practices enable immigrants to bring relatives to the United States and provide them a source of income, but employment in small businesses like laundries, restaurants, and grocery stores also allowed Chinese immigrants to claim mercantile status and thereby avoid deportation under the Chinese Exclusion Act. Over the next decade, Chin Foin would provide similar employment opportunities to family members through his restaurants, paying forward the benefits once extended to him by the social network and community of Chinatown.

Chin first became involved in the restaurant industry in 1904, when he became the proprietor and manager of the King Yen Lo restaurant, located at the corner of

Clark Street and Van Buren Street. Though not quite the kind of opulent eatery Chin would ultimately become renowned for in Chicago, King Yen Lo nonetheless amounted to a more elaborate and "classy" establishment than most Chinese restaurants of its time. The restaurant was a "chop suey emporium" that capitalized on the nascent fad among American urbanites for chop suey, a hodgepodge dish that experienced growing and widespread popularity in Chicago in the years prior to the eatery's establishment.[5] Despite its location above the first-floor saloon of alderman Michael "Hinky Dink" Kenna, a famously corrupt Chicago politician and "Lord of the Levee" alongside fellow ward boss John Coughlin, it was yet considered by urban consumers relatively respectable, upscale, and safe for middle- and even upper-class patronage.[6] Chin Foin's first foray into restauranting thus began to establish his reputation in Chicago as a respectable restaurateur, and laid the groundwork for his future success in the industry.

The 1900s were a particularly opportune decade for Chin to launch his restaurateur career, as Chinese restaurants had reached an unprecedented level of popularity in Chicago at the turn of the century. Throughout much of the nineteenth century, racially informed stereotypes of Chinese restaurants imagined the eateries as sinister dens of iniquity, sites of taboo interracial and cross-class mixing, and hosts to vices like opium smoking, gambling, and the prostitution and enslavement of white women. Following these stereotypes, the food served in these restaurants was frequently described as containing pets and vermin, such as dogs, cats, and rats, or as being totally incomprehensible to Western eaters for its barbarousness. The concerns over Chinese eateries largely reflected the racial anxieties felt by many Americans concerning Chinese immigration since the 1850s. These stereotypes began to shift, however, at least in respect to cuisine, during the "chop suey craze" of the late 1890s, in which urban consumers in many American cities patronized Chinatown restaurants in much larger numbers than ever before. The craze, underwritten by the United States' increasing interaction with China on the world stage and by the gastronomical appeal of chop suey to the American palate, was ushered in by the much-feted arrival of Chinese minister Li Hongzhang to New York City in 1896. During his visit, New Yorkers flocked to Chinatown in droves to consume Chinese culture and to try the dish that New York newspapers alleged Li insisted on eating over Western cuisine.[7] The impulses and desires that drove New Yorkers to venture into their local Chinese enclave compelled similar behaviors among urban Americans across the country in the late 1890s and early 1900s. By 1904, Chinese restaurants and chop suey had become widely popular and unprecedentedly mainstream in cities like Philadelphia, Boston, and Chicago, gaining a widespread tolerance and affection they had never received from most Americans before.

In that same year, Chin took the first step in starting a family in the United States when he married a young Chinese American merchant's daughter, Yoklund Wong, in San Francisco. Her father, Wong Duck, was an established and influential importer on the West Coast and provided the supplies for Chin's Chicago grocery.[8] By all contemporary accounts other than race, Yoklund was a very Americanized woman. She was born in the United States, to a mother who had also been born in the United States, and was thus an American citizen by birth. According to a newspaper description of the young bride, Yoklund "[wore] American dresses and [had] American habits." Even the headline of the article announcing her marriage to Chin Foin, "Fair Chinese Bride Wears American Clothes and Hats," emphasized her typically "American" attire.[9] However, while both bride and groom were described as particularly Americanized, their wedding ceremony and celebration, held in Chinese fashion in San Francisco's Chinatown, also reflected the transnational cultural heritage typical of many Chinese Americans at the time, and which Chin ultimately employed in the spaces of his restaurants to appeal to white American customers.

Beyond a source of income, Chin Foin's restaurants also served an important social function in the lives of his nascent family. Only weeks after their marriage in California, Chin and his wife held a separate postnuptial celebration at King Yen Lo, following their relocation to Chicago. Hundreds of guests attended the celebration, including prominent Chinese merchants, city officials, and Chin's political friends and patrons.[10] In November 1907, one month after Yoklund gave birth to the couple's first son, a large and elaborate banquet was held in the boy's honor at King Yen Lo. The extensive guest list consisted of very well-to-do white and non-white attendees, including doctors, lawyers, politicians, former Chicago mayors, prominent Chinese merchants, and even the acting Minister of the Chinese government, who traveled from D.C. to attend the celebration.[11] Chin Foin's first son, much like his restaurants, was a child of transnational cultural interaction: his full name was Theodore Chin Chungow, "Chungow" being a more traditional Chinese name chosen by the acting Minister, and "Theodore" being chosen in honor of the American president.[12]

Following upon the success of King Yen Lo, Chin began expanding his career as a restaurateur. In December 1906, he opened his second restaurant, King Joy Lo, on the 100th block of Randolph Street, several blocks north of the Chinese enclave. Chin set out to make his second restaurant far more extravagant than his first, and to make the rest of Chicago aware of this opulence. Advertisements for King Joy Lo described it as a "beautifully decorated and sumptuously furnished American and Chinese Restaurant," and featured detailed descriptions of the restaurant's interior décor, including its magnificent chandelier, picturesque carvings and embroideries, miniature Chinese theater, and elegant fountain at the center of the main floor (Figure 9.1).[13] The advertising campaign surrounding the restaurant's grand opening also made particular mention of the $130,000 Chin and other investors had spent on its decoration.

Those who first dined at King Joy Lo in the winter of 1906 were treated to what was likely the most elegant experience they had ever had in a Chinese restaurant, or even considered possible for such an establishment. To be sure, the food on offer was overall not terribly distinct from that served by most other Chinese restaurants in the early twentieth century. The menu's Chinese offerings included a wide variety of Americanized dishes, such as chop suey, chow mein, and egg

FIGURE 9.1 Advertisement depicting the interior of King Joy Lo. *Chicago Tribune*, 1906.

foo young, while the "American Style" half of the menu—longer than the Chinese half—included such familiar fare as mutton chops, fried spring chicken, and "Ham and Eggs, Country Style."[14] The eatery's real elegance, however, lay in its atmosphere. The ground floor of the restaurant featured a grand main hall, marked by high ceilings supported by decorated pillars, a brilliant chandelier hanging over a mosaic fountain, and surrounding mirrored walls framed in teakwood, with an elegant staircase in the back of the hall leading to the second floor. This upper level partially operated as a gallery, from which diners could watch "the interesting throngs of people coming and going on the main floor." A screen on the second floor hid from view the orchestra that played the elegant music that permeated the restaurant. Also included on the second floor were private dining rooms, mostly enclosed by carved screens, which allowed patrons the opportunity to dine in semi-privacy if they so desired. Little expense was spared in giving the restaurant an opulent interior décor that included several Asian features and designs meant to evoke a sense of the exotic Orient, including a miniature Chinese theater, carved pagodas, embroideries, and teakwood carvings lining the walls.[15]

While Chin aimed to give his restaurant an "Oriental" atmosphere, King Joy Lo was also designed to be particularly accommodating to non-Chinese patrons. Those dining at the restaurant could order Chinese or American dishes, a strategy of accommodation that dated back to some of the earliest Chinese restaurants in San Francisco, and both chopsticks and Western silverware were made available for use. Advertising for the restaurant emphasized that it used modern ranges and refrigerators in the kitchens, which, potential customers were assured, were open to inspection at any time. The "well dressed men and women" who thronged the restaurant in December of 1906 would thus have felt quite comfortable and safe in Chin's restaurant, rendered that much more trustworthy than the vilified Chinese restaurants of the previous century.[16] Chin's reputation in Chicago was already established by this point but King Joy Lo, with its accommodating yet still sufficiently "Oriental" features, further enhanced his image in Chicago society as a provider of respectable and elegant Chinese dining experiences.

The establishment and subsequent success of King Joy Lo also served to expand and solidify Chin Foin's widening network of social and political connections, as his position in Chicago society and the city's Chinese American community continued to rise. Although the restaurant was partially funded by local white investors who knew and did business with Chin, King Joy Lo received significant financial support from the Chinese Empire Reform Association (*Baohuanghui*). Founded in 1899 in Canada by Kang Youwei, the reformist organization operated outside mainland China in the pursuit of restoring the Guangxu Emperor to power following his ouster by the Empress Dowager Cixi.[17] The emperor had initiated the Hundred Days' Reform in 1898, with the goal of modernizing China following its decades of military defeat at the hands of European powers. Although he left behind no written records of his political leanings, Chin Foin himself was clearly sympathetic, or at least not actively opposed, to the Chinese reform movement, given his ownership and management of King Joy Lo, a restaurant established to generate revenue for the Reform Association. Kang Youwei himself was even directly involved in the restaurant, assisting in the naming and decorating of the eatery and attending the opening ceremony.[18] Among Chinese reformers, the Chinese American community, and local Chicagoans, Chin Foin enjoyed an enormous boost in prestige as a result of his association with and management of King Joy Lo.

In 1911, Chin established his next and most famous upscale Chinese restaurant: the Mandarin Inn café, located at 414 and 416 South Wabash Avenue. By this time, due to the success of King Yen Lo and King Joy Lo, and the prominence he enjoyed in Chicago society, Chin's own name and close personal involvement with the enterprise, as general manager and as president of the newly formed Mandarin Inn Company, was a key selling point in advertising for the new restaurant. Reflecting his reputation in Chicago as a renowned Chinese restaurateur, the announcement for the restaurant's opening night included the boastful proclamation: "Chin F. Foin's name stands for the best in Chinese and American restaurant operation."[19]

The Mandarin Inn included all the splendor of King Joy Lo and more. Chin's latest restaurant also followed a multi-story design, with the second floor including balcony seating that looked over the luxurious main floor. The opening ceremony, a visually and aurally spectacular affair, featured Chinese artwork and live musical performances, as well as "fountains playing, birds singing, [and] flowers adding their glory to the scene." Much of the interior décor was once again crafted in a Chinese fashion, featuring dragon fixtures and imported Chinese furniture "of the most luxurious type."[20] As with other "Orientalized" entertainment sites of this period, patrons of the Mandarin Inn likely experienced a feeling of being instantly transported to an imagined China as they crossed the threshold from the streets outside into the opulent restaurant interior.

Like advertisements for King Joy Lo, the announcement for the Mandarin Inn prominently featured Orientalist imagery, including Chinese dragons and an image of an entryway with pagoda-style architecture. However, advertising for Chin's latest restaurant tended to accentuate its luxury over its Asian ambiance. To

FIGURE 9.2 Newspaper announcement for the opening of the Mandarin Inn. *Chicago Tribune*, 1911.

emphasize the upscale nature of the establishment, words like "luxury," "excellence," and "magnificent" were repeatedly invoked in advertisement descriptions, and the need for reservations was also implied.[21] Advertising also emphasized the live singing and orchestral music that was to be featured in the restaurant, while large drawings of the restaurant's opulent interior were placed alongside and above the Chinese dragons and pagoda. Although both were obviously important elements of the restaurant's appeal, the Mandarin Inn's luxuriousness seemed to represent a greater selling point than its "Oriental" exoticism.

The announcement for the restaurant's opening also emphasized the Mandarin Inn's distinctiveness next to other Chinese restaurants in the city (Figure 9.2). Design choices not common in Chinese eateries at the time, such as linen table cloths, were highlighted, as was the introduction of a Chinese afternoon tea service, which allegedly could not be found in any other Chinese restaurant in Chicago.[22] Publicity for the restaurant also contended that its food, the bulk of which certainly included chop suey, chow mein, and Euro-American cuisine, was more authentic than that of its competitors. Although this sort of claim was not uncommon among turn-of-the-century Chinese restaurants, and though most observers today would scoff at the idea of considering chop suey "authentic" Chinese food, advertising for the Mandarin Inn made this point rather strongly, such as by printing in capital letters that Chin Foin's establishment served "THE ONLY CORRECT CHINESE MANDARIN COOKING IN CHICAGO."[23] As an upscale Chinese restaurant, Chin's most recent venture was meant to be, or at least appear to be, unparalleled.

The Mandarin Inn matched, if not exceeded, the accommodation strategy reflected in both the King Yen Lo and the King Joy Lo restaurants. The adoption of an English name for the eatery, for example, represented a clear indication of the restaurant's intended clientele, as well as a dramatic marker of the increasing prominence of Chin Foin's restaurants in Chicago society; Chin's latest establishment would be specifically tailored towards non-Chinese Americans and would appeal to them quite literally on their own terms. Persisting in making available safe gustatory options for Western diners, the menu of the Mandarin Inn offered a "limitless variety" of both Chinese and American dishes, while at the same time the restaurant's serving of European, American, and Chinese alcoholic beverages was also emphasized.[24] Meanwhile, the establishment's "perfect" ventilation system, which allegedly ensured patrons' comfort in all types of weather, as well as the professionalism of the wait staff, were all touted in the restaurant's advertising campaign.[25] These attributes in particular would have been seen as a reflection of modernity, as well as a definitive departure from the negative stereotypes associated with Chinatowns and Chinese food elsewhere. As such, Chin's newest restaurant, as his older establishments had done, created a space in which white Chicagoans could comfortably partake of what they considered to be Chinese culture and Chinese food, even as they simultaneously dined on American steak and European champagne on Wabash Avenue, in an environment that combined luxury entertainment with a safe and respectable aura of exoticism. For white Chicagoans, in the safety and opulence of Chin Foin's restaurants, the Yellow Peril did not exist.

Granted, Chin Foin's establishments were not the first Chinese American restaurants that were designed to accommodate and attract an otherwise wary white clientele. As Erica J. Peters has detailed, Chinese immigrant restaurateurs in San Francisco employed various strategies in their eateries, such as offering dishes from a variety of cuisines other than Chinese, to draw in "a desirable class of white patrons" as early as 1849. According to Peters, these immigrants sought to deliberately "reach out" to potential white customers, including those of influence in society, such as wealthy businessmen, politicians, and newspaper editors, in the hopes that food would create for them "a path to acceptance over time."[26] During the chop suey craze of the 1890s and 1900s, meanwhile, Chinese restaurateurs up and down the East Coast and in the Midwest opened numerous "chop suey joints" beyond the barriers of Chinatown in order to make patronizing Chinese restaurants that much easier for non-Chinese customers.[27] Furthermore, as Anne Mendelson has argued, even the creation of chop suey itself represented an act of strategic invention on the part of Chinese restaurateurs; the dish was a "quasi-Chinese culinary idiom," invented during a time of great hardship and constant threat to deliberately appeal to the preferences of the non-Chinese majority, thus representing "a historic turning point in race relations."[28] Although not all eateries that served chop suey were considered "high-class" during the chop suey craze, relatively upscale Chinese restaurants had certainly been established as early as the 1880s, including Bun Sun Low and Hang Far Low in San Francisco and Yu-ung-Fang-Lau in New York.[29] However, although they were not unprecedented within the national context of Chinese American restaurant history, Chin Foin's establishments did fall among the earliest and most successful upscale Chinese restaurants to cater to middle- and upper-class white patrons in Chicago, alongside other eateries like Guey Sam and Wee Ying Lo.[30] Moreover, as will be discussed below, the professional and social career of Chin Foin stands as a stark demonstration of the impressive potential benefits that such accommodation in restaurant spaces could offer for some Chinese American immigrants during the Exclusion era.

To be sure, the success of the Mandarin Inn and Chin's other restaurants did not necessarily reflect a coinciding shift in public opinion toward *all* Chinese restaurants and immigrants. On the contrary, his establishments succeeded largely in spite of the persistent negative stereotypes surrounding Chinese restaurants (or, arguably, *because of* their subsequent fetishization by white urbanites). In particular, concerns that the activities taking place in Chinese restaurants threatened the purity of white women who ventured into them remained prevalent into the first decade of the twentieth century, even despite the contemporaneous emergence of the chop suey craze. For example, in 1905, as Chin was preparing to open his second restaurant, this gendered anxiety briefly scandalized his first establishment. When the chef of King Yen Lo eloped with a 19-year-old white girl, the girl's mother identified the corrupting influence of Chinese restaurants, which she deemed "stepping stones from the home to the saloon," as responsible.[31] Though the personal reputation of Chin Foin remained remarkably unaffected by the scandal, its occurrence speaks to the enduring influence of the negative stereotypes surrounding the ethnic establishments that Chin and other Chinese immigrants operated, even as Chinese restaurants became increasingly popular in Chicago. As late as 1910, a *Chicago Daily Tribune* article entitled "Chinese Mix Sin with Chop Suey" alleged that Chinese restaurants remained corrupting venues through which white women were being introduced to "smoking, drinking, and other evils destined to make them slave wives of Chinamen, or drag them down to lives of more open shame."[32] While Chin Foin's restaurants received patronage from men and women alike, this patronage occurred alongside persistent reports of the dangers that Chinese restaurants, and Chinese men in general, posed for white women.

Although fears of Chinese corruption became even more exacerbated in cities across the country following the murder of Elsie Sigel in 1909, such concerns were generally not extended to Chin Foin and his restaurants, in part because he was seen as a member of the "better element" of Chinese immigrants, rather than of the more dangerous, less assimilable class. Throughout the nineteenth century, both natives in China and Chinese immigrants in the United States had been perceived by many (though certainly not all) American and European observers as varying in character and "quality," rather than as universally undesirable. Depictions of Chinese people in locations such as the Chinese Museum in Philadelphia, or in European travel writings in imperial China, portrayed the Chinese as divisible into two classes: the poorer rabble, including migrant laborers from Guangdong, and the wealthier "gentlemen" class.[33] Beyond differences in socioeconomic status, these two "classes" were also seen as distinguished by their diets, refinement, and behavioral proclivities. Such characterizations were also extended to the Chinese in Chicago; indeed, when Elsie Sigel's murderer was believed to have fled to Chicago, the police partially relied on the "better element" of the city's Chinese community in order to apprehend the fugitive.[34] As a result of his growing wealth and obvious Americanized status, Chin Foin had begun to be identified as part of this better element as early as 1905, referred to by Chicago newspapers as a "Chinese gentleman," a "plutocrat," and born to wealth and privilege in China.[35]

Not only was Chin Foin himself seen as a better class of Chinese immigrant but his restaurants, the Mandarin Inn in particular, were generally perceived as distinguishing sites of consumption. Although prices at the Mandarin Inn were advertised as "extremely moderate," there is no indication that the consumers who frequented the restaurant were anything other than middle- and upper-class. In a 1913 article attributing the success of the Mandarin Inn to Chin Foin's management, the restaurant was described as Chicago's first "high-class" Chinese eating-house, patronized by "discriminating Chicago citizens."[36] The nightly musical entertainment provided by an organ player and vocalist, both of whom were listed by name and pedigree in the article, was also described as upscale. Furthermore, in the 1917 publication of *Engelhard's New Guide to Chicago*, a small, cursory guide-book of places of interest for visiting sightseers and residents, all three of Chin Foin's restaurants were included among the six establishments listed under "Chop Suey Restaurants" as worthy of interest. Further still, of these six restaurants, only to the Mandarin Inn was there addended the qualification, "Select clientele."[37] Evidently, Chin's latest restaurant was not only considered distinctive in comparison with other Chinese restaurants in the city, but was also recognized as catering to the privileged and aesthetically discerning of Chicago.

Ultimately, Chin's status as a provider of a socially distinguishing and upscale commodity strengthened his perception as a Chinese immigrant of distinction, facilitating his upward social mobility in Chicago. This social ascent reached a dramatic spatial pinnacle in the fall of 1912, when he moved his family into the Clarence Knight mansion in the South Side.[38] The mansion, located on Calumet Avenue between Thirty-Third and Thirty-Fifth streets, was part of an exclusive and "fashionable" neighborhood reported to house many of the leaders of Chicago society.[39] Naturally, for a Chinese immigrant in racially and residentially segregated Chicago, this move was not easily accomplished. According to the Chinese-American Museum of Chicago, Chin faced bureaucratic challenges in securing the deed for the mansion, as well as the obstinate opposition of the neighborhood to having a non-white family among them.[40] In order to mollify his prospective neighbors, Chin launched a public relations campaign which emphasized his wealth, his reported graduation from Yale, and his ability to maintain the house and grounds. Though his purchase of the Knight mansion was still described by a *Chicago Tribune* article in terms of an invasion, an "incursion" into white space, Chin's status as a "high caste Chinese" seemed to have a significant mitigating effect on his neighbor's concerns, who came to view his presence among them as delightfully cosmopolitan. His wealth and class, and his subsequent ability to maintain the mansion's interior and exterior elegance, ultimately trumped any apprehensions neighborhood residents might have had about Chin's race. As one resident tellingly remarked, "If Chin Foin is a gentleman, we shall welcome him."[41]

It is worth noting here that Chin Foin's move from his family's previous apartment at 500 East 31st Street took place simultaneously as Chinatown was being relocated from the Loop to the South Side, in what is today Armour Square. Between 1911 and 1915, the main Chinese business district, which up to this point had been located along Clark Street between Van Buren and Harrison, shifted south to its current position on Cermak, Archer, and Wentworth Avenue. While a multitude of reasons for the shift have been put forth and debated, it is likely that anti-Chinese sentiment among white Chicagoans significantly contributed to the relocation, which was brought about by property owners in the Loop who forced out Chinese residents and businesses by raising the rents.[42] In 1911, the media framed Chinatown's pending move to Armour Square as a Chinese invasion of an otherwise white neighborhood, and Chinese business owners found it difficult to win over their tentative new neighbors.[43] Chinese Americans spotted in the new location before the move officially took place were likened to reconnaissance scouts for an invading army, highlighting the extent to which Chinese Chicagoans remained relegated to an otherized, alien status. Nonetheless, the move eventually did take place; by as early as 1913, official celebrations such as Chinese New Year were reportedly being held in "the Arthur avenue [sic] Chinatown rather than on Clark Street."[44] As the city's Chinese community was further relegated to the margins, however, Chin Foin was relocating himself still *deeper* into the city's white spaces, purchasing a home on Calumet Avenue and operating a Chinese restaurant on the 400th block of Wabash Avenue. Evidently, Chin and his family were considered a much more distinct and acceptable "type" of Chinese immigrant, one whose presence in white society was not considered threatening or undesirable.

Chin's identity as acceptably high-class and Americanized was likely enhanced more by his association with the Mandarin Inn than with any of his previous establishments. The Mandarin Inn, by August of 1912, was arguably the most accommodating upscale Chinese restaurant established to date in the city of Chicago. Throughout the 1910s, the restaurant remained unmatched by other Chinese eateries in the city in terms of its reputation and prominence. Indeed, that his Americanized status was not *hampered* by his occupation as a Chinese restaurateur in early twentieth-century Chicago, but instead improved by his association with the Mandarin Inn, is a testament to the perceived safety and distinction of the luxury Chinese restaurants of which Chin Foin was a pioneer. Insofar as the restaurant not only expanded his fortune, but also demonstrated his distinct "gentleman" status vis-à-vis other Chinese immigrants and his competence in engaging with middle- and upper-class white American culture, the Mandarin Inn played a significant role in enabling Chin Foin's upward social mobility as an appropriately Americanized member of the "better element" of Chinese America.

In the wake of his financial and social accomplishments, the historical record seems to indicate that Chin Foin's success in the restaurant industry also enabled his children to live relatively comfortable middle-class lives. The historical record indicates that Chin and Yoklund had six children together by 1924.[45] The first-born son, Theodore Chin Foin, went on to receive a degree in Chemical Engineering from the Armour Institute of Technology, a technical school in Chicago which later became the Illinois Institute of Technology. By the mid-1930s, his prospects for obtaining an advanced degree were such that he turned down a job in Kansas City as a Chinese interpreter in order to attend graduate school at the University of Michigan.[46] Chin Foin's daughters, Gladys and Louise, born September 19, 1911, and April 9, 1917, respectively, did not reach Theodore's level of academic achievement, though they were educated. The two sisters attended public school in Chicago until 1925, at which point they were sent to live in China for a number of years as part of their cultural education.[47] In the late 1930s, Gladys married Gung Hsing Wang, a famed Chinese diplomat, and returned to Chicago, where her husband created the Chinese American Civic Council and was responsible for the twentieth-century revitalization of Chicago's Chinatown. Finally, Victor Chin Foin, born December 19, 1918, followed a path very similar to that of his eldest brother. Victor received a bachelor's degree in mechanical engineering from the University of Michigan, Theodore's alma mater, in 1941.[48] Unfortunately, Victor died the next year in New Orleans, at the age of 23.[49] More regrettable still, little is known about Frances, the second-oldest son, and Warren, the youngest, who was born in 1922.

Although Chin Foin almost certainly wanted his children to be educated and enjoy all the benefits of upper-middle-class living, he did not live long enough to see these aspirations come to pass; Chin died prematurely in 1924, leaving the burden of leading their family to his wife, Yoklund. Chin Foin's death was tragic and accidental: on the evening of March 29, he fell down a darkened elevator shaft in his Mandarin Inn restaurant, and died a few hours later at the Post-Graduate hospital.[50] In the months leading up to his death, he had been planning to travel to China with Yoklund and their children. After his death, which was followed in just five years by the onset of the Great Depression, life became particularly burdensome for Yoklund. Much of the family's fortune and businesses were lost in bank foreclosures, and she and the children relocated from their upper-class mansion on Calumet Avenue to a smaller residence on South Grand Boulevard, nearly twenty blocks south. To alleviate their financial troubles, Yoklund found work as a tailor in a Jewish upholstery shop. This financial burden also factored into her decision to send Gladys and Louise to China in 1925. Despite the troubles that befell her in the years following Chin's death, Yoklund proved remarkably resilient, continuing for years to provide for her children and eventually for her grandchildren as well.[51]

Chin Foin's restaurants, as successful as they were in the short term, proved not to be as equally resilient. The property that housed King Yen Lo was razed in the 1910s, although by this time Chin had moved on to establishing and running his more elaborate restaurants.[52] After his death, King Joy Lo and the Mandarin Inn were both transferred to new owners. In 1926 it was announced that King Joy Lo would be remade into an even more luxurious "Oriental" restaurant called the Rialto Gardens, which remained one of the more prominent upscale Chinese restaurants in the city into the 1930s.[53] The Mandarin Inn, meanwhile, fell into the capable hands of Don Joy, another Chinese immigrant who himself was a notable figure in the world of Chicago restaurants. Don Joy played an integral role in Chin Foin's restaurant career from its beginning: he had worked as the chef of King Yen Lo and was an investing partner in King Joy Lo.[54] By 1913, he opened his own upscale Chinese eatery, Joy Yet Lo, on North Clark Street, further establishing his reputation as a provider of Chinese fine dining. However, despite his obvious skill and experience, Don Joy could not indefinitely sustain Chin Foin's greatest restaurant. The Mandarin Inn closed in 1928, only four years after the death of its founder, and was replaced with a nightclub. Ironically, this club went on to be replaced in the 1950s with another Chinese restaurant, Jimmy Wong's, which remained in operation until 1997.[55]

Though his restaurants did not outlive their founder for very long, Chin Foin yet made a noticeable impact on Chicago's restaurant culture in the first decades of the twentieth century. Chin helped pioneer the upscale Chinese restaurant in Chicago, introducing the city to a dining experience that Chicagoans would previously have had to journey to New York or San Francisco to enjoy. His restaurants, especially the Mandarin Inn, likely inspired similar establishments like the Golden Pheasant Inn, which opened in 1916 and became one of the largest Chinese restaurants in Chicago in the 1920s.[56] As is evident in the career of Don Joy and the success of the Golden Pheasant Inn, the luxury Chinese restaurant remained a viable business model and a visible feature of Chicago's restaurant scene for nearly two decades following the establishment of the Mandarin Inn. Through his establishments, Chin Foin demonstrated how to cater Chinese restaurants to appeal both to desires for "Oriental" exoticism and to demands for respectable luxury dining options that catered to middle- and upper-class women and men.

Chin's notable success in creating a brand of upscale Chinese dining establishment that accommodated and appealed to the tastes and demands of Chicago's wealthy classes depended on a number of factors that coincided at that precise moment in American history. The first was the unprecedented popularity Chinese restaurants enjoyed at the turn of the twentieth century following the chop suey craze, and the fetishization of the eateries that had resulted from decades of persistent fears of and negative stereotypes surrounding Chinese immigration. Although Chinese restaurateurs had engaged in various strategies to "reach out" to potential white patrons since the 1840s, such outreach did not by itself bring about a profound shift in the status and appeal of Chinese restaurant cuisine in American culture overall. Such a shift did not begin to occur until the late 1890s and early 1900s, in cities like New York, Philadelphia, and Chicago, largely in response to the changing nature of Chinese immigration to the United States as well as the country's increasing interaction with China, and Asia more broadly, on the world stage. Within two decades of the passage of the Chinese Exclusion Act, and roughly contemporaneously with the emergence of the American empire in the Pacific, Chinese American restaurants had gone from denigrated loci of cultural corruption, immigrant vice, and Asian invasion, to mainstream sites of titillating "Oriental" consumption for white consumers. Many of these consumers were members of the newly moneyed urban middle class, who were also seeking distinctive consumption opportunities to distance themselves from the working class. Chinese fine dining establishments conveniently catered to this demand. Finally, luxury Chinese restaurants like Chin Foin's offered in a safe and respectable form the type of "Oriental" exotic spectacle and experience that many Americans craved in the decades surrounding the turn of the twentieth century. Americans at this time had largely embraced a new "culture of empire," in which white Americans increasingly turned to visual spectacles that played on Orientalist concepts of cultural difference and exoticism, in venues like the World's Columbian Exposition's Midway Plaisance, as a means of confirming their own position of relative superiority and establishing greater order in their lives. Establishments like the Mandarin Inn, helmed by a "high caste Chinese" like Chin, made such "Oriental" spectacles and exotic delights respectable for middle- and upper-class white consumers.

The case study of Chin Foin's restaurants and his move into the mansion on Calumet Avenue also demonstrates the narrow pathway available to certain Chinese American immigrants to achieve upward social mobility during the Exclusion era. Chin was able to move into an exclusive, mostly white neighborhood because he rendered himself an "acceptable" Chinese immigrant to his white neighbors. He accomplished this in large part through his restaurants, which enabled him to amass a great deal of wealth in one of the few industries Chinese immigrants could safely work in, as well as to further demonstrate his distinct status in contradistinction to other, less desirable Chinese immigrants by crafting luxurious "Oriental" restaurant spaces that stood out in sharp contrast to other, more low-class Chinese restaurants of the era. Furthermore, his last and most renowned restaurant, the Mandarin Inn, allowed him to turn his Chinese ethnicity (otherwise a stigma in most other arenas of American society at the time) to his advantage by positioning himself as a culturally competent insider who could provide other members of the cultural high classes access to a safer, more luxurious version of the "Oriental" culture Americans had become so fascinated with at the turn of the twentieth century.

Though the restaurant industry was not the only avenue for Chinese immigrants to become wealthy or prove their status, it was perhaps the most convenient means to do so, given Chinese restaurants' surge in popularity during this period and their ability to render "Chineseness" into a form of cultural capital rather than a marker of racial inferiority. Through crafting a brand of successful restaurant spaces that rendered Chinese culture, embodied in restaurant food and luxurious décor, safely consumable for middle- and upper-class white patrons, Chin Foin demonstrated to a city-wide audience of restaurant-goers his membership in the "better element" of Chicago's Chinese population, and was thus able to better facilitate his family's access to spaces in American society otherwise barred to Chinese immigrants. In this way, the story of Chin Foin's Chinese restaurants represents a poignant and illuminating chapter in the history of Chinese American immigration during the Exclusion era, as well as that of American restaurant culture.

Key Terms

Orientalism: According to Edward Said, "a style of thought based upon an ontological and epistemological distinction made between 'the Orient' and (most of the time) 'the Occident.'"[57]

Chinese exclusion: The desired prohibition on the immigration and/or entry of Chinese laborers and women into the United States, as well as the barring of Chinese Americans from enjoying the full rights and privileges of citizenship, based on racial animus.

Upscale: Relatively expensive and designed to cater and appeal to affluent and distinguished customers.

Discussion Questions

1. What does Chin Foin's experience tell us about the nature of racial identity in the United States? Why was his class identity seemingly more important than his racial identity?
2. Would a Chinese immigrant like Chin Foin have been able to achieve a similar feat of upward social mobility by establishing and operating other kinds of businesses (e.g. laundries)? Why or why not?

3. Chinese food is currently the most popular "ethnic cuisine" in the United States. What does this case study possibly reveal about why Chinese restaurants have become so popular among Americans? Why is the history of these establishments so different from that of other immigrant-operated eateries?

Notes

1 "Testimony of Chin F. Foin," 1906, Chinese Exclusion Case Files, Record Group 85, National Archives and Records Administration—Great Lakes Region; "Application for Preinvestigation of Mercantile Status of Chin Foin," 1924, Chinese Exclusion Case Files, Record Group 85, National Archives and Records Administration—Great Lakes Region.

2 United States Census Office, *Compendium of the Eleventh Census* (Washington, DC: Government Printing Office, 1892).

3 "Testimony of Chin F. Foin."

4 "Testimony of Chin F. Foin"; "Testimony of Chin Yun Quay," 1906, Chinese Exclusion Case Files, Record Group 85, National Archives and Records Administration—Great Lakes Region.

5 "Chop Suey Fad Grows," *Chicago Tribune*, July 19, 1903; "Georgia Belle Marries Rich Chinese Merchant," *Oakland Tribune*, March 16, 1907.

6 Adam McKeown, *Chinese Migrant Networks and Cultural Change: Peru, Chicago, and Hawaii, 1900–1936* (Chicago and London: The University of Chicago Press, 2001), 194–205; Huping Ling, *Chinese Chicago: Race, Transnational Migration, and Community since 1870* (Stanford, California: Stanford University Press, 2012), 121.

7. Andrew Coe, *Chop Suey: A Cultural History of Chinese Food in the United States* (New York: Oxford University Press, 2009).

8 "Fair Chinese Bride Wears American Clothes and Hats," *The Inter Ocean*, May 19, 1904.

9 "Fair Chinese Bride Wears American Clothes and Hats."

10 "Fair Chinese Bride Wears American Clothes and Hats."

11 "Chinese Baby Is Guest of Honor at Banquet of Chicago Celestials," *The Inter Ocean*, November 7, 1907.

12 "Chinese Envoy Is Coming for Christening of Baby," *Chicago Daily Tribune*, November 2, 1907.

13 "King Joy Lo Advertisement," *The Inter Ocean*, December 20, 1906; "King Joy Lo: The Finest Chinese-American Restaurant in the World," *The Chicago Daily Tribune*, December 22, 1906.

14 "King Joy Lo Mandarin Restaurant Menu," n.d., Digital Collections, Los Angeles Public Library.

15 "King Joy Lo: The Finest Chinese-American Restaurant in the World."

16 "King Joy Lo: The Finest Chinese-American Restaurant in the World."

17 McKeown, *Chinese Migrant Networks and Cultural Change: Peru, Chicago, and Hawaii, 1900–1936*, 205.

18 McKeown, 205.

19 "Mandarin Inn Grand Opening Tonight," *Chicago Daily Tribune*, August 16, 1911.

20 "Mandarin Inn Grand Opening Tonight."

21 Mandarin Inn Advertisement, *The Chicago Daily Tribune*, December 31, 1912.

22 "Mandarin Inn Grand Opening Tonight."

23 "Mandarin Inn Advertisement"; "Mandarin Inn Grand Opening Tonight."

24 "Mandarin Inn Grand Opening Tonight."

25 "Mandarin Inn Grand Opening Tonight."

26 Erica J. Peters, "A Path to Acceptance: Promoting Chinese Restaurants in San Francisco, 1849–1919," *Southern California Quarterly* 97, no. 1 (2015): 5–6.

27 Coe, *Chop Suey*, 160–72.

28 Anne Mendelson, *Chow Chop Suey: Food and the Chinese American Journey* (New York: Columbia University Press, 2016), xvi–xix.

29 Peters, "A Path to Acceptance: Promoting Chinese Restaurants in San Francisco, 1849–1919," 16–17; Coe, *Chop Suey*, 159.

30 Ling, *Chinese Chicago*, 72–73.

31 "Two Girls Wed Chinamen," *The Inter Ocean*, September 23, 1905.

32 "Chinese Mix Sin with Chop Suey," *Chicago Daily Tribune*, March 27, 1910.

33 *"Ten Thousand Chinese Things": A Descriptive Catalogue of the Chinese Collection in Philadelphia* (Philadelphia, 1839); Robert Fortune, *A Residence Among the Chinese: Island, On the Coast, and at Sea* (London: John Murray, Albemarle Street, 1857).

34 "Expect to Arrest Sigel Girl Slayer in Chicago," *The Inter Ocean*, June 20, 1909.

35 "Randolph Street Lease," *The Inter Ocean*, December 24, 1905; "Fair Chinese Bride Wears American Clothes and Hats"; "Mandarin Inn Success Tribute to Management," *The Inter Ocean*, December 28, 1913.

36 "Mandarin Inn Success Tribute to Management."

37 *Engelhard's New Guide to Chicago: Designed for the Use Both of Visitors and Residents* (Chicago: G.P. Engelhard and Co., 1917), 63.

38 Pierre Bourdieu, *Distinction: A Social Critique of the Judgement of Taste* (Harvard University Press, 1984), 1–2.

39 "Chinese Boniface Buys Old Mansion in Society Center," *The Inter Ocean*, August 28, 1912.

40 "1912: Chin Foin Wins a Civil Rights Battle," Chinese-American Museum of Chicago, n.d., www.ccamuseum.org/index.php/en/research/research-1900-1949/117-1912-chin-foin-wins-a-civil-rights-battle.

41 "Chinese Family Takes a Fine Home," *The Chicago Tribune*, August 28, 1912.

42 Ling, *Chinese Chicago*, 51.

43 "Chinatown Plans to Move Two Miles to the South," *Chicago Tribune*, November 24, 1911.

44 "Chinese Keep New Year's," *Chicago Tribune*, February 6, 1913.

45 The couple may have had a seventh child, a son, who died before this time, though the historical record is not clear on this point.

46 *General Register*, vol. 2 (Ann Arbor, Michigan: University of Michigan, 1936), 123; "Letter to the District Director, United States Immigration Service," September 18, 1935, Chinese Exclusion Case Files, Record Group 85, National Archives and Records Administration—Great Lakes Region.

47 "Application for Preinvestigation of Citizenship Status of Louise Foin Chin," February 4, 1924, Chinese Exclusion Case Files, Record Group 85, National Archives and Records Administration—Great Lakes Region; "Application for Preinvestigation of Citizenship Status of Gladys Foin Chin," February 4, 1924, Chinese Exclusion Case Files, Record Group 85, National Archives and Records Administration—Great Lakes Region; Adrienne Drell, ed., *20th Century Chicago: 100 Years, 100 Voices* (Chicago: Sports Publishing LLC, 2000), 37.

48 *The Michigan Alumnus*, vol. 49 (Ann Arbor, Michigan: University of Michigan Libraries, 1942), 47.

49 Chin Foin had two other children, Warren and Francis, though details of their lives are not as well-known as those of Chin's other children.

50 "Rich Chinese Dies," *Chicago Tribune*, March 30, 1924.

51 Ling, *Chinese Chicago*, 121.

52 "Anatomy of a Restaurateur: Chin Foin," *Restaurant-Ing through History* (blog), November 1, 2011, https://restaurant-ingthroughhistory.com/2011/11/01/anatomy-of-a-restaurateur-chin-foin/.

53 "King Joy Lo Cafe to Be Remade into 'Rialto Gardens,'" *Chicago Daily Tribune*, May 9, 1926.

54 *The University of Chicago Magazine*, vol. 1 (University of Chicago, Alumni Association, 1908), 50; "Randolph Street Lease."

55 Charles A. Sengstock, *That Toddlin' Town: Chicago's White Dance Bands and Orchestras, 1900–1950* (Urbana: University of Illinois Press, 2004), 127.
56 Ling, *Chinese Chicago*, 74.
5/ Edward W. Said, *Orientalism* (New York: Vintage, 1979), 10.

References

"1912: Chin Foin Wins a Civil Rights Battle." Chinese-American Museum of Chicago, n.d. www.ccamuseum.org/index.php/en/research/research-1900-1949/117-1912-chin-foin-wins-a-civil-rights-battle.

"Anatomy of a Restaurateur: Chin Foin." *Restaurant-Ing through History* (blog), November 1, 2011. https://restaurant-ingthroughhistory.com/2011/11/01/anatomy-of-a-restaurateur-chin-foin/.

"Application for Preinvestigation of Citizenship Status of Gladys Foin Chin," February 4, 1924. Chinese Exclusion Case Files, Record Group 85. National Archives and Records Administration—Great Lakes Region.

"Application for Preinvestigation of Citizenship Status of Louise Foin Chin," February 4, 1924. Chinese Exclusion Case Files, Record Group 85. National Archives and Records Administration—Great Lakes Region.

"Application for Preinvestigation of Mercantile Status of Chin Foin," 1924. Chinese Exclusion Case Files, Record Group 85. National Archives and Records Administration—Great Lakes Region.

Bourdieu, Pierre. *Distinction: A Social Critique of the Judgement of Taste.* Harvard University Press, 1984.

"Chinatown Plans to Move Two Miles to the South." *Chicago Tribune*, November 24, 1911.

"Chinese Baby Is Guest of Honor at Banquet of Chicago Celestials." *The Inter Ocean*, November 7, 1907.

"Chinese Boniface Buys Old Mansion in Society Center." *The Inter Ocean*. August 28, 1912.

"Chinese Envoy Is Coming for Christening of Baby." *Chicago Daily Tribune*, November 2, 1907.

"Chinese Family Takes a Fine Home." *The Chicago Tribune*. August 28, 1912.

"Chinese Keep New Year's." *Chicago Tribune*, February 6, 1913.

"Chinese Mix Sin with Chop Suey." *Chicago Daily Tribune*, March 27, 1910.

"Chop Suey Fad Grows." *Chicago Tribune*. July 19, 1903.

Coe, Andrew. *Chop Suey: A Cultural History of Chinese Food in the United States.* New York: Oxford University Press, 2009.

Drell, Adrienne, ed. *20th Century Chicago: 100 Years, 100 Voices.* Chicago: Sports Publishing LLC, 2000.

Engelhard's New Guide to Chicago: Designed for the Use Both of Visitors and Residents. Chicago: G.P. Engelhard and Co., 1917.

"Expect to Arrest Sigel Girl Slayer in Chicago." *The Inter Ocean*. June 20, 1909.

"Fair Chinese Bride Wears American Clothes and Hats." *The Inter Ocean*, May 19, 1904.

Fortune, Robert. *A Residence Among the Chinese: Island, On the Coast, and at Sea.* London: John Murray, Albemarle Street, 1857.

General Register. Vol. 2. Ann Arbor, Michigan: University of Michigan, 1936.

"Georgia Belle Marries Rich Chinese Merchant." *Oakland Tribune*, March 16, 1907.

"King Joy Lo Advertisement." *The Inter Ocean*. December 20, 1906.

"King Joy Lo Cafe to Be Remade into 'Rialto Gardens.'" *Chicago Daily Tribune*. May 9, 1926.

"King Joy Lo Mandarin Restaurant Menu," n.d. Digital Collections. Los Angeles Public Library.

"King Joy Lo: The Finest Chinese-American Restaurant in the World." *The Chicago Daily Tribune*, December 22, 1906.

"Letter to the District Director, United States Immigration Service," September 18, 1935. Chinese Exclusion Case Files, Record Group 85. National Archives and Records Administration—Great Lakes Region.

Ling, Huping. *Chinese Chicago: Race, Transnational Migration, and Community since 1870*. Stanford, California: Stanford University Press, 2012.

"Mandarin Inn Advertisement." *The Chicago Daily Tribune*. December 31, 1912.

"Mandarin Inn Grand Opening Tonight." *Chicago Daily Tribune*, August 16, 1911.

"Mandarin Inn Success Tribute to Management." *The Inter Ocean*. December 28, 1913.

McKeown, Adam. *Chinese Migrant Networks and Cultural Change: Peru, Chicago, and Hawaii, 1900–1936*. Chicago and London: The University of Chicago Press, 2001.

Mendelson, Anne. *Chow Chop Suey: Food and the Chinese American Journey*. New York: Columbia University Press, 2016.

Peters, Erica J. "A Path to Acceptance: Promoting Chinese Restaurants in San Francisco, 1849–1919." *Southern California Quarterly* 97, no. 1 (2015): 5–28.

"Randolph Street Lease." *The Inter Ocean*, December 24, 1905.

"Rich Chinese Dies." *Chicago Tribune*. March 30, 1924.

Said, Edward W. *Orientalism*. New York: Vintage, 1979.

Sengstock, Charles A. *That Toddlin' Town: Chicago's White Dance Bands and Orchestras, 1900–1950*. Urbana: University of Illinois Press, 2004.

"Ten Thousand Chinese Things": A Descriptive Catalogue of the Chinese Collection in Philadelphia. Philadelphia, 1839.

"Testimony of Chin F. Foin," 1906. Chinese Exclusion Case Files, Record Group 85. National Archives and Records Administration—Great Lakes Region.

"Testimony of Chin Yun Quay," 1906. Chinese Exclusion Case Files, Record Group 85. National Archives and Records Administration—Great Lakes Region.

The Michigan Alumnus. Vol. 49. Ann Arbor, Michigan: University of Michigan Libraries, 1942.

The University of Chicago Magazine. Vol. 1. University of Chicago, Alumni Association, 1908.

"Two Girls Wed Chinamen." *The Inter Ocean*. September 23, 1905.

United States Census Office. *Compendium of the Eleventh Census*. Washington, DC: Government Printing Office, 1892.

10

CHOP SUEY, P.F. CHANG'S, AND CHINESE FOOD IN AMERICA

Haiming Liu

With more than 40,000 Chinese restaurants in the United States, Chinese food is an important component of the American restaurant market. The two largest, most visible Chinese restaurants are Panda Express and P.F. Chang's China Bistro. Panda Express was founded in 1983 as a fast-food chain with about 2,000 stores by 2018, while P.F. Chang's was established in 1993 as a full service, sit-down Chinese restaurant with 210 stores in the same year. Neither of them has stores locating in or close to Chinese concentrated neighborhoods or communities. Both catered mostly to mainstream American customers and claimed to offer real Chinese food, as most other Chinese restaurants did. Their rapid expansion marked an important change in the American restaurant market. Chop suey as Americanized Chinese food lost its historical appeal. Chinese restaurants in America began to offer real Chinese food to both Chinese and non-Chinese customers. The dominant success of P.F. Chang's in the Chinese restaurant business is a mixed blessing for Chinese Americans. (In this chapter, I will focus on P.F. Chang's only as Panda deserves another research study.) As corporate business, it has significantly changed the image of Chinese food in America. Different from chop suey houses, however, P.F. Chang's is not part of Chinese American food culture. This chapter documents the significance of chop suey in American food history and analyzes the meaning of P.F. Chang's in the Chinese restaurant business.

Chop Suey as Chinese American Food

Chinese immigrants were pioneers in the food business in California. Founded in 1849, Canton Restaurant was one of the earliest fine dining restaurants in San Francisco catering to customers of all nationalities and classes but the growth of Chinese restaurants was slow. In the 1870s, San Francisco had a thriving restaurant business. There were "baked beans garnished with crispy pork" from New

England, Indian-meal pudding, the corn pone of Virginia, the chicken gumbo of New Orleans, and the "side-meat" of Missouri, or New York's chicken pie.[1] By 1878, there were only 11 Chinese restaurants in the city. The number grew to 28 in 1881 but dropped again to 14 in 1882 when the Chinese Exclusion Act was passed.[2] Chinese restaurants did not thrive in America until after 1900 when the chop suey meal became popular.

On January 29, 1900, *The New York Times* reported: "Judging from the outbreak of Chinese restaurants all over town, the city has gone 'chop-suey' mad."[3] When Liang Qichao, a reformist leader and a famous Chinese intellectual, visited the United States in 1903, he was surprised to notice that there were more than 400 chop suey houses in New York alone.[4] In the early 1900s, New York City was experiencing an explosive growth of chop suey houses. According to the 1903 *New York Times* article, the first Chinese who opened a chop suey house outside of Chinatown was a Chinese man named "Boston." He closed his restaurant at Doyer Street in Chinatown and opened a new one on Third Avenue and Rivington Street. "He did so well that soon many other Chinese followed him."[5] Charley Boston, also known as Lee Quong June (or Li Quen Chong), was a wealthy Americanized Chinese merchant, and a leader of the famous On Leong Tong in New York's Chinatown.[6] Boston and his followers made a breakthrough in American restaurant history. Chop suey houses moved out of Chinatown and grew rapidly across America as a popular ethnic food.

Reflecting his impression of New York upon arrival in the 1910s, a Jewish immigrant said: "I felt about Chinese restaurants the same way I did about the Metropolitan Museum of Art—they were the two most strange and fascinating places my parents took me to, and I loved them both."[7] When millions of Jewish immigrants landed in America, chop suey was attractive to many of them because it was an iconic food of New York City. In 1929, American artist Edward Hopper accomplished his masterpiece *Chop Suey* after his frequent patronage of a chop suey house in Columbus Circle, Manhattan. In the forefront of his painting, two fashionable women sit, eying each other in silence. On the table is a purple, square-shaped clay teapot and a greenish blue porcelain bowl. Behind them is a man sitting in the shadows looking down with a cigarette. Opposite him is a young woman looking at him with inquiring eyes. With three of the customers being women, the painting indicated that restaurants were no longer a man's world. Of Hopper's works on American urban life, *Chop Suey* was his most iconic painting, which was sold at a record-breaking price of $29 million at a Christie's auction in November 2018.

Chop suey houses spread from New York to New Jersey, Connecticut, Long Island, Boston, and other cities and states on the East Coast, as well as to the Midwestern and Western United States. In 1900, Chicago had only one Chinese restaurant. By 1905, Chicago had 40 Chinese restaurants, and only five were in Chinatown. In 1915, the number grew to 118 and only six or seven of them were in Chinatown.[8] Between 1929 and 1949, the number of Chinese restaurants in San Francisco increased from 78 to 146.[9] Most of them offered chop suey, egg foo yong, and chow mein. A few served stir-fried dishes, different types of noodles, and Cantonese dim sum food. Their restaurant names could be Wong Coffee House, Lee Noodle Shop, or Peking Restaurant, but they were all chop suey houses in the eyes of American customers. They all had chop suey business signs or banners outside. Most of them located outside of Chinatown. Before 1900, there were only a couple of Chinese restaurants in Los Angeles Chinatown frequented almost exclusively by Chinese customers. In 1910, the number grew to fifteen.[10] Most of them offered chop suey meals and located outside of Chinatown. Interestingly the largest Chinese restaurant in Los Angeles in the 1920s was Crown Chop Suey Parlor in Pasadena owned by Mr. Kawagoye, a Japanese immigrant.[11]

When chop suey house spread across America, restaurant operation became a major occupation for Chinese immigrants. For more than six decades, the chop suey meal was a popular ethnic food in America. In 1920, there were as many Chinese working in the restaurant business as in the laundry business. According to Ching Chao Wu, while 11,534 Chinese were laundrymen, 6,943 were cooks, 2,766 were waiters, and 1,688 were managers.[12] In the 1930s, Chinese in Fall River, Massachusetts placed fried chow main in between a hamburger-sized bun and created the famous chow mein sandwich. Since then, many local restaurants, Chinese and non-Chinese, in southeastern Massachusetts served hot chow mein sandwiches with brown gravy. The St. Paul sandwich in St. Louis, Missouri was another Chinese creation. The Wonder bread had deep-fried egg foo yong patty as the key component slathered with mayonnaise, optional pickle, sliced tomato, and icy lettuce. The egg foo yong patty consisted of whipped eggs, bean sprouts, and minced white onions. In a hybridized format, the chow mein sandwich and the St. Paul sandwich became popular local American restaurant food. In the late 1940s, there were about 4,300 Chinese restaurants in the mainland United States and 7 percent of the American population frequented them. In the 1950s, the number of Chinese restaurants increased to 4,500 with over 20 percent of Americans frequenting them. In 1959, New York City alone had about 750 Chinese restaurants.[13] Chop suey houses was synonymous with Chinese restaurants in America.

What Chinese immigrants created in chop suey was not a Chinese delicacy but a resilient ethnic food in America. Based on a humble dish of rural origin, Chinese immigrants invented a series of fast-food types of American meals like chicken chop suey, beef chop suey, pork chop suey, fish chop suey, vegetable chop suey, chow mein, egg foo yong, paper-wrapped chicken, and many others. Most chop suey houses were individually owned small businesses. They provided almost standardized chop suey meals. Their similar menu was a reflection of Chinese restaurant operators' understanding of the American restaurant market at that time rather than a culinary consideration. They knew that their food had to satisfy both American customers' taste and their social expectations of Chinese cuisine. The niche they had in the American restaurant market was not a fine dining opportunity but a low-end ethnic meal choice. Chop suey was the right commodity because it was a cheap, tasty, and Americanized Chinese food. Its flavor and culinary format met American customers' expectation of Chinese cuisine.

With Six You Get Eggroll was a popular movie in 1968. It had nothing to do with Chinese but was a family comedy about a remarried middle-aged white couple with four children. Its title reflected American customers' expectation of Chinese restaurants. "Just pick up the kids from school, head over to the local Chinatown and order the Number 2 Special."[14] The Special included large portions of chop suey, egg foo yong, moo goo gai pan, and egg drop soup. In the 1960s, a dinner for a family of six at a Chinese restaurant cost no more than 15 dollars. American customers were not interested in authentic or high-end Chinese cuisine.

Chop suey houses had such fans of the popular food as President Eisenhower as an individual and American Jews as a collective. When Dwight D. Eisenhower was a major and stationed in Washington D.C. in the 1930s, he was a regular customer with his wife and young son at the Sun Chop Suey Restaurant on Columbia Road owned by Jew Gam On. World War II interrupted his dining habit for a few years. When he became the President of the United States from 1953 to 1961, he resumed his patronage. His favorite food was chicken chop suey with a simple request—be good and hot.[15] By then chop suey was no longer an exotic "Oriental" food but a common restaurant meal that many Americans liked. American Jews were the most enthusiastic and faithful customers of Chinese food as a collective. Similar to other Americans, early Jewish immigrants liked Chinese food for its flavor and modest price. Different from other American customers, they discovered a deeper meaning in consuming Chinese food and incorporated it into their own culture. In their view, the chop suey house was part of the metropolitan New York life. Through Chinese food, they became more adapted to American urban life. For many American Jews, eating Chinese was their Christmas dinner, their childhood memory, and their family tradition. The Jewish humorist Molly Katz once wrote: "Never mind chicken soup; when Jews need comfort, solace, or medicinal nourishment, we dive for Moo Shu Pork."[16]

Changes in the 1970s and 1980s

In 1962, Cecelia Chiang opened her Mandarin Restaurant on Polk Street in San Francisco's Chinatown. Born in Beijing and raised in Shanghai, she had tasted many well-known Chinese dishes. She wanted to offer authentic Chinese food in America. Her menu listed over 300 items, including sizzling rice soup, smoked tea duck, beggar's chicken, and Mongolian lamb. During the first year and a half, the Mandarin Restaurant attracted little business. In the 1960s, Cecelia Chiang was probably the only restaurateur in San Francisco to serve authentic Chinese cuisine.[17] She was losing money and close to bankruptcy. Johnny Kan of the famous Kan's Restaurant in Chinatown kindly advised: "Change your cooking style. People are happy with chop suey. Besides, nobody has even heard of pot-stickers." Chiang's sister even suggested that she close the restaurant.[18] Offering real Chinese food by a Chinese restaurateur seemed rare and strange in San Francisco where Chinese had come as early as 1849.

At a point when Chiang was beginning to feel hopeless and desperate, Herb Caen, a Pulitzer Prize-winning columnist for the *San Francisco Chronicle*, dropped by and tasted her food. A few days later Caen declared his discovery of real Chinese food in the Mandarin Restaurant. Chiang immediately received hundreds of phone calls for reservations. Her business took off overnight. Eight years later, the Mandarin Restaurant moved out of Chinatown to Ghirardelli Square and became a high-end restaurant with 300 seats. On its grand opening, a $250 per person dinner banquet was completely sold out.[19] No Chinese restaurant in America had ever charged that much. The Mandarin's golden days began with the banquet. Businessmen, celebrities, tourists, and middle-class families all came to eat Chiang's authentic Chinese food. Chiang's success was a bittersweet story. Mainstream American customers frequented her restaurant in droves only after Caen's endorsement. The previously slow business was obviously not a flavor or culinary issue. The customers had no problems accepting Chiang's dishes but needed to be assured by their own food and cultural critics that it was all right to eat real Chinese food.

In 1975, Chiang opened another Mandarin Restaurant in Beverly Hills, Southern California. Her son, Philip Chiang, joined her and then took over the management. Philip faced similar attitudes of American customers when he offered authentic Chinese food. When he stopped using ketchup and decreased the use of starch in order to bring out a more authentic flavor of his popular dish, Sweet-and-Sour pork, his customers became panicked and phoned him, saying: "What is going on here? We liked it the way it was!" When he replaced Western-style broccoli with Chinese broccoli, or string beans with Chinese long beans, customers would stop him and complain. They reminded him: "Well, you're a Chinese restaurant right? You're supposed to have chow mein."[20] Philip was fighting many losing battles when offering authentic Chinese dishes. In 1988, he rebuilt his restaurant after a fire hazard. In the new restaurant with an open kitchen, customers could watch Peking duck pulled from the oven, with its skin brown, crispy and delectable.[21]

Paul Fleming, owner of four Ruth's Chris Steak House stores, discovered Philip's restaurant during a business trip. Like Herb Caen, he enjoyed real Chinese food and was impressed by Chiang's restaurant. He wanted to establish a high-end chain restaurant featuring authentic Chinese food for mainstream customers. Chiang was a good partner. From steakhouse to Chinese restaurant was quite a change of business interest. As a restaurateur, Fleming noticed changes taking place in the Chinese restaurant business in the 1970s and 1980s due to the influx of Chinese immigrants. After the Immigration and Nationality Act of 1965, waves of Chinese immigrants entered America from Taiwan, Hong Kong, and mainland China. New York and California attracted Chinese immigrants most. The number of Chinese restaurants rapidly grew in New York, California, and other metropolitan regions. By the 1980s, ethnic restaurants constituted 10 percent of all restaurants in the United States; Chinese, Italian, and Mexican represented 70 percent of them; and Chinese restaurants made 30 percent of the total number of ethnic restaurants in the United States.[22]

On July 27, 1973, *The New York Times* carried a huge advertisement on two newly opened Hunan restaurants; one was "supervised" by Uncle Peng and the other by Uncle Tai. Both were celebrated chefs in Taiwan. While Peng's was located at 219 East 44th Street, Tai's was at 1059 3rd Avenue.[23] In the 1970s, many Hunan or Sichuan flavored Chinese restaurants appeared in New York. In 1974, ABC news station in New York did a segment on Peng Garden restaurant. Reporter Bob Lape visited Chef Peng in the kitchen and video-taped how he cooked General Tso's chicken, the most famous dish in Hunan cuisine in Taiwan. After the segment ran, about 1,500 people wrote in and asked for the recipe.[24] Peng was a master chef specializing in Hunan cuisine. After he arrived in Taiwan from mainland China, he allegedly cooked for the Nationalist leader Chiang Kai-shek. In 1955, Peng created his iconic dish called General Tso's chicken.[25] His Hunan Garden was one of the most famous restaurants in Taipei. The city had several hundred Huanan restaurants. They all featured General Tso's chicken.

When Peng opened his Hunan Garden in New York, other Taiwanese immigrants followed suit. Historian Lynn Pan noticed that many Hunan restaurants appeared in the 1970s and "there would have been fewer good Hunanese restaurants if there had been fewer immigrants from Taiwan, and there would certainly have been no Cuban-Chinese restaurants at all if there hadn't been a wave of migration of Chinese from Cuba."[26] Food historian Michael Luo observed that in the 1970s: "Hunan and Sichuan restaurants in New York influenced the taste of the whole country. Dishes like General Tso's chicken and crispy orange beef caught on everywhere."[27] General Tso's chicken replaced chop suey as the most famous Chinese dish. *New York Times* food critic Mimi Sheraton wrote in 1977: "For the last several years one of our very best Chinese restaurants has been Hunan, featuring the hot, spicy and gingery cuisine of the province for which it is named."[28] In November 1980, *The New York Times* reported: "In the last year, more than a half-dozen Chinese restaurants have opened in southern Westchester, and every one has to be commendable in one way or another."[29] In July 1981, *The New York Times* reported again:

> As recently as three years ago, there were few, if any, Hunan-style Chinese restaurants in Connecticut. Since then, at least three or four have sprung up in Fairfield County alone. This peppery and oily style of Chinese cooking has caught on, as has its near neighbor Sichuan. The newest Hunan restaurant is Hunan Garden.[30]

In New York City, the number of Chinese restaurants in 1958 was 304. Thirty years later, it grew to nearly 800.[31]

Since the late 1980s, San Gabriel Valley in Southern California has become a Chinese congregated area and restaurant business, the most visible ethnic enterprise by post-1965 Chinese immigrants. Before 1965, Monterey Park, a suburban city close to Los Angeles Chinatown, had only one Chinese restaurant. In 1983, the number of Chinese restaurants in Monterey Park grew to 40 after Chinese moved into the city.[32] Four years later, Chinese restaurants grew to 60, representing

75 percent of the dining business in the city.[33] Harbor Village and Ocean Star, located on Atlantic Boulevard, became two of the largest city revenue generators in Monterey Park. Ocean Star, owned by Robert Y. Lee, had 800 seats and was one of the biggest Chinese restaurants in San Gabriel Valley, Southern California.[34] By 1990, the Chinese population in Southern California rose to 324,274, making San Gabriel Valley the largest Chinese congregated area in the nation. By 2000, the Chinese population in Southern California increased to 523,597.[35] About 50 percent of them congregated in the San Gabriel Valley and dispersed into cities like Alhambra, Rosemead, San Marino, South Pasadena, San Gabriel, Arcadia, and all the way east to West Covina, Hacienda Heights, Rowland Heights, Diamond Bar, and Walnut. The most visible dining destination, however, is not a single city but Valley Boulevard, which goes through Alhambra, San Gabriel, and Rosemead.

> The boulevard—a bustling swath of Asian supermarkets, about 100 Asian restaurants and scores of small shops selling products as varied as woodsilk towels and chrysanthemum tea—is not only a regional shopping district, but also has put San Gabriel on the international destination map.[36]

In 2004, as a home to over 240,000 Chinese residents, San Gabriel Valley had more than 2,000 Chinese restaurants.[37]

Most Chinese restaurants were small, family-owned business and catered to mostly Chinese clients. As sociologist Min Zhou observed, 90 percent of customers of Chinese restaurants in New York were Chinese. Chinese customers, rich or middle-class, frequented Chinese restaurants "to feel the cultural atmosphere associated with their home country."[38] The rapid growth of Chinese restaurants meant more options for Chinese customers because different Chinese restaurants could feature different regional flavors and offer their own special dishes. Food items on their menu could be a dim sum dish for $1 or a bird's nest soup for $75 or more. With prices ranging from 50 cents to 50 dollars per dish for a dinner, proprietors tried to maximize customer traffic flow. Sometimes, cutthroat competition affected food quality and price. Many Chinese restaurants in Chinese congregated areas had mediocre furniture and filthy restrooms while only a few were stylish and elegant. Their selling strategy was not a pleasant dining environment but special flavored dishes and competitively priced food.

P.F. Chang's in the American Restaurant Market

While hundreds of Chinese restaurants appeared in New York in the 1970s and in Southern California in the 1980s, many middle-class American customers did not know where to go when they wanted to eat real Chinese food. Fleming noticed an opportunity for high-end Chinese restaurant in the American food market and wanted to grab it. As an executive of P.F. Chang's acknowledged, "We looked at the restaurant universe and Chinese wasn't represented. . . . There were only independent operators. The whole country was available for the concept."[39] Dining out in a Chinese restaurant was a different experience between a Chinese customer and a non-Chinese customer. Eating in a Chinese restaurant made Chinese customers feel at home especially if it served real Chinese food. For non-Chinese customers, Chinese food was just one of their dining out options in America. A high-end restaurant was not just a place for food but also a destination for social gathering. When middle-class Americans ate in a full-service restaurant, it was often for a business lunch, a family event, a weekend retreat, or a romantic date. Middle-class Americans expected a similar dining environment when they ate in a full-service Chinese restaurant. They also needed waiters to explain dishes in fluent English. Fleming's vision was to establish a Chinese restaurant that served American customers who were culturally different from Chinese customers and had different expectations.

In 1993, Fleming opened his first P.F. Chang's China Bistro in the Fashion Square shopping center in Scottsdale, Arizona and claimed to offer authentic Chinese food. Fleming insisted that places like Phoenix would be a good gauge of Chinese food for American customers.[40] "P.F." stood for Paul Fleming and "Chang" for Chiang. P.F. Chang's China Bistro is an obvious Chinese restaurant name for American customers. It was an obvious Chinese restaurant name. Philip purposely changed "Chiang" into "Chang," a more contemporary way of the Romanization of his last name.[41] Cecilia, along with Barbara Tropp, created the menu for P.F. Chang's. Tropp was a restaurateur and author of *The Modern Art of Chinese Cooking*, which won the prestigious Julia Child Award for Best International Cookbook.[42] P.F. Chang's claimed to feature five Chinese regional cuisines: Guangdong, Hunan, Mongolian, Shanghai, and Sichuan. As early Chinese immigrants came from Guangdong, Cantonese cuisine had more influence in America than any other Chinese flavors. Brought over by immigrants from Taiwan, Hunan cuisine was also popular from the 1970s. Mongolian lamb and some Shanghai dishes were long-term house specials on the Mandarin's menu. "We're constantly confirming that we're keeping it as close to what they're doing in China as possible," said, P.F. Chang's executive chef, Paul Muller. Initially, Muller modified some traditional Chinese dishes but then decided to prepare his food as closely to what he saw and learned in China. He observed that some of his patrons frequently commented: "This is way too salty. This is way too oily."[43] Yet they kept coming back. Like what happened to Cecilia Chiang's Mandarin restaurant after Caen's endorsement, mainstream American customers had no difficulty accepting real Chinese dishes at P.F. Chang's, a corporate restaurant business.

P.F. Chang's as a Corporate Business

Paul Fleming's business vision was to establish a high-end chain restaurant featuring real Chinese food across America. In 1996, he purchased back all its original stores partially owned by other people, and hired a management team with Richard Federico as president and Robert Vivian as chief financial officer. He then opened new stores in Denver, Las Vegas, Houston, and Irvine. In 1998, when Fleming had ten P.F. Chang's stores, he filed an IPO at $12 a share for his business. The price jumped to $32.75 per share in March 2000. By then, the chain had established 39 stores and had another 13 in development.[44] Its speed of growth was set at 13 to 15 new restaurants per year. As of December 2017, P.F. Chang's was operating 210 full-service Bistro restaurants and 200 quick casual Pei Wei restaurants across the country.[45] It was the first and the only full-service, sit-down Chinese restaurant that became a publicly traded stock on Nasdaq. Together with California Pizza Kitchen or Cheese Cake Factory, P.F. Chang's was often an anchor restaurant in a high-end American mall like Newport Beach Mall in Southern California.

P.F. Chang's had a comfortable dining atmosphere for middle- and high-class American customers. As a chain restaurant business, the size of P.F. Chang's stores ranged from 4,500 square foot to 8,000 square foot and had inside seating to accommodate 210 to 225 customers; some locations offered patio dining. Each store had an open kitchen and standardized operation procedure. One executive said: "We're not having to go in and figure out how to operate. All functions are identical."[46] Describing P.F. Chang's store in Irvine, California, a *Los Angeles Times* article in 1996 observed:

> this place is simply stunning. The main dining area, as big as a Vegas show-room, includes a parquet floor, replicas of Xi'an terra-cotta statuary standing guard on pedestals, . . . The inspired concept of this place is to fuse authentic Chinese cooking with the amenities of a fine Western restaurant.[47]

Though each chain store's exterior and interior design could be different, none of them looked like a traditional Chinese restaurant in Chinatown. There was no Buddha figure at the entrance as many Chinese restaurants had. The stylish interior featured hand-painted murals depicting ancient Chinese landscapes and sculptures representing the life and society of the Tang (618–907) and Ming Dynasties (1368–1644). The hardwood furniture and the stone floor gave a contemporary feel.

In flavor and cookery, P.F. Chang's claimed that it tried to be as close as possible to Chinese food tradition. Fleming hired Paul Muller as his executive chef who had no Chinese background before he worked for P.F. Chang's. He came from a chef family and grew up in Long Island, New York. His grandfather was a chef at Hellman's Deli in New York. After graduating with a culinary degree from the New York Institute of Technology, he won a fellowship to teach at the school. He had also worked at the Manhattan's Waldorf-Astoria hotel as chef-tournant and rotated through the hotel's various kitchens. In his early days at P.F. Chang's, Muller had a hard time learning to use a wok. When he worked at the company's third store in La Jolla, Southern California, Muller recalled:

> The wok handles are three times the diameter of a saute pan, so I always would grab everything so tightly. Sometimes at the end of my training day, in the middle of the night, my hands would just curl up into a claw shape and cramp up.[48]

Muller had no experience cooking Chinese in his previous chef job. Fleming promised to establish the executive chef position only after Muller successfully learned Chinese cooking and could manage a store's kitchen well. To help Muller learn Chinese cooking, Philip Chiang arranged for him to spend time with the chefs at the Mandarin, took him to tour Chinatowns across the United States, and let him visit Hong Kong and mainland China for several months. There Muller met Chiang's relatives "and really got to understand that what we were doing at P.F. Chang's was authentic and traditional but still innovative."[49] Philip knew that Muller would not learn Chinese cooking well without knowing Chinese culture. As the chain's director of culinary operations and the corporate executive chef, Muller traveled to China every 14 to 16 months to follow culinary development there and to visit the chain's manufacturers and purveyors. "Its water chestnuts and bamboo shoots still come from China and so do many of its sauce bases, such as black-mushroom soy, plum and hoisin."[50]

In terms of hygiene standards, P.F. Chang's did a lot better than many independently owned Chinese restaurants did in Southern California. The Los Angeles County Department of Health Services regularly sent health inspectors to score restaurants on a 100-point scale. Inspectors would check everything from inadequate cooling or heating of food to the chef's personal hygiene, the use of leftovers, or unclean equipment. An A grade is granted when a restaurant gets scores of between 90 and 100 points, a B for 80 to 89 points, and a C for 70 to 79 points. Below 70, a restaurant will be ordered to close.[51] According to a 2009 study, almost all P.F. Chang's and Panda Express stores were grade A restaurants. In comparison, a high percentage of Chinese restaurants in San Gabriel Valley failed to reach the A grade. Many independently owned Chinese restaurants in Chinese congregated areas had hygiene problems.[52]

P.F. Chang's emphasized that MSG was absolutely forbidden in its cooking, which obviously tried to address a major concern of American customers when eating in a Chinese restaurant. Many Chinese restaurants had allegedly used MSG in cooking. P.F. Chang's also emphasized its use of fresh ingredients. "That includes all meats, seafood and poultry. Vegetables are all hand cut every day. Every dumpling, every spring roll is made by hand every day. We probably use 40-some sauces plus and we make every one of those every day."[53] Food at P.F. Chang's was, however, not necessarily as healthy as many customers expected. As Professor Susan Bosego Carter of UC Riverside pointed out, food at P.F. Chang's

> is high in calories, sodium, sugar, and fat—including trans-fat. P.F. Chang's "Small Plate" serving of "Crispy Green Beans" contains 1040 calories, over 70 percent of them from fat. Its delicate-sounding "Chicken Lettuce Wraps" have 580 calories and 2590 mg of sodium, "Cantonese Style Lemon Chicken" contains almost half a cup of sugar! Calories, fat, sodium, and sugar counts at Panda Express are somewhat lower, which is about comparable to the offerings at McDonald's. Let us hope that the next chapter in the

engaging story will bring truly healthy, authentic, Chinese regional cooking to a large and appreciative American public.[54]

Food as a Commodity and Culture

Food at P. F. Chang's is still different from its counterpart in China. Many dishes at P.F. Chang's are actually Chinese-inspired food rather than real Chinese food. What Fleming created in P.F. Chang's was a compelling business concept to sell Chinese food at a high-end chain restaurant across the country. P.F. Chang's China Bistro has made real Chinese food a visible high-end dining option in the American restaurant market and available to a wide range of middle-class American customers. It has accomplished a dream that many Chinese American restaurants failed to achieve. As a corporate food business, P.F. Chang's restaurants provided a trendy, comfortable dining environment that attracted mainstream middle-class American customers, which most small or medium-sized, family-owned, Chinese restaurants could not afford.

While P.F. Chang's was an impressive culinary success representing Chinese food in America, it was unrelated to Chinese American identity and culture. Corporate business created the food concept and produced food as a commodity. When food becomes a commodity, it is no longer an inherited culture and does not necessarily belong to those who originated it. To sell authentic Chinese food as a commodity in the American restaurant market requires no ethnic association or intrinsic linkage to the Chinese American community. Culture is hereditary or primordial; commodity is not. Displaying ethnic resilience, chop suey was a culinary innovation out of an American racial environment. It was a food commodity as well as a significant piece of Chinese American culture. Though Americanized in flavor and culinary format, chop suey was a real ethnic food and a cornerstone business for the Chinese American community. Its formation and popularity reflected how American popular palates shaped, transformed, and even altered Chinese food. At the same time, chop suey as a popular ethnic food also helped shape the American diet. Its history shows how Chinese in America negotiated with racial environment, explored job opportunities, and adapted to American society. Chop suey looked like a case of assimilation but it is in fact a story of ethnic resilience.

P.F. Chang's has presented a new image of Chinese food in America but its success is a mixed blessing for Chinese Americans. Through its expansion, more and more American customers get to know real Chinese food while they tend to stay away from independent, small, and family-owned Chinese restaurants for social dinners. P.F. Chang's success poses a serious question to Chinese in America: could Chinese American restaurateurs in future open their own high-end chain stores to non-Chinese clients in America and other countries? P.F. Chang's has also expanded internationally. As Yong Chen noted in another chapter of this volume, P.F. Chang's had 220 stores in 21 countries including 25 stores in Mexico by 2017.[55] In December 2017, Cheese Cake Factory as a prominent American restaurant opened its first store in Shanghai and then in a high-end mall in Beijing the following year. In April 2018, P.F. Chang's matched Cheese Cake Factory with its own first store in Shanghai and then another store in Beijing.[56] Its overseas expansion poses a challenge to P.F. Chang's itself. In 1928, a chop suey restaurant opened in Beijing but closed shortly after because Chinese customers showed no interest in Americanized Chinese food.[57] Can Chinese customers today accept P.F Chang's Chicken Lettuce Wraps, Dynamite Shrimp, Asian Caesar Salad, or Asian Angus NY Strip? As the largest full-service Chinese restaurant in America, what role can P.F. Chang's play in the largest Chinese restaurant market?

Key Terms

Chop suey: An Americanized Chinese restaurant dish, which contains chopped meat with stir-fried bean sprouts, bamboo shoots, and onions, served with rice.

P.F. Chang's China Bistro: A high-end Chinese American restaurant chain that caters to mainstream or non-Chinese Americans that was developed by Paul Fleming and Philip Chiang.

Chinese food in America: A general term in the chapter including both Americanized Chinese food and authentic Chinese food in America.

Discussion Questions

1. How do you understand the statement, "Chop suey looked like a case of 'assimilation' but in reality, it is ethnic 'resilience?'"
2. How and why is the P.F. Chang restaurant a significant breakthrough in the American restaurant market?
3. How and why is P.F. Chang's restaurant success a mixed blessing for Chinese Americans?

Notes

1 Noah Brooks, "Restaurant Life in San Francisco," *Overland Monthly and Out West* (Vol. 1, Issue: 5, November 1868), 473.
2 Tonia Chao, "Communicating through Architecture: San Francisco Chinese Restaurants as Cultural Intersections, 1849–1984" (PhD diss., University of California, Berkeley, 1985), 226, Table 4.
3 "Heard About Town," *The New York Times*, January 29, 1900.
4 Liang Qichao, *Xindalu Youji* (Diary of Traveling in the New World) (Japan: Xinming-chonghao, 1904; reprint, Changsha, China: Hunan Renming Chubanshe, 1981), 52.
5 "Chop Suey Resorts," *The New York Times*, November 15, 1903.
6 Bruce Edward Hall, *Tea That Burns: A Family Memoir of Chinatown* (New York: Free Press, 1998), 158–159 and Mary Ting Yi Lui, *The Chinatown Trunk Mystery: Murder, Miscegenation, and Other Dangerous Encounters in Turn-of-the-Century New York City* (Princeton, NJ: Princeton University Press, 2005), 65.

7 Gaye Tuchman and Harry G. Levine, "'Safe Treyf': New York Jews and Chinese Food" in Barbara G. Shortridge & James R. Shortridge, eds. *The Taste of American Place: A Reader on Regional and Ethnic Foods* (New York: Roman and Littlefield, 1997), 173.

8 Huping Ling, *Chinese Chicago Race, Transnational Migration, and Community since 1870* (Stanford, CA: Stanford University Press, 2012), 24–57.

9 Chao, "Communicating through Architecture," 95.

10 William Mason, "The Chinese in Los Angeles," *Museum Alliance Quarterly* 6, no. 2 (Fall 1967): 16 (Los Angeles County Museum of Natural History).

11 Pasadena City Directory (1920), 268.

12 Ching Chao Wu, "Chinatowns: A Study of Symbiosis and Assimilations" (PhD diss., University of Chicago, 1928), 87.

13 Mai (Him Mark Lai), 393.

14 Linda Loi, "So We Don't End Up Like Chop Suey: Searching for Authentic Chinese Food in L.A.," www.sscnet.ucla.edu/aasc/classweb/fa1197/M163/loi5.html accessed in December, 2009.

15 "Eisenhowers Keep Yen For Chop Suey: Send Out for Dish to Capital Restaurant that Has Been Their Favorite Since 1930," *The New York Times*, August 2, 1953.

16 Molly Katz, Jewish a Tuchman and Levine, "Safe Treyf," 73 (New York: Workman, 1991), 67.

17 Johnny Kan's Kan's Restaurant (Guan Yuan) was a rare high-end Chinese restaurant that Herb Caen and other celebrities frequented in San Francisco. As an American-born Chinese, Kan featured mainly Cantonese cuisine, and many dishes were Americanized in flavor. According to Madeline Hsu, however, Kan's Restaurant in San Francisco's Chinatown was the first Chinese restaurant to push for authentic Chinese food. See Madeline Y. Hsu, "From Chop Suey to Mandarin Cuisine: Fine Dining and the Refashioning of Chinese Ethnicity during the Cold War Era," in *Chinese Americans and the Politics of Race and Culture*, ed. Sucheng Chan and Madeline Yuan-yin Hsu (Philadelphia: Temple University Press, 2008), 173–193.

18 See www.asianpacificfund.org/awards/bio_chiang.shtml accessed in December, 2009.

19 Ibid.

20 Loi, "So We Don't End Up Like Chop Suey."

21 Ibid.

22 Donna Gabaccia, *We Are What We Eat: Ethnic Rood and the Making of Americans* (Cambridge, MA: Harvard University Press, 1998), 218.

23 *The New York Times*, July 27, 1973.

24 Jennifer 8 Lee, *The Fortune Cookie Chronicles: Adventures in the World of Chinese Food*, (New York: Hachette Book Group, USA, 2008), 81–82.

25 Dunlop, Fuchsia (February 4, 2007). "Human Resources," *The New York Times Magazine*: Section 6, Page 75. Browning, Michael (April 17, 2002). "Who Was General Tso and Why Are We Eating His Chicken," *The Washington Post*. Retrieved February 24, 2007. Text available at Wired NewYork.com

26 Lynn Pan, *Sons of the Yellow Emperor: A History of Chinese Diaspora* (New York: Little, Brown and Company, 1990), 334.

27 Michael Luo, "As All American As Egg Foo Yong," *The New York Times*, September 24, 2004.

28 Mimi Sheraton, "Restaurants," *The New York Times*, December 16, 1977.

29 M.H. Reed, "Sichuan Cuisine: Another Source," *The New York Times*, November 9, 1980.

30 Patricia Brooks, "Skillfully Spiced Hunan Fare," *The New York Times*, July 12, 1981.

31 Min Zhou, *Contemporary Chinese America: Immigration, Ethnicity, and Community Transformation* (Philadelphia: Temple University Press, 2009), 105.

32 Steve Harvey, "Sings the Blues without Locust's Song," *Los Angeles Times*, April 5, 1983.

33 Mark Arax, "Monterey Park Nation's 1st Suburban Chinatown," *Los Angeles Times*, April 6, 1987.

34 Shawn Hubler, "'A Feeding Frenzy in the 'New Chinatown'; The Glut of Restaurants Has Made the San Gabriel Valley the Nation's Chinese Food Capital," *Los Angeles Times*, December 5, 1995.

35 Asian Pacific American Legal Center of Southern California, *The Diverse Face of Asians and Pacific Islanders in Los Angeles County* (2004), 49.

36 Stephanie Chavez, "New Look Reflects an Old Pattern," *Los Angeles Times*, July 25, 2004.

37 David Pierson, "Selling the Taste of Chinatown," *Los Angeles Times*, June 16, 2004.

38 Min Zhou, *Chinatown: The Socioeconomic Potential of an Urban Enclave*, Philadelphia: Temple University Press, 1992, 99.

39 Cynthia Mines. "Chinese Chain: Steaming with Success," May 1, 2000 http://retailtraf ficmag.com/mag/retail_chinese_chain_steaming, accessed December, 2014.

40 Joel Kotkin, "Will Chinese Food Go the Way of Pizza?" *The New York Times*, March 26, 2000.

41 Ibid.

42 Barbara Tropp, *The Modern Art of Chinese Cooking Techniques and Recipes* (New York: William Morrow, 1982).

43 Bret Thorn, "Paul Muller: Creating a Stir and Frying Up a Storm at P.F. Chang's China Bistro," *Nation's Restaurant News*, January 27, 2003, www.findarticles.com/p/articles/mi_m3190/is_4_37/ai_97314555/pg_1

44 Kotkin, "Chinese Food."

45 Company Information: P.F. Chang's China Bistro, Inc. in *The New York Times* (Business edition), September 12, 2009.

46 Ibid.

47 Max Jacobson, "P. F. Chang's Explores New Dimensions but Stays Flat in Places," *Los Angeles Times*, March 21, 1996.

48 Ibid.

49 Ibid.

50 Ibid.

51 See the Los Angeles County's website: www.lapublichealth.org, retrieved in July 2007.

52 Liu, Haiming and Lin, Lianlian, "Food, Culinary Identity, and Transnational Culture: Chinese Restaurant Business in Southern California," *Journal of Asian American Studies*, Vol. 12, No. 2 (June, 2009), 135–162.

53 Ibid.

54 Review of *From Canton To Panda Express: A History of Chinese Food in the United State* by Haiming Liu, Susan Boslego Carter, *Southern California Quarterly* (Vol. 98, No. 3), pp. 372–388 (The Historical Society of Southern California).

55 Yong Chen, "Surveying the Genealogy of Chinese Restaurant in Mexico: From High-end Franchises to Makeshift Stands," chapter 6 in this vol

56 Jessica Meyers, "P.F. Chang's Come to Shanghai, but You Really Sell American Chinese Food to the Country that Invented the Wok," *Los Angeles Times*, May 29, 2018.

57 "Chop Suey Café in Peking Fails—Untraveled Chinese Don't Know About Dish; It's American," *Los Angeles Times*, October 28, 1928.

PART III

Person-Centered Narratives

11

CHINESE RESTAURANTS AND JEWISH AMERICAN CULTURE

Jacob R. Levin

> You know, like all Jews, I was probably in a Chinese restaurant.
>
> Supreme Court Justice, Elena Kagan

The above quote will be put in a much larger and much longer context, but first I want to reference an old comedy bit performed in the 1950s and 1960s.[1] Lenny Bruce, perhaps comedy's most controversial, if not influential, Jewish comedian (his birth name was Leonard Alfred Schneider), had a bit in his stand-up act discerning the difference between "Jewish" and "goyish."[2] *Goy* (*goyim* plural) is a Hebrew word to refer to a non-Jewish person.[3] Here is a section of that piece that explores the Jewish practice of seeing the world divided between things that are Jewish and culturally foreign to ourselves:

> Dig: I'm Jewish. Count Basie's Jewish. Ray Charles is Jewish. Eddie Cantor's goyish. B'nai Brith is goyish; Hadassah, Jewish. Marine corps—heavy goyim, dangerous. Kool-Aid is goyish. All Drake's cakes are goyish. Pumpernickel is Jewish, and, as you know, white bread is very goyish. Instant potatoes—goyish. Black cherry soda's very Jewish. Macaroons are very Jewish—very Jewish cake. Fruit salad is Jewish. Lime jello is goyish. Lime soda is very goyish.[4]

At the risk of exhibiting the great hubris historians sometimes practice by imagining how our subjects in the past might respond to our inquiries, I believe undoubtedly that if asked, Lenny Bruce would assure his audience that Chinese food is inherently the most Jewish of the non-Jewish foods. Why write a chapter starting with a quote from an Associate Justice of the Supreme Court of the United States, and an imagined response to a comedy bit about the most Jewish and non-Jewish aspects of American culture decided by a famous comedian who was notoriously on the wrong side of the law most of his professional life? Because that quote might serve as the most high profile example of the historical roots of the relationship leaping into the references of modern American culture.

So why would there be a need for a Supreme Court Justice to respond to an inquiry about her whereabouts on Christmas? Why would Senator Lindsey Graham, Republican from South Carolina, ask such a question of a U.S. Solicitor General going through her 2010 confirmation hearings to earn an appointment to the highest court of the land? My guess is because he knew it would garner an expected response that would lead to laughter and lighten the mood in the room during a particularly intense exchange between Justice Kagan and members of the Senate. But why would Senator Graham expect such a predictable response from Justice Kagan? Because just about every year many religious, secular, national, and local press outlets do a story that is some variation of "Can anyone explain why Jews eat Chinese food every Christmas? We have the answer!"

Some of the pieces are more thorough than others by being rooted more deeply in exploring the origins of the relationship, speaking with culinary experts, and speaking with food historians. Some address the religious and culinary traditions that bind the two communities.[5] Others explore the geographic and population statistics to explain how the groups became culinarily bonded.[6] Still some decide to include less-flattering traditions and stereotypes like Jews enjoying inexpensive food because of their well-known "thriftiness" and the fact that Chinese takeout is a commonly less expensive fare than Italian or other similarly imported cuisines.[7] There have simultaneously been both academic musings and pop culture references on the bond between the two communities spanning decades that are a multitude when submitted for review all together. All of these things will be fused together in the following study, examining the historical and the cultural roots that brought these two large non-Christian minority communities together, not just for Christmas dinner, but at kitchen tables and great dining halls across the country.

My personal relationship between my Jewish heritage and Chinese food on Christmas was a little unorthodox and winding to forge. I was raised as a Reform Jew in Columbia, Maryland, a suburb between Baltimore City and Washington, D.C. Most of our little neighborhood shopping centers had some form of Chinese restaurant. We loved our local restaurant in town, Hunan Manor, for big family dinners. I have childhood memories of walking past the koi ponds and the Golden Buddha statue in the waiting room, past the huge fish tanks with crabs, lobsters, and other delights swimming around before being chosen for their respective dishes. Recently, a family friend and neighbor came back into town from her home in Florida and when we asked her where she wanted to go out for dinner, her immediate reply was, "Chinese! I can't get any good Chinese down where I live." I will admit my first thought was, "Oh, there must not be a big Jewish population where she lives on the coast."[8] So we took her to Hunan Manor, a first time for my wife and I in over a decade, and feasted on pork egg rolls, Peking duck, and spicy, garlic string beans.

As a young teenager, my still-go-to Chinese restaurant, Hunan Legend, opened in the neighborhood shopping center about a mile from my childhood home. It became as regular a dining option for take-out dinners as frequently as one would order a pizza for a last-minute supper. My parents hosted my surprise eighteenth birthday dinner in Hunan Legend's private dining room. When a blizzard struck in my time home during winter break from college, my friends and I would trek up unplowed streets because we knew all of our specific dietary needs (vegan, vegetarian, and pork-lovers) could be met at Hunan. When my wife's family arrived in town to celebrate our wedding weekend last summer, we took all of my mother-in-law's siblings and their spouses there for dinner.

In researching for this chapter, my wife and I went to sample some Kosher Chinese food from David Chu's China Bistro in the heavily Jewish suburb of Baltimore, Pikesville. With some minor protein substitutions (and rather strict kosher rules), we greatly enjoyed our beef egg rolls and Dry Shredded Chicken, which is a misnomer since as the menu describes the dish, it is "White meat chicken light breaded and fried until crispy then sautéed with celery, carrots in chef's special delicious sauce."[9] There will be a more involved discussion of the history and cultural relevance of the development of Kosher Chinese food later in the chapter. Chu's Bistro was significant because its clientele that night for dinner was a noticeable mix of observant Orthodox Jews who would pick that specific establishment for its compliance with their extensive dietary laws, and people of a variety of racial, ethnic, or religious backgrounds who were at Chu's that night because it was simply their regular neighborhood spot for Chinese.[10]

However, when I was younger, my family did not eat Chinese food on Christmas Day. My Jewish family would travel to the Midwest to celebrate Christmas with close family friends who were raised Catholic and went all out on Christmas family celebrations. Big pot-luck feasts, family games, waking up on Christmas morning for gift exchanges, sledding on frozen hillsides, and definitely no Chinese food. My unique experiences with Chinese food during Christmas started in my teenage years when I would travel to San Francisco with my family to visit friends on the Pacific coast. Unlike in Ohio, while in San Francisco over the holiday, we would wake up and head into the historic Chinatown district of the city. We would wait in line, surrounded in a cloud of smells of unknown ingredient or origin. We would sit at a big table in the Hong Kong Tea House on Pacific Street enjoying a Dim Sum Christmas brunch. My family recollects seeing a sign in the front window of the Tea House with this text:

> The Chinese Rest. Assoc. of the United States would like to extend our thanks to The Jewish People we do not completely understand your dietary customs . . . But we are proud and grateful that your GOD insist you eat our food on Christmas. Happy Holidays!"[11]

This tradition allowed us to be engulfed in an array of dumplings, steam buns, soup, and noodle dishes with both common (to American palates) and exotic meats and seafood as carts swirled around us on a seemingly momentary basis.

As an adult it is a given that I will enjoy my favorite cuisine on Christmas Eve or Christmas Day, as a sheer habit of my adult life. Since getting married and now spending Christmas in Florida with my wife's family, her parents have enjoyed incorporating a trip on Christmas Eve or Christmas Day lunch to their favorite local Chinese restaurants as a way of including some of my traditions in with their Christmas practices. But the story of the ties that bind American Jews and Chinese Cuisine in America has significant historical and cultural roots, dating back over a century.

This chapter will examine the historical origins and chronological developments that helped make Chinese food and Chinese restaurants probably the "most Jewish" of the "non-Jewish" foods in Jewish American culture. The foundation rests in first- and second-generation Eastern European immigrants traveling from the American Jewish epicenter in the Lower East Side neighborhood in New York City, which was practically next door to Chinatown. Over the next century it evolved into several generations of both communities adapting to their respective audiences, and popular culture embracing that an acceptable part of Christmastime celebrations would include Chinese food, and perhaps a trip to the movies.

Historical Narrative

There are myriad historical reasons why American Jews would gravitate towards Chinese food as one of their chosen ethnic cuisines in America. Like practically all stories examining the Jewish American experience, it begins in Manhattan, the Lower East Side, with a flood of Eastern European Jews in the decades between 1880 and the 1920s. Individual Jews and small communities have been in the New World since before the United States' founding. The oldest congregations date back to the 1600s, and the oldest continually standing synagogue, Touro Synagogue in Newport, Rhode Island, has stood since 1763.[12] Like all groups and communities in America, there is no technical, singular version of an "American Jew." Many of the earliest arrivals in America were of a Sephardic background, originating in Spain, Portugal, Northern Africa, and the Eastern Mediterranean. In the early- to mid-nineteenth century, a wave of wealthier German Jews arrived. Many were cosmopolitan, educated, and not very observant of strict religious code, but rather swept up in the capitalist Enlightenment Age central European movements. The first Reform temple in America was built in Baltimore, Maryland in 1849.[13] The Second Wave of Jewish immigration began with Russian and Eastern European pogroms in the 1880s, and until new federal immigration laws in 1924 cut off Jewish immigration from Eastern and Southern Europe, around two million Jews came into the country, almost all of them through New York's Ellis Island. Many of these immigrants established roots in New York City. By 1930, there were approximately 1,765,000 Jews out of New York's 5,970,800 residents.[14]

While the majority of these Russian and Eastern European Jews were Ashkenazi Orthodox and fairly homogenous in their beliefs and practices, the modern American Jewish community is a diverse mosaic of divergent groups. There are splits between Sephardim, those whose roots originate in the Mediterranean and Iberian regions, and the Ashkenazi of Central and Eastern Europe. Major religious communities include those who identify as Orthodox, Conservative, Reform, and Reconstructionist. Even within those groups there are near endless subdivisions of affiliations and practices down to basically a personal level. Certain affiliations require adhering to kosher laws, like the Orthodox and ultra-Orthodox, while Reform Jews rarely keep kosher though some make the personal choice to avoid certain banned proteins without practicing the intensive and countless requirements of those who keep to the strictest levels of Kashrut.

With these millions of new residents also came their cultural and religious practices and requirements. For Jews, that meant subscribing to the Laws of Kashrut, or kosher dietary restrictions. The basic tenets of kosher law require certain slaughtering practices of certain types of acceptable animals. Beef and lamb are acceptable, pork is banned. Seafood with fins and scales are acceptable, shellfish (crabs, shrimp, lobster) are not allowed. Most famously there is a biblical decree that a kid cannot be boiled in its mother's milk, a refutation of a Pagan practice, which modern rabbinic law extended to the complete separation of all meat and dairy in kosher cooking, alternately known as "no mixing milk and meat."[15]

The unique dietary restrictions meant that American Jews could rarely eat beyond bakeries, butchers, and groceries specifically tailored to the needs of their own communities. Many of the first- and second-generation immigrants rarely went out to eat, as it was seen as an extravagance, or they rarely had the spare income to do so. However, as some extra income came into the household, and younger generations began to rebel against their parents by exploring outside of their relatively insular communities and cuisines, Jewish New Yorkers could see virtually as many different cuisines as possible in their own city. So why gravitate to Chinese food as opposed to the other dozen cuisines available in the city at the time?

Besides Eastern European/Jewish cuisine, the other European-based foodways would be particularly problematic. Italian and French cuisines frequently mixed milk and cheese with their meat dishes. Germanic (and other central-European cuisines) are especially pork-centered for their proteins. Mexican and other Latin American cuisines incorporated milk and meat in their dishes. Chinese food, on the other hand, rarely included any dairy in its menu. This exclusion allowed many Jews, venturing out of their restrictive home culinary traditions, were granted a certain level of comfort that they would not be violating their religious law if they indulged in these foreign delights. The lack of dairy would jive with kosher consideration, but what about the pork and shellfish frequently centered in Chinese cuisine, one could ask.

Gaye Tuchman and Harry Gene Levine published "New York Jews and Chinese Food: The Social Construction of an Ethnic Pattern" to examine just this inherent paradox about Jewish American embrace of Chinese food.[16] In their analysis and subsequent study, Tuchman and Levine coined a phrase to the unique middle-ground with which Jews viewed and rationalized Chinese cuisine for a variety of reasons, that being "safe *treyf*." *Treyf* is the Yiddish word for a food that does not comply with kosher law, unkosher. Tuchman and Levine believed that through the "hiding" of the *treyf*, a basic masking through shredding preparations, covered in savory and garlic-heavy dark brown sauces, Jewish immigrants and their children were more accepting of violating religious law for the new delicious offerings from the other side of the globe.[17] It was almost as if these consumers could eat a dish knowing its contents violated their religious restrictions, but, because they were "hidden," they were somewhat acceptable. They claim that by mid-century, as many immigrants had grandchildren in New York, the finely chopped and minced shrimp and pork in their egg rolls were simply imagined by consumers as not there. While the sight of a whole lobster or meat in a cream sauce would physically revolt most Jews who, even if non-practicing had most likely had never consumed them, the preparation of shredding meats and shellfish into dishes appealed to Jewish palates. Much of Eastern European Jewish cuisine also shared elements with Cantonese cuisine of the Chinese immigrants. Tuchman and Levine believed there was a "gastronomical resonance" between the two. Both enjoyed a taste for the sweet and sour palates. Both cuisines favored chicken, chicken soup, seasoning with garlic, celery, and onions.[18] Tuchman and Levine ultimately decided a taste for chicken soup, sweet and sour dishes, and tea (without milk) all resonated with the Jewish eater.[19]

Beyond the culinary similarities in ingredient and food preparation, the space of a Chinese restaurant meant many different things to American Jews. They viewed eating Chinese food as something uniquely "American" that they could do to begin their assimilation process. Jewish immigrants saw their Chinese hosts as fellow American "outsiders" simply starting businesses and working to feed their families. They were fellow non-Christian minorities, and Jews could eat in Chinese establishments without experiencing the anti-Semitism common in Italian and other Christian-owned establishments.[20] It was that same anti-Chinese sentiment in American society that also made some Jews feel "more American" simply by being served by a more recent immigrant in a perceived lower position on the American social hierarchy. This did lend itself to some bad behavior of some Jewish patrons, including one of Tuchman and Levine's interviewees recalling an incident in the 1950s where her Jewish uncle repeatedly mimicked the Chinese waiter's accent to his face.[21] Often the Chinese proprietors lumped Jewish customers into the broader whiteness of America, but that did not mean they weren't a specific target for Chinese restaurateurs.

So far, all of the discussion in this section has been about the Jewish immigrant affinity for Chinese food, however, this was no one-sided affair. Chinese business owners actively sought out Jewish customers for their restaurants. There were several motivations for the Chinese immigrants to seek out Jewish customers. The center of the Jewish community in New York was on the Lower East Side, right next to Chinatown. Sheer proximity between the groups promoted a relationship. Chinese restaurants began branching into other Jewish neighborhoods in the Boroughs and surrounding communities. Yong Chen's study of American Chinese food, *Chop Suey, USA: The Story of Chinese Food in America*, included a chapter on "the makers of American Chinese food." In Chen's section on Jewish affinity for the cuisine, one respondent named Eleanor who frequented Chinese restaurants once a week growing up in 1930s New York, replied, "You can tell whether it is a Jewish neighborhood or not by the number of Chinese restaurants."[22]

Chen further examined why perhaps other ethnic populations did not court the Jewish palate as strongly as the Chinese restaurateurs. Looking at New York population breakdowns for 1910, there were more than 340,000 native Italians, but a much smaller pool of roughly 4,000 Chinese immigrants as potential native customers. Additionally, there were very limited employment opportunities for Chinese immigrants beyond laundry services or the restaurant industry, which offered higher wages.[23] Jewish patronage of Chinese restaurants was crucial for their survival and eventual flourishing, especially on the East Coast. Chen wrote, "In the early 1930s, some Chinese knowledgeable about the restaurant business in New York and Philadelphia estimated that Jews accounted for 60 percent of the white clientele at their establishments in the two cities."[24]

Large group tables where dishes were shared communally fostered loud discussion and debate, which many Jewish families felt quite familiar with at their tables. Simply ordering from the extensive menus offered a chance for debate, disagreement, and eventual submission to suggestions from the collective group, a hallmark practice of Jewish religious study. Tuchman and Levine recorded a response from a Protestant man from the Midwest who married a Jewish New Yorker and described going out for Chinese food with a group of Jewish friends during which they "discussed the menu with an enthusiasm which eluded me."[25] There was an underdog character to the foreign immigrant that resonated with second- and third-generation American Jews, and getting a good bargain on an abundantly overflowing table of food appealed to the thriftiness practiced by most immigrant groups.

Tuchman and Levine do point out that, as previously discussed concerning the non-monolithic character of "American Jewry," there are some Jews who never latched on to the Chinese food craze, and some who have drifted away from it. Both the earliest and most recent Jewish immigrant communities never bonded with Chinese cuisine like their Eastern European brethren. In mid-nineteenth century, the first wave of Jewish immigration came from Germany, and largely lived uptown, far away from the Eastern European and Chinese immigrants. They frequently viewed their coreligionists of a lower class and often remained more closely aligned with German cuisine and culture than anything else. Many of them moved and settled in the Midwest and never found roots in New York. The most recent wave of Jewish immigrants from the Soviet Union and Israel have mostly concentrated in specific areas of New York City, primarily dining in restaurants serving their own ethnic cuisine.[26] Lastly, they argue that the large group of Jews from the Northeast United States who settled in Florida to retire have pulled away from their ties to Chinese cuisine and much more frequently scope out and eat at "Early Bird Specials" than Chinese or even Jewish delicatessen food. Great deals and large social eating arrangements leave them comfortable in establishing a new identity, not just that of an American Jew, but as a retired American, a Floridian, living with "the boredom and pleasures of perpetual vacation."[27]

Ultimately, factors like having practically no dairy on the menu, relatable flavor palates, and a willingness of younger generations to stretch or abandon what was considered acceptable dietary practices allowed Chinese food to become a staple favorite among American Jews. Additionally, the restaurants were open on Sundays and Christmas, and practically never had any of the Christian iconography or anti-Semitic antagonism of Italian restaurants which made Jews feel like Chinese restaurants were safe spaces. For some Jews, eating Chinese food was a way to feel more American, to make themselves feel closer to non-Jewish white Americans by "othering" the Chinese immigrants who worked at the restaurant.[28]

Although in 2018 observant Jews can find certified kosher delicacies from sushi to Oreos, sodas, candies, and a variety of cuisines stretching from Thai to French, for much of the twentieth century observant Jews could only consume Jewish ethnic fare. With the proliferation of both the koshering industries and food product corporations eager to reach a yet-untapped market, the palates of kosher-observant Jews could travel the culinary world. As the Jews looking to test Chinese food would flood down into Manhattan's Chinatown, one owner of a kosher delicatessen thought to capture some of the desire amongst his own kosher-observant customers and began making Chinese dishes that still passed his strict kosher requirements. The earliest kosher Chinese food, according to *The New York Times*, was located in New York City, at 135 Essex Street. Solomon Bernstein, proprietor of a kosher delicatessen, chose to attempt to capture some of the Jewish market for the already-popular Chinese cuisine well established on the East Coast. Since his deli specialized in spiced and smoked meats, he began preparing his own egg rolls, using veal instead of the pork called for in the recipe. Other Chinese dishes became "koshered" and, except for dishes explicitly calling for shellfish, many if not much of the Cantonese menu would rapidly become a favorite among East Coast Jewish palates.[29]

Today practically everywhere there is a significant Jewish population you can find kosher Chinese restaurants. A simple internet search will garner dozens and dozens of responses in cities ranging from New York, Boston, Miami, Los Angeles, Philadelphia, and Baltimore. As mentioned earlier, in preparation for this chapter, my wife and I sampled some local kosher Chinese food. A few blocks away from Baltimore's largest kosher supermarket, sits the popular David Chu's China Bistro in the Pikesville suburb of Baltimore. The smells and dishes filling our table mirrored any Chinese restaurants you've enjoyed—piles of noodles and rice, and saucy meats and vegetables piled high as customers noshed and chatted in ever-increasing volume. We ordered the egg rolls, made with beef instead of pork or shrimp, and for our main course we picked the (unfortunate and not accurately depicting the deliciousness) Dry Shredded Chicken. The restaurant was packed full of patrons on a Friday afternoon ranging from large Orthodox families, to businessmen wearing suits and yarmulkas, to patrons for whom one could imagine this was simply their neighborhood spot. Our meal was delicious.

The ties between Jewish Americans and Chinese food and culture are so strong that for nearly two decades the Museum at Eldridge Street in the Lower East Side of Manhattan has hosted a street festival to celebrate the diverse neighborhood in which it's located. It originally started as the "Egg Rolls and Egg Cream Festival." The museum describes it as the most popular event they host every year, and it recently expanded to include the growing local Puerto Rican population in the neighborhood and is now the "Egg Rolls, Egg Creams, and Empanadas Festival" starting in June 2018. According to the museum's website, the festival has served several purposes. First, to:

> celebrate the diverse ethnic communities of the Museum at Eldridge Street's Lower East Side/Chinatown neighborhood! With the Museum's home, the landmark Eldridge Street Synagogue, as its centerpiece, this neighborhood festival spills out onto the street with a mash-up of Jewish, Chinese and Puerto Rican tastes, traditions, sights, and sounds.

The festival features hallmarks of Chinese and Jewish culture including kosher egg roll and dumplings and challah demonstrations, and plenty of cultural performances from singing to Hebrew and Chinese scribes demonstrating the ancient languages. Yiddish-language newspaper and media outlet *Forverts* sent a correspondent to the festival in 2012 and they put out a mini-documentary celebrating the welcoming nature of the organizers and participants and diversity of the festival.[30]

The festival also celebrated one of the more unique crossovers between the two communities—the game of mah jong.[31] Mah jong is a very popular game within the Jewish community. Jewish women in the 1920s and 1930s picked it up as a game of leisure and viewed it as exotic Orientalia. An American businessman named Joseph P. Babcock brought it back from China and began importing mah jong sets. A National Mah Jongg League was formed in 1937, and most of the first members were Jewish women of German decent. It is still popular amongst American Jewish women who gather to play cards and a modernized version of the Chinese game.[32]

Cultural References

As I said previously, there are no shortages in popular culture of the special affinity Jewish Americans have for Chinese cuisine, on Christmas and otherwise. From serious dramas to comedies, movies to television sitcoms, stand-up routines to late-night talk show appearances, it can be found near and far that the producers of American culture know how Jews love Chinese food. There is an old joke of unknown origins common amongst Jewish storytellers and comedians. The essential root of it is this: "The Jewish calendar goes back about 5,700 years, and the Chinese calendar goes back about 4,600 years. Do you know what that means? It means the Jews survived without Chinese food for over a thousand years!"[33] Jewish actors and comedians, like Billy Crystal, would joke with late night hosts about how he felt "so Jewish" that he had to go out and order Chinese food.

In the film *My Favorite Year*, the lead character, a young Jewish writer, said to his obviously non-Jewish date, "Katherine, Jews know two things: suffering, and where to find great Chinese food."[34] Previous scholarship on this unique bond between American Jews and Chinese food has pointed out Philip Roth's novel character Alexander Portnoy reinforced an important point expressed in the previous section about the duality of Chinese restaurants being a safe place for Jews since they did not face the anti-Semitism perceived to be directed their way from others in public, while also being a place where Jews could be assumed as "white" by the Chinese staff whom they could mock for not speaking English well enough.[35]

More recent pop culture has jumped on the topic as well. *Saturday Night Live*'s animated shorts were a staple for over a decade, primarily run by comedian and writer Robert Smigel. In December 2005, singer Darlene Love provided vocals for his clay-mation short, entitled *Christmastime for the Jews*. The video included all sorts of stereotypes of what Jews would do on Christmas "when they controlled the town." Other notable lines include:

> Well it happens every year around Christmas Eve, when all the happy Christian people take their leave; the streets are deserted and that's big news, its Christmastime for the Jews; . . . they can finally see King Kong without waiting in line, they can eat in Chinatown and drink their sweet-ass wine.[36]

This line was accompanied by the visual of basically caricature versions of white Jews (curly hair, big noses, glasses) sitting at a restaurant table being served food by an Asian woman with slanted eyes and a man swirling his glass of wine to aerate it before tasting. The "sweet-ass wine" would probably refer to Manischewitz, a popular kosher wine which is particularly sweet. It is also growing in popularity among Asian drinkers (mostly South Koreans, and immigrants from Northern China) in America and around the world.[37]

Gilmore Girls, a popular female-created and -led drama, had an episode entitled "Jews and Chinese Food," though it had little to do with that particular religious group and their dining habits in the context of the episode.[38] Amy Sherman-Palladino, who wrote and ran *Gilmore Girls* would return to television a decade later with another show, this time explicitly focusing on Jewishness and comedy. In 2017, Amazon Studios released an original series entitled *The Marvelous Mrs. Maisel*, centered on the life of Ms. Miriam "Midge" Maisel, living with her Jewish family on the Upper West Side of Manhattan. It was arguably the "most Jewish" show of 2017, and among the many stereotypes both reinforced and challenged by the show, one is clear. When it came to celebrating a big achievement with the family, there was no place to go besides the iconic Chinese palaces of New York City. In this case, it was Ruby Foo's, where the family sat surrounding the big round table, eating decidedly un-kosher foods like pork spare ribs and egg rolls with pork and shrimp.[39] Ruby Foo's was a Chinese restaurant on West 52nd Street in Manhattan which has since closed, but authors and patrons still remember their pork spare ribs as being the best they ever tasted.[40]

In November 2015, Columbia Pictures released a holiday buddy comedy starring Joseph Gordon-Levitt, Seth Rogen, and Anthony Mackie entitled *The Night Before*.[41] The basic premise of the movie is that young Ethan (Gordon-Levitt) tragically lost his parents as a young teenager and his two best friends Isaac (Rogen) and Chris (Mackie) have spent each Christmas with him in order to help him through his holiday grief. The Christmas in the movie would be their last together so they had to relive all of the things they did every year to celebrate the holiday. The movie centers on Christmas Eve, with the three stars all wearing "ugly Christmas sweaters," visiting FAO Schwartz Toy Store, visiting the Christmas tree at Rockefeller Center, and going out for Chinese food for dinner. As Seth Rogen, donning an "ugly Christmas sweater" of blue and white with a large Star of David across the chest, leads his fellow stars into the Chinese restaurant, opening his jacket to acknowledge the shared experience with a group of Hasidic Jews sitting at a table they pass by, one of his partners says off-camera, "It's not Christmas Eve until you've had Chinese."

One of the most popular sitcoms of the twenty-first century, *The Big Bang Theory*, aired an episode entitled "The Matrimonial Metric," where two of the engaged stars of the show, Sheldon and Amy, played by Jim Parsons and Mayim Bialik, are working to plan their wedding. In a subtle reference to the "Jews and Chinese Food" connection, when the cast gathered to eat their take-out dinner, a plot point in many, if not most, episodes, the Chinese food order was incomplete, leaving out the fried rice. Howard Wolowitz, the only explicitly identified Jewish character on the show (Mayim Bialik is a practicing Orthodox Jew herself, but her character is not), calls the restaurant to complain about the incorrect order, and to the shock of his surrounding friends, has a conversation in "Chinese" (I am unsure as to whether it was an accurate translation of either Mandarin or Cantonese, so I would not speculate which language he was speaking, or if it was a bad television trope of a made-up foreign language with English subtitles). It's a subtle reference to the fact that not only would the one Jewish character call the Chinese restaurant to correct the order, but that he would be so "in" that he would use their first language to correct the order while also making a "roast" style insult of his friend, Raj Koothrappali.[42]

A simple YouTube search returns videos galore of people exploring the links between Jews and Chinese food, and documentary treatments about the connections between Jews and Chinese food, like the one entitled "Christmas at Shalom Hunan," posted in December 2007.[43] Yiddish language publication *Forverts* posted a video by Shmuel Perlin entitled "'Egg Rolls and Egg Creams': A Jewish-Chinese

Street Festival" on YouTube in July 2012, touring the festival discussed in the previous section.[44] There are dedicated groups of Jewish friends who for years have sampled dozens of restaurants around Long Island, New York in the desire to find the best Chinese food, who have donned their experiment "The Chinese Quest."[45]

To bring this exploration back to where it began, most recently, Jewish publican *Tablet Magazine*, released an online edition of the "100 Most Jewish Foods" representing all roots and regions of Jewish cuisine from around the world. To draft the short piece on the importance of Chinese food, *Tablet* went to rapper, author, and food expert Action Bronson, a New York Jew, to describe the Jewish love of Chinese cuisine. Some of his more notable lines include, "Chinese food is as Jewish as matzo ball soup in New York City." Referencing the breaking of Kashrut law, he said, "They can be Jewish, but they'll still eat that Chinese rib. They'll still eat that roast pork. They'll still eat that fried rice." My personal favorite dish, he referred to like this, "Lo mein is heavy-duty in the Jewish community." Finally, the eloquent writer's side came out in his declarative closing statement, "Chinese food is not a phase. This is forever, this is a lifestyle—a Jewish lifestyle."[46]

I couldn't agree with Bronson more. I finished drafting this chapter on a Friday night, writing past sundown in violation of Shabbat observance rules. My next task will be calling in the order to my favorite Hunan spot, where I will rush out, pick up sweet and sour pork to deliver to my mother, some wonton chicken soup for my under-the-weather spouse, and some lo mein and moo-shi chicken to enjoy for myself. Chinese food is inescapably Jewish.

Key terms

Kosher: The collection of dietary restrictions (laws) followed by observant Jewish people around the world. The most commonly known and followed of these rules bans the consumption of shellfish and pork products. It also forbids the combination of dairy and meat products in a single meal.

Pogrom: The persecution of a specific ethnic or religious group, often associated with state-sanctioned or condoned violence and murder against Jewish communities. Most commonly associated with Russia and other Eastern European destruction of Jewish communities, seizure of Jewish property, and mass murder of Jewish individuals.

Ashkenazi Jews: Jewish communities who lived in Central and Eastern Europe, making up the great majority of Jewish immigrants to the United States from 1880–1924.

Discussion Questions

1. Why does American Chinese cuisine lend itself to American Jewish dietary needs better than other global cuisines like Italian or French? What are some

commonalities between the Eastern European Jewish cooking styles and American Chinese cuisine? What are the other factors besides flavor profiles and common ingredients that drove American Jews to explore Chinese cuisine when dining out over other, more popular styles of food, especially in large American cities?

2. What are the earliest historical roots of the American Jewish community and Chinese restaurants? Has the relationship between the two communities changed over the last century? Is the bond two-sided between both communities, or is it a more one-sided affinity by Jews for Chinese cuisine? Why do you think it is still so popular today among both observant Orthodox Jews and non-kosher American Jews? Why do you think food is so important to Jewish Americans?

3. In what ways has popular culture recognized and presented this unique intergroup relationship? Are there other popular representations of inter-group bonds, historical or current, that you can think of that mirror the relationship discussed in this chapter?

Notes

1 Acknowledgments and thanks: My primary motivator and biggest supporter is my wife, Alicia Brands, so all scholarship I produce is dedicated to her. She is also my best editor and critic, always helping me to improve my work. Perhaps most importantly, for this project, she assisted me in my research into local kosher Chinese restaurants around Baltimore, accompanying me for several research trips and working lunches. Also, a special thanks to the gracious and patient editors of this collection, Dr. Jenny Banh and Dr. Haiming Liu, who helped me shape and complete my contribution.

2 "Lenny Bruce, Uninhibited Comic, Found Dead in Hollywood Home: His Nightclub Acts Blended Satire with Scatology and Led to Arrests." *New York Times*, August 4, 1966, p. 32. Found online at Proquest Historic Newspapers Database, https://search-proquest-com.proxyau.wrlc.org/hnpnewyorktimes/docview/117324411/3D914EAF8E81491DP Q/9?accountid=8285.

3 *Goy*, *goyim*, and *goyish* can be used by Jews in a derogatory tone as well, but the basic definition/translation of the term simply refers to a person or thing that is non-Jewish.

4 There are several versions of the joke available online. This transcription was from a website on Jewish comedy history about the bit found at www.myjewishlearning.com/article/jewish-and-goyish/. There is also a recorded one available that has different qualifiers for the joke found at www.youtube.com/watch?time_continue=192&v=uD6Oi2kySSU, both accessed January 9, 2018.

5 Kimberly Yam, "The Reason Jews Eat Chinese Food on Christmas Is Rooted in Solidarity: Chinese and Jewish People Both Understood 'What It's Like to Be Outsiders' on Christmas." *HuffPost*, December 22, 2016. www.huffingtonpost.com/entry/why-jews-eat-chinese-food-on-christmas_us_585968b9e4b08debb78b4d92 accessed January 10, 2018.

6 Melissa Kravitz, "Why Do Jews Eat Chinese Food on Christmas? How the Tradition Has Evolved over 100 years." *Mic.com*, December 14, 2016, https://mic.com/articles/161093/why-do-jews-eat-chinese-food-on-christmas-how-the-tradition-has-evolved-over-100-years#.js2WBhXC2. Accessed January 10, 2018.

7 Josh Ozersky, "Why Do Jews Love Chinese Food?" *Time Magazine*, September 14, 2011. Accessed online January 10, 2018, http://ideas.time.com/2011/09/14/why-do-jews-love-chinese-food/.

8 This off-the-cuff thought is corroborated by some recent population data. The American Jewish Yearbook from 2008 listed the population of Brevard County where she lives with around 5,000 Jews, compared with the three Southeast Florida Counties (Miami-Dade, Broward, Palm Beach) which had a total of over 527,000 of the state's 655,235 Jews. American Jewish Yearbook 2008, p. 189. American Jewish Committee Archives, found online at www.ajcarchives.org/AJC_DATA/Files/AJYB806_USPopulation.pdf. Accessed January 10, 2018.

9 www.davidchuschinabistro.com/#/menu/C; Accessed January 10, 2018.

10 An obvious point of discussion in response to this statement would be that without asking every individual what their ascribed religion or ethnicity was, how could I know? There is a healthy population of non-white Jews of Color, but an assumption that people wearing crucifix necklaces are not Jewish would seem fair. Much more discussion on the complex multitudes that make up "American Jewry" will continue later in the chapter.

11 There is a complex "history" of the sign around the internet. Some websites describe it as a hoax, or based on a popular Jewish writer's thoughts on the phenomenon, but my family stands by the memory of seeing the sign in the restaurant window before going in on Christmas to eat.

12 Ben Sales, "Who Owns America's Oldest Synagogue? It's a 350-year-old Argument." Jewish Telegraphic Agency, August 4, 2017. www.jta.org/2017/08/04/news-opinion/united-states/who-owns-americas-oldest-synagogue-its-a-350-year-old-argument. Accessed January 10, 2018.

13 "Historical Timeline of Baltimore Jewry: 1657–1849." Jewish Museum of Maryland. http://jewishmuseummd.org/exhibits/timeline/timeline-1657-1849/ Accessed January 10, 2018.

14 American Jewish Year Book, 1930, Volume 32, p. 224. American Jewish Committee Archives, www.ajcarchives.org/AJC_DATA/Files/1930_1931_7_Statistics.pdf. Accessed January 10, 2018.

15 Geoffrey Wigoder, "Keeping Kosher: Food Laws in the Bible," *My Jewish Learning*, www.myjewishlearning.com/article/food-laws-in-the-bible/, accessed January 9, 2018.

16 Originally published as "New York Jews and Chinese Food: The Social Construction of an Ethnic Pattern" by Gaye Tuchman and Harry G. Levine. *Contemporary Ethnography*. 1992: 22(3), 382–407. This author was only able to obtain this version of their original release of the paper online, so future page citations will match the online .pdf document found here: Tuchman, Gaye, and Harry G. Levine. "New York Jews and Chinese Food: The Social Construction of an Ethnic Pattern." Queens College. Web. Archived March 19, 2013, at the Wayback Machine, http://dragon.soc.qc.cuny.edu/Staff/levine/SAFE-TREYF.pdf, accessed January 10, 2018.

17 Tuchman, Gaye, and Harry G. Levine. "New York Jews and Chinese Food: The Social Construction of an Ethnic Pattern." Queens College. Web. Archived March 19, 2013, at the Wayback Machine.; pp. 3–4, 7; http://dragon.soc.qc.cuny.edu/Staff/levine/SAFE-TREYF.pdf, accessed January 10, 2018.

18 Tuchman, Gaye, and Harry G. Levine. "New York Jews and Chinese Food: The Social Construction of an Ethnic Pattern." Queens College. Web. Archived March 19, 2013, at the Wayback Machine. p. 9; http://dragon.soc.qc.cuny.edu/Staff/levine/SAFE-TREYF.pdf, Accessed January 10, 2018.

19 Tuchman, Gaye, and Harry G. Levine. "New York Jews and Chinese Food: The Social Construction of an Ethnic Pattern." Queens College. Web. Archived March 19, 2013, at the Wayback Machine, p. 9.

20 Yong Chen, *Chop Suey, USA: The Story of Chinese Food in America* (New York: Columbia University Press, 2014), 117.

21 Tuchman, Gaye, and Harry G. Levine. "New York Jews and Chinese Food: The Social Construction of an Ethnic Pattern." Queens College. Web. Archived March 19, 2013, at the Wayback Machine.; p. 9; http://dragon.soc.qc.cuny.edu/Staff/levine/SAFE-TREYF.pdf, Accessed January 10, 2018.

22 Yong Chen, *Chop Suey, USA*: *The Story of Chinese Food in America* (New York: Columbia University Press, 2014), 116.

23 Yong Chen, *Chop Suey, USA*: *The Story of Chinese Food in America* (New York: Columbia University Press, 2014), 117.

24 Yong Chen, *Chop Suey, USA*: *The Story of Chinese Food in America* (New York: Columbia University Press, 2014), 119.

25 Tuchman, Gaye, and Harry G. Levine. "New York Jews and Chinese Food: The Social Construction of an Ethnic Pattern." Queens College. Web. Archived March 19, 2013, at the Wayback Machine, p. 11.

26 Tuchman, Gaye, and Harry G. Levine. "New York Jews and Chinese Food: The Social Construction of an Ethnic Pattern." Queens College. Web. Archived March 19, 2013, at the Wayback Machine, p. 15.

27 Tuchman, Gaye, and Harry G. Levine. "New York Jews and Chinese Food: The Social Construction of an Ethnic Pattern." Queens College. Web. Archived March 19, 2013, at the Wayback Machine, pp. 14–15.

28 Tuchman, Gaye, and Harry G. Levine. "New York Jews and Chinese Food: The Social Construction of an Ethnic Pattern." Queens College. Web. Archived March 19, 2013, at the Wayback Machine, p. 9

29 Daniel B. Schneider, "F.Y.I.," *The New York Times*, April 16, 2000. Accessed online December 27, 2017, www.nytimes.com/2000/04/16/nyregion/fyi-788643.html

30 "Egg Rolls and Egg Creams: A Jewish-Chinese Street Festival," YouTube, accessed February 8, 2018. www.youtube.com/watch?v=KR-n1memRtc

31 www.eldridgestreet.org/event/eggrolls/

32 Scarlet Chang, "When Jewish Women Embraced Mah-jongg," *The Los Angeles Times*, May 13, 2012; online edition, http://articles.latimes.com/2012/may/13/entertainment/la-ca-mah-jong-20120513. For a short video explanation, MyJewishLearning published a video, February 6, 2017, entitled "How Mah-Jongg became a Jewish Game," www.youtube.com/watch?v=lE9eETsQwq8.

33 Yong Chen, *Chop Suey, USA*: *The Story of Chinese Food in America* (New York: Columbia University Press, 2014), 114.

34 Yong Chen, *Chop Suey, USA*: *The Story of Chinese Food in America* (New York: Columbia University Press, 2014), 114.; *My Favorite Year*, directed by Richard Benjamin (Culver City, CA: Metro-Goldwyn-Mayer Studios, 1982), film.

35 Tuchman, Gaye, and Harry G. Levine. "New York Jews and Chinese Food: The Social Construction of an Ethnic Pattern." Queens College. Web. Archived March 19, 2013, at the Wayback Machine, p. 9.

36 David Brooks, *Saturday Night Live*, "TV Funhouse: Christmastime for the Jews" www.youtube.com/watch?v=BGzO1ghRKp4, accessed online December 26, 2017; Written by Robert Smigel, Scott Jacobson, Eric Drysdale, Julie Klausner; Music Produced by Steven M. Gold; Vocals by Darlene Love.

37 "Beyond the Seder Table: Manischewitz Wine Popular Among Asian Americans," *Jerusalem Post*, May 2, 2016. Accessed February 10, 2018. www.jpost.com/Not-Just-News/Beyond-the-Seder-table-Manischewitz-wine-popular-among-Asian-Americans-452979

38 Amy Sherman-Palladino, *Gilmore Girls*, "Jews and Chinese Food," directed by Matthew Diamond (Burbank, CA: Warner Brothers Burbank Studios, February 22, 2005), television.

39 Amy Sherman-Palladino, *The Marvelous Mrs. Maisel*, "Mrs. X at the Gaslight," directed by Scott Ellis, (Amazon Studios, original series, 2017), streaming television.

40 Patricia Volk, "A Love Affair, Dumplings on the Side," *The New York Times*, March 26, 2006, online edition, accessed March 8, 2018. www.nytimes.com/2006/03/26/nyregion/thecity/a-love-affair-dumplings-on-the-side.html

41 Jonathan Levine, *The Night Before*, directed by Jonathan Levine (2015; Burbank, CA: Columbia Pictures/Sony Pictures Home Entertainment, 2016), film.

42 Mark Cendrowski, *The Big Band Theory*, "The Matrimonial Metric" (Burbank, CA: Warner Brothers Burbank Studios, 4 January 2018), television.

43 "Christmas at Shalom Hunan," YouTube, accessed February 8, 2018. www.youtube.com/watch?v=9ApHwQqLycg

44 "Egg Rolls and Egg Creams: A Jewish-Chinese Street Festival," YouTube, accessed February 8, 2018. www.youtube.com/watch?v=KR-n1memRtc

45 "About Us: The Chinese Quest," accessed February 8, 2018. www.thechinesequest.com/about-2/; Erica Marcus, "Five Long Island Men on a Quest for Great Chinese Food," February 18, 2015, www.newsday.com/lifestyle/restaurants/five-long-island-men-on-a-quest-for-great-chinese-food-1.9924167, accessed February 10, 2018; "5 Jewish Guys on a Chinese Food Quest," YouTube, accessed February 10, 2018. www.youtube.com/watch?v=ETArmtiR2fk

46 Action Bronson, "Chinese Food: 100 Most Jewish Foods," *TabletMag*, https://100jewishfoods.tabletmag.com/chinese-food/ accessed March 8, 2018 online.

12

LAST TANGO IN ARGENTINA

Cheuk Kwan

"Would you like to retire to China?" I ask the 71-year-old man sitting next to me as our taxi meanders down the streets of Buenos Aires. A light rain falls.

"I can't go home. It's too complicated. There are too many problems every time I go back,"[1] says Foo-Ching Chiang (江福清) from the shadowy interior of the cab. Through rain-splattered windows, yellow streetlight dances across his weathered face. Chiang has been in Argentina for more than half of his life. Today is the feast day of Santa Ana and we have just come from a San Telmo church concert that opened with the national anthem. I ask whether he calls Argentina home.

"Yes and no. For me the concept of home is fading," says Chiang. "I empathize with your internationalism. It's the only way out. The Earth is so small and our time here so quick. I see myself as a member of this Earth so, for me, the concept of national boundaries is troubling."

"A lot of people want to be buried in China," I say, not expecting an answer. The older generation of Chinese immigrants has a deep-seated desire to be returned to China when they die, even if only as bones and ashes.[2]

"I told my children to scatter my ashes to the sea," Chiang replies emphatically. The rain is pelting harder against the taxi window and I've found my kindred spirit.

Finding Mr. Chiang

There are 40 million of us in the Chinese diaspora,[3] and it's serendipitous how we find each other in unexpected corners of the world. We instinctively forge connections across the blurred landscape of other human beings.[4]

Fifteen years ago, in a city then known as Leningrad, I met a stocky, elderly Chinese man not unlike Chiang. He was walking on the other side of a bridge that spans the Neva River. After we nodded to each other, I made a point of crossing over to chat with him, and he invited me to his Soviet-era apartment. After dinner with his grown daughter and his Russian wife of 40 years, he shared the story of how he had come to live in the Baltic city so far from home and of the trials they faced in an inter-racial marriage in the Soviet Union. Chance encounters like these are precious moments in our life journeys, where we connect with each other across geography, history and politics.[5]

I found Chiang through six degrees of separation. My sister has a friend whose aunt, Eileen, lives in Rio de Janeiro. It was during a lunch with Auntie Eileen, within view of Pão de Açúcar, that she brought up that her stepson lives in Buenos Aires. This connection in Argentina prompted me to send Kwoi Gin (甄國健), the cinematographer for my *Chinese Restaurants* film series, to scout for a Chinese restaurant owner in the land of tango.[6] Kwoi was in a cyber-relationship with a woman from Buenos Aires, and I was all too happy to send him there for his Christmas "getting-to-know-you." That was when he connected with Auntie Eileen's stepson Stephen Wu (吳冷輝), who took him to meet his good friend of many years, Chiang.

Paris of South America

Kwoi and I land in Buenos Aires early this August morning in 2003. We are nearing the end of our 4-year, 5-continent, 13-country odyssey to tell the stories of restaurant owners around the world.[7]

The soft winter light, faint smell of *Gauloise* in the air, and misty vistas of a lush green countryside on the ride from the airport remind me of taxi rides from Paris' Charles de Gaulle airport. With its cosmopolitan air, fashion sense, architecture and boulevard cafés, Buenos Aires lives up to its reputation as the Paris of South America. Even its Jewish garment district, with *milongas* in abandoned lofts, reminds me of Paris' 13th District—not to mention the obelisk standing in the middle of Plaza de la Republica, just like its counterpart at Place de la Concorde.

Through another three degrees of diasporic separation, Kwoi found us a gorgeous Parisian-style apartment that belongs to a French diplomat Valerie. Valerie and her Chinese writer-husband, whom she met during a previous posting in Beijing, is on vacation with their toddler son—leaving us this luxurious apartment that comes with a maid who dutifully lays out breakfast every morning.

Ajay Naroonha and his wife Sarada are already waiting for us in the apartment. Ajay is the cousin of my Goan-Canadian friend Christine in Toronto and I engaged him to be my sound recordist and second camera during our shoot in India earlier in the year. The couple came all the way from Mumbai on this shoot, arriving the day before via Air Canada's nightly Toronto to Sao Paolo non-stop. It's the only way I could get our Indian nationals to South America without transiting through the post-9/11 United States.

Luz Algranti arrives last, just as we are sitting down for breakfast. She's our local fixer and interpreter whom Kwoi found through his now former cyber-girlfriend. The Argentina film crew falls into place like pieces of a jigsaw puzzle.

FIGURE 12.1 Tango dancing in La Boca.

Casa China

Casa China is a three-story building on Calle Viamonte, just a few blocks from Teatro Colón in the heart of Buenos Aires. Two heavy red doors, each adorned with the Chinese character for "fortune," open to a sky-lit inner courtyard decorated with Chinese artifacts and motifs. A half-moon arch, like those in classical Chinese gardens, leads to the restaurant hall. Kwoi makes a mental note that the courtyard would be a perfect backdrop for Chiang's interview.

Chiang conceived the concept of Casa China a few years after he arrived in Argentina in 1964. He imagined it as a home away from home for the handful of Taiwanese families who lived there at the time. It would become a gathering place for future generations to enjoy the food and to socialize with each other.

"The future of the world rests with those who can hand over to future generations the essence of life and hope," Chiang wrote in his essay "The Casa China Story."[8] He also envisioned that once the People's Republic of China established diplomatic relations with Argentina,[9] more Chinese would make their way to here and Casa Chinas would become vibrant Chinese cultural centers. In this remaining Casa China in Bueno Aires, *tai chi*, cooking, and Chinese medicine classes are held on the second floor. There's even a Sunday evening tango class for Chinese immigrants. Chiang lives on the third floor.

Maria Alejandra Gerolami has been working at Casa China for four years. This evening, dressed in a blue Chinese tunic, she's demonstrating the iconic Chinese culinary export *chow fan*, fried rice. She works quickly and offers up cooking tips—always use leftover rice, break up the rice chunks with your spatula, cook the harder vegetables first then beat in the eggs. As she melds ingredients such as water chestnuts, bamboo shoots, and dried Chinese mushrooms into the dish, Maria describes the culinary alchemy of arriving at the right mix of colors, taste, and aroma.

"Everyone is very happy when they leave here," Maria explains. "The food is prepared based on where people are coming from. There're people who like more vegetables, there're people who don't eat pork, or spicy food. It all depends on who's here. Okay, I will write it down step-by-step for you. *Sin preocupaciones.*" No worries.

Chiang takes us to the basement kitchen to meet his chief cook Yafang Jiang (江亞芳). He introduces the woman as his niece from Mainland China, and there's no reason to doubt him. After all, they have the same surnames—Jiang and Chiang being the Mainland and Taiwanese romanization[10] respectively of the Chinese character for "river." However, this kind of family relationship can sometimes be stretched. Chinese restaurant owners around the world have been known to bring over distant relatives—even unrelated people with the same surnames from their own villages—to work at their establishments.[11] It's a way out of China, and immediate livelihoods, for these new immigrants.

Chiang now proves that he is still the master of making spring roll skin. "The secret is when you mix the flour with the water, it should neither be too dry, or too wet. You have to wait a few hours, then you can do it." He spreads a dollop of dough onto a flat round pan. "The temperature of the pan has to be just right. If it's not hot enough, the dough will stick."

"The dough is a little wet today," comments Yafang, to no one in particular. So, the flour mix can be different from day to day. And the art of making paper-thin spring roll skin lies in adjusting to the variations in every batch depending on the ambient moisture. Chiang continues to make more skin on the flat stove as he talks, until his niece asks him to stop.

"I kind of do this as a daily physical exercise," he laughs. "I feel that as long as we have these skills, we'll have no problem surviving here."

A Bit of History

Chiang was born in 1931 in Jiangsu Province in eastern China and was orphaned at a very young age. It was during the early stages of the Chinese Civil War between Chiang Kai-shek's (蔣介石) Nationalist government and insurgent Communist forces.

On December 13, 1937, at the outbreak of the Sino-Japanese War, Japanese soldiers marched through the city gates of Nanjing (Nanking), then capital of the Republic of China, and, in a matter of weeks, killed more than 200,000 civilians in what is known today as the Nanking Massacre.[12] Shortly after the massacre, the

7-year-old Chiang was sent there to live with relatives. By that time, Nanjing had become the seat of the collaborationist government in Japanese-occupied territory. No one in his family talked about the horrific event, not even years later. Chiang brushes aside my asking about his recollection of this momentous event.

Following the end of the Second World War, Chiang lived for a short time in Shanghai before moving to Taiwan in 1947, when he was 16. Two years later, Chiang Kai-shek's Nationalists fled to Taiwan when it was evident that mainland China was all but lost to Mao Zedong's (毛澤東) Chinese Communists. The Nationalists controlled the social, cultural, and political agenda in Taiwan, an island off mainland China populated by Chinese who had mass migrated across the Taiwan Strait after Dutch colonizers were expelled in 1662. The Dutch called the island Formosa, a name that was commonly used until the 1970s.

Life in Taiwan was not happy for Chiang. He never finished school and only held odd jobs. When asked to join the governing Nationalist Party, the Kuomintang (國民黨), he refused, not wanting to be drawn into the "whirlpool of politics." Kuomintang's preoccupation in the 1960s was to recover Chinese mainland from "Communist bandits." Chiang's sympathies, however, lay with local Taiwanese who resented the new arrivals from Mainland.

"It was very childish. You were either a friend or an enemy, there was no in-between," Chiang says, evoking the sentiments of a young generation in Taiwan at that time. The Communists had already established a new republic on the mainland and these young people didn't see the point of fighting over a lost cause.

Chiang was soon conscripted and served on the tiny island of Jinmen, the first line of defense in southwestern Taiwan within shelling distance of China's guns across the strait. He brought along an English dictionary and a copy of *The Old Man and the Sea*. Like his hero Hemingway, Chiang has always been his own man—self-taught, a loner, a romantic, and non-conformist. It was during his time in the barracks that Chiang wrote a 38-page love letter to his fiancée detailing the cruelties and injustices of war. For his pacifist rebellion, he landed in solitary confinement for four months.

Chiang married his fiancée after his discharge but could not hold down regular jobs. After the birth of their two children in the late 1950s, Chiang saw no future in Taiwan and wanted to leave the island when traveling abroad was restricted. An Argentine diplomat couple he had met in Taipei arranged for the family to migrate to Argentina.

A Brave New World

La Boca once was a working-class *barrio* settled by Italian immigrants from Genoa. Now it's an artists' colony and tourist destination with rows of brightly painted houses by the dock. The rough neighborhood is home to Maradona's equally rough Boca Juniors *fútbol* team—two policemen come by to tell us to watch our camera gear. I bring Chiang to the dockside in the old port—close to where his family would have disembarked 40 years earlier after their month-long sea journey from Taiwan—and ask about his first impression of the New World.

"*Las chicas como estrellas en el cielo*," Chiang enthuses. Girls were like stars in the sky. I am interviewing Chiang in Spanish through our interpreter, Luz. I grew up in an English-speaking world and am always fascinated by Chinese diasporic communities who speak in languages other than English. Chiang's Spanish is serviceable, using mostly the present tense, dropping plurals, and mixing up the genders. All this I would learn from my translator weeks after I came back from South America. It's okay, I would tell her, the Chinese language has no conjugated verbs or gendered nouns.

"We didn't know that Buenos Aires was so modern and so beautiful," Chiang continues. "And in truth, I have a lot of faith because the city is so big and it surely has space for us."

When he arrived, there were only about 200 Chinese in Buenos Aires, mostly Cantonese. Chiang noticed they were not well off, "so they have to work very hard." I ask about the Chinese grocery and electronic goods stores in Barrio Chino at Belgrano.[13] "That came later, settled by immigrants from Taiwan and China in the eighties," Chiang tells me about Buenos Aires' Chinatown.

After a few months of odd jobs, Chiang moved his family to the provincial capital of Cordoba, where the city is smaller, people closer and friendlier. When he approached the American consulate for work, he was told there were no jobs for him because he did not speak Spanish. But, could he cook? Just like that, he was hired to prepare family meals at the consulate. Chiang thus joined a long line of Chinese immigrant cooks who do not have a culinary background.

Like so many Chinese immigrants before him, Chiang also became a small-scale purveyor of *empanaditas*, turnovers, made from his home kitchen. It was the consul-general who encouraged him to turn these little *empanadas* into spring rolls. Soon, with the help of his wife, he set up a mini-factory making up to 600 spring rolls a day. Chiang eventually moved his family back to Buenos Aires, convinced that there was a bigger market there. With word-of-mouth and publicity, he began to mass-produce frozen spring rolls for supermarket chains, becoming the Spring Roll King of Argentina.

The Chinese Diaspora

The journey to South America had opened Chiang's eyes to the world of the Chinese diaspora. The freighter that took his family from Taiwan stopped in Hong Kong, Singapore, Malaysia, Mauritius, Mozambique, and South Africa before rounding the Cape of Good Hope to South America. He was surprised to find Chinese settlers everywhere: Port Louis, Maputo, Durban, Cape Town, even São Paulo, and Montevideo.

Taiwanese of Chiang's generation, who came in the 1950s and 1960s, were not the first Chinese immigrants to settle in Argentina. The first wave, mostly Cantonese-speaking from southeast coastal regions of Kwangtung province, came between 1919 and 1949.[14] But Chiang now tells me that a tribe of Chinese of unknown provenance had come from France after the First World War to settle in the northeast region of Chaco, near Paraguay. They became *gauchos*, Argentine cowboys.

It was the Chinese in Chaco who made a profound impression on Chiang. When he made a trip there, he saw children two generations removed who could not speak Chinese. He thought about his own children: "If they don't speak Chinese, the Chinese culture will be lost."

I now bring up the more than 140,000 Chinese Labour Corps[15] recruited by the British and French during the First World War to provide support work and manual labor behind front lines.[16] Most of them were repatriated back to China after the war, but could some of them have made their way to Argentina? Chiang is aware of them but insists that those who came to Chaco were not from the same province in China as those behind the frontlines in Europe, nor had they ever served in France.

In the late 1960s, Chiang made several extensive trips around the world "to look at how other Chinese migrants live." It's this curiosity into the Chinese diaspora that informed his worldview. He, for example, learned about racism that led Chinese railroad workers to migrate from the United States to Central and South America[17]—but not to Brazil or Argentina, he hastens to add, because of two continental barriers: the Andes and the Amazon.

After his travels, Chiang crafted a cultural manifesto that he sent me before I arrived in Argentina. The document, written in Chinese and translated into Spanish and English, offers his vision of Chinese culture playing a big part in "life

FIGURE 12.2 Finishing a *parrilla* meal in San Telmo, from left to right: Chia-Yin, Chiang, Kwan, Kwoi, Luz, and Sarada.

harmony and world peace." It delves into, among other things, the *yin* and *yang* of life forces and the preservation of 5,000 years of Chinese culture—drawing inspiration from *Future Shock*, *The Aquarius Conspiracy* and the philosophies of Russell and Krishnamurti.[18] Chiang also cites Beethoven's Ninth Symphony as a major influence in his life, quoting Friedrich Schiller's poem *Ode to Joy* that Beethoven used in the final choral movement of the symphony:

> *Thy magic power re-unites*
> *all that custom has divided*
> *all men become brothers*
> *under the sway of thy gentle wings.*

"Within four seas, all men are brothers," I quote back a Chinese saying.

The Daughter

"It's just a short hop across the Andes," says Chia-Yin Chiang (江嘉音), who flew in from Santiago de Chile in the morning for one of her frequent visits with Chiang. She comes to see her father to have "one of these long conversations that both of us enjoy having from time to time."

In her mid-forties, having lived the past 15 years away from home, Chia-Yin appreciates the opportunity to spend time with her father. I find all this very touching and tell her so. Chinese men are not usually open and expressive enough to have long chats with their daughters like that.

"Our family has become disjointed, we don't have time to meet each other. One lives in the north, the other in the south. How do we maintain our family unity?" she adds. Our interview is on the balcony overlooking the sky-lit courtyard just outside Chiang's living quarters. While setting up, Kwoi peeks inside. The room is filled with old and dusty furniture, unkempt, stockpiled with old Chinese newspapers. It reminds Kwoi of depressing places where "elderly uncles" lived their remaining years in 1950s Hong Kong.

"My father had rough times in life, first in his childhood during the Sino-Japanese War, and later in Taiwan during the Cold War, then coming to Argentina without knowing anyone," Chia-Yin continues. "But I think that has strengthened him instead of weakened him. It has provided him with unbounded optimism about life."

"Argentina is not an easy country to live in, and last year we had the worst situation," she adds. Chia-Yin, an UN economic development specialist, is referring to the country's economic crisis in 2002 in which the peso lost more than half of its value.[19] "Every time I call and tell him that I worry for him, he would say 'Why worry? This is normal. We've always lived like this, in uncertainty, in chaos, so you shouldn't be too worried.'"

Chia-Yin stood out as *china*. When they were growing up in Cordoba, she and her younger brother Chia-Erh (江嘉爾) were the only Asians among the 2,000 students in their school. Classmates came up to her to stroke her hair and look at her eyes. "I felt like a Martian," she recalls. "In fact, I escaped from school one time feeling uncomfortable and unwanted."

Chia-Yin did not date during her adolescence and was always helping out in the restaurant, working at the dessert table when she was 9, and helping out in the dining room at age 13. When she was 19, she was left in charge of the restaurant for three months while Chiang went on a world tour with her brother—"those were the hardest months of my life."

"Yes, of course, my father expected me to marry a Chinese," Chia-Yin anticipates where I'm going next with the interview. "When I was 21, he went to China and brought the son of a childhood friend of his to Argentina, thinking probably that we could hit it off." She didn't dislike the young man—they spoke the same language and he was very pleasant. However, he had grown up in China while she's from the West. "We didn't have the same outlook in life. We were just incompatible."

Partly to get away from her father trying to find her a prospective *Chinese* husband, Chia-Yin left to study in New York. She was in her twenties, and found the city exhilarating. "It was the 1980s, New York was on top of the world. I was stimulated by the diversity of people, hearing these different beautiful languages spoken."

When the Falklands War broke out in 1982, the situation back home made it impossible for her family to support her. A friend urged Chia-Yin to apply for work at the United Nations, since she could speak three official UN languages. She accepted the only position available, a secretarial job. Chia-Yin worked by day and completed her graduate studies in the evening at New York University. The UN eventually promoted her to a permanent job as an economic development specialist, posted in Geneva.

Even though Chia-Yin was in her thirties and living in Europe, Chiang tried again to interest his daughter in a prospective husband from Taiwan. Again, she thought the young man was interesting but, again, incompatible. After seven years in Switzerland, Chia-Yin became homesick and wanted to be near her father. She applied for a job at the UN's Latin American headquarters in Santiago de Chile. By that time, she had met an American physicist.

"As our friendship turned into a romance," she recalls. "He decided that Geneva was no longer interesting without me there and would come with me to Chile—that's when we decided to get married."

What Is Love?

Chiang was introduced to Yongfen Liu (劉永芬) when she was in junior high school. He was only four years older than her and treated her like a little sister. They were, however, married several years later, in 1957.

"It was her mother's idea," Chiang recalls, speaking in Mandarin. "Her mom liked me a lot. She was a great woman. She even came to live with me in Argentina in her eighties and told me, 'I would like my life to end with you beside me.'"

But immigrant life in Argentina was not a happy one for Liu.

"I found my mother crying one day when I was a child," Chia-Yin recalls. "My mother comes from a very comfortable and well-to-do family. She was sad because there was no money to go back to Taiwan."

Chiang and Liu soon grew apart in Argentina and Liu eventually moved to the United States with their son in 1981. "I wanted to set her free, so I made no effort to retain her," Chiang explains. "She spent an hour every day doing her make-up, living like an aristocrat. I just wanted to live a simple life."

"People are excited to be married before their twenties; but after a while, when you started having responsibility, you would not be as impulsive as before," Chiang continues. "In our times, responsibility was very important to us. And I still feel a sense of responsibility for my wife and my mother-in-law."

Chia-Yin confides to me that if she were to choose between her father being alone and uncared for, or having someone care for him in his old age, she would choose the latter, "for his own good." She also told her mother that if she ever finds a suitable companion in New York, to "go ahead."

"I don't feel like they should limit their choices because of some traditional Chinese views of family life. We're all adults. I think what matters the most is their happiness. And if they're happy whether living alone or with someone else, that's up to them. That's their choice."

Stephen Wu

Stephen Wu and Chiang have been friends for as long as Chiang has been in Argentina—40 years. This morning, seven of us, including Wu's father-in-law, pile into an old Mercedes and make our way to Wu's country house just outside the city.

Porteños is a generic Spanish word meaning "port people," but residents of Buenos Aires have adopted the term for themselves. *Porteños* country houses are essentially family homes with large yards just outside city limits, far away from the port area. Wu's plot is larger than most, fenced in by walls and trees, with a stream running through it. In the front yard, to one side, is an abandoned circus trailer. Wu was a magician and ran a circus, which is where he met his Italian wife, a trapeze artist. They have been married for 46 years. One of their sons now runs the circus. Wu became a successful businessman—he talks business non-stop in the car with his father-in-law.

Auntie Eileen told me very little about her stepson when we met in Rio de Janeiro last year, even less about how he ended up in a circuitous way in Argentina. It seems that Wu comes from a wealthy and well-connected family. His father was a high-ranking military officer during the Sino-Japanese War when Nationalists and Communists were busy fighting the Japanese, and with each other. Names of Nationalist leader Chiang Kai-Shek and collaborationist leader Wang Jingwei (汪精衛) crop up in our conversation, but Wu gives no indication which side his father was on.

"The whole society was like a fishnet—everything was connected but hard to tell who's good and who's bad," Wu quotes his father.

In 1949, on the eve of Communist victory, Wu's family moved to Brazil with a large group of émigrés, including the modern expressionist painter and gourmet, Zhang Daqian[20] (張大千). I always wondered how the artist ended up in Brazil—and now this also explains how Auntie Eileen, Wu's stepmother, ended up there as well.

Helpers are now laying out a *parrilla* feast, various beef parts cooked to perfection in the backyard brick grill. Kwoi jokes we are about to consume half a side of cow in one sitting, enough meat to feed an entire village in China. The atmosphere is idyllic, the conversation jovial. The winter sun shines warmly and spreads a golden hue across the garden. Beer, wine, and liquor flow freely.

After lunch, we walk around with glasses of brandy, picking fruits from the trees. I am drunk with the scene. Thousands of miles away from China, at the other end of the world, we meet as long-lost friends. Wu is in the mood to talk, which prompts Chiang to open up as well. They speak of love and mistresses, about Chiang's separation from his wife, the universe and the world, and liberation from family entanglements.

"All his friends hope he and his wife can get back together as soon as possible," Wu tells me in a loud enough voice to make sure that Chiang hears it.

"You've to respect a person's choice. A person has her right to do things she wants," Chiang rejoins. "It is not appropriate to use family to bind two people together."

"I have lots of girlfriends, but I still want to be with my wife all the time," says Wu. I'm not sure whether he's saying it in jest.

"I told my wife that she has three choices," Chiang says. "If she wants to live with our daughter, she can go live with our daughter; if she wants to stay with me, we can live together; and if she wants to live with our son in New York, she can live with our son." Chiang elaborates for us his concept of love, of the romantic or platonic varieties, and about the need for a companion to take care of him at his age. When I ask him whether he's still in love with his wife, he answers only in generalities, with comments like "what's love anyway?"

"I don't have female friends," Chiang adds. "Why? Because they're going to fight for sure! It's not necessary. My time is valuable. I had one once, a girl who helped me sell things, but it was a disaster. She wanted to be with me all the time. I didn't think it was going to work out."

Sunday in San Telmo

San Telmo, with its colonial buildings and cobblestone streets, is the oldest *barrio* of Buenos Aries. Sunday is when *Porteños* and tourists descend onto the area to eat, shop, and have a good time. As we walk through the area filled with antique shops, flea markets, and tango dancers in the street, Chiang becomes animated and explains how he came to open his own curio shop in the *barrio*.

"I have been to many Chinatowns, but the souvenir shops are all small and crowded, unlike mine," Chiang says proudly as he walks us into his store. This is where we meet his long-time friend, the 70-year-old shopkeeper Shouchang Wang (王壽昌). Wang shows me the products on the shelves. Chiang is right. They are laid out like gallery pieces.

I suggest we all go to the café-bar next door where a handful of men are nursing their coffees and their Camparis; pictures of Carlos Gardel, the patron saint of tango, hang on the walls; and a football game is on the television.

"I jumped ship in the 70s. Nothing really to worry about, I wasn't robbing them," Wang speaks to us in Cantonese. "Argentina is resource rich and that attracted me right away." He uses the Chinese expression "jump ship" to describe how illegal immigrants, often working in merchant marines, would go ashore and vanish into a foreign country.

"Right now, my wife, my children, and my grandchildren are all *ghosts. Así es la vida* [That's life]." Here Wang uses a part-derogatory, part-endearing Cantonese term *gwei*, ghost, for white Europeans—Chinese see themselves as "humans" in the Celestial Empire, all others are "ghosts."

Wang is Hakka and lived in the Kwangtung province before emigrating to Taiwan—he makes a point of distinguishing his Hakka identity from that of early Cantonese immigrants in Argentina. Hakka, literally "guest families," are the Jews of China. Driven by war and famine, they migrated from the central plains of China 1,000 years ago to the southeastern part of the country, settling in and around several counties in Kwangtung and Fujian provinces. From there, many emigrated all over the world, mainly to India and the Indian Ocean, South Africa, the Caribbean, and the Americas.

Wang left his wife and children back in Taiwan when he "jumped ship" in Argentina. After his wife died, his relationship with his children back in Taiwan ended. "I lost contact with them." Wang reminds me of older Chinese who left China as young men. Living apart from their original families—often in hardship— and in countries with restrictive immigration policies, these men would marry and have second families in the new world. I encounter these stories everywhere I go in the Americas.[21]

Bar Sur

I've always liked the tango, its seductive and sensuous music, and the eroticism and sexual longing in the dance. And I've always wanted to find a Chinese restaurant owner who could tango the night away. Sadly, Chiang does not, and I'm reduced to filming him trying to dance with the rest of the tango class in Casa China or watching a pair of tango school students dancing in a bar-restaurant in La Boca.

Bar Sur is a tango parlor in San Telmo. Its checker-tiled floor hosts nightly tango shows for tourists arriving by the busload. On our last night in the city, after yet another *parrilla* meal with more drinking, we walk with Chiang to Bar Sur. He stands at the entrance but doesn't go in.

FIGURE 12.3 Filming Chiang in front of Bar Sur.

The lighting near the entrance is a warm orange glow. Cobblestones glisten after the rain. It is cool and Chiang instinctively pulls up his collar, a cigarette dangling from his mouth. Kwoi now back-steps with his camera, like a human dolly, to pull wide on Chiang. Through the camera, I see a loner standing in front of a tango bar, in the country that gives us the melancholic dance.

Afterwards, we call a taxi to take Chiang home. As the car disappears into the mist, hurrying into the night, I'm overcome with sadness.

Key Terms

Diasporic ethnography: Writing the personal experiences of Chinese people in their diasporic communities.

Food culture: The customs, practices, and attitudes towards the production, procurement, circulation, and consumption of food.

Hybridity: The synthesis of multiple forms (experiences, medias, world views, etc.) to create new ways of understanding conventional or traditional frameworks.

Discussion questions

1. Chiang appears to be a humble, hard-working man—like many other Chinese who fled the wars in China. What does Chiang's life story signify about the aging Chinese population in the Chinese diaspora? What does the preservation of these stories signify?
2. How does the concept of hybridity and cross-cultural interaction affect the lives of those in the Chinese diaspora? What elements of hybridity help enhance or alter understandings of traditional Chinese culture? Internal to most cultures, food is a vital element for understanding the survival of its people. The case is no different for Chinese people. What do the hybrid elements of food, diaspora, and personal journey say about Chinese people in Argentina?
3. The author uses local colors and socio-cultural references to contextualize the story geo-politically and historically. How do these elements enhance your understanding of the space and its relationship to the characters?

Notes

1 All quoted texts are from English transcripts of video recordings or my production notes.
2 "It was general practice for overseas Chinese to exhume the remains after seven years, clean and dry the bones and then ship them back to China for burial." From "Chinese Cemetery at Harling Point," Old Cemeteries Society of Victoria, accessed April 15, 2018, www.oldcem.bc.ca/cem_ch.htm. See also "Chinese Cemetery," District of Oak Bay, accessed April 15, 2018, www.oakbay.ca/explore-oak-bay/points-interest/chinese-cemetery
3 Chee-Beng Tan, ed., *Routledge Handbook of the Chinese Diaspora* (Routledge, 2012).
4 My observation and personal experience. See also Jiaming Sun, Scott Lancaster, *Chinese Globalization: A Profile of People-Based Global Connections in China* (Routledge, 2013).
5 Having grown up as a member of the Chinese diaspora, I have always wanted to tell the stories and explore the inter-connectedness of the varied components of this global migration phenomenon. As a world traveler, I often seek out Chinese restaurants and wonder how their owners ended up in far-flung corners of the world speaking different languages, living in different cultures.
6 Two events inspired me to make the *Chinese Restaurants* documentary series: my 1976 visit to Istanbul's China Restaurant that was owned, according to my guidebook, by a man who "walked from China" (this story became the Turkey episode in my documentary); and my 1982 visit to Fort Jesus Museum in Mombasa, Kenya where Chinese artifacts and connections are on full display, from Ming porcelain retrieved from shipwrecks off the coast of East Africa to influences of Chinese rudder design on the East African dhow. I am also inspired by a 1999 article by Nicholas Kristof that reported how Ming Dynasty Admiral Zheng He's (鄭和) sea expeditions had reached the east coast of Africa as early as 1415, and shipwreck survivors were found to have settled and intermarried with indigenous people on Pate Island off Lamu, Kenya. See Nicholas D. Kristof, "1492: The Prequel," *The New York Times Magazine*, June 6, 1999, accessed April 15, 2018, www.nytimes.com/1999/06/06/magazine/1492-the-prequel.html.
7 My 15-part *Chinese Restaurants* documentary series (www.ChineseRestaurants.tv) tells the stories of the Chinese diaspora through the lens of family-run Chinese restaurants. The films explore issues in history, geo-politics, migration, family, identity as well as food and culture. The series was filmed between 2000 and 2003 in five continents, from the Amazon to the Arctic. Six countries in the Americas are featured: Argentina, Brazil, Canada, Cuba, Peru, and Trinidad & Tobago.
8 Personal fax communication from Chia-Yin Chiang on July 2, 2003, the essay "The Casa China Story" written by Foo-Ching Chiang.

 9 Diplomatic relations established on March 19, 1972. See "Argentina-China relations," Wikipedia, accessed April 15, 2018, https://en.wikipedia.org/wiki/Argentina%E2% 80%93China_relations

10 People's Republic of China uses *pinyin* while Taiwan, Hong Kong, and other Chinese communities use the Wade-Giles system of romanization.

11 Anecdotes and personal stories told to the author by family-run Chinese-Canadian restaurant owners. See also Ronald Takaki, *Strangers from a Different Shore: A History of Asian Americans, Updated and Revised Edition* (First Back Bay, 1998).

12 Iris Chang, *The Rape of Nanking: The Forgotten Holocaust of World War II* (Basic Books, 1997).

13 "Barrio Chino (Buenos Aires)," Wikipedia, accessed April 15, 2018, https://en.wikipedia. org/wiki/Barrio_Chino_(Buenos_Aires)

14 "Chinese Argentines," Wikipedia, accessed April 15, 2018, https://en.wikipedia.org/ wiki/Chinese_Argentines

15 "Chinese Labour Corps on the Western Front," The National Archives, accessed April 15, 2018, http://blog.nationalarchives.gov.uk/blog/chinese-labour-corps-western-front-2/

16 "The Forgotten Army of the First World War: How Chinese Labourers Helped Shape Europe," *South China Morning Post*, accessed April 15, 2018, http://multimedia.scmp. com/ww1-china/

17 Robert Chao Romero, *The Chinese in Mexico, 1882–1940*, 2nd ed. (University of Arizona Press, 2012). Scott Zesch, *The Chinatown War: Chinese Los Angeles and the Massacre of 1871* (Oxford University Press, 2012).

18 From interviews and conversations with Chiang, as well as Chiang's "Cultural Manifesto" that he shared with me in July 2003.

19 "Argentina's Collapse: A Decline without Parallel," *The Economist*, February 28, 2002, accessed April 15, 2018, www.economist.com/node/1010911

20 After 1949, Zhang Daqian resided in São Paulo and Mogi das Cruzes, Brazil; Mendoza, Argentina; then Carmel, California before settling in Taipei, Taiwan in 1978. See "Zhang Daqian," Wikipedia, accessed April 15, 2018, https://en.wikipedia.org/wiki/ Zhang_Daqian. Zhang Daqian was a gourmet who employed and trained his private chefs, many became well known after they left his employ. The Sichuan dish Daqian Chicken is attributed to him. In 1975, I was invited by one of Zhang's former chefs running a Sichuanese restaurant in Santa Cruz, California to visit the artist's studio-residence inside 17-Mile Drive in Monterey County, California. The artist was taking a nap and I never met him. See also "Zhang Daqian and the Art of Fine Dining," Christie's, accessed April 15, 2018, www.christies.com/features/Zhang-Daqian-and-the-art-of-cuisine-8918-3.aspx

21 Anecdotes and personal stories told to me by Chinese Canadian families, as well as film interviews in Canada, Cuba, and Trinidad. For the complexity and transnational nature of these relationships, see for example "From Harlem to China: How an African-American Tracked Down her Chinese Grandfather," *South China Morning Post*, May 16, 2017, accessed April 15, 2018, www.scmp.com/lifestyle/families/ article/2094342/harlem-china-how-african-american-tracked-down-her-chinese

13

CHINESE RESTAURANT KIDS SPEAK ABOUT LABOR, LIFEWAYS, AND LEGACIES

Jenny Banh

Prologue

"I have an accent in every language I speak," my uncle Luhk Suk (Six Uncle) would joke with me when I expressed exasperation at my mother's family members who did not identify as solely Chinese.[1] We own Chinese restaurants, so of course we are part of the Sino-tribe, which has over 1.35 billion members in Mainland China and around 40 million in the diaspora.[2] We have suffered for having Chineseness in our marrow. We had to flee Vietnam because my family was part of the Chinese business class[3] and all businesses were nationalized.[4] I guess Luhk Suk was trying to reassure me that we were not oddballs and that it was normal for our family to immigrate four times from four nation states in four generations. There are many peculiar things about my Chinese restaurant family: we compare food item deals incessantly, we predict the probability of the restaurant's demise, we figure out how the dish was made, we order off-menu dishes, and we always tip well. Senior male family members are often friends with various waiters, which leads to further discounts. We often do not pay for tea services at Dim Sum houses where my family knows the restaurant managers. In our family, being ascetic and getting a good deal on food items is tantamount to sainthood. I asked my uncle why we kept migrating to different countries and he said, "We have always moved around."

Our family is originally from Three Rivers Guangdong, China and my grandfather moved to Saigon Vietnam in his late teens. There have been historical flows of ethnic Chinese people into Southeast Asia for centuries.[5] Grandfather's parents later sent for my very young grandmother from China to marry him. My grandfather and grandmother had eight children and became extremely successful through owning an export company.[6] "On March 24, (1978) the Hanoi government announced henceforth all 'bourgeois trade' in the south would be nationalized . . . the new policy applied to small traders [and large enterprises]."[7] Eight years earlier, before the Vietnam War was ended in 1975, my grandfather had sent all his children abroad, including my father, but he stayed behind in Vietnam to manage his business. After this decree, he had to give up the company, and his four-story home. He died very soon after of cancer.[8]

In the early 1970s my father was already an adult when he moved to Hong Kong. He then moved to New York and eventually to Belleview, Illinois.[9] The shadow history[10] of our family's time in Southeast Asia would never be discussed in my household.[11] In Cantonese, my mother would say, "*Baba* moved to Illinois because there were no Chinese or Asian people and people could not tell what real Chinese food was. There was too much competition in New York." This was the response I got from my mother when I asked her why my sister Kate and my cousins, Lucas and Sandy, were raised in Catholic schools and in predominantly Anglo and African American communities. There is a lot of silence and misdirection in her statements to me. Dare I say resistance?[12] She withholds many things from me and I have to guess or imagine what she means. I think my family history consists of many imaginaries within and between the generations. Maybe within me as well, which is why I wanted to have an oral 'history in their own words' directly from Chinese kids who grew up in restaurants.

This is not a story of *all* Chinese restaurant families as there are over 50,000 Chinese restaurants in the United States alone.[13] This chapter is not about a famous Chinese chef cooking delicate recipes[14] or a sojourning Chinese male hiding lurid tales of having double families on different continents,[15] or even racism.[16] Instead this chapter adds to the literature of how kids of a struggling immigrant family felt, the life-long effects, and what they experienced as they grew up in a Chinese restaurant.

Using first-person family oral history, I trace my family lineage from Guangdong, China to Saigon, Vietnam to Hong Kong (then a British colony), to Ferguson, Missouri and Belleville, Illinois. I also ask a series of question of my older sister Kate and two cousins, Lucas and Sandy who also grew up in Chinese American restaurants in nearby Ferguson, Missouri. Kate, Sandy, Lucas, and I were all born between the mid-1970s and mid-1980s in Vietnam, Hong Kong, and New York. We were all originally sponsored by New York families and moved again to the Midwest. This moving was not through advertisements but instead by word-of-mouth and Sino-ethnic honeycomb networks.[17]

Chinese restaurant business became a lifeblood to my multiple generational family as it helped maintain ethnic language maintenance, ethnic pride, and physical proximity. All four of us are now professionals and college educated with families. I will highlight the jobs that I and my cousins did in the restaurants and the legacy that a lifetime of working in a Chinese restaurant bestowed on us as children, now adults. For example, a major effect was the development of an intense work ethic, cultural sensitivity, risk taking, customer service abilities, grit, and knowledge of

Chinese diasporic networks. Issues of "authenticity" will be answered from the perspective of Chinese restaurant kids.

Questions and Answers

What are your names and how are we all related?

Jenn: My parental grandparents have eight surviving children. We are all cousins and our parents are siblings. Our father is the older brother to Sandy and Lucas's mother. My sister Kate and I grew up with Sandy and Lucas in the Midwest and our families shared meals, although we were located in Belleview, Illinois and they were in Ferguson, Missouri.

Do you know your grandparents' immigration story?

Lucas: Grandparents were born and raised in China, along with their siblings.

My grandma's side, I'm not too familiar with. There is another sibling on her side, but they were at a young age when their families immigrated and migrated to Vietnam. At that time, it was economic opportunities. I think when they immigrated, it was during war time in China. They opened a grocery store in Vietnam.[18]

Kate: No.[19]

Sandy: So, I can go back I think to my great Grandfather who had two brothers. He was the oldest of three brothers. My Great Grandfather was the youngest and his older brother went to Vietnam to start businesses. I'm not quite sure, I think he ended up owning a lot of stores, and some land. He brought his two younger brothers over to help him, and to give them some property. So, they all prospered. My Great Grandfather ended up having three or four kids, two brothers, and a sister that I know of. I know my Grandfather went back to China for art school. He's a great artist. He went back, and then I think at some point in time he got married in Hong Kong. And, then after he got married, they went back to Vietnam. I'm a little fuzzy after that. I know that my Dad and his two sisters were born in Vietnam. And, then my Dad ended up going out of Vietnam because of the war and he landed in Hong Kong. And, then from Hong Kong he made his way to the US.[20]

Jenn: My grandfather is from Three Rivers Guangdong, China. As an 18-year-old, he did not want to be a turnip farmer as his father and grandfather were before him. And so, his uncle left for Vietnam, and said, "Why don't you go to Vietnam to work with me?" And so, he left at age 18 to go to Vietnam and he became very successful. He sold steel. He developed many businesses and he had a large four-story house. And he went back to China when he was in his twenties and met my grandmother, who actually had two moms and she was an only child.[21] And later, they had eight children.

What were your parents' jobs in the USA?
Business opportunities?

Lucas: My dad had several jobs in New York. He had three jobs at once. He worked in the cafeteria of a nursing home. That was his day shift. At night, he would go to the malls and clean up, scrub the elevators. Yeah, on the weekends he would go with my mom to rake leaves for people. My mom at the time was working in the factory, an electronics factory. Yeah and so my dad friends were working in a restaurant business in St. Louis, Missouri. And, they basically told my dad – urged my dad to go over to Missouri as times were good over there.

Kate: Mom was a factory worker as a seamstress, and dad was a janitor at a department store. They later moved to Illinois and owned a restaurant: *Banh Chop Suey.* Because there were not that many Chinese people there, not much competition. We had a restaurant in Belleville, we lived in Belleville, Illinois but then we had a restaurant, after *Banh Chop Suey* because dad had it in downtown somewhere, I don't remember where, but it was downtown. We were living in Belleville, Illinois. *Banh Chop Suey* was the first restaurant, then *Diamond Chop Suey*, and then *Hunan Wok* was third.

Jenn: And then, in Hong Kong, they're waiting for their refugee status to go into the United States, where we moved to New York, Long Island, where my father was a janitor and my mother worked at a sweat shop. And then later, they had a friend named Robert who said "Okay, why don't you open a Chinese restaurant?" They had no cooking background; absolutely no knowledge of the restaurant business in the United States and did not speak English.

And they moved to Illinois and Missouri, where we lived as, together, maybe 10 to 12 people in two bedrooms. It was a fun time. And then we moved to open a restaurant and that restaurant was *Banh Chop Suey.* I think as part of the Chinese diaspora from Vietnam we had a psychological advantage over SE Asians who were part of the majority population.[22]

Additionally, as a family, we had what Sucheng Chan would call "Social Capital." We lost all our money back in Vietnam, but we had intergenerational business skills and psychological armor that we developed when we had been discriminated against in Vietnam. Chan defines social capital as each individual's or family's unique combination of "language competence, education, occupational skills and transferrable work experience."[23] I'm not sure if I'm remembering this quote exactly but Aiwha Ong interviewed a Chinese diasporic businessman and he said, "I can live anywhere in the world as long as it is near an airport."[24] My family branch was never "Vietnamese" so it was easier for us to start over in a new country. Even now I think if I have to leave the country immediately and start all over, I can and I will. This is what I want to teach my children.

What were your jobs in the restaurant?

Sandy: Sure. I started probably around age eight. And, we started off doing little stuff, like, passing the menus out, and bringing water or drinks to the guests. It gradually became full waitressing. So, as I got older, I was doing full waitressing, at the cashier. I didn't help to do any of the cooking. I sometimes helped with the preparation, cutting the vegetables. I did some dishes. But mainly I was in front of the house.

Lucas: I worked a lot of roles. I waited tables, bussed tables, was a cashier, and worked in the back. I helped my mom—helped my mom prepare all the ingredients to make the dishes. I didn't do much of the cooking, but I did do a lot of the frying of the crab Rangoon and eggrolls.

Kate: I prepared the sandwiches with mayonnaise and lettuce and tomatoes, wrapped the wontons and put the noodles in the cups and took orders.

Jenn: We peeled shrimp, like frozen shrimp; our fingers would be frozen. And, I think we were, like nine? They, they don't really care about child labor; you just have to do it, and you don't get paid. Our parents did let us buy a Dairy Queen ice cream sometimes as a reward. We folded together wontons. I don't think I cut vegetables. I just remember a lot of knife accidents and lots of blood.

What food did you serve in the restaurant?

Lucas: Kung Pao chicken and General Tso chicken. It's a spicy plate in a dark sauce. It has a variety of vegetables. It's like broccoli, carrots, bean sprouts. And the usual rice, soy sauce, salt and pepper, sugar and all that. Crab Rangoon, egg rolls, fried wonton, wonton soup, hot and sour soup, cashew chicken, sweet and sour chicken and the St. Paul Sandwich. It's made out of mostly four or five eggs.

Kate: Americanized Chinese food. Chop Suey, St. Paul Sandwich, wontons, eggrolls, fried rice.

Sandy: We served a mix of . . . we had American food, so we served burgers, fried chicken. We had of course the American style of Chinese food: Sweet and sour chicken, egg foo young, all that stuff. Egg foo young is basically an egg patty. So, it's eggs. It has a lot of bean sprouts, and vegetables, and meat. And, basically, we crack an egg over it, put a little corn starch, mix it all up, and we deep fry it. Yeah. So, egg foo young are like a couple patties over gravy, you eat it with rice. And, a St. Paul Sandwich is the same patty in between two slices of white bread. I did not like the egg foo young. But I love the fried rice. I love the egg drop soup. Oh, my Mom made the best hot grays chicken. Hot grays chicken is basically chicken wings, breaded and deep fried. And, my Mom covers it in this sweet, spicy, spicy, garlicky sauce.

Jenn: We sold egg foo young, wontons, and fried rice to our customers who were primarily African American. We never ate the food we served unless someone left the order, but that was rare.

Do you want your kids to work in a Chinese restaurant?

Lucas: Seeing how our parents toiled in restaurants . . . absolutely not! I don't think even our parents wanted us to work in one either. Sure, you learn life skills and build character but they can acquire that in other jobs.

Kate: No because the heat in the kitchen was extremely hot, and it's a lot of hard work, I'd rather let her use her brain and have a professional job than to work at a restaurant.

Sandy: I don't care, as long as they work. They need to work.

Jenn: No, it is an honest job but very hard to endure. I hope they have a choice about what they want to do. They have to work hard though.

Did working in a Chinese restaurant help you to maintain language fluency?

Lucas: I credit both to working in a Chinese restaurant and at home to maintaining my Chinese language fluency.

Kate: No, I think being with our parents and being with our grandparents maintained our Chinese language. Not necessarily the Chinese restaurant because at the Chinese restaurant you have to speak English all the time. Yeah, yeah, you were forced to speak Chinese to your parents.

Sandy: I don't think the restaurant had an effect. I think two things had a major effect, one, my Grandparents lived with us, and they knew no English. So, we were forced to speak to them. And, then the other was I really got into like the whole Chinese drama stuff.

Jenn: Yes, I think working is a Chinese restaurant and watching Kung Fu movies was the way I was able to maintain some Cantonese fluency. We would get video tapes from Lucas and Sandy's parents' little grocery[25] store and I watched them incessantly.

Should Chinese food that's Americanized be treated the same as Chinese food from China?

Lucas: I guess, it depends on the dish, because I know the dish does exist on both sides of the ocean, both in China and the US. It's . . . I guess what makes it authentic, I think, is the way it's made. In the US, let's take Kung Pao chicken again. So, the spices we use are a lot heavier, because the spices we use . . . we put more spices in there. It may be saltier, because we put more salt and MSG in it. In the American version. Americans love the Chinese food we serve because of the MSG, right. It's the secret ingredient to everything. So, that's the secret ingredient, right. But in the Chinese version, we may lighten up on the spices. We may put less sugar, less soy sauce and probably no MSG at all. And, probably make it spicier too, because the Chinese like food spicier.

Kate: No, not the same, because it's a different caliber, because when you eat real Chinese food like the soups, like the real . . . eight-hour soups. You can really taste the ingredients in the soup and it's not oil based or vinegar based, or soy sauce based. There are no oils, soy sauce, or anything in there. And if you eat the Chinese food that we eat, the food it's more herbs and they use more like other vegetables to enhance the flavors. We don't eat like a lot of the sauce-based stuff.

Sandy: It's different but I still like Panda Express.

Jenn: It depends on the audience and the restaurant needs to make food that customers will eat. So traditional Chinese food for Mainland Chinese and Americanized Chinese food for the midwestern American customers.

What is your relationship with Panda Express?

Lucas: You know, my wife loves Panda Express. I always dread it when she wants to go there, because I always argue with her, why you want to eat that? So, I mean . . . because with me . . . growing up in the restaurant, I know how everything's made.

Kate: We like that. We like it. I like their orange chicken.

Sandy: I still eat at Panda Express. Like sometimes when we go out, we're at the mall or somewhere, and we eat Panda Express, whatever. It's not our first instinct, but yeah sometimes. I think, I think it's, I'm not sure, I really don't have much thought. Yeah. I'm pretty neutral, no negative, for me it's a fast food option. Do I think it's authentic? No, I don't think it's authentic. For me, it's just another American fast food option. Do I consider it Chinese food? No, I probably don't consider it Chinese food.

Jenn: I would not choose it over traditional Asian food but I would over other ethnic foods. I usually get the beef and broccoli bowl, but with no beef. Cows are too hard working to eat, but . . . those burps. Cow burps are killing our environment.

Did you experience racism?

Lucas: Oh, of course. Yeah. I mean, they face racism even when before they came to the States. In Vietnam, the Chinese communities are considered the stereotype of Jewish people. From what my parents told me, they faced a lot of discrimination in Vietnam.

Sandy: Yes, I had young kids make the "Ching Chong" comments.

Kate: Not here because they don't actually understand the experience that we experienced over there. I think over there you experience much more racism and much more disapproval over there.

Jenn: I remembered people made fun of my parents' accent and, just lots of different painful things. But, as a kid, you just don't understand, so I didn't understand. My parents understood but ignored it, put their head down and kept going. And, you know, I just ignored it just like my parents. But my parents always say, "Don't care about it, just keep going. Don't care about it."

Have you met other Chinese restaurant kids?

Lucas: I have a good friend—I have a good friend here in Dallas. He's a—he's an ABC. He was born and raised in the US. He was born and raised in a small town, Durant in Oklahoma. It's like in a boomtown. He's transferred from Fujian. They came here—he went to Oklahoma and they started a restaurant business just like a Chinese restaurant—like an Americanized Chinese restaurant. Just like what my parents did.

Sandy: Sure. We grew up with a bunch of them.

Jenn: I have bumped into quite a few restaurant kids and workers over time. And one thing I've noticed is that they're all professionals and they all have a huge drive and work ethic.

What did you learn from working in the Chinese restaurant? Lifelong legacy effects?

Lucas: I learned to have a good work ethic, be a risk taker, and have good customer skills. I was not just working there by myself but I also watched my parents work. I saw the stresses of being a small business owner where my parents had to wear many hats and take risks in order to make enough sales to cover operating costs. And closing up at night with the risk of robbery. It's tough working at a restaurant because you work by standing all day. You take all the risks and you get up at 7 a.m. and don't come back until 10 p.m. at night. And, most of the time, you know, you are standing.

Kate: I liked the fact that it gave you good work ethic. I disliked the fact that it was a lot of hard work. My dad and mom had to work from 10 a.m. to twelve o'clock midnight six days a week with Sunday off. Well, I mean I consider it's pretty low to work at a restaurant because my mom and dad only made $30,000, $25,000, $20,000 a year. And see how hard work that they had to endure and how the treatment they had with customers. With theft and how people were so rude sometimes to them. The money was just so little compared to what they had to do just to survive.

Sandy: No. I don't really have any phobias about the restaurant business. It was fun. I actually enjoyed working and talking to the customers. I don't think there was anything hugely negative. We had a sense of obligation and responsibility as a family. I know how it feels to be in a hot kitchen, so I understand where my parents are coming from. It's a tough, you know restaurants . . . it's a tough life. So, I think the biggest thing is, for me, look-ing at my kids, I definitely want them to have a strong work ethic. So, when they are of age, definitely getting a job is very, very important to me. Once they can get their work permit at 14, they should get a job, any job. Cause they need to understand. Right? They need to understand all the impacts of the work ethic. It's not easy. Some get a sense of entitlement, you know? Because things are coming way too easy for my kids. So, they need to understand, they need to understand the front-line people, and the values they will need in order to be a good person. And, if they want to be a good leader, they will need to understand at that level.

Jenn: I always tip when eating out because my father said the waiters and wait-resses worked very hard and they don't get paid enough.[26] My father said that we were treated poorly but not as bad as other ethnic groups, so as a young child I was hyper-aware of different classes of people. Catholic school was very isolating. We just saw African-Americans and Anglos and we saw no Asians. The only Asian people we saw on the weekends were our relatives. So even now when I see Asian people, I sometimes think they are my relatives and I have to help them.

Thank you so much for taking the time to give this oral history of Chi-nese kids who grew up in Chinese restaurants.

Key Terms

Chinese restaurant kids: Chinese children who were raised in a Chinese restaurant with their family members. They often worked at a very young age in the restaurant doing odd jobs such as answering the phone, taking orders, peeling shrimp, and cleanup.

Chinese Vietnamese: Chinese people who settled in Vietnam over many centuries. In the late 1970s their businesses were nationalized and many fled to various countries.

Social capital: Social capital refers to each individual's or family's unique combination of language competence, education, occupational skills, and transferrable work experience.

Discussion Questions

1. Why did the Chinese who lived in Vietnam leave the country after the fall of the Vietnam War? What jobs did they tend to do in Vietnam?
2. What were the long-term effects on Chinese kids growing up in a Chinese Restaurant?
3. How do Chinese who are originally from SE Asia have a psychological advan-tage over other populations from that country? What social capital did these restaurant families bring with them from SE Asia?

Notes

1 Trieu, Monica. *Identity Construction among Chinese-Vietnamese Americans: Being, Becoming, and Belonging.* El Paso: LFB Scholarly Publishing, 2009.

2 Schiavenza, Matt. A Surprising Map of the World Shows Just How Big China's Population Is. August 13, 2013. www.theatlantic.com/china/archive/2013/08/a-surprising-map-of-the-world-shows-just-how-big-chinas-population-is/278691/

3 Karl Marx would call us part of the Petite Bourgeoisie since different sides of the family owned steel companies, gas stations, and school supply stores.

4 Pan, Lynn. *The Encyclopedia of Chinese Overseas.* Cambridge: Harvard University Press. 1998 (see pp. 228–233).

5 Sar Desai, D.R. *Southeast Asia: Past and Present.* Boulder: Westview Press. 2009.

6 According to my aunt my grandparents had nannies for each of their eight children and paid extra money for an ethnically Chinese one instead of an ethnically Vietnamese nanny. They also were taught Chinese characters and spoke only Cantonese in the household. This contrasts with my mother's side of the family who were upper middle class and therefore interacted and went to school with local Vietnamese children. Thus, on this side of the family my youngest uncle and aunt can mostly speak Vietnamese and could only pass the Vietnamese language to their children. My cousins accordingly identify as a mixture of Chinese-Vietnamese to Vietnamese while I identify as Cantonese only. To make my SE Asian students identify with me there are times I will state I am Chinese-Vietnamese.

7 Chan, Sucheng. *The Vietnamese 1.5 Generation: Stories of War, Revolution, Flight, and New Beginnings.* Philadelphia: Temple University Press. 2006.

8 I do recall my mother saying that he was a very hard worker and very honest. Apparently, he loved my sister a lot. His story reminds me of how things can be taken away from you very quickly even after a lifetime of hard work and integrity.

9 Now the majority of my family resides in California. The majority of Asian Americans live on the coasts and Hawaii.

10 Because of my parents' defensiveness I have not broached the topic with them. They have stated they never want to talk about this dark, sad time. Sometimes they will say that they lost everything there and will become very sad. I learned as a young child and adult to never ask them about this time.

11 I cannot say this silence was because of traumas or just my idiosyncratic family norms. I never truly understood my family was from Vietnam until I had a college roommate who asked me if I was Chinese-Vietnamese. Another notable memory was when a UCLA professor asked me if I was a "boat person" and I said no. My family is a quite silent and evasive family. We were encouraged to not ask questions or talk too much.

12 Scott, James. *Weapons of the Weak: Everyday Forms of Peasant Resistance.* New Haven: Yale University Press. 1987.

13 See Ferdman, Roberto and Christopher Ingraham. We analyzed the names of almost every Chinese restaurant in America. This is what we learned. *Washington Post.* April 8, 2016. www.washingtonpost.com/news/wonk/wp/2016/04/08/we-analyzed-the-names-of-almost-every-chinese-restaurant-in-america-this-is-what-we-learned/?utm_term=.5ccca1539dff

14 Yan, Martin. *Martin Yan's Chinatown Cooking: 200 Traditional Recipes from 11 Chinatowns Around the World.* William Morrow Cookbooks: An Imprint of Harper Collins Publishers, 2002.

15 See Chan, Bernice. "From Harlem to China: How an African-American Tracked Down Her Chinese Grandfather." *South China Morning Post.* May 16, 2017. www.scmp.com/lifestyle/families/article/2094342/harlem-china-how-african-american-tracked-down-her-chinese

16 Jung, John. *Sweet and Sour: Life in Chinese Family Restaurants.* Yin and Yang Press. 2011.

17 Ngai, Pun. *Made in China: Women Factory Workers in a Global Workplace.* Durham: Duke University Press. 2005. See her explanation on how rural factory workers find jobs through word of mouth using honeycomb networks (chapters 1–2).

18 Lucas [pseudonym], "'I Have an Accent in Every Language I Speak': Chinese Restaurant Kids Speak About Labor, Lifeways and Legacies." Interview by Banh, Jenny. July 8, 2017.

19 Kate [pseudonym], "'I Have an Accent in Every Language I Speak': Chinese Restaurant Kids Speak About Labor, Lifeways and Legacies." Interview by Banh, Jenny. December 11, 2017.

20 Sandy [pseudonym], "'I Have an Accent in Every Language I Speak': Chinese Restaurant Kids Speak About Labor, Lifeways and Legacies." Interview by Banh, Jenny. December 11, 2017.

21 My great grandfather kept getting new wives because they couldn't have any boys so my grandmother grew up relatively wealthy and very spoiled. So he married her and then took her back to China again, because she's a little too spoiled.

22 See Chan, Sucheng. *Survivors: Cambodian Refugees in the United States*. Urbana: University of Illinois Press, 2004.

23 Ibid. Although she talks about this "social capital" in terms of the Cambodian Chinese, I think it can apply to the Vietnamese Chinese as well.

24 Ong, Aihwha. *Flexible Citizenship: The Cultural Logics of Transnationality*. Durham: Duke University Press. 1999.

25 It should be noted that my cousins had a grocery store in Vietnam and came penniless to the United States but later they managed to also own a grocery store in the Midwest. This is what Sucheng Chan would call "social capital." You can easily see this in how the Cambodian Chinese have dominated the donut businesses in California.

26 I even tip in Hong Kong and Beijing where they don't really know what to do with the money but whose workers work to the bone.

14

CHINESE AMERICAN CHEF MING TSAI

Life of East and West Hybridity

Jenny Banh

Introduction

The opening first-minute sequence of the cooking show *East Meets West* shows Chef Ming Tsai, wearing a white martial arts robe, bowing, then immediately switching to playing tennis, flipping vegetables on a fiery wok, and then walking through a local Chinatown.[1] Growing up in in the Midwest, Ming Tsai seemed to my 9-year-old self like an affable Mr. Rogers mixed with a chef knife-wielding Batman. He spoke perfect English, looked like my cousin, and cooked Chinese food like my dad. There are over 40,000 Chinese Restaurants in the United States alone and many are family run.[2] I imagine I was not the only Chinese American restaurant kid mesmorized by this iconic Chinese American chef who has appeared on American television with *Simply Ming*, now in its sixteenth season.[3]

In many ways, he was similar to me as we were both raised in the Midwest and in Chinese American restaurants. He worked in his family-owned restaurant called *Mandarin Kitchen* and this is where, as a child, he learned about the ins and out of running a Chinese restaurant. He attended a series of prestigious schools on the east coast. First, Phillips Academy in Andover, Massachusetts for high school and, second, Yale University as an engineering major while also attending the Le Cordon Bleu cooking school in the summer. He then went on to graduate from Cornell University with a master's degree in Hotel Administration and Hospitality Marketing.

His first Chinese restaurant, *Blue Ginger*, opened in 1998 to much acclaim from patrons because of the East–West flavor combinations. Then came a series of awards: Best New Restaurant by *Boston Magazine*, Chef of the Year by *Esquire*, 2002 Best Chef Northeast, and Top 5 of Most Popular Restaurants. In 2007 *Blue Ginger* received the Ivy Award and in 2009 the Silver Plate Award for overall restaurant excellence. In addition, Ming had written five cookbooks: *Blue Ginger: East Meets West Cooking with Ming Tsai*, *Simply Ming*, *Ming's Master Recipes*, *Simply Ming One-Pot Meals*, and *Simply Ming In Your Kitchen*.

Interview with Chef Ming Tsai

What is your first memory of being a kid in a Chinese restaurant?
My first memory of being a kid in a Chinese restaurant includes large tables with big lazy Susan's in the middle surrounded with a lot of family and more food than you could imagine.

Did you have a job as a kid in the Chinese restaurant and what was it? Did you have any siblings or cousins who also worked in Chinese restaurants?
At *Mandarin Kitchen*, I was the restaurant manager at 15 or 16 years old. When you are the owner's son, the manager also means you are the dishwasher, janitor, rice cooker, egg roll cart boy, and anything else mom deemed necessary. I definitely had the title, but certainly without the riches.

One thing that has bothered me in the literature about Chinese food is that it often leaves out the females and children who toil in the restaurant who are not paid. For example, my mom worked just as hard as my dad and she ran the restaurant by herself. Can you go in depth of what your mom did and what you did in a Chinese restaurant as a kid? Your siblings? Cousins?
Unlike your experience, my mom was front and center and I remember her picture in the *Dayton Daily News* when the restaurant opened. My dad was actually in the background, though he was also busy at his full-time job designing B-1 bombers at Wright-Patterson Air Force Base nearby. But my dad always let my mom have the limelight because she really was the chef/owner.

What is the migration story of your father and mother and how did they come to own a Chinese restaurant in Ohio?
Both of my parents came here to go to college. My dad came in 1948 to attend Yale (class of 1952). My mom came because her father taught music at Yale. They actually met in New Haven when my mom was 16 and he was about 19 or 20 years old.

Both my brother and I went to prep school and therefore left home four years earlier than most kids. When my brother and I were at school, my mom actually started teaching local cooking classes. People loved her classes and encouraged her to open her own restaurant, which eventually led to *Mandarin Kitchen*.

Who were your patrons in your family restaurant and what were the popular orders that they had?
The restaurant was located in Dayton Arcade, which was in the center of town so it attracted a lot of business and administrative workers that worked in downtown Dayton.

The most popular dishes were definitely the Mongolian Beef, Sweet & Sour Pork and Mom's Famous Eggrolls. She actually got her start by demonstrating how to make her eggrolls in high school. People loved it so much and encouraged her to open a restaurant. All the while, my dad created a new system for the kitchen to make it a more efficient process. I like to think he invented batch cooking, which is essentially what the Chipotle's of the world use now. My dad would cook ten orders of beef, put them into a hotel pan to keep them warm and then sauté and dish up with rice and all the accompaniments when the order came in. We would make 10–15 orders of everything, plate it up with rice and noodles and then serve it so that so plate up was under 15 seconds and we could get dishes out fast.

What is a hidden story or something you want patrons to know about working in the Chinese restaurant? For example, Anthony Bourdain said US American Kitchen is the underbelly of atypical individuals. Who works in a Chinese Restaurant and why? US? Abroad?

Ironically enough, we had mostly Asians working there and most were actually Japanese. They were wives of people who worked at Wright-Patterson Air Force Base. I think that was partially luck and happenstance. We hired one, then their friend came and on and on. They were incredibly loyal and stayed with us until the day we closed. The hardest position to keep was the dishwasher. My motivation was always to hire one because when we didn't have one as the manager, I became the dishwasher!

Do you think there is a so called "authentic" Chinese Food? What is your definition of "real" Chinese food? Do you see any changes in Chinese Restaurants in the past 50 years?

There are finally in the last 10 years some really truly authentic regional Chinese restaurants. The reason they are authentic is because the chef is from Sichuan, can get all the flavors, spices, and produce. In reality, it's actually even better than what you would get in China because the quality of the ingredients are better here. The wok and cooking techniques are the same, ingredients are better quality, but the chef is the same. The "mistake" that was made when Chinese food was introduced to this country, and this is similar for a lot of other ethnic foods, is that it gets dumbed down to conform to the American palate. It was primarily done for one reason—business because it ensured that people would come back and buy it again. But over the last 10 years palates are changing because of TV, travel etc. and people are demanding more authentic flavors form China including traditional Cantonese dim sum, super mala Sichuan, Hokkien cuisine, true Hunan, Chengdo. Just like in Italy and Mexico, every region has their specific type of cuisine.

What is the story behind you opening your first restaurant? You have a BA in Engineering from Yale, were your parents disappointed you pursued food instead of your major?

I realized at a young age, probably 8 or 9 that you could make people happy through food. When I realized that I no longer wanted to be a mechanical engineer and instead wanted to become a chef, I just knew that it was the right path. My parents have always been incredibly supportive and that never changed. I graduated from Yale with a Mechanical Engineering degree and from there attended Le Cordon Bleu cooking school in Paris. I was very fortunate to train under renowned Pastry Chef Pierre Hermé in Paris and with Sushi Master Kobayashi in Osaka. I've cooked across the US in Chicago, San Francisco, and New Mexico and received a Master's degree from Cornell University in Hotel Administration and Hospitality Marketing. Eventually I realized that I wanted to work for myself and own my own restaurant. In 1998 I opened *Blue Ginger* in Wellesley, MA focusing on East–West Cuisine. I officially closed the restaurant on June 3rd of 2017 after 19 years of incredible service. *Blue Ginger* provided me with a national platform to make thousands of people happy through food, but also created a true family among staff, managers, and regulars. In 2013, I opened my second restaurant, *Blue Dragon*, an Asian gastro-pub located in the Fort Point Channel of Boston now in its sixth year of service. For more information check out BlueDragonBos.com.

What led to your famous Chinese food television shows? Where do you think Chinese restaurant food reception is going around the world?
I actually don't have a "Chinese" food television show, it's East–West, bringing in Chinese and Western influence. About 30 to 40 percent of the recipes do focus on Chinese flavors as a way to introduce them, but I don't limit it to just Chinese flavors, rather I incorporate all Asian flavors. I was originally discovered through Food Network and became their Asian expert. I was truly at the right place at the right time doing the right style of food.

In 2018, there seems to be an Asian zeitgeist with films like **Crazy Rich Asians, Searching** *etc. You certainly see this in food too with famous Asian chefs on television like David Chang, Roy Choi, and Kristin Kish. In particular, do you think Asian American chefs have an easier time with Americans being more open with their palates? Or do Asian chefs face the same issues?*
The American palate is getting more sophisticated and they are demanding more complex and traditional flavors. When they say spicy, they truly mean spicy. But don't forget that travel has helped us achieve this recognition for traditional flavors. Americans are traveling more and the more exposed they are to world cuisine and flavors, the more the demand the flavors they are seeing and tasting on the road.

Back to the beginning and future of Chinese food and American Chinese restaurants: What long-term effect did you see from working at a Chinese restaurant as a child to you now as an adult? Do you want your children to work in Chinese restaurants? What is the future for you and Chinese American restaurants?[4]
I think that working at a Chinese restaurant is more typical than you'd think today. As a son that worked in my mom's restaurant, I developed work ethic early on and it truly helped teach me the value of money. Once I got a job, I started paying for things like gasoline, movies, etc. I also learned that if I wanted

to live as well as my parents do, I needed to study hard, get good grades, and do well. I think it was more of a reality trip, and it really taught me to value money. Being in a restaurant also taught me how to deal with people including working with those who had positions both above and below you and how you deal with customers. The daily interactions with anywhere from 50 to 200 people greatly defines your character and helps you develop the skills to develop with all different types of people. I think that's one of life's greatest challenges too though. It's so important to learn how to deal with all different types of people and how to find the best in everyone.

Key Terms

Palate: A person's appreciation of taste and flavor, especially when sophisticated and discriminating.

Le Cordon Bleu: Prestigious cooking school in Paris.

Dim sum: A style of Chinese cuisine that is usually served during breakfast and lunch and prepared as small bite-sized portions of food.

Discussion Questions

1. How has Chef Ming Tsai said the American palate has changed? Do you find in your own life that you are more exposed to different ethnic cuisine? What kinds of cuisine are you exposed to and how have you encountered them?
2. Chef Tsai says he was the manager of *Mandarin Kitchen* when he was 15 or 16 years old. What jobs did he have to do and why? Have you ever had to work when you were young and what did that experience teach you?
3. At a young age Chef Tsai realized you could make people happy through food. Have you ever experienced that? What was the dish that brought happiness?

Notes

1 See East Meets West with Ming Tsai: Chiles: www.youtube.com/watch?v=U3sLmeKR7hg
2 See Passu, Charles (August 26, 2015) "Meet the Pilot Who Doubles as Block Island's Chinese-Food Delivery Guy. Regional Airline Brings Chinese Takeout, Sushi and Pizza to Popular Summer Resort." *The Wall Street Journal*, p. A1.
3 See Ming Tsai's personal website to learn more about him, including his social media accounts. www.ming.com
4 Thank you Sanjay Soundarajan, my Fresno State graduate student research assistant for all your help on this chapter and this book.

15

CULINARY AMBASSADOR CHEF MARTIN YAN SPEAKS

Life, "Authenticity," and the Future of Chinese Restaurants

Jenny Banh

Introduction

I grew up watching the *Yan Can Cook* television show in our family-owned American Chinese restaurant in Belleview, Illinois. I just remember how funny Chef Martin Yan was and his showmanship with his gigantic Chinese chef's knife. I had never seen anyone Asian before who was not a family member, so he was intriguing to me. He was similar to my parents in that he made Chinese food, but only later did I learn the Chinese food we made was for non-Chinese customers and did not contain "traditional" Chinese flavor profiles. Mom said we had to move far away to a place where people did not know what "real" Chinese food was, as my parents were not trained Chinese chefs. We never ate the food that we sold ourselves unless someone skipped out on an order. As a family that immigrated from Hong Kong, via Vietnam, I am certain that we must have watched his show as a family unit at least once.

One might say that Martin Yan is one of the most famous Chinese American chefs globally, but that would neglect to give him credit for also being one of the funniest TV chefs. Besides his iconic *Yan Can Cook* television show, he was once a guest on a Cartoon Network show called *Space Ghost*. He is shown comically berating the cartoon Space Ghost by rhythmically saying, "You talk too much and I'll put an apple in your mouth, Shut Up!" The other cartoon characters and television viewers, like myself, are at this point laughing hysterically. Yan follows up by saying, "You are such a nice guy. I would *never* do that to you!"

Later Space Ghost berates Martin and says, "You killed the Chicken." Martin responds, "No I didn't, I am just dissecting him. This chicken is nervous because he has never had a close encounter with Space Ghost."[1] Martin then says the chicken has to relax and proceeds to take both wings and twirl them around in circles. Of course, later he shows his incredible knife skills while humorously dissecting the raw chicken, making the chicken "exercise." Truly, there is no Chinese American chef like this iconic culinary ambassador and he was also a Chinese restaurant kid like me.

Interview with Chef Martin Yan

Great. It's a wonderful privilege to interview you. I'm actually a Chinese restaurant kid. I grew up in a Chinese restaurant in the Midwest.[2]
Oh, really? I just came back from checking out some well-established Chinese restaurants in Atlanta, Georgia.

Interesting, my cousins and I we all grew up in a Chinese restaurant, but now I'm a professor.
I'm sure your parents are very happy for you and your eventual career path—the restaurant business is pretty tough for family, as well as normal lifestyles.

[laughing] Yes, and so, my book is called **American Chinese Restaurants***, so we would love to include an interview with a famous Chinese chef.*
My English name is Martin Yan: M-A-R-T-I-N Y-A-N, and my actual Chinese name is Man Tat: M-A-N-T-A-T [甄文达]. I have been involved with Chinese food and Chinese restaurants since I was 13. I do hope one day I will be famous.

And what year were you born and do you have siblings? Migration story?
I was born in Guangzhou, Southern China in December 1948. I left China at age 13 and went to high school in Hong Kong. While attending high school. I worked at my distant uncle's restaurant. The restaurant was also where I slept every day.

I have a brother who was also trained as a chef; he resides in Toronto, Canada.

What high school in Hong Kong?
I attended a Christian high school, Munsang College near my uncle's restaurant where I worked throughout my high school years, which was located in the web of Chinese restaurants in Kowloon City with the most diverse cuisines. I had a good taste and palate for a variety of Asian flavors. It really opened my mind for my future career path.

And you came alone?
Yes, I left Guangzhou without any money. I had no direct relatives in Hong Kong so I became part of my uncle's restaurant family.

What's the story behind your first Chinese restaurant experience?
My father owned a restaurant in Guangzhou, and my mother ran a grocery store. As a child, I hung around my father's restaurant and my mother's store, and later, my uncle's restaurant in Hong Kong. I developed a good feel for the food

business—being among the smells and the tastes of a restaurant. We actually lived in the back of the grocery store where I also was exposed to traditional Chinese ingredients at a very young age.

What type of Chinese food did your dad cook in his restaurant?

They had a small neighborhood restaurant that was known for clay pot, one-meal dishes. Clay pot cooking is comforting and easy to prepare and serve. Even now, I still enjoy clay pot dishes at home and when I eat out at a restaurant.

How comforting. What about your mother and her store?

The food you eat when growing up as a child is always the most comforting. My mother's grocery store carried all sorts of traditional food and ingredients, like dried squid and salted fish. If you go to New York or San Francisco Chinatown, you will still find small stores like my mom's—which carry all the basic seasonings and dried ingredients.

Were your mom and dad both good cooks? So, let's go back a little bit to your father. Your father came to America before you, and then he worked in Oregon?

My parents were pretty decent cooks, but definitely not master chefs as they had no formal training. My father traveled to Portland, Oregon in the early 1920s where he opened a small café, barber shop, and jewelry store. Because there was a period of discrimination and the Chinese were not allowed to own property, many Chinese eventually returned to China to settle down—my father, too. He returned to China where he bought some property and opened a restaurant and grocery store for my mother before I was born.

The Chinese Exclusion Act of 1882. Do you know what year your dad came to the US?

I believe it was maybe in the 1920s or 1930s. When he returned to China, he was probably in his sixties. Those days, it was common to have multiple families—one in America and another in China.

And then, what about when you came to the US, did your parents ever want to come back to the US with you?

My father passed away when I was very young, about 5. I left Guangzhou and went to Hong Kong; my mother stayed in China. After graduating from high school, I made my way to Canada then the US where I received my Master's degree at UC Davis, California. Later on, I managed to get my mom and my brother and his family to immigrate.

This is when you opened your first Chinese restaurant in the United States?

I have been around the restaurant business since I was young, but I did not open a restaurant until much later. After graduating from UC Davis, I went back to Hong Kong and worked for a food manufacturing company. I eventually returned to

Alberta, Canada where I helped a friend open a restaurant. In 2006 I opened my own restaurant, and in 2012, we opened M.Y. China in downtown San Francisco.

Oh, interesting. Can you speak a little bit about your first restaurants?
In 2006, I partnered with a restaurant operator for my first restaurant *Yan Can China Bistro*. It was fast-casual dining—once your order is placed, the food is cooked to order.

At one point, we had about eight to ten locations throughout California. Later on, we also opened *Martin Yan's Sensasion* restaurant. It was unfortunate that due to my restaurant partner's sudden death in 2008, the money chain was disrupted, and we eventually ended up closing and selling most of the restaurant units.

There seems to be more respect to Asian food with people like Anthony Bourdain highlighting it and giving it respect.
In the US, there are more Chinese restaurant operations than all the fast food chains combined. There are well over 52,000 restaurants serving Chinese food. The growth of Chinese restaurant businesses has continued in leaps and bounds. They also outnumber the combination of Korean, Thai, Vietnamese, and Japanese ramen and sushi bars. Chinese food is affordable and offers a variety of ingredients and flavors—there's something for everybody. Of course, celebrity chefs like Anthony Bourdain have brought Asian food awareness to the public.

Now, you mentioned Panda Express, you mentioned Pick Up Sticks. My parents did something like that, as well, but not as nice. Do you think that American palettes will open up to more traditional flavors? I don't want to say "authentic" but things like Din Tai Fung or maybe like Sichuan flavors?
Panda Express has done very well and built a large following. Now you see them everywhere. For the last 35 years with programs like the *Yan Can Cook* on air, practically everybody has a wok in their kitchen—everybody knows how to use the chopsticks. Most people have tasted Chinese food and Asian dishes. The acceptance of Chinese food in America is no longer just fast food anymore.

Nowadays, diners have different expectations—you have all kinds of palettes as well as dietary preferences. In recent years, there are more and more regional Chinese restaurants serving a variety of traditional food.

Interesting. Have you been to San Gabriel Valley?
Yes, I have many friends who live in that vicinity which probably has the highest concentration of new immigrants from Taiwan, Hong Kong, and various parts of China. That's the reason why in San Gabriel, Monterey Park, and Rowland Heights you will find different regional Chinese cuisines—Beijing, Shanghai, Hunan—it's supply and demand.

When you visit the San Francisco bay area or Flushing, New York or Queens, you'll also see the same trend—a high concentration of Chinese, and you will see countless traditional regional Chinese restaurants.

I guess, I want to go back to your television show. You talked about specialization. You said that at UC Davis you were teaching.

Yes, I taught Chinese cooking classes through the UC Extension program to pay my way through college. I introduced a variety of common and exotic ingredients and a great deal of regional cuisines in my classes. It was through my teaching experiences at UC Davis that led the way to eventually getting into the TV media arena.

I have to say, I have been mesmerized by you since I was a child.

I was fortunate to be in the right place at the right time! There's a Chinese saying. 天时、地利、人和[3] tiān shí dì lì rén hé, translated to "right time, right place, and right people."[4] If you don't have all these, you may not succeed. In the US alone, there are a lot of talented chefs, actors, actresses, and singers but why are there just a few who become really successful? Timing, making the right connections and the right decisions as well as working hard—these are all important ingredients for success. I consider myself as being one of the luckiest and fortunate ones. Perhaps that's why I want to share my life journey with others, particularly the Chinese and Asian communities.

Thank you for saying that, and your work ethic is incredible.

I do work very hard, often six to seven days a week and I travel a great deal around the globe. First and foremost, I consider myself a culinary ambassador, not only for Chinese cuisine, but for Asian cuisine in general. I am most fortunate to be doing something I really love and have a passion for—that's why it doesn't feel like work.

Wow. How did you hook up with the PBS people? I mean, that was a long time ago.

My first cooking shows were produced in a commercial television station in Calgary, Alberta—a total of about 500 programs in 4 years. When someone told me there was an opportunity in Los Angeles, I moved to Southern California. During my short stay in Los Angeles—about 6 months, I made quite a few good contacts such as producers and directors and was offered a number of opportunities. Around the same time, I was approached by the PBS station, KQED, in San Francisco to do a new cooking series. Eventually I moved to Northern California. The rest is history. Since 1982 with PBS, we have co-produced and worked together to create well over 2,000 episodes.

I love that you said you are a culinary ambassador.

I do consider myself as an ambassador of food. Food brings people together—it has no national boundaries. As I said, it's a matter of timing, hard work, opportunity—and a bit of luck. There are a lot of chefs who are just as good or better than me and work just as hard. I love the opportunity to introduce Chinese and Asian food and culture to the general public.

Yeah. I love that, that's such a truism, and I noticed that you travel the world.
In the last decade, I've been traveling close to 250 days a year. I travel worldwide, learning from master and home chefs alike, sharing my experiences with countless chefs and the general public. I give lectures and seminars and am involved in charities and fundraising events—raising money for an orphanage in Vietnam, for the Agent Orange victim, for Buddhist temples all over Asia. Just a couple weeks ago, I was the guest chef for the WildAid charity event in Los Angeles. I find it most gratifying—it gives me a sense of personal satisfaction and a meaning to life.

Great. I know that you have, must have seen, many Chinese restaurants around the world. I know your TV show, actually, goes over that, as well. Have you, is there any insight that you have, having traveled to so many Chinese restaurants around the world? Do you see any commonalities among those Chinese restaurants that you see globally?
As I travel around Chinese restaurants, I see chefs are developing, using ingredients that are seasonal and accessible in their particular area. If you live inland, you will find less seafood dishes. If you are near the ocean, you will find more variety of seafood dishes. It all depends on what's available locally. Chefs are like magicians—they never stop creating new dishes with new ingredients, like crocodile, for instance.

Different restaurants will target different types of audiences. In various parts of the work, they cater to the local palate. In Chinatown, you will find Chinese old-timers enjoying home style dishes that are not on the menus of Panda or PF Chang. Yet, all are cooking with similar techniques and seasonings.

So, in terms of global versus the local; is there a flavor difference?
It depends on where you are. I just came back from India and dined at one of the upscale Chinese restaurants there. Chinese restaurants in India are basically a fusion of Cantonese cuisine with a little twist of Indian flavor. That's localization of flavors. Chefs around the world are creating new flavors using local ingredients and seasonings.

So in traveling around the world, did you find the Chinese restaurant food to be a fusion of Cantonese food and whatever the local flavor was?
In recent years, due to the explosion of Chinese immigrants from different parts of China, you will see more and more traditional and regional dishes. In early years, most of the immigrants were from southern China so they opened mostly Cantonese restaurants.

Interesting. So, you have been a chef, now, for many years, many decades.
Food is my passion—I love to cook and share. I consider myself more than just a chef. I am bridging the cuisines, as well as lifestyles, of the West and the East. If you watch the *Yan Can Cook* shows, it's not just about cooking and teaching

you how to cook a few dishes, I take you on a journey to the place where I film. I share my personal experiences with you—the people, the tradition, heritage and culture, the food and the lifestyles. I have been doing this for decades and will continue to do it.

I know you are ethnically Chinese. What do you think of Chinese restaurants that are not Chinese owned? You know, what I've been reading is P.F. Chang's is not Chinese-owned, right?

There are many Chinese restaurants that are not operated by Chinese. *P.F. Chang*'s owner is Paul Fleming ("P.F.") who also owns the famous Fleming steakhouse. And "Chang" refers to my good friend, Philip Chang. His mother, Cecilia Chang, owns a very famous restaurant in Ghirardelli Square, San Francisco and also in Los Angeles, *The Mandarin*. Philip is also a top chef. I know that Paul Fleming loved *The Mandarin*. Perhaps that's how they ended up naming the restaurant *P.F. Chang*. It is not important whether a Chinese restaurant is Chinese-owned or not, as long as they are doing a good job, it's a good Chinese restaurant. All restaurants have a target clientele.

So, what do you think of these restaurants. Is it fusion?

I have visited a few *PF Chang* restaurants. Their menu and flavor profile is a bit different than that of a traditional Chinese restaurant in Chinatown diners. It is not really fusion but more mainstream. And they use woks and traditional seasonings.

As long as you can please your guests, you will be a successful restaurant.

It was in Belleville, Illinois, and Ferguson, Missouri. There were no Chinese there.

All the Chinese live in Chicago.

Yes.

Fusion is not the same thing as being "authentic" or "traditional." In those cities where are few Chinese, most likely you will find chop suey and chow mein on the menu.

And that is okay, too. For some operators, this is their livelihood. As long as they can provide good service and keep their customers happy, it is a good day's work. So, we can only say "traditional"— it's the local taste, catering to the local palette.

Right, that's true.

Because you're not always cooking for yourself, you're cooking for your customers. If you insist on serving the most authentic dishes, you know what? You're going to lose most of your customers.

What is your favorite food to cook for your family?

My favorite meal still remains the dishes that my mom cooked years ago—clay pot cooking or one-pot meals. I cook the rice first. When the rice is just about done, I throw in some chicken, mushrooms, and Chinese sausage. When the rice is done, everything is done. We cook and eat from the pot.

Of course, of course, yes. Especially in Hong Kong, yes. What do you think will be the future global reception of Chinese restaurants and food?
I expect that there will be more Chinese restaurants opening up in many parts of the world—more than any other ethnic restaurant. It has already been happening in the last quarter of a century. Chinese cuisine offers a great deal of variety. It's relatively healthy cooking—a lot of vegetables and a variety of small amounts of protein. Besides, it is affordable and has something to offer for everyone.

Wow, okay. Interesting. Well, that's all my questions. Is there anything else you'd like to add?
As a new generation of young chefs is getting into the business, you will see more creative and exciting flavors.

To me, it is about serving fresh, healthy, and delicious food. For those who come after me, follow your instincts and passion.

Even though the restaurant business is tough, many still want to be in the restaurant business. If this is what you love, it is a place to showcase your skills and creativity.

I love to hang around my downtown San Francisco restaurant, *M.Y. China*, because I get to see old and new friends from around the world. It gives me pleasure to see our customers enjoying every bite of our creations.

Thank you so much for your insights, Chef Yan. Thank you.[5]
It's been my pleasure. Good luck with your career.

Key Terms

> **Traditional**: The transmission of customs or beliefs from generation to generation, or the fact of being passed on in this way.
> **Authentic**: Of undisputed origin; genuine.
> **Chinese American restaurant**: Most popular restaurant in the United States, numbering over 52,000, which is more than McDonald's, KFC, and Burger King combined.

Discussion Questions

1. Chef Martin Yan talks about the multigenerational migration patterns of his father. What did his father do in the United States and why did he come back to China? How is your family migration pattern similar to or different from Chef Yan's?
2. Chef Martin Yan talks about how he was raised by parents who owned a Chinese restaurant and grocery store, which exposed him to specific flavor and ingredient profiles. Are there any other examples in which the family influences their kids' occupational choices?

3. On first glance, it may seem that Chinese restaurants are everywhere and quite successful but, in reality, it is a very hard business to survive in. What does Chef Yan say that makes the Chinese restaurant so hard to keep open? Can you think of why it is so hard to maintain restaurants, gyms, and magazines?

Notes

1 See Space Ghost C2C 34 Cookout Emeril Lagasse, Nathalie Dupree, Martin Yan Yan Can Cook: www.youtube.com/watch?v=fLhcMOy7Q8U&t=639s
2 The interview with Chef Martin Yan took place on October 20, 2018 and was transcribed at 10,000+ words. It was edited down to 5,000 words for clarity. We went back and forth to get the precise answers to the questions.
3 Thank you to David Yu 余樹泉 for all Cantonese translations.
4 天时、地利、人和 (tiān shí dì lì rén hé) can be translated also as *"the time is right, geographical and social conditions are favorable (idiom); a good time to go to war."*
5 Thank you Sanjay Soundarajan, my Fresno State graduate student research assistant, for all your help on this chapter and this book.

PART IV
Comics

PROLOGUE
What Number Did We Get?

Written by Isha Aran
Illustrated by Karl Orozco

#372 and #1
A Winning Combo

Written by Isha Aran, Daniel Tam-Claiborne,
Sophia Park and Julian Tucker
Illustrated by Karl Orozco and Sophia Park

#249
Dim Sum Drama

Written and Illustrated by Isha Aran

#818
First In Our Hearts

Written and Illustrated by Amelea Kim

PART V
Visual Analysis

17

A VISUAL HABITAT STUDY FOR CHINESE RESTAURANTS IN A CALIFORNIA CONURBATION

Nicholas Bauch and Rick Miller

Southern California's San Gabriel Valley (SGV) is home to one of the most pro-lific agglomerations of Chinese restaurants in the Americas.[1] However, this region (including at its core the cities of Monterey Park, Alhambra, Rosemead, and San Gabriel) radiates few of the visual-architectural cues that normally distinguish other such areas as "Chinatowns."[2] This expansive area retains an unpronounced ver-nacularism typical of Southern California's post-World War II suburban housing boom (Figure 17.1).

This chapter uses photographs and text to explore the spatial connections between the restaurants (as points of broad regional and international appeal) and the banal, seemingly forgotten infrastructures of dwelling in the SGV. These spaces of habitation, we contend, compose a necessary urban milieu for restaurant-going that offers a micro-economic rationale for the very existence of the restaurants in the first place. One should not, that is, look at Chinese restaurants here without also looking at the houses that cover the vast majority of the land mass in this multi-city region. Ours is a story of connecting adjacent built environments—restaurants and houses—to show that each cannot exist without the other.

While visually unassuming,[3] this built environment has over the past 30 years become home to a range of Chinese cuisines. From this perspective, the tastes found in SGV restaurants exist in blithe indifference of their vernacular surround-ings of suburban streets and homes, responding instead to the palates of the people who dwell in these neighborhoods. Here, the visual cues that might normally signal "Chinatown" for outsiders are largely non-existent.

The crux of our story is that one can read the SGV's culinary economy not by looking directly at restaurant menus, nor by mapping out their spatial distribution, but instead by raising one's head to the liminal space between the restaurant edifices and the nondescript housing stock indicative of the SGV landscape. Focusing on the spatial proximity between these two defining events—the domestic Siniciza-tion of the SGV and the installation of a renowned culinary scene into the existing

FIGURE 17.1 The San Gabriel Valley is architecturally known for its mass vernacular, suburban neighborhoods. It is a landscape dominated by dwelling places. Near S. Granada Ave. and E. Adams Ave., Alhambra.

Source: Photo by N. Bauch, 2017.

planscape—allows us to see how dwelling has remained "hidden in plain sight" in the discourse surrounding this cultural-culinary phenomenon. Those who live in the SGV might appreciate the proximity of restaurants, but often overlook the immediate adjacencies between commercial and residential zones, while those who travel to the SGV for its food seldom step away from the restaurant to witness the built environment of dwellings that sustain the food phenomenon with customers, knowledge, language, capital, and, not least, labor.

Methods in Cultural Geography

This move—a raising of one's head and a moving of one's feet to the neighborhoods surrounding the strip restaurants—has a parallel in geographic thought. Namely, it is a move from the lens of place to the lens of landscape. If place is the shared accumulation of emotion, memory, sensory observations, conversations, lives lived and reflected upon, then landscape is a step back from this, answering not so much "What is this place?" but instead "What is the connection between this place and the larger geographic context of social and economic forces that allows it to function?" It is a matter of methodological entry point, as both place and landscape are geographic lenses that ultimately seek to uncover and explicate the surface of the earth as modified by humans.[4] A "place" methodology is inductive, starting with fine-grained details like an analysis of the food itself, or a recording of long interviews, eventually painting a picture that deepens one's understanding of the layers upon layers of meaning that accrue, transforming a dot on a map into a family restaurant.[5]

A "landscape" methodology, on the other hand, often lends itself to deduction, meaning that researchers start with general premises or observations, then move toward a conclusion. Deduction is helpful when working in a visual medium (e.g. photography) because it encourages the crafting of a poetics, where "conclusion" is really closer to an "articulation" of the starting premise itself. Photographs, in a landscape study such as this one, and in contradistinction to remote sensing, are not usually employed to discover something new with optical technology, but to write a visual script that communicates the researchers' observations. Walking through the SGV neighborhoods with cameras in hand, therefore, is as much a record of our process and journey as it is about capturing the right information.

In this chapter, we start with a general observation about the architectural banality of suburban housing in the largest Chinatown (by land area) in the United States (Figure 17.2).

FIGURE 17.2 Typical urban housing in the largest Chinatown (by land area) in the United States.

Source: Photo by Rick Miller, 2017.

Part of this starting premise is asking specifically what it looks like when the restaurants—magnets of cultural spectacle for locals and non-locals alike—geographically collide with the everyday lives of people who more often than not have nothing to do with the restaurants. That is, an average patron in a SGV restaurant would not likely be aware that s/he is within meters (Figures 17.8–17.11) of the edge of an enormous and ongoing residential real estate transition that continues to see upward pricing pressure due to foreign demand.

Brief Social History of the SGV

Historically, the SGV has steadily progressed from a series of towns that were largely white in the 1950s to a recognition of an Americana that is as diverse spatially as it has been ethnically. The common post-war dichotomy of white suburbs ringing a city filled with immigrants had long been challenged by historical realities in the SGV. The city of San Gabriel itself had been home primarily to Mexican-Americans and Japanese-Americans, which would see the area redlined after an April 17, 1939 Area Report prepared by the Home Owners Loan Corporation, which designated both groups as "subversive" nationalities, though acknowledged nearly all residents were American-born.[6]

In the late 1970s, a Chinese-American real estate developer named Frederic Hsieh began to purchase land in Monterey Park, at the time a predominantly white and Latino suburb about 5 miles east of downtown Los Angeles. He predicted that emigration from China—in particular from Hong Kong and Taiwan—to Los Angeles would intensify as those with means were seeking to escape the effects of Mao's communist regime. Hsieh intentionally set out to make a new Southern California Chinatown in Monterey Park, utilizing his networks to Chinese banks and employing booster-ish advertising campaigns such that to Chinese immigrants, the three most recognizable cities in the United States were New York, Los Angeles, and Monterey Park.[7] Frequently dismissed in the 1970s as someone with too grandiose a vision, by 1987 Monterey Park was home to 12 Chinese banks, as well as the highest concentration (40 percent) of Chinese residents in any city in the United States.[8] This influx of Chinese immigrants dramatically changed the cultural and economic makeup of the city within a decade, as housing prices soared and new businesses (including restaurants) began catering to Chinese-speaking clientele. This type of suburbanization—dramatically different from the 1950s story of "white flight"—predicted how much of the North American suburban landscape would develop in terms of immigration hot spots and ethnic diversity.[9] Such a dramatic change did not come without controversy, as the Chinese immigrants experienced waves of racism from existing residents whose city was being transformed at a rapid pace. Today, Asians and Asian-Americans make up a little over a quarter of residents in the SGV, while Hispanics comprise a plurality of 45 percent and non-Hispanic whites another quarter of overall population.[10]

FIGURE 17.3 Outdoor dining area at Szechuan Impression restaurant, looking south into the Ethel Park neighborhood; W. Valley Blvd. and S. Ethel Ave., Alhambra. This is a rare example in the SGV where sidewalk seating bleeds almost seamlessly into the tree-lined residential street, the thin sun screens serving as metaphorical borders between the commercial strip and the places of habitation.

Source: Photo by N. Bauch, 2017.

Brief Geography of the SGV

The spatial organization of restaurants within the SGV follows a commercial zoning pattern that consolidates businesses along major transportation corridors. On these linear zones one finds the vast majority of Chinese restaurants in our study area that, like any line of storefronts, tend to host the majority of vehicle and foot traffic. The architectural and urban planning histories of the region have led to a proliferation of strip malls, which dominate the built environment along the retail commercial zones (Figure 17.4).[11]

This geographical pattern is echoed in the zoning plans for these SGV cities, as witnessed, for example, in the city of San Gabriel's Valley Blvd. plan (Figure 17.5).

Here, the legacy of a linear north-south and east-west street lattice is punctuated with major arterial roads that host nearly all commercial and retail activity in the SGV. One remarkable geographical observation about Chinese settlements in the SGV is the retention and repurposing of this quintessentially American city plan.

FIGURE 17.4   Looking south to the Valley Plaza and Lu's Garden, across the street from China Taste Restaurant. At Lafayette St. and E. Valley Blvd., San Gabriel.

Source: Photo by N. Bauch, 2017.

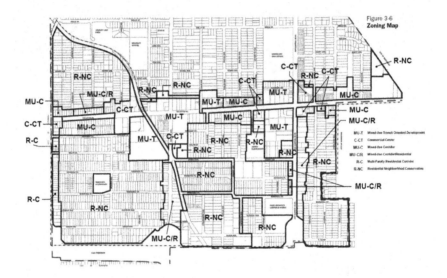

FIGURE 17.5   City of San Gabriel zoning map, focusing on Valley Blvd. (running east-west) and San Gabriel Blvd. (running north-south). Important to note is that all commercial activity takes place along these strips; there is almost no mixed land use once "inside" a neighborhood.

As one journalist in 1987 put it, noting the repurposing of existing new world infrastructure by Chinese immigrants already well underway, "it's an old culture in a brand new place"[12] (Figure 17.6).

This lattice-like geographic form of restaurant distribution in the SGV is the observation that has piqued our curiosity about the interiors—or spaces in the middle—of the general structure of the SGV city plans. In particular, we are interested in the boundary conditions between the busy avenues and boulevards that have made the SGV known among global Chinese networks (e.g. Valley Blvd. or

FIGURE 17.6 The use of existing infrastructure, as well as the construction of new strip malls since the late 1970s by Chinese investors in the SGV, has prompted the observation that in this suburban Chinatown, customs are lifted from their original sites of practice and planted in architectural forms that were designed for an idyllic lifeway.

Source: Photo by Rick Miller, 2017.

Atlantic Blvd.), and the hundreds of square miles of residential real estate that fill in the space between these dominating lines of travel. Given that traffic density wanes toward the middle of the square sections between the major arterials, questions arise about the look, shape, and feel of this "ethnoburb."[13]

Reading Restaurant Economies from Liminal Space

The SGV eschews the easy, kitschy symbols that dominate most other Chinatowns in North America. Between the commercial strips and the housing zones, the liminal space is the space the restaurant must capture to maintain independence from the kitsch. Here we make two observations, using photographs to build a "habitat study" for Chinese restaurants in the SGV. As such we are not so much interested in tracking Chinese restaurants per se, but are instead focused on what the built environment looks like immediately surrounding some of the iconic restaurants. We offer a reading of Chinese restaurants through the lens of the residential patterns that abut the restaurants themselves.

Observation 1: Spatial Proximity

The first point is that the distance between Chinese restaurants and housing is usually small. The transition zone between the backs of restaurants and the beginnings of dwelling units tends to signify the increasing density of the built environment in the SGV and the increasingly intense real estate market (Figures 17.7 and 17.8).

What can one glean about Chinese restaurants in the SGV by looking at the edges of the buildings as they quickly transition into housing? What is productive about this method? Perhaps most fundamentally it reminds us how exactly the SGV is a revolution from the nineteenth- and early-twentieth century urban organization indicative of American Chinatowns that persist in many places still today. In this "classic" model—found most prominently in San Francisco and New York—Chinese immigrants developed multi-generational, monocentric, spatially concentrated enclaves, the economies of which were tied as much to the locale as they were to Chinese and Taiwanese banks.[15] However, when Chinese immigration to Los Angeles began to explode in the 1970s, it took on a different urban form, multi-nodal in nature, mirroring the wider urban pattern of southern California that was the opposite of dense concentration.[16] As sociologist Timothy Fong points out, there was no precedent for a *suburban* ethnic enclave, especially one still undergoing Anglo-American resettlement to the southwest region of the country from eastern states.[17] The Sinicization of the SGV, therefore, has long confounded the Anglo narrative of white settlement in southern California, even if only in a relatively small area. Starting in the 1970s, the ethnic transition happened so quickly there was no time to replace the look of the post-World War II "American dream" stock housing.

FIGURE 17.7   Alley behind Chengdu Taste, near W. Valley Blvd. and S. 9th St. in Alhambra, looking west. To the right is the loading zone for the restaurant, which by 2013 had become known for its style of cooking that was "freed from the tyranny of Sichuan cooks preparing only the cuisine of Chongqing."[14] To the south, on the other side of the alley, immediately begins residential garages and apartment units.

Source: Photo by N. Bauch, 2017.

FIGURE 17.8   Behind Tasty Noodle House, at N. Mission Dr. and W. Las Tunas Dr. in San Gabriel. The sharp edge of the strip mall directly abuts the manicured front lawn, driveway, and fencing of a single-family residence along a street running perpendicular to the commercial artery.

Source: Photo by Rick Miller, 2017.

Observation 2: Border Types

This second observation is a typology of borders that shows the various ways borders between Chinese restaurants and housing units are made and maintained in the SGV.

Stemming from her investigation into U.S.–Mexico border artworks, Ila Sheren points out that, by the late twentieth century, "in the world of visual art, borders came to represent a space of performance rather than a geographical boundary, a cultural terrain meant to be negotiated."[18] Though here used in a completely different context, this insight remains useful because it distinguishes physical boundaries from "spaces of performance" that are continuously culturally negotiated. How is the liminal space *performed* in the SGV?

As it relates to our case study of the SGV, we are guided by the question of what these physical, liminal landscapes look like. One thing a reader might learn from this photo-text chapter is how to recognize vernacular liminality, i.e. the everyday urban areas one can inhabit while being neither in a tourist-commercial restaurant zone nor a residential neighborhood. The notion of liminality has a longstanding role in theorizations about space. Geographer Dominique Moran, for example, recently wrote that liminality traditionally conveys "the specific spaces of betweenness, where a metaphorical crossing of some spatial and/or temporal threshold takes place."[19] In this view, it follows that liminality requires the existence of two states of being, the liminal space, as it were, being neither state fully while maintaining some elements from each. These kinds of in-between spaces, as Moran hints at, take on their own identities; for example in her case she shows how prison visiting rooms are neither prison nor the "outside" world, and therefore tend to accrue their own customs, laws, and lifeways. As such, a key point in thinking through borderlands is that liminality is not a linear transformation from one state to another. One can permanently or semi-permanently inhabit a liminal space, or borderland, without necessarily moving toward one of the two purported binary poles. It is important to note that "spaces of liminality" are often used metaphorically, as in "she lives in a liminal space between freedom and imprisonment." But the crux of this for geographical investigation is that the in-between states are instantiated in the material landscape; that is, they become areas one can embody for varying amounts of time.

With these photographs we are trying to present the look of a conurbation that is in many ways defined by its liminal zones, physical manifestations of the metaphorical between-ness of Chinese-American culture (housing) and its

FIGURE 17.9 Rural Drive south of Garvey Avenue in Monterey Park. View is eastward into the alley behind Beijing Piehouse.

Source: Photo by Rick Miller, 2017.

commercialization (restaurants). This is true if for no other reason than many of the restaurant laborers, customers, owners, knowledge brokers (chefs), must cross this liminal zone when they move from dwelling to restaurant, in a way that a tourist from Los Angeles or out of state would not. Culinary tourism in the region is by and large channeled along the commercial strips and freeways, seldom with a need to venture to the back lots and neighborhoods that make the restaurant scene possible (Figures 17.9 and 17.10).

Liminality is crucial for the social life of cities to function. As de Certeau might have put it, they are the places in which "leakiness," or slippage between informal lifeways and the state, most often occurs.[20] Using the camera's eye to expose the backs of commercially successful restaurants on major SGV streets—and the alleyways that bridge them to dense suburban housing just steps away—reminds viewers that this multi-nodal ethnic enclave is a Southern California conurbation. It peels back the facade of the tourist-driven quest for authenticity found in other types of Chinatowns, and reminds viewers that the dwelling patterns of the SGV

FIGURE 17.10   Abbot Ave. in San Gabriel looking north toward W. Valley Blvd. The wall on the right side of the photo is the edge of San Gabriel Square, an outdoor shopping center which includes dozens of restaurants, anchored by a 99 Ranch Market grocery. The spatiality of the SGV's conurbation, which gives rise to shopping plazas and parking lots, stands in counterpoint to the Chinatowns in urban centers elsewhere.

Source: Photo by N. Bauch and R. Miller, 2017, 4 × 5-inch color film.

FIGURE 17.11 More commonly, attempts are made to elide the proximity between the restaurant industry and places of dwelling in SGV by visual and physical barriers. Location: S. Atlantic Blvd. and W. Valley Blvd., Alhambra.

Source: Photo by N. Bauch, 2017.

are truer to the core of immigrant diaspora motivations indicative of Southern California. In this case, adopting existing, affordable housing infrastructure was reflective of a motivation to settle, not to reproduce the Chinatown model of other North American cities (Figure 17.2). Glimpsing this through the anchor of restaurants reminds us that there exists a unique geographical answer to questions about the historical becoming of any landscape.

Further Research

This research is a starting point that we hope sparks further work along two lines. The first is empirical research in the form of ethnography and surveying. It would be helpful to know, for example, what percentage of restaurant patrons are local and what percentage are visitors to the SGV. The same goes for ethnic identity, place of origin, and time lived in the SGV. The other line of future research is methodological, namely to deepen how a visual, photographic approach can contribute to geographical understanding of the meaning and formation of landscapes.

In this introductory study, we have focused on the transitional borderlands (the liminal space) between Chinese restaurants in the SGV, and the suburban housing stock that has fueled the growth of Southern California for nearly 100 years. We hope by looking at these photographs, readers gain a deeper understanding of the significance of otherwise banal "back-alley" scenes that at once divide yet connect the visible imprint of Chinese restaurants to the overlooked landscapes of domestic inhabitation which allow these expressions of taste to thrive.

Key Terms

Photographic research methods: A set of activities involving cameras and photographs through which questions are posed and knowledge is generated within the social sciences and humanities.

Suburban landscapes: These denote the conjoined natural and built environments—the land as altered by human activity—in urban areas that are less dense than traditional city centers.

Liminality: A state of existence in between two recognizable phenomena, in which new properties tend to emerge that had beforehand not existed.

Discussion Questions

1. How might a visual approach to suburban landscapes supplement one's understanding of Chinese restaurants in the San Gabriel Valley? How do the authors use a "landscape" approach that might differ from the ideas of "place"?
2. Examining the images presented in this chapter, how are Chinese restaurants presented as distinct or indistinct from their vernacular context?
3. What kinds of spatial relationships do the images present between restaurants and their surrounding suburban fabric? Some spatial relationships to consider are: contrasting building types (consider the size, material, and forms of buildings to think about how buildings are used), the juxtaposition of different building types within the same image, and the separation (by alleys, by walls or fences, by strategic uses of plantings) between these building types.

Acknowledgements

The authors would like to thank Jenny Banh and Haiming Liu for their sage advice as we developed this idea into a chapter.

Notes

1 A simple search on the Yellow Pages website yields at least 1,186 unique Chinese restaurants in the cities that compose the San Gabriel Valley. www.yellowpages.com, accessed June 7, 2018.
2 Wong, Bernard P., and Tan Chee-Beng, eds. 2013. *Chinatowns Around the World: Gilded Ghetto, Ethnopolis, and Cultural Diaspora.* Boston: Brill. The SGV eschews the stereotypical visual markers of Chinese identification at work in various Chinatowns in the Americas: pagoda rooflines, dragon gates, and similar forms of kitsch.
3 This is changing as real estate marketing takes to visual cues to retain the attention of home-buyers. See: Hawthorne, Christopher. 2014. "How Arcadia is Remaking itself as a Magnet for Chinese Money." *Los Angeles Times,* December 3, Architecture.

4 Marsh, George Perkins, and David Lowenthal. 2005 [1885]. *Man and Nature: The Earth as Modified by Human Action*. Cambridge, Mass.: Belknap Press.

5 For a helpful discussion on narrating place, see: Bodenhamer, David J. 2015. "Narrating Space and Place." In *Deep Maps and Spatial Narratives*, edited by David J. Bodenhamer, John Corrigan and Trevor M. Harris. Bloomington: Indiana University Press.

6 For a rich ethnography of the SGV in the twenty-first century, see: Cheng, Wendy. 2013. *The Changs Next Door to the Diazes: Remapping Race in Suburban California*. Minneapolis: University of Minnesota Press.

7 Klein, Karen E. 1991. "Cultural Diversity Springs from Asian Influx." *Los Angeles Times*, October 13, At Home.

8 Arax, Mark. 1987. "Monterey Park: Nation's 1st suburban Chinatown." *Los Angeles Times*, April 6, B1.

9 Keil, Roger. 2017. *Suburban Planet: Making the World Urban from the Outside In*. Malden, Mass.: Polity Press; and Lerup, Lars, and Jesus Vassallo. 2017. *The Continuous City: Fourteen Essays on Architecture and Urbanization*. Zurich: Park Books.

10 Data from http://maps.latimes.com/neighborhoods/region/san-gabriel-valley/#ethnicity, based on U.S. census tracts last accessed June 12, 2018.

11 Sherman, Roger. 1995. *Re: American Dream: Six Urban Housing Prototypes for Los Angeles*. New York: Princeton Architectural Press.

12 Arax, Mark. 1987. "Monterey Park: Nation's 1st Suburban Chinatown." *Los Angeles Times*, April 6, B1.

13 Li, Wei. 1999. "Building Ethnoburbia: The Emergence and Manifestation of the Chinese Ethnoburb in Los Angeles' San Gabriel Valley." *Journal of Asian American Studies* 2 (1):1–28. Here, Li helpfully complicates the definition of ethnoburb to include its global economic factors; it is more than a "suburban Chinatown." At its simplest, however, she defines ethnoburb as an "ethnic suburb," a phenomenon divergent from the dense populations of immigrant settlements common to North American cities in the nineteenth and twentieth centuries.

14 Gold, Jonathan. 2013. "Chengdu Taste Serves Down-Home Sichuan." *Los Angeles Times*, August 3, Counter Intelligence. http://articles.latimes.com/2013/aug/03/food/la-fo-gold-20130803

15 Nee, Victor, and Bratt de Bary Nee. 1990. *Longtime Californ': A Documentary Study of an American Chinatown*. Stanford: Stanford University Press.

16 Tseng, Yen-Fen. 1994. "Chinese Ethnic Economy: San Gabriel Valley, Los Angeles County." *Journal of Urban Affairs* 16 (2): 169–189.

17 Fong, Timothy P. 1994. *The First Suburban Chinatown: The Remaking of Monterey Park, California*. Philadelphia: Temple University Press.

18 Sheren, Ila Nicole. 2015. *Portable Borders: Performance Art and Politics on the U.S. Frontera since 1984*. Austin: University of Texas Press; p. 3.

19 Moran, Dominique. 2013. "Between Outside and Inside? Prison Visiting Rooms as Liminal Carceral Spaces." *GeoJournal* 78 (2): 339–351; quote on p. 342.

20 de Certeau, Michel. 1984. *The Practice of Everyday Life*. Berkeley: University of California Press.

18

REDEFINING AND CHALLENGING THE BOUNDARIES OF CHINESE CUISINE

A Visually Based Exploration of Uyghur Restaurants in the United States

Christopher Sullivan

Introduction

The United States is home to an increasing number of restaurants specializing in Uyghur cuisine. The Uyghur[1] are a Turkic Muslim population that predominantly live in China's northwestern Xinjiang province (see Figure 18.1). Outside of China, countries including Germany, Turkey, Kazakhstan, and the United States are also home to Uyghur diasporic communities—yet the majority of China's (and the world's) ethnic Uyghur population resides in Xinjiang province. The Uyghur are one of 56 state-recognized ethnic groups in the People's Republic of China. The largest ethnic group, the Han, constitutes approximately 92 percent of China's population with over 1.2 billion members of the world's population.[2] The remaining 55 ethnic minority groups, including the Uyghur, make-up approximately 8 percent of China's population—around 300 million people. According to official census data, the Uyghur are one of China's largest ethnic minority groups with between 10–11 million residents in China. Outside of China, estimates of the size of the Uyghur population are uncertain. One advocacy group estimates there are between 1–1.6 million Uyghur outside of China, with the largest concentration of Uyghur expatriates found in Central Asia.[3]

Uyghur restaurants in the United States serve Uyghur dishes one might find in Xinjiang's capital, Urumqi, or the far western city of Kashgar. Traditional Uyghur dishes include bowls of long hand-pulled wheat noodles served underneath piles of vegetables and lamb meat (*laghman*); skewered lamb kebabs seasoned with cumin and other spices; rice pilaf cooked with carrots, lamb and seasoning (*polo*); warm nan bread with a dash of spices and sesame seeds; and cold vegetable dishes seasoned with garlic and salt. Uyghur cuisine has been heavily influenced by countries surrounding Xinjiang province and regions along the historic Silk Road—including Central Asia, the Middle East—and of course, China.[4] One distinguishing feature of Uyghur

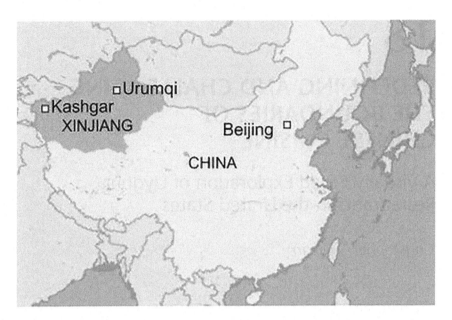

FIGURE 18.1 Map of Xinjiang Province, People's Republic of China.

Source: Accessed November 15, 2018, www.bbc.com/news/world-asia-china-33251572

cuisine is its emphasis on preparing and serving halal foods.[5] As most Uyghurs identify as Muslim, Uyghur restaurants prepare and serve food in accordance with Islamic
Law. This includes not serving pork products or alcoholic beverages.

To date, the majority of Uyghur restaurants in the United States are clustered in
larger, urban metropolitan centers and surrounding suburbs, including New York
City, Los Angeles, the San Francisco Bay Area, and Washington DC. The location
of Uyghur restaurants in the United States reflects both the migration trajectories
of Uyghur diasporic communities and, to some extent, the desire to increase the
presence (and profits) of Uyghur food in the United States by appealing to an urban
"foodie" clientele beyond Uyghur, Chinese, and Chinese-American customers. As
a recent article in the *Washington Post* highlights, one Uyghur restauranteur expects
"Uyghur food is going to be the next big thing in the United States."[6]

Historically, the label "Uyghur" was not used until the early twentieth century.
Detailed historical research has shown how the development and popularization of
the term "Uyghur" started around 1920.[7] The label "Uyghur" referred to Turkic-
speaking residents of what is now known as Western China. Prior to the label
"Uyghur," residents referred to themselves as "Muslims" or "locals," or, alterna-
tively, as residents of the "six cities" or Altishahri in the Uyghur language.

As the term "Uyghur" is relatively recent, Uyghur cuisine is itself a constructed
concept. This chapter explores this construction of Uyghur cuisine through a
visually based analysis of food served at restaurants that advertise themselves as
"Uyghur." It explores conceptions and limitations of the broader term Chinese
cuisine and its relationship to Uyghur cuisine. While some dishes served at Uyghur

restaurants might find themselves at home either in Chinese restaurants in mainland China or in the United States, other dishes might be more reminiscent of food served at Turkish or Central Asian restaurants. Academic works on Chinese cuisine(s) often conflate Uyghur cuisine with either food from the Xinjiang region or food of Western China more broadly. In some circles, Uyghur cuisine and Xinjiang cuisine are used more-or-less interchangeably.

Uyghur restaurants in the United States navigate a complex culinary terrain. They challenge progressive American diners ("foodies") to push the boundaries of their conceptions of Chinese food. In doing so, they stake out a unique culinary identity in the minds of American diners. At the same time, Uyghur restaurants do not travel too far away from their connections to mainland China—perhaps out of concern for alienating their Chinese expatriate and Chinese-American customer base. Uyghur restaurants further carve out a distinct culinary identity by appealing to a broader Muslim restaurant-goer in advertising themselves as "Halal." Uyghur restaurants use different strategies in attracting each of these broad groups of restaurant goers.

Uyghur Food, Restaurants and Identity

Scholars in the social sciences and humanities have explored how food, eating practices and eating locations (including restaurants) are important markers of identity, national belonging, and ethnic boundaries. At the same time, food, eating practices and eating locations also serve as sources that reinforce, challenge, and maintain power imbalances. Appadurai highlighted this point in the South Asian context:

> With the elaboration of cuisine and its socio-economic context, the capacity of food to bear social messages is increased. As many anthropologists have shown, food, in its varied guises, contexts, and functions, can signal rank and rivalry, solidarity and community, identity or exclusion, and intimacy or distance.[8]

In his view, food had two opposing functions: it served to bring people and groups together, creating intimacy and solidarity. But food also maintained relations of inequality and exclusion.

While most Han Chinese in mainland China are familiar with Uyghur food, many Americans have not yet heard of the Uyghur people, let alone Uyghur cuisine. While there are disagreements over how many regional cuisines exist within the broader umbrella of "Chinese cuisine" in China,[9] traditionally Uyghur food has been grouped together with foods from the Western part of China. Within China, restaurants serving Uyghur food (sometimes referred to as "Xinjiang food") can be found across the country. Wu and Cheung note:

> In China eating mutton and selling mutton on the street practically testified Muslim identity. In Beijing, mutton, kebab, pilaf, spice and tomato on rice,

all became ethnic markers distinguishing the Uygur sojourners of Xinjiang Autonomous Region of Northwest China from the Han Chinese.[10]

Noting the considerable disagreement and subjectivity inherent in creating regional cuisines within China—Uyghur food has typically fallen under a "Western" style of Chinese cuisine (including labels connected to Sichuan province, and Xinjiang province more specifically). T.C. Lai's *At the Chinese Table* elaborates on this broader term "Chinese cuisine":

> True Chinese cuisine is said to have developed in the Song dynasty (960–1279). "Cuisine" may be defined as a "manner or style of cooking", but the development of a cuisine is made possible only by the availability of a wide variety of ingredients, and by considerable body of cooks and eaters who are prepared to experiment with and partake of these foodstuffs, and who enjoy eating.[11]

Lai discusses a traditional division of Chinese cuisine into *fan* and *cai*: the former referring to rice, noodles, breads; while the latter refers to meats, vegetables, fruits, and other food items eaten with *fan*.[12] Lai further distinguishes Chinese cuisine for its emphasis on particular taste combinations, visual harmony, and texture; as well as the use of certain spices and styles of cutting and preparing food.[13] In regards to seasonings, Lai writes of "five-spice powder" as a typical seasoning used in Chinese cuisine. It is a mixture of star anise, cinnamon bark, brown peppercorns, fennel, and cloves.[14]

Some Uyghur dishes, like cold crushed cucumber served with garlic, are similar to dishes found in many Chinese restaurants. What distinguishes Uyghur cuisine from other types of Chinese cuisine? Aside from the emphasis on preparing foods in accordance with Islamic Law, the use of cumin spice has historically separated Uyghur cuisine from other cuisines in China.[15] The heavy use of lamb meat, and absence of pork, further distinguishes Uyghur cuisine from other regional cuisines in China.

In the United States, a lack of name or cultural recognition among many Americans means Uyghur food appeals to an "exotic" element characteristic of "foodie" culture.[16] Studies of food, taste, and identity in the social sciences have been heavily influenced by Bourdieu's *Distinction* (1979/1984).[17] Bourdieu and researchers in this tradition have explored how food and cuisine can serve as important markers of social status through differentiated practices of cultural consumption. Research has shown how a taste for the "exotic" can serve as a marker of an individual's class position, and social distinction.[18]

For many American diners, Chinese food represents a monolithic cuisine. Are Uyghur restaurants in the United States changing (and broadening) Americans' perceptions of "Chinese food"? Or are Uyghur restaurants staking out a separate identity—one that is socially and culturally distinct from "Chinese food" and Han Chinese-ness? Using a visually based analysis of five Uyghur restaurants in the United States, this chapter argues that Uyghur restaurants carve out a unique culinary identity, which asserts itself as distinct from Chinese cuisine to "foodie" restaurant goers. At the same time, these restaurants must also appeal to their mostly Han Chinese clientele by emphasizing their geographical connection to China's Xinjiang province. Finally, Uyghur restaurants' emphasis on Halal preparation appeals to a broader Muslim restaurant goer.

Methodology

Growing up as a white, middle-class kid from a small town in upstate New York, food was the primary link to my own ethnic identity and heritage. My mother's family is Polish-American—and holidays and special events were filled with my grandmother's pierogi, borsch, gwumpki, kielbasa, and Polish pastries and desserts. My connection to my family's ethnic heritage was linked to foods that my friends and classmates might have considered "exotic," or outside the standard Anglo-American diet. Food offered a limited window into Polish culture and heritage and provided opportunities to learn more about my maternal family's immigration to the United States in the early twentieth century.

An undergraduate study abroad trip first took me to China in the year 2000, where I learned more about China's non-Han ethnic minority populations. Subsequent trips and extended stays in China brought me to Xinjiang province, and later to intensive language training in beginning Uyghur, Turkish, Farsi, as well as Mandarin Chinese. In graduate school, my dissertation explored ethnicity and inequality in China through quantitative and ethnographic perspectives. These experiences have contributed to my interest in exploring how food, cuisines, and restaurant spaces intersect with my broader research interest in ethnicity and inequality in China.

For this project, I visited five Uyghur restaurants in the United States—two on the west coast and three on the east coast—to examine characteristics of Uyghur restaurants that distinguish them from Chinese restaurants. Broadly speaking, two of the Uyghur restaurants were located in urban areas, while three were in more suburban areas. At each restaurant I took photographs of the food, menu, interior décor, and exterior. While there was variation in the quality and presentation of food across the five restaurants, there were also similarities in the interior décor and exterior signage. Each visit focused on the visual presentation of the food and material objects inside and outside the restaurant, as well as the choice(s) of language and linguistic marketing/advertising used by the restaurant. Of particular interest were objects that visually signaled Uyghur restaurants as being "Uyghur" (and not Chinese), including the ways in which Uyghur restaurants advertised themselves and positioned themselves vis-à-vis Chinese restaurants to a diverse set of restaurant goers.

The Restaurants

The first Uyghur restaurant, Restaurant One, was part of a larger chain of "Chinese-Uyghur" restaurants headquartered in mainland China. According to the restaurant menu, its mainland Chinese parent company has opened several chain locations in the United States, with plans for continued expansion. The exterior signage featured both English language text and Chinese characters. The Chinese text on the exterior signage advertised itself as a "Xinjiang Restaurant." It was the only restaurant in the group to advertise itself in English as "Chinese-Uyghur" as opposed to "Uyghur" (see Figure 18.2). The menu detailed how ownership of this particular restaurant was connected to mainland China—and, as such, it is interesting to point out the choice to refer to the restaurant as "Chinese-Uyghur." Given recent reports of violence and mass internment in Xinjiang province,[19] as well as China's changing historical relationship to the Xinjiang region (home to the majority of the world's Uyghur population)—this linguistic move is a clear attempt to connect Uyghur cuisine, culture, and food to mainland China and Chinese identity. In contrast, all four remaining restaurants described themselves as "Uyghur" restaurants and made stronger reference to the ancient "Silk Road."

Restaurant One was in an urban neighborhood on the west coast. It was located several blocks from the city's more famous Chinatown. The signage in the front of the restaurant advertised traditional Uyghur dishes like "Polo," "Kebabs," and "Laghman" (advertised in English as the "House Specials"), along with food that might be more familiar to American audiences—including Honey Walnut Shrimp, Broccoli Beef, and Orange Chicken. Restaurant One featured a mixture of both traditional Uyghur cuisine and popular dishes that one might find at a Chinese restaurant that caters to American tastes.[20] The restaurant had the largest seating area of any of the six restaurants visited and featured bright colored textiles above booth seating. A large dividing wall awkwardly separated the restaurant in half.

FIGURE 18.2 Exterior signage of Restaurant One.

FIGURE 18.3 Interior of Restaurant One.

It had fewer decorations on the walls compared with other restaurants visited (see Figure 18.3). The walls were painted a drab, neutral color, and featured traditional Uyghur musical instruments and artwork sporadically hung on the walls. The blaring music did not sound Uyghur, but vaguely international and featured non-Chinese, non-Uyghur language singers.

Hand-pulled wheat noodles, or "laghman," was a traditional Uyghur dish ordered at each of the five restaurants. The laghman at Restaurant One was oily and the noodles did not taste freshly made. The dish featured a tomato-based sauce with fungus, green and red bell peppers, and sliced onions. The noodles were uniform in size—an indication they were likely not prepared by hand. The texture of the food was soggy and the vegetables soft. Similarly, the nan bread, while warmed, tasted like it had been sitting out for a day or two. The cold cucumber dish featured a light and flavorful sauce that was salty and sour (see Figure 18.4). Overall, the food tasted pre-packaged and less fresh compared with that of the other restaurants visited.

The second restaurant on the West Coast, Restaurant Two, was owned and operated by a Uyghur family from Xinjiang Province. It was located in a suburban strip mall surrounded by other Chinese and Asian restaurants. Restaurant Two had a much smaller dining space, with six or seven tables crammed into a restaurant in the middle of a suburban shopping plaza. The exterior advertised the restaurant as serving "Uyghur Food—the Tastes from Xinjiang" in English, as well as indicating that the restaurant was Halal. The languages on the exterior of the restaurant featured Chinese characters, English, and some Arabic letters. The name of the restaurant, and most of the information about the restaurant, was written in English. The Arabic script advertised the restaurant was Halal, while the Chinese text described the restaurant as serving "Xinjiang cuisine."

FIGURE 18.4 Crushed cucumber with garlic at Restaurant One.

Restaurant Two was packed full of diners when I visited. Judging by the language spoken (Uyghur and Mandarin Chinese), the patrons were a mixture of mostly Uyghur and Han Chinese customers. The décor featured carpet wall hangings, vibrant textiles, paintings, traditional Uyghur men's hats, and musical instruments, while the television played Uyghur music videos (see Figure 18.5). The menu featured traditional Uyghur cuisine options written in English and Chinese only. It featured the phrase "Uyghur Cuisine" written in English and "Xinjiang Cuisine, unique taste" written in Chinese characters. The English text on the menu described the food as "Uyghur" while the Chinese text referred to the food as being from Xinjiang province.

The "laghman," or hand-pulled noodle dish, featured many of the same vegetables as Restaurant One—but the noodles tasted fresh and were less uniform in size. The dish was less oily and featured a wider selection of vegetables. In addition to the onions and peppers, it also contained diced tomatoes (see Figure 18.6) The cold dish featured cold gelatinous rice noodles, herbs, and chickpeas in a spicy chili sauce. Both dishes tasted freshly made. The busy kitchen featured several employees working in a cramped space—and I noticed some staff members hand-pulling the noodles.

On the east coast, I visited three Uyghur restaurants. Restaurant Three was located in a suburban shopping mall near a large Asian supermarket, and surrounded by restaurants offering a variety of Asian cuisines. The restaurant's exterior featured the name of the restaurant in English, along with a description of the restaurant in

FIGURE 18.5 Restaurant Two interior.

FIGURE 18.6 Hand-pulled noodles ("laghman") at Restaurant Two.

FIGURE 18.7 Restaurant Three signage.

Chinese (see Figure 18.7). Other text written in English made explicit reference to the historic Silk Road. The menu featured English language only descriptions of the dishes. Unlike Restaurant One, the menu offered limited options of what one might find at a Chinese restaurant in the United States, and instead featured more traditional Uyghur dishes.

Restaurant Three was nearly empty when I arrived. The interior décor featured several wall hangings, including carpets and needlepoint work, Uyghur men's hats, as well as framed textiles. The walls were a vibrant red color, and matched a dark red brick interior. The restaurant featured traditional Uyghur music in the background. The owners were also a family from Xinjiang province, and the waitstaff featured both Uyghur and Han Chinese individuals.

The "laghman" dish featured long, hand-pulled noodles that were uneven in size – a likely indication they were hand-made at the restaurant. The noodles were served with sliced onions, green and red peppers, and tomatoes. Typically, "laghman" is served with slices of lamb or beef (and in some cases, chicken), but I ordered the dish without meat. The tomato sauce was light and salty, with just a hint of spice. The nan bread was served at room temperature, and had a thick, doughy texture. The cold cucumber salad was heavy on the garlic and chili peppers, served in an oily vinegar dressing.

Restaurant Four was also located on the east coast, but in a more urban locale. It was situated in an upscale part of town, close to a subway station. From the outside, there was no clear indication it was a Uyghur restaurant (see Figure 18.9).

FIGURE **18.8** Nan bread at Restaurant Three.

FIGURE 18.9 Exterior of Restaurant Four.

The exterior of the restaurant featured the restaurant's name in English, with no Chinese characters or Arabic script visible from the street. A glass enclosed box featured a menu with only English language descriptions of the food.

The restaurant's interior featured bright textiles and pillows, wall hangings, Uyghur hats, and paintings. The seats and tables were crammed closely together. I was seated next to a large party of Uyghur diners, and soon the restaurant filled up with a mixture of Uyghur, Han Chinese, and Caucasian patrons. The menu featured some food options not available at the other restaurants. For example, it was the only restaurant that offered tofu in place of lamb or beef in the traditional "laghman" dish (see Figure 18.10).

The food was more expensive at Restaurant Four, with slightly smaller portion sizes than those of the other restaurants. The hand-pulled noodles tasted fresh and featured a colorful assortment of vegetables. The seasonings were less flavorful and had a mild taste. The cold cucumber dish was well seasoned with garlic, salt, vinegar, and oil, and the nan bread was served warm. Together with Restaurant Five, the presentation of the food reflected the posh surroundings of the restaurant. Smaller portions, beautifully presented in an upscale, if tightly packed, space.

Restaurant Five was located in a more suburban location on the east coast. It featured a larger dining space and fresh looking interior. Like its urban neighbor just discussed, this last restaurant advertised its name only in English. It did not feature any Chinese characters or Arabic script on the exterior of the building. Both Restaurant Four and Restaurant Five were less embedded in Chinese or

FIGURE 18.10 Hand-pulled noodles with tofu at Restaurant Four.

FIGURE 18.11 Interior at Restaurant Five.

Asian Ethnic Enclaves—and were both located in upscale neighborhoods and had a mixture of Uyghur, Han Chinese, and Caucasian diners.

The interior featured a brightly colored textile trim around the tables, several traditional paintings featuring all male musicians, and some more abstract themed paintings. It was a large space, mostly empty when I visited, but it soon became more crowded (see Figure 18.11). The owner and manager was also Uyghur, with an Uyghur server.

The presentation of the food at Restaurant Five was more similar to Restaurant Four in the sense the portions were slightly smaller than in the first three restaurants. The food was beautifully presented, with a unique presentation of the cold cucumber salad (see Figure 18.12). The hand-pulled noodles were thin but clearly hand-made, and the dish was well seasoned with a similar range of vegetables.

Discussion and Conclusion

The growth of Uyghur restaurants in the United States offers an important entry into discussions of how food is not only connected to eating, but to what John-ston and Baumann refer to as the "cultural politics of belonging, exclusion, and status."[21] For many American diners, Chinese food represents a monolithic cuisine.

FIGURE 18.12 Cold cucumber, onion and tomato at Restaurant Five.

However, in China, and increasingly in the United States, the idea of a single "Chinese cuisine" is problematic. As Wu and Cheung note:

> Chinese gourmets used to argue about whether there should be three, four, six, or eight major high cuisines in China, but the post-modern food scene in China . . . has obscured all the boundary markers, because of migration, innovation, modern communication, creolization and globalization. Maybe the question of what Chinese cuisines is can be answered more satisfactorily today in the foreign, global, or transnational context, when our studies show Chinese cuisine is more readily identified in Australia, the Philippines, Indonesia, Japan, or the US.[22]

While Wu and Cheung argue the boundary markers over what separates Chinese food from non-Chinese food has been obscured in mainland China, they simultaneously point to places like the United States for hope in providing a clearer, if not more limited, conception of what constitutes Chinese cuisine. However, the growth of Uyghur restaurants in the United States challenges this hope in bringing clarity to the boundaries of what constitutes Chinese cuisine—and instead, offers diners in the United States an expanded conception of food from Western China.

The five visits offered an opportunity to begin to search for visual signs that serve to demarcate the boundaries of Uyghur restaurants (and cuisine) from Chinese restaurants (and cuisine). The presence of signage in three (and sometimes four) languages, including English, Chinese, Uyghur, and Arabic was one visible difference from Chinese restaurants. All five of the restaurants advertised themselves as "halal"—something rarely found in most Chinese restaurants in the United States.

While Restaurant One sought to emphasize Uyghur cuisine as being part of a broader Chinese cuisine landscape, the other four restaurants sought to emphasize Uyghur cuisine on its own terms. Restaurant One also offered the most "cross-over" menu items, including orange chicken and chow mien traditionally served at (more Americanized) Chinese restaurants in the United States. Other menu items—including cold, crushed cucumber with garlic—are typically found at Uyghur and non-Uyhur restaurants in mainland China. All of the restaurants offered dishes that many would consider uniquely Uyghur—the "laghman" and "polo" dishes are distinctly different from Chinese cuisine, and the lamb kebabs, while popular in China, reference cuisines in the Middle East and Central Asia.

The description and analysis presented here, while limited, begin to explore how Uyghur restaurants both challenge and redefine the broader landscape of Chinese cuisine for multiple dining audiences. Uyghur restaurants navigate a complex food landscape by appealing to customers in quite different ways. Four of the five restaurants I visited actively rejected the Chinese restaurant label in their English language signage and menus, and sought to assert Uyghur cuisine as its own independent culinary identity. Beyond linguistic forms of representation, all five restaurants expanded on American notions of Chinese food by offering menu options unavailable at conventional Chinese restaurants. Foods like laghman, polo, and lamb kebabs are not typical of mainstream Chinese restaurants in the United States. The interior and exterior décor of these five restaurants featured traditional Uyghur material objects like musical instruments, men's hats, and wall hangings that further signaled a unique Uyghur identity.

In the broader context of Uyghur positionality within Chinese politics and society, the identity of Uyghur cuisine and restaurants in relationship to Chinese cuisine and restaurants takes on an added level of meaning. Uyghur restaurants have uniquely positioned themselves within the broader landscape of United States restaurants by appealing to several different groups of restaurant goers. In doing so, Uyghur restaurants in the United States have redefined and challenged American diners' views on Chinese cuisine; appealed to Chinese regionalism and Muslim identity to broaden its customer base, while at the same time carving out a space for a unique Uyghur culinary identity distinct from the broader label of Chinese cuisine.

Key Terms

Uyghur: A Turkic Muslim ethnic minority group in China. The Uyghur predominantly live in China's northwestern Xinjiang province.

Foodie: Term used to describe a person with a strong interest in food. A "foodie" enjoys food for pleasure, or out of an interest or hobby, rather than simply out of hunger. A gourmet.

Halal: Meaning sanctioned by Islamic law. It involves preparing, serving, and selling food in accordance with Islamic law.

Discussion Questions

1. What makes Uyghur restaurants and food different from Chinese restaurants and food?
2. What "customers" do Uyghur restaurants appeal to? What strategies do Uyghur restaurants use to market to each of these different restaurant-goers?
3. In what ways are food and identity connected to each other?

Notes

1 Alternative spellings include "Uighur" and "Uygur." For consistency, I make use of the spelling "Uyghur" throughout this chapter.
2 According to the 2010 Population Census of the People's Republic of China. Accessed November 15, 2018 (in Chinese), www.stats.gov.cn/tjsj/pcsj/rkpc/6rp/indexch.htm. See also the University of North Carolina Chapel Hill's "Chinese Ethnic Groups: Overview Statistics" (in English), Accessed November 15, 2018 https://guides.lib.unc.edu/china_ethnic/statistics
3 Number of Uyghur expatriates outside of China, according to the World Uyghur Congress, as cited by "Nowhere to Hide" (March 31, 2018). *The Economist*, 426, 58. Retrieved from https://search.proquest.com/docview/2019985096?accountid=10349
4 See E.N. Anderson, *The Food of China* (New Haven: Yale University Press, 1988).
5 The term halal comes from Arabic, where it translates as lawful or permitted. Halal refers to food that has been prepared in accordance with Islamic Law. Practically, this means food was prepared free of ingredients prohibited under Islamic Law (e.g. pork products, alcohol); and prepared using utensils and machinery cleansed in accordance with Islamic Law.
6 Maura Judkis, "Is their crossroads cuisine the 'the next big thing'? Uyghurs hope so," Accessed November 17, 2018, www.washingtonpost.com/lifestyle/food/theyre-chinese-and-muslim-and-they-want-you-to-try-their-crossroads-cuisine/2017/03/03/906638bc-f91e-11e6-bf01-d47f8cf9b643_story.html
7 See Rian Thum, *The Sacred Routes of Uyghur History* (Cambridge and London: Harvard University Press, 2014).
8 Arjun Appadurai, "Gastro-politics in Hindu South Asia," *American Ethnologist* 8, no. 3 (1981): 494.
9 See Sidney Cheung and David Wu, eds. *The Globalization of Chinese Food* (London and New York: Routledge, 2002).
10 David Wu and Sidney Cheung, "The Globalization of Chinese Food and Cuisine: Markers and Breakers of Cultural Barriers," eds. Sidney Cheung and David Wu (London and New York: Routledge, 2002), 7.
11 T.C. Lai, *At the Chinese Table*, (Hong Kong: Oxford University Press, 1984).

12 Lai, *At the Chinese* Table, 18.

13 Lai, *At the Chinese* Table.

14 Lai, *At the Chinese* Table, 19.

15 Kongshao Zhuang, "The Development of Ethnic Cuisine in Beijing," eds. Sidney Cheung and David Wu, (London and New York: Routledge, 2002), 73–74.

16 Josée Johnston and Shyon Baumann, *Foodies: Democracy and Distinction in the Gourmet Foodscape*, 2nd ed. (New York: Routledge, 2015).

17 See Pierre Bourdieu, *Distinction: A Social Critique of the Judgement of Taste*, Translated by Richard Nice, (Cambridge: Harvard University Press, 1979/1984).

18 For example, see Alan Warde, Lydia Martens, and Wendy Olsen, "Consumption and the Problem of Variety: Cultural Omnivorousness, Social Distinction and Dining Out." *Sociology* 33, no. 1 (February 1999), 105–127.

19 For example, see Cat leaves bag (2018, Oct 20). *The Economist*, 429, 60. Retrieved from https://search.proquest.com/docview/2123019906?accountid=10349

20 For a discussion of the social history of Chinese restaurants in the United States and how Chinese cuisine has been modified for an American palette, see Haiming Liu, *From Canton Restaurant to Panda Express: A History of Chinese Food in the United States* (New Brunswick, NJ: Rutgers University Press, 2015).

21 See Josée Johnston and Shyon Baumann. *Foodies: Democracy and Distinction in the Gourmet Foodscape*. 2nd ed. (New York: Routledge, 2015).

22 David Wu and Sidney Cheung, "The Globalization of Chinese Food and Cuisine: Markers and Breakers of Cultural Barriers," eds. Sidney Cheung and David Wu (London and New York: Routledge, 2002), 4.

19

DIASPORIC COUNTERPUBLICS

The Chinese Restaurant as Institution and Installation in Canada

Lily Cho

You walk in and consider sitting down at one of the orange artificial leather booths, but then the shiny counter catches your eye. You see a row of stools in front of it. Behind the counter, there is an old cash register, shelves neatly stacked with an assortment of teas and candy bars. The coffee machine is plugged in. A mixture of elaborate paper lantern-style lights and bright fluorescent tubes illuminates the space. There is a glass jar filled with fortune-cookie fortunes. Everything feels a bit too familiar, right but not quite right. You are not sure if you should sit down. Welcome to one of Karen Tam's Gold Mountain Restaurants.

These restaurants are a series of installations that Tam has done from 2002 to the present. So far, she has installed more than ten of them across Canada. Even though some of them have been in art spaces in major urban centers such as Centre A in Vancouver and the MAI in Montreal, most of the Gold Mountain Restaurants have been in small cities and towns across the country. She has shown at the Alternator Gallery in Kamloops, British Columbia, the Southern Alberta Art Gallery in Lethbridge, the Forest City Gallery in London, Ontario, and so on. Each of the installations is different. Each has its own name, its own furniture and signs and menus. Each one is also similar despite, and perhaps because of, their differences. They bear a resemblance to each other. They are recognizable as a particular kind of restaurant. They are not just Chinese restaurants, but a specific genre of Chinese restaurant characterized precisely by their lack of cosmopolitanism.

Such restaurants are ubiquitous in small towns in Canada. There is almost no small town that does not have at least one Chinese restaurant. They are a legacy of Chinese immigration to Canada during the building of the Canadian Pacific Railway in the nineteenth century. Chinese workers were brought in to help construct the railway that would bind the nation from the Pacific to the Atlantic Ocean. After their labor was no longer needed, a series of increasingly punitive legislative measures was put into place, under the auspices of the *Chinese Immigration Act*, and

Chinese workers were left to construct lives far away from family and community. The Chinese restaurant in small towns is a reminder of the hardship of this period but also of the extraordinary ways in which Chinese migrants built vibrant spaces of community despite the discrimination and racism they encountered. Tam's Chinese restaurant installations brilliantly reprise this history by transforming art galleries into fake restaurants and thus posing important questions about public space.

Through these installations, Tam also opens up the question of the restaurant as a public space of critique. In this chapter, I argue that Tam's installations illuminate precisely both the ways in which interaction between and across cultural divides. In so doing, in transforming this institution of small town life into an installation within the cosmopolitan spaces of contemporary art, she animates the Chinese restaurant as a diasporic counterpublic.

In the spirit of Michael Warner's idea of the counterpublic, I suggest that Tam does not simply recreate restaurants. She makes a space, albeit a temporary, contingent, and fragile one, that highlights the mutually transformative relations between communities, between cooks and customers, between Chinese and non-Chinese. In that the Chinese restaurant is not a purely oppositional space, Warner's notion of a counterpublic must be delineated from Nancy Fraser's idea of a subaltern counterpublic. He notes that "Fraser's description of what counterpublics do— 'formulate oppositional interpretations of their identities, interests, and needs'— sounds like the classically Habermasian description of rational-critical publics, with the word 'oppositional' inserted."[1] Instead, Warner argues that "counterpublics are 'counter' to the extent that they try to supply different ways of imagining stranger sociability and its reflexivity; as publics, they remain oriented to stranger circulation in a way that is not just strategic but constitutive of membership and its affects."[2] Warner's idea of counterpublics is especially salient to thinking about how diasporic communities are distinct publics that engage with dominant culture through specific modes of address that may or may not always be heard or understood. Diasporas do not always, and usually do not, have coherent political or even social agendas, but they nevertheless continue to make spaces in which there is a sense of a community beyond that of the diasporas themselves. Disparate and dispersed, small town Chinese restaurants in Canada create a space that is nonetheless constitutive of a recognizable public that persists in addressing strangers and the strangeness of dominant culture through an invitation to sit down, to open up the menu, to consume something familiar and different. Tam's installations distill this function of the restaurant and re-present it to her audience as yet another space of "stranger circulation."[3]

It is crucial that counterpublics remain neither hermetically insulated from larger, dominant public culture nor infinitely open to the incursions of that culture. The tension produced by the closed and yet open space of address is, at least in part, indicative of a counterpublic. Counterpublics do not merely speak to and among themselves. Nor are they addressing just any stranger. Warner offers the example of a queer public as such a counterpublic. A diaspora might be another.

While there are important differences between a queer public and a diasporic one, the latter is also nonetheless a public that is acutely aware of the tension of its existence in relation to a larger, dominant public. The focus on the question of power and dominance makes Warner's conception of the counterpublic especially useful for thinking about diasporas. He understands that the public sphere is not simply a strategy of domination through exclusion of those who are not white, propertied, and male. Merely extending membership to women, non-white people, people who do not own land, and so on, is not necessarily the way to make the public sphere more public. For Warner, "the projection of a public is a new, creative, and distinctively modern mode of power."[4] Warner emphasizes the ways in which counterpublic life is an engagement with relations of power. This emphasis is particularly salient in understanding the formation of diasporic subjects and communities. Diasporic counterpublics, I suggest, recognize the distinctly modern mode of power embodied in projection of a public even as they remain acutely aware of their subordinate status. The point is not for them to take over, but for them to articulate a distinct space of relation despite the horizons marked out by a dominant public culture.

In suggesting that the Chinese restaurant is a diasporic counterpublic space, I am distinguishing the idea of a diasporic community from that of a diasporic counterpublic. A counterpublic is a space of address. It is the creation of a world in which relations of power are always present but are also always under negotiation. It is a space that calls out to other members of the diasporic community through a mutually recognizable form of address—Chinese food—and invites the transformations of subjectivity that come out of the requirements of public circulation. The Chineseness of the Chinese food is always under question at these restaurants but it is this very uncertainty, the persistence of it, that is so productive of diasporic counterpublic culture. Chineseness in diaspora is not smugly certain of its authenticity, of its connection to some ancestral or originary root. That is a good thing. Small town Chinese restaurants demand what amounts to the experience of a perpetual double take. Is this Chinese or is it not? Isn't it just like that one in the other town, or is it not? Karen Tam's installations capture this experience and recreate it. Is this a restaurant, or is it not?

Tam's installations create a public space within a public space. She produces a restaurant inside an art gallery. Through this act of doubled publicness, she shows her audience how difficult it is to cross the divide across the shiny space of the arborite counter, through the swinging doors. It takes more than just sitting as a customer in the restaurant to fully experience its publicness. It is not that the restaurant isn't a public sphere, but that its publicness is a mediated one. To get to the Chinese restaurant's true publicness, Tam suggests, one must simultaneously step away from and move further into the space of the restaurant. Her installations invite their audiences to do that. By taking the restaurant out of the restaurant and installing it into the space of the gallery, she allows her audience to step away from it even as they are asked to enter further into the restaurant by inviting them behind the counter to examine the cash register and, through the swinging doors, into the kitchen, even though they may not feel as though they should be there. Days Lee points out in a catalogue essay for *Gold Mountain Restaurant*, that Tam

> has noticed that people who have worked in a restaurant tend to go behind the counter to examine the cash register, the dishes, and the coffee machine. Then, they walk through the swinging doors to inspect the kitchen where often a stove, a deep fryer, and even a sink are installed. However, the non-Chinese are hesitant to explore these spaces.[5]

As she tells Lee, she asks people who may have only experienced the restaurant as customers to consider "what life was like inside."[6]

But Tam's installations are not simply mimetic creations. They pose questions rather than answer them. Françoise Belu argues that "through her mimetic *mis en abyme*, Karen Tam temporarily mystifies viewers in order to show them, first of all, that the Chinese restaurants of North America are themselves mystifications."[7] These are mystifications with a function. They create the spaces of interaction and connection that produce diasporic culture. The installations extend this function by bringing together unlikely communities and provoking conversation across the space of the counter. As the documentation of the Gold Mountain Restaurants project on her website attests, Tam's installations draw a wide range of attendees into one space. People who had little interest in the abstractions of contemporary art are suddenly wandering in and out of her installations. Old-timer Chinese restaurant owners sit at a bench at the doorway to the restaurant. In a challenge to the idea of museums and galleries as sacrosanct spaces, school kids are eating their lunches there. Even the curators are doing it. In my own experience of attending one of her openings, I found that I was as likely to chat with a family member of Tam's or a former restaurant owner as with an arts administrator, artist, or curator. It is not just that Tam democratizes the space of the contemporary art gallery. It is also, and more importantly, that she makes the public space of the gallery more public by making it more private.

The restaurant installations are intensely private by all kinds of measures. First, Tam is not reticent about her own personal, private experience with Chinese restaurants. In interviews, and throughout the material for her catalogue, she talks about growing up with the restaurant she considers her "second home," the Restaurant aux sept bonheurs in east Montreal.[8] It was her attempt to document her parents' restaurant when they decided to sell it that was the catalyst for what would eventually become the *Gold Mountain Restaurant* project. In some ways, you could say that Tam has been recreating her parents' restaurant over and over and over again as a project of private memorialization. Tam's installations are also private in the ways in which they invite interactions with the art that are highly personal. "Visitors to her installation," Belu notes, "can no longer confine themselves to looking; they are plunged instead into another world in which they must dwell."[9] They have to enter into the installation, confront the invitation to sit down, to go past the swinging doors into the kitchen. Further, the installations shy away from grand statements about art, or race, or society. "Karen Tam practices a veritable social art that is diametrically opposed to general statements about society."[10] In this movement away from the general, Tam's installations demand a more intimate, more specific social engagement. Finally, the restaurant installations also transform the public space of the gallery into the privatized space of a commercial restaurant. This transformation highlights one of the contradictions of public spaces such as art galleries: despite their public status, they often function like private spaces in that their claims to high culture limit those who might enter. On the other hand, Chinese restaurants, despite being private businesses, have often functioned as public gathering spaces.

This tension between public and private that runs throughout the installations makes possible a set of dialogues and interactions that are, according to Warner, one of the central characteristics of publics and counterpublics. Tam's installations create this effect of inhabiting the very public space of the restaurant while demanding a very private series of reflections. Visitors to Tam's installations shuttle constantly between the public address of the art and its invitations to the personal and the private. As Belu observes of these restaurants where no food is served:

> The practical goal—eating—that makes a person go to a restaurant is omitted here: no meals are served, and viewers logically come to ask themselves questions about the context. For it is up to them to get to "the very marrow" by asking themselves questions about their relationships with others and, specifically, with those others who are the most different from themselves, the foreigners. Social art, which can operate only through singularity, is always participatory.[11]

In that they are hyper-real recreation of the restaurant as a public space, Tam's installations make the gallery more public by delving into the tension between publicity and privacy that marks the constitution of the public sphere. In so doing, these installations insist upon a series of interactions and connections that form a diasporic counterpublic.

It is not just the installations themselves that perform this function of interaction and connection, but also the process Tam engages in for each and every installation. *Gold Mountain Restaurant* is not a traveling exhibition in the traditional sense. Tam does not pack up the "restaurant" into boxes after each show. It is not simply crated and then shipped to the next gallery. On the contrary, when each installation is taken down, the contents return to their various owners in the local community. Tam relies upon the generosity and the idiosyncratic possibilities of the objects that she finds within each host community in order to construct her installations. Each one is built to suit the specific space in which it will be housed. Each has its own specificity from the name to the furniture to the features that can be found. Some might have a counter. Some might have a deep fryer. Some might have booths. Some might not. They all share in the same process of construction and installation wherein Tam arrives at each site and enlists the help of local (sometimes retired) restaurant owners, artists, and random passers-by.

Tam relies upon the involvement of a range of people from diverse communities. When Tam installed the version of *Gold Mountain Restaurant* in London, Ontario (*Old Silver Moon Restaurant* installed at the Forest City Gallery in 2006), I remember feeling a distinct sense of panic (which Tam obviously didn't share) when she outlined her process and asked me if I knew of people who might have some old signs, chairs and tables, lights, props, and so on. Of course, there are such things in every town. But what if she couldn't find them in time? What if people wouldn't lend their things out? Of course, the artist knew better. Her installations come together every time, and every time they draw together a range of unlikely conspirators in the project of making contemporary art.

Tam's process, from the ways in which she assembles each restaurant installation to the range of spaces that her installations have migrated out into, echoes that of the development of the restaurants themselves. Chinese restaurateurs find themselves scattered across the country. They must construct a restaurant out of the materials they find. They rely upon a mixture of an existing network of business associations and local passers-by. Even though the installations resemble the restaurants, after stepping into one of Tam's restaurants, one could just as easily say that the restaurants resemble art installations. Tam draws a connection between the space of the contemporary art gallery and the space of the Chinese restaurant.

Thinking about diasporic counterpublics shifts discussions of diaspora away from classification and membership, and towards a recognition of the contingencies and dynamism of diasporic culture. Diasporic culture is contingent upon the conditions of dispersion and arrival. It cannot know in advance what it will be, just as people in diaspora cannot know in advance what kind of home they will make, what kinds of resources and communities they will find, what the forms of cultural survival will be and how they will flourish. The diasporic counterpublic recognizes how diasporas are communities that look both inward and outward.

Let me illustrate more clearly through the Chinese restaurant how a diasporic counterpublic is made up of both diasporic and non-diasporic members. As a gathering of diners and those who prepare and serve the food, it is a public that never fully claims universalism. It is too marked by race and too aware of its subordinate status. In this sense, it is not like the hockey rink or the community center. But it is like them enough to make some claims to publicness. Its address is not merely to other Chinese diasporic subjects. That it is a business, a restaurant, necessitates an address that extends beyond the Chinese community. The restaurants are spaces where a range of people will, at least for a moment, be eating Chinese. Through the consumption and production of something that will be called Chinese food, a series of interactions and negotiations unfold. Even though the exchanges are mediated by capital, and perhaps even overdetermined by merchant–consumer relations, I suggest that there is something there that exceeds that a purely commercial relationship.

It is a relationship that produces a sense of a public that has a specific membership but is not closed or limited. What draws this public together is an ongoing agreement around the production and consumption of Chinese food. That food is mutually acknowledged as Chinese but it is also constantly changing, mutating and responding to ideas of Chineseness and Canadianness among both Chinese and non-Chinese people. The food represented on the Chinese restaurant menu is a textual testament to the basis of this public. It is not an agenda so much as it is an index of cultural interaction. The food that you will find at these restaurants, the easy juxtaposition of egg foo yong with beef dip sandwiches, would not exist without the unique coming together of Chinese and non-Chinese appetites in small towns across the country. Indeed, it is hard to find egg foo yong anywhere else and even the beef dip sandwich is hard to come by outside of a small town Chinese restaurant. Of course, because it is a counterpublic, there is nothing so blatant as a statement that the Chinese restaurant menu will represent Chineseness in diaspora. Given the diversity of Chineseness in diaspora, that would be an impossible claim to make. But the menu offers some sense that some kind of quiet, mutual pact has been made that the Chinese restaurant will be a gathering of a whole constellation of varying tastes and cravings that will come to constitute this institution of small-town life. It is a counterpublic of culinary expression. Its discourse is not that of the rational dialogue and debate that characterizes the bourgeois public sphere, but it has a shared discursive sensibility nonetheless.

As crucial as the offerings on the menu are, a Chinese restaurant is not entirely about the food. It is also a physical space with its own architecture and interior. Tam's *Gold Mountain Restaurant* installations perfectly capture this specific physicality. Even though each of her installations is different, taken together as an entity, the Gold Mountain Restaurants evoke through borrowed and found materials the ways in which these restaurants form a particular genre of their own. It is not easy to identify the specific elements that constitute these spaces. The typography of the signage? The swinging doors? There is no prescriptive and coherent list of physical elements that mark these restaurants, and yet we know one when we see it. The originary spaces of diaspora are fraught with problems of definition and delineation. These are spaces remade through memory and some sense of what "home" should and could be. Sometimes, there is a sense that this "home" is itself more imaginary than the relationships that tether those in diaspora to it.

In many ways, diasporas are characterized by the lack of physical space, the loss of home and homeland. Further, in the spaces of arrival, diasporas struggle with issues of isolation on the one hand and ghettoization on the other. In terms of the Chinese restaurant as a diasporic counterpublic, I am aware that some publics need spaces but not all of them do. Thinking about diasporas in terms of publics and counterpublics makes the issue of space particularly poignant.

As diasporic counterpublics, Chinese restaurants stage over and over again the delicate negotiations and interactions that constitute their publicness. They carve out a distinctly Chinese space within a landscape that would otherwise offer no reference whatsoever to their difference. At the same time, they remain persistently open to non-Chinese presence in the form of actual bodies within the restaurant and the catering to the tastes and hungers of these bodies in the form of the menu. The restaurants enact diasporic displacement in their overt claiming of difference, of Chineseness. They do offer their customers some sense, however problematic, of entering a space that is clearly not Euro-Canadian. It is a space that is identified as Chinese by both the Chinese and non-Chinese members of the community. What that Chineseness is, whether or not it is an accurate or authentic reflection of Chinese culture, is not the point. It is the very openness to interpretation, the very fact that these restaurants do not offer a static and authorial claim to Chineseness, that renders them as such fine counterpublic spaces. They do not constitute a republic of difference, but rather a counterpublic of uncertain and constantly negotiated differences. In this sense, they do not resolve the problem of home and homelessness for diaspora. Instead, they offer a crucial mediating space through which that problem can be staged and navigated.

Tam's installations stage and animate the Chinese restaurant as a counterpublic sphere. By taking her audience to a place that they already know, Tam asks them to reconsider what they do know about Chineseness, about hunger, about immigrant labor, about what it means to make a place even when one is displaced. Walking into one of Tam's Gold Mountain Restaurants is as much an experience of mild dislocation (you are in an art gallery that has become a restaurant that has become art) as it is one of emplacement. Her restaurants, and the process through which she constructs them, show how, as Warner suggests, a public can be "a poetic world making."[12] Her restaurants illuminate how the Chinese restaurants that are her inspiration can be a transformative, not merely replicative, space of circulation. It is the circulation of identities and difference that makes Chinese restaurants such a rich site for the kinds of relationships and interactions out of which diasporic culture is forged. Diasporas and diasporic cultures are not static objects of study. Let me suggest, though, that the other side of these diasporic practices, how diasporic people sustain and create relationships to the places in which they have found themselves is just as important. This chapter is an exploration of one example of such a process. So much emphasis has been placed on the relationship to the spaces from which diasporas have been dispersed and yet so much of the work of diasporic cultural survival depends upon the relationships diasporic communities build in the spaces of arrival. As an institution of small town life, and as an installation in contemporary art galleries across the country, Canadian Chinese restaurants are a diasporic counterpublic. They invite you to come inside, take a seat, look around, wonder, talk to someone, eat something, and engage in diaspora.

Key Terms

Counterpublic: A community that exists as a counter to a dominant or mainstream community.

Chineseness: Having qualities that can be identified as Chinese.

Canadianness: Having qualities that can be identified as Canadian.

Discussion Questions

1. What is the difference between a Chinese restaurant in a small town and Chinese restaurant in an urban space?
2. If a Chinese restaurant in a small town is a kind of community space, what does it mean to think of a private business as a space for community?
3. What makes a Chinese restaurant? The food? The people who cook the food? The people who eat the food? The décor? All of the above? If it is all of the above, is any one of these things more important than another?

Notes

1 Warner, Michael. *Publics and Counterpublics*, p. 118.
2 Ibid. pp. 120–121.
3 Ibid.
4 Ibid., p. 108.
5 Lee, Days. "Memories of a Chinese-Canadian Restaurant," p. 40.
6 Ibid.
7 Belu, Françoise. "The Empire and the Middle Kingdom, or the Dream Exchange," p. 16.
8 Lee, p. 39.
9 Belu, p. 17.
10 Ibid.
11 Belu, p. 17.
12 Warner, p. 114, emphasis removed.

Works Cited

Belu, Françoise. "The Empire and the Middle Kingdom, or the Dream Exchange." In *Gold Mountain Restaurant Montagne d'Or*. Montreal: MAI (Montréal arts interculturels), 2006. 8–20.

Fraser, Nancy. "Rethinking the Public Sphere: A Contribution to the Critique of Actually Existing Democracy." In *Habermas and the Public Sphere*, ed. Craig Calhoun. Cambridge, MA, and London: MIT Press, 1992. 109–142.

Lee, Days. "Memories of a Chinese-Canadian Restaurant." In *Gold Mountain Restaurant Montagne d'Or*. Montreal: MAI (Montréal arts interculturels), 2006. 37–49.

Warner, Michael. *Publics and Counterpublics*. New York: Zone Books, 2002.

20

TOY'S CHINESE RESTAURANTS

Exploring the Political Dimension of Race through the Built Environment

Hongyan Yang

Restaurant architecture, with its malleable physicality, connotes different cultural meanings, demonstrating the plasticity of race. This chapter explores the racial representations of Chineseness by closely examining the built environment of three Chinese restaurants in Milwaukee, Wisconsin that were owned by the Toy family. Scholarship on Chinese immigrants in the United States tends to focus mostly on populations living on the east and west coasts. Despite being smaller, the history of Chinese immigrants in the Midwest can be dated back to the late nineteenth century. The history of Chinese immigrants in Milwaukee has not received considerable scholarly attention despite its significance.[1] To enrich the history of Chinese immigrants in Milwaukee, this chapter traces the evolution of the built environment of three Chinese restaurants that were operated in different time periods: The Toy Building (1913–1946), Toy's Chinatown Restaurant above Walgreens (1938–1968), and Toy's Chinatown Restaurant on North Third Street (1968–1992).

With particular attention to the built environment, I conducted material culture analysis of the restaurants' historical photographs, postcards, and architectural plans. Other primary and secondary sources, such as newspaper archives and works of Chinese immigration and ethnic food histories, helped contextualize and explain the changes. I argue that the Toys' representations of Chineseness can be seen through the built environment, constantly changing in different time periods. The built environment of Chinese restaurants shaped and was shaped by the social issues of race as well as broader economic, social, and cultural contexts. This chapter highlights the significance of architecture in studying Chinese restaurant histories and how that can be done through tracing one immigrant family's restaurant businesses over time.

The Toy Building (1913–1946)

In 1913, a six-story building in downtown Milwaukee was constructed, which included a 300-capacity restaurant, a ballroom, and a 460-seat theater, as well as offices and living quarters. This building (see Figure 20.1) featured a Chinese architectural style and was reported as the largest and most luxurious Chinese restaurant in the world at the time. Green enameled terracotta—the conventional color of bricks in China—appeared throughout the building, except the two roofs. The three dormers on the top roof featured a Chinese imperial pavilion style. Additionally, there was a complete pavilion on top of the building. Reading up and down, from cornice to balcony, was a Chinese poetic couplet in Chinese characters: "Everybody welcome" and "Good time, good cheer." In the middle of the balcony on the fourth and fifth floors there was the shop sign proclaiming, "Shanghai Building."[2] Architecturally, the exterior of this building clearly distinguished itself from the other surrounding buildings.

At the restaurant's center, a bazaar featured silks, china, and other imported goods for sale. This $200,000 building was designed by Chicago architect R.T.

FIGURE 20.1 The Toy Building in 1932.

Source: Photograph courtesy of the Milwaukee County Historical Society.

Newberry. It was recorded that "the company Arthur I. Richards Co. arranged every detail from the very beginning, consulting Mr. Toy throughout, and the new building is a monument to the ability and taste of the members of the Richards company and of their fidelity to the interests of their clients."[3] Thus, the Chinese architectural features were reflections of both the owner Charlie Toy's wishes to display the Chinese culture and the western clients' curiosity towards the Orient. The luxury of the restaurant was beyond people's imaginations. It was a dream of Charlie Toy, who determined to erect a building that was not only the finest in the country, but in the world.

On March 22, 1913, the Toy Building was covered in an extensive story across five pages in *The Milwaukee Journal* (for an image of the first page, see Figure 20.2). The article, titled "Toy Building is Designed Like a Chinese Temple," noted it as:

> A veritable Chinese temple in exterior design, the building would attract notice and admiration anywhere. It is Chinese in every line, from the great green dragons which frown from the skyline at the top of its six stories, to the smaller dragons which guard the balcony of the restaurant floor and the entrance to the main stairway leading thereto.[4]

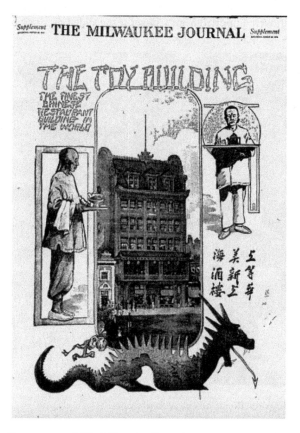

FIGURE 20.2 Cover page of *The Milwaukee Journal*.

The restaurant was located on the second floor of the Toy Building. The interior finishing also featured exotic Chinese cultural images and materials. Figure 20.3 shows that the golden dragon appeared on the principal posts and pilasters that supported the ceiling, creating a highly exotic experience. The paneled ceilings were elaborately enriched with filigree ornamentation. The teak wood tables were trimmed with mother of pearl. On the table, there was no western dining ware like knives and forks. All you could see was typical Chinese seasonings such as soy sauce in very ornate bottles, whose shape was similar to a fancy Chinese porcelain vase. The mosaic floor was also richly colored. The decorations of the whole second floor were recorded to have been arranged by Mr. Toy, including the wood carving and the hand-embroidered silk panels that were wrought in the highest style of Chinese art, and all done in China a year prior.[5] The light system was described as:

> The indirect system of lighting is used. A fine, soft glow is obtained by the use of mirror reflectors in fixtures designed from Chinese lanterns, the filigree part of the fixture being covered with Chinese silk in many colors. Bracket lights on the posts and panels, with glass bead and mirror effects, make a distinctive feature. There are also many elaborate lantern fixtures suspended from the ceiling which were imported from China for the added decoration of the room.[6]

FIGURE 20.3 Toy's restaurant on the second floor.

Source: Photograph courtesy of the Milwaukee County Historical Society.

Such luxurious finishing was not simply rich in wealth, but also rich in culture. The detailed decoration was also encoded with Chinese philosophy. One example was the Chinese apricot blossoms and bamboo that appeared in wood carvings, silk embroideries, paintings, and light fixtures. Apricot flowers symbolize noble qualities and represent luck. Bamboo is green all year round, which symbolizes immorality and good luck in Chinese culture. Another example is the peacock figures used in the panels of silk embroideries that covered the wall.[7] Although in western culture the peacock is sometimes personified negatively as one making a proud display of oneself, it represents fortune, peace, and happiness in Chinese culture. It is the incarnation of the phoenix in mythos, representing the harmony of Yin and Yang as well as women's beauty.

The performance stage is at one corner of the main dining room. The stage had the same carved fixture and silk embroidered panels as the dining room. The Chinese lanterns were hanging down to light up the stage. A band, consisting of seven white men, performed for the customers (Figure 20.4). The performance was broadcast through the radio program WTMJ, sponsored by *The Milwaukee Journal*, at noon, dinner hour, and midnight. The name of the artist and the song were noted on the back of the band's photograph: "Joe Gumin plays Jingle Bell in all languages." Joe Gumin is a well-known artist based in Milwaukee in the

FIGURE 20.4   The band on stage.

Source: Photograph courtesy of the Milwaukee County Historical Society.

1920s and 1930s. While listening to the available recording of this song online today, it is not hard to imagine the familiar festive atmosphere the band created for western customers to enjoy while eating Chinese food. This demonstrated the efforts of Charlie Toy to cater to the western customers' tastes and cultural comfort.

The Toy Building's evocations of Chinese culture, both on the exterior and interior, created an exotic yet comfortable attraction for native-born Americans. Gregory Filardo remarked about the Toy building, "Dining at the original Toy's restaurant was an exotic experience. As one might easily surmise from this picture, what with winged dragons crouched beneath ceiling beams as if to strike out the unwary guest."[8] Toy's public decorative architectural choices to resemble Chinese culture were shaped by his genuine adoration and preservation of Chinese culture. He also conveyed the importance of Chinese education to his descendants. He went back to China with his family in 1923 and 1937 to provide his grandchildren a chance to learn the Chinese language and culture. Three of his grandchildren, Elizabeth, Edward, and Marjorie attended college in China.[9]

Toy's adoration of Chinese culture was one important motivation for him to preserve it through the restaurant's built environment, but that was not the only motivation. His awareness of Americans' curiosity towards oriental cultures also led him to purposely exoticize the restaurant's built environment to fulfill the stereotype in Americans' eyes in order to receive attractions. In the eighteenth century, the American society had a romantic fascination with Chinese-style luxury artifacts, which were considered crucial to the formulation of a new American individual and nation. Although in the first half of the nineteenth century admiration for China decreased as a result of direct trading contact, Chinese products were still popular. Repulsive attitudes towards the Chinese rose around the mid-nineteenth century. Although the Chinese were not welcomed in American society, their cultural artifacts seemed nonthreatening and pleasing to the dominant culture. Despite American society's concerns with the Chinese labor issues, middle-class Victorian American families still highly valued Chinese artifacts. For example, they displayed Chinese porcelains and luxuries in their homes to convey social status and to distinguish themselves from the working-class immigrants.[10] The oriental imagination relied heavily on the Chinese goods circulated in the American market. In the 1870s and 1880s, popular culture became a way through which the western perceived the "orient."[11] Charlie Toy and the local architectural firm understood this social attitude towards Chinese artifacts, so they combined Chinese artifacts with familiar American musical settings. This created a new experience for the non-Chinese customers to consume the exotic oriental culture. What this exemplifies is a necessary balance of marketing Chinese and safe, familiar space for American consumers.

Toy's keen observation of Americans' fetish for Oriental objects helped his restaurant ironically survive the racist atmosphere in the late nineteenth and early twentieth centuries. At that time, anti-Chinese sentiment was prevalent on a national level. The Chinese Exclusion Act suspended the immigration of many Chinese laborers to the United States for ten years. Succeeding legislations extended this act until 1943. White Americans used derogatory and racist comments against Chinese immigrants. *The Annual Report of the Health Department of the City and County of San Francisco* in 1888 noted, "The Health Officer stereotyped the Chinese as dirty and the Chinatown in which the Chinese immigrants have been socially segregated is described as 'unfit for human habitation.'"[12] In the late 1860s and 1870s, the Chinese restaurants in San Francisco did not draw much attention from the American public even with elaborate food being prepared by the finest chefs from Canton. Influenced by the sentiments expressed in the *Chinese Repository* decades earlier, local Americans still considered Chinese food inedible.[13] Western descriptions of Chinese food in the late nineteenth and early twentieth centuries reported on indecent foods such as dogs, cats, and rats.[14] Milwaukee was no exception to this racism. Although Chinese immigrants were only beginning to arrive in Milwaukee in the 1880s, local society also witnessed strong anti-Chinese sentiment.[15] The growing racism in Milwaukee led to the violent anti-Chinese riot in 1889.[16] Charlie Toy's success shows us a different facet of racism: although hate and fear towards Chinese people based on their race was prevalent, Americans had racial fetishism towards their cultural artifacts such as Chinese food and built environments. He profited from western customers' fetishizing of the Orient by providing them with classy imaginings of China through the luxurious environment of his restaurant. He enhanced the visibility and cultural distinctiveness of the Toy Building with exotic exterior architectural features and interior finishing.

Toy's Chinatown Restaurant (1938–1968)

During the Great Depression, the bleak economic condition severely reduced Toy's import business, so he had to give up the Toy Building. The building was later demolished. He opened a new, smaller restaurant called Toy's Chinatown Restaurant that was located above Walgreens at the intersection of North Third Street and West Wisconsin Avenue. Most likely due to economic constraint, instead of purchasing the ownership, Toy chose to rent the second floor of the Walgreens Drug Store. In contrast with the previous building, the restaurant sign was barely noticeable; it was hidden on the first floor, displaying the English word "CHINA-TOWN" instead of the Chinese characters. The exterior of the building's second floor did not feature Chinese architecture like his previous restaurant. The Chinatown Restaurant merged indistinguishably into the building architecturally as a result of the disappearance of both Chinese characters and architectural features.

The reduction of Chinese architectural elements also affected the interior (Figure 20.6). It showed Toy's efforts to save money by doing minimal renovation. Except for the Chinese dragon featured between the wallpaper and ceiling, the dining setting at the new location was quite a standardized American dining place. The most noticeable new feature was the cutlery. Knives and forks were displayed on every table, with a combination of decorative, folded napkins at the center

FIGURE 20.5   Toy's Chinatown Restaurant in 1945.

Source: Historic Photo Collection/Milwaukee Public Library.

of the table. The soy sauce bottles and other seasonings containers did not feature decorative Chinese styles and were quite simple compared with the ones in the Toy Building. The plain-carpeted floor contrasted with the previous delicate mosaic floor in the Toy Building. This restaurant was demolished in 1968 because of downtown renovation and a new Federal Building slated for its spot.

The reduction of Chineseness in Toy's Chinatown Restaurant, both on the exterior and interior, is a reflection of economic constraints of restaurant businesses nationwide. During the Great Depression, restaurant businesses across the country struggled. Less expensive restaurants became the mainstream.[17] The bleak economy greatly influenced Toy's imported business and directly led to the Toy Building closing. Toy's second restaurant was not able to be as luxurious as the previous building perhaps because the economy was crashing and simultaneously people's desire to eat at such upscale restaurants reduced. In light of this, he chose to rent the second floor of the Walgreens building and used locally accessible standardized American furnishing and decorations, as importing Chinese artifacts would have cost more.

Toy's simplified Americanized dining setting was not only a reflection of his economic constraint, but also his social attitude towards the American culture. Although importing Chinese artifacts became more difficult during the Great Depression, the family chose not to utilize the Chinese artifacts from the previous Toy Building

FIGURE 20.6 Toy's Chinatown Restaurant above Walgreens.

Source: Photograph courtesy of the Milwaukee County Historical Society.

to manifest Chineseness. Instead, the family created a standardized American dining environment, which demonstrated their embracement of American culture and the changing diplomatic relationship between China and the United States. In the late 1930s and early 1940s, the image of Chinese Americans improved because of China's alliance with the United States during World War II. The United States and China became allies to fight against Japanese aggression in late 1941. It was also recorded that many Chinese Americans served a tour of duty in the American army forces during World War II to show their support.[18] The Toy family was also well represented in the War service. One of Charlie Toy's sons, three of his grandsons, and the wife of one of his grandsons served in the U.S. military.[19] The Chinese Exclusion Act was also repealed in 1943. The changing diplomatic relationship between the United States and China not only affected the restaurant, but also made it easier for Chinese property owners to coexist with white neighbors.

Additionally, Toy's choice in setting up a standardized, American built environment demonstrated his awareness of the social attitude towards ethnic cuisines on the national level. The Great Depression raised concerns over the dietary inadequacy American children faced. The concern about national strength and health drove the reformation of foreign foodways.[20] Besides, during World War II, the United States relied on mostly simple foods to survive food shortages with rations. Perhaps both influenced the Toy family's choice to present a more Americanized and simplified dining environment that the local customers found more comfortable.

Toy's Chinatown Restaurant (1968–1992)

Toy's Chinatown Restaurant continued to operate its business in a new location at 830 North Old World Third Street (See Figure 20.7) from 1968. The building stands today, but the space has been occupied by a Thai restaurant, The King and I, since 1992. This new location demonstrates the Toys' effort to revive Chinese architecture features but in a more subtle and culturally comfortable way. The overall figure of the building is similar to Chinese gate towers, which were often erected in China to mark entryways to major structures such as an official building, a temple or even a city. The restaurant's circular entrance is a Moon Gate, a traditional Chinese architectural element that can commonly be found in Chinese gardens. It represents joy and happiness in Chinese culture, and this kind of doorway marks the architecture as Asian for American observers. The gate creates a kind of ceremonial experience as customers enter the restaurant. Additionally, the pagoda style rooftops are Chinese in a more obvious way. These Chinese architecture features are still commonly found in Chinese restaurants in the United States today,

FIGURE 20.7 Toy's Chinatown Restaurant in 1984.

Source: Photograph courtesy of the Milwaukee County Historical Society.

showing the owners' efforts to demonstrate their cultural pride. While architecturally this building is nearly all Chinese, the restaurant sign was still in English, showing its dedication to welcoming the native born Americans.

The interior of the new location also featured design elements from Chinese culture, some having been saved from the original 1913 building. After walking into the restaurant, there is an octagonal lobby, which is the waiting area. The postcard below (Figure 20.8) shows that the octagonal lobby was guarded by a ring of multi-colored dragons staring down from the ceiling onto a stone-like patio floor. The taiji symbol on the ceiling represents the fusion of yin and yang, symbolizing the inclusion of everything to reach to a sublime stage. Posts in the lobby were Chinese red and sparkled with flecks of gold. Perhaps the Toy family was worried that the exotic octagonal lobby might be too strange for western customers. The first page of the restaurant menu greeted the customers:

> Honorable customers, welcome to Toy's. Be not afraid of the fire-breathing dragon on the menu cover; he is our Toy family symbol or chop mark ... We consider our dragon a symbol of our promise that you will enjoy the finest in Cantonese and American cooking during your visits.[21]

This demonstrated the family's awareness of cultural difference, which led them to maintain a careful balance between presenting the exotic Chinese culture and creating a culturally comfortable environment for the customers.

FIGURE 20.8 The Garden of 24 Dragons at Toys Restaurant 830 N Old World 3rd Street.

Source: From the Archives Department, University of Wisconsin-Milwaukee Libraries.

Much like the exterior of the building, the interior was markedly Chinese. The east and west walls of the dining area were adorned with heavy silken tapestry-like wallpaper imported from Hong Kong.[22] The architectural plan in 1968 shows the detailed decorations of the interior walls, which featured many Chinese cultural symbols. For example, the west wall of the main dining room showed the four Great Inventions from ancient China: compass, gunpowder, papermaking, and printing.[23]

Customers were fascinated by the Chinese atmosphere and cultural artifacts in the restaurant. The Toy family imported tapes from Hong Kong and aired oriental music in the restaurant. The decorations of the restaurant displayed the family's dedication to presenting Chinese culture:

> There are embroidered silk paintings from China, ceiling beams decorated in the Chinese fashion by artist Kurt Schaldach, beautiful wood carvings from the original Toy restaurant, massive Chinese lanterns, and even an ornately embroidered valance which was once the skirt around the bandstand at Charlie Toy's. A homey touch I hadn't discovered before was the first names of all the Toy Children in Chinese brush symbols on the ends of the ceiling beams. Laura Toy did the calligraphy for these.[24]

While dedicated to traditional Chinese culture, the interior also shows the new-generation Toy family members' nuances in displaying new Chinese culture. Charlie Toy's grandson Moy and Moy's two sons, Ernest and Edward, were in charge. While maintaining the value that Charlie Toy placed on Chinese culture, they showcased a lightened Chinese decorative style that exhibited the progress made necessary because of modernization. One newspaper article noted, "changing tastes are much in evidence . . . The exotically mysterious atmosphere of earlier Toy restaurants has been lightened. Teak and ebony fixtures are merely suggested in the new dining room."[25] In an interview, Ernest Toy explained the influence of modernization on the new decorative choices: "Once people were looking for atmosphere . . . we had hard teak wood chairs and marble top tables so ornately carved that you couldn't get your legs under them. Now people want comfort."[26] While the Chinese atmosphere was still highly appreciated by the customers, the balance between culture and comfort became more important in modern society. Due to the influence of modernization, the family made a conscious effort to combine tradition with modern tastes. The gleaming new kitchens had a Chinese stove, which was specially made in San Francisco to accommodate Chinese woks for traditional Chinese cooking. The new restaurant was a demonstration of what a modern Chinese restaurant could be like in America. Because Moy Toy and his two sons received an American education, we might see the nuanced decorative choices as their efforts to negotiate between Chinese and American cultures as well as between tradition and modernization.

The Toy family's exhibition of their cultural pride in this new era reflects another chapter of ethnic history in the United States, the beginning of ethnic revival.

Historian Donna Gabaccia noted this significant change in ethnic food history. She wrote, "the ethnic revival that began in the 1960s was a cultural and political reaction of long-time Americans against the Cold War and its intensely national- ist celebration of cultural consensus."[27] Ethnic groups began to undo the efforts of assimilation of the previous generations and started celebrating their cultural roots.

The change in immigration policy made the celebration of ethnicity possible. The 1965 Immigration and Nationality Act liberated the immigration of many eth- nic groups. Chinese from a wide range of backgrounds and regions began to enter the United States. This brought a variety of regional cuisines to the United States. Besides the mainstream Cantonese food, Chinese food in America expanded to include food from Szechuan, Hunan, Beijing, and many other regions of China. During the late 1950s and early 1960s, family-run American-Chinese and Can- tonese style cuisine became one of the most popular ethnic foods in the nation.[28] A survey in the 1960s shows that Cantonese food was the favorite gourmet food of thousands of Milwaukeeans and Wisconsinites. The popularization of Chinese food, on the one hand, provided a suitable environment for the Chinese in Milwaukee to actively express their cultural traditions; on the other hand, this no longer required the restaurants to use extraordinary exotic oriental features to enhance their archi- tectural visibility to attract customers. Chinese food had already established itself as a naturalized American culture. Carrying the love and nostalgia for their home coun- try all these years, the Toy family represented a subtle revival of Chinese culture in the built environment of the Toy's Chinatown Restaurant at the new location. Whereas the first restaurant fetishized and marketed Chineseness, this restaurant seemed to embrace the Chinese culture in more genuine and subtle ways.

Conclusions

This chapter shows that the Toys' representations of Chineseness through the built environment were not consistent, but changed based on the economic, social, and cultural contexts over time. The first restaurant shows us that when facing anti- Chinese sentiment in the late nineteenth century and early twentieth centuries, Charlie Toy—the first-generation immigrant in the family—catered to his western clients' classy orientalist imaginations of China through a luxurious built envi- ronment. He enhanced the visibility and cultural distinctiveness of the building, overly emphasizing Chineseness. The second restaurant above Walgreens—Toy's Chinatown Restaurant—went in the opposite direction, showing more efforts of the family in embracing the American mainstream culture and a reduction of Chi- neseness. The dining setting was quite a standardized American dining environ- ment. This could be attributed to a combination of multiple factors including the family's economic constraints during the Great Depression, Toy's embracing American culture, and the family's awareness of the national concern over foreign foodways. Quite different from that, the third Restaurant on North Third Street featured a revival of Chineseness, staging and celebrating the Chinese culture. This reflected the nationwide ethnic revival trend that began in the 1960s. Influenced by modernization and the popularization of Chinese food, the representation of Chineseness in the built environment appeared in a more subtle manner.

Through examining the built environment of three Chinese restaurants, this chapter enables us to observe the changing meanings of Chineseness in different time periods.[29] Architecture serves as a powerful medium through which the Toy family exhibited their shifting racial identities. Previous studies on Chinese restaurants and ethnic food histories have contributed to our understandings on how the social phenomenon of race affected ethnic food choices.[30] This study introduces an underexplored yet vibrant architectural aspect of Chinese restaurants. Besides the social environment, it shows that local economy, cultural perception, and the passage of time also influenced the racial representations in the built environments. The Toy family used buildings to tell us what it meant to be Chinese and how to visually represent Chinese restaurants in these contexts.

Key Terms

Built environment: Man-made structures, features, and facilities viewed collectively as an environment in which people live and work.

Material culture: The everyday mundane cultural artifacts that appear in buildings and landscapes. It is significant in revealing specific social mentalities and behaviors of groups in different cultures.

Racial representation: The portrayal of certain races through various mediums.

Discussion Questions

1. What are the roles of the built environment and other material culture in revealing the history of the Chinese restaurant and immigrant experiences?
2. How did Chinese restaurant owners choose to represent their identities based on their observations of the social environment and economic conditions?
3. How do you relate the making of Chinese restaurants to the social phenomenon of race, local economy, and many other factors?

Notes

1 David Holmes and Wenbin Yuan, *Chinese Milwaukee* (Charleston, Chicago and San Francisco: Arcadia Publishing, 2008), 7–57.
2 Ibid.
3 Unknown, "Toy Building is Designed Like a Chinese Temple," *The Milwaukee Journal*, March 22, 1913.
4 Ibid.
5 Ibid.
6 Ibid.
7 Ibid.
8 Gregory Filardo, *Old Milwaukee: A Historic Tour in Picture Postcards* (Vestal, NY: Vestal Press, 1988), 70.
9 Holems and Yuan, *Chinese Milwaukee*, 45–65.

10 John Kuo Wei Tchen, *New York Before Chinatown: Orientalism and the Shaping of American Culture, 1776–1882* (Baltimore, MD: Johns Hopkins University Press, 1999), 24–275.

11 Mari Yoshihara, *Embracing the East: White Women and American Orientalism* (Oxford: Oxford University Press, 2003), 8–9.

12 San Francisco Board of Health, *Annual Report of the Health Department of the City and County of San Francisco*, (San Francisco, 1888), 11.

13 Andrew Coe. *Chop Suey: A Cultural History of Chinese Food in the United States* (Oxford: Oxford University Press, 2009), 125–126.

14 Coe. Chop Suey, 24. Barbas, Samantha. "'I'll Take Chop Suey': Restaurants as Agents of Culinary and Cultural Change." *The Journal of Popular Culture* 36, no. 4 (2003): 671. Gabaccia, Donna. *We Are What We Eat: Ethnic Food and the Making of Americans* (Cambridge: Harvard University Press, 1998), 103.

15 Maurine Huang, "Chinese without a Chinatown," PhD diss., University of Wisconsin, Milwaukee, 1988, 90–92.

16 Victor Jew, "Exploring New Frontiers in Chinese American History: The Anti-Chinese Riot in Milwaukee, 1889," in *The Chinese in America: A History from Gold Mountain to the New Millennium*, ed. Susie Lan Cassel (Walnut Creek, CA: AltaMira Press, 2002), 77–90.

17 Marcello Signore, "The Great Depression . . . In the Kitchen," *Fine Dining Lovers*. May 19, 2011; available at www.finedininglovers.com/blog/curious-bites/great-depression-kitchen/

18 K. Schott Wong, "From Pariah to Paragon: Shifting Images of Chinese Americans during World War II," in *Chinese Americans and the Politics of Race and Culture*, ed. Madeline Hsu and Sucheng Chan (Philadelphia: Temple University Press, 2008), 153–172.

19 Charles Toy Manuscript Collections, MSS-1461, Milwaukee County Historical Society.

20 Gabaccia. *We Are What We Eat*, 124.

21 Restaurant menu; available at the Humanity Department, Milwaukee Public Library, Central Library.

22 Jay Joslyn, "A New Home for an Old Restaurant," *Milwaukee Sentinel*, November 30, 1968.

23 This information was obtained from the 1986 architectural plan of the restaurant, which is available from the City of Milwaukee Records Center.

24 Marian Hahn, "Toy's Chinatown Restaurant—A Three-Generation Success," in Box 1, Folder 7, Chinese-American Collection, Milwaukee County Historical Society.

25 Joslyn, "A New Home for an Old Restaurant."

26 Ibid.

27 Gabaccia. *We Are What We Eat*, 176.

28 John Jung, *Sweet and Sour: Life in Chinese Family Restaurants* (US: Yin and Yang Press, 2010).

29 Michael Omi and Howard Winant, "Racial Formation Rules: Continuity, Instability and Chang," in *Racial Formation in the Twenty-first Century*, ed. Daniel Martinez Hosang et al. (Berkeley, Los Angeles and London: University of California Press, 2012), 308–331.

30 To name a few studies: Liora Gvion and Naomi Trostler, "From Spaghetti and Meatballs through Hawaiian Pizza to Sushi: The Changing Nature of Ethnicity in American Restaurants," *The Journal of Popular Culture* 41, no. 6 (2008): 950–974; Donna Gabaccia, "Food, Mobility, and World History," in *The Oxford Handbook of Food History*, ed. Jeffrey M Pilcher (Oxford and New York: Oxford University Press, 2012), 305–323.

References

Barbas, Samantha. "'I'll Take Chop Suey': Restaurants as Agents of Culinary and Cultural Change." *The Journal of Popular Culture* 36, no. 4 (2003): 669–686.

Coe, Andrew. *Chop Suey: A Cultural History of Chinese Food in the United States*. Oxford: Oxford University Press, 2009.

Filardo, Gregory. *Old Milwaukee: A Historic Tour in Picture Postcards*. Vestal, NY: Vestal Press, 1988.

Gabaccia, Donna. *We Are What We Eat: Ethnic Food and the Making of Americans*. Cambridge, MA: Harvard University Press, 1998.

Gabaccia, Donna. "Food, Mobility, and World History." In *The Oxford Handbook of Food History*, edited by Jeffrey M Pilcher, 305–323. Oxford and New York: Oxford University Press, 2012.

Gvion, Liora and Naomi Trostler. "From Spaghetti and Meatballs through Hawaiian Pizza to Sushi: The Changing Nature of Ethnicity in American Restaurants." *The Journal of Popular Culture* 41, no. 6 (2008): 950–974.

Hahn, Marian. "Toy's Chinatown Restaurant-A Three-Generation Success." In Box 1, Folder 7, Chinese-American Collection, Milwaukee County Historical Society.

Holmes, David and Wenbin Yuan. *Chinese Milwaukee*. Charleston, Chicago and San Francisco: Arcadia Publishing, 2008.

Huang, Maurine. "Chinese without a Chinatown." PhD diss., University of Wisconsin, Milwaukee, 1988.

Jew, Victor. "Exploring New Frontiers in Chinese American History: The Anti-Chinese Riot in Milwaukee, 1889," in *The Chinese in America: A History from Gold Mountain to the New Millennium*, edited by Susie Lan Cassel, 77–90. Walnut Creek, CA: AltaMira Press, 2002.

Joslyn, Jay. "A New Home for an Old Restaurant." *Milwaukee Sentinel*, November 30, 1968.

Jung, John. *Sweet and Sour: Life in Chinese Family Restaurants*. US: Yin and Yang Press, 2010.

Kuo, John and Wei Tchen. *New York Before Chinatown: Orientalism and the Shaping of American Culture, 1776–1882*. Baltimore, MD: Johns Hopkins University Press, 1999.

Omi, Michael and Howard Winant, "Racial Formation Rules: Continuity, Instability and Chang." In *Racial Formation in the Twenty-first Century*, edited by Daniel Martinez Hosang et al., 308–331. Berkeley, Los Angeles and London: University of California Press, 2012.

San Francisco Board of Health, *Annual Report of the Health Department of the City and County of San Francisco*. San Francisco, 1888.

Signore, Marcello. "The Great Depression . . . In the Kitchen." *Fine Dining Lovers*. May 19, 2011. Available at www.finedininglovers.com/blog/curious-bites/great-depression-kitchen/.

Unknown. "Toy Building is Designed Like a Chinese Temple." *The Milwaukee Journal*, March 22, 1913.

Wong, K. Schott. "From Pariah to Paragon: Shifting Images of Chinese Americans during World War II," in *Chinese Americans and the Politics of Race and Culture*, edited by Madeline Hsu and Sucheng Chan, 153–172. Philadelphia: Temple University Press, 2008.

Yoshihara, Mari. *Embracing the East: White Women and American Orientalism*. Oxford: Oxford University Press, 2003.

AFTERWORD

E. N. Anderson

My first Chinese food, in my childhood in Nebraska, was chop suey out of a can. My first serious eating of Chinese dishes was done in Berkeley and San Francisco in the glorious 1960s. At that time, the vast majority of Chinese restaurants in the United States clung to chop suey (Cantonese *tsap seui*, "miscellaneous leftovers"), chow mein (*chao min*, "fried noodles), egg foo young (*fuyung tan*, "narcissus egg"), won ton soup (*won ton*, "original chaos from which the universe emerged"—a great description of the soup), and the other old favorites of a now-vanishing world. It was a more or less Americanized version of the food of the rural districts south of Guangzhou city. The people who ate in these "chop suey houses" were most often stalwart working men and women, Chinese or Anglo.

San Francisco's Chinatown then centered on Grant Street, known in Cantonese as *Tong Yan Kai*, "Cantonese Street." I discovered much more elaborate dishes and preparations, to say nothing of what we now call "fusion cuisine"—such as ginger ice cream and baked almond cookies.

Chinese food led me down a path to Hong Kong, where I did field work in 1965–66 and 1974–75 with my family. The restaurants there were even better than fame alleges; the best food was often in small, unpretentious, family places, or even street stalls, rather than the big "wine palaces" that got media attention. Here, again, there was fusion cuisine. One favorite of ours was dan ta (*tan ta*, "egg tarts"), a small custard pie originally from Belem, Portugal, which entered Cantonese cuisine via Macau, at that time a Portuguese colony.

I returned to an America just waking to the realization that Cantonese was not the only Chinese food. The first Sichuan restaurant in Los Angeles, the Chungking, opened in the westside, near where I grew up in Santa Monica. It had a good run until replaced by better ones. A Shanghainese restaurant opened on Wilshire Blvd. about the same time.

Today, of course, there are countless superb restaurants in Los Angeles and other large American cities, serving cuisines from all over China. The food is often indistinguishable from that in the homeland, and indeed some restaurants are branches of firms there. Riverside, where I have lived most of my adult life, was long a cultural laggard hosting only nostalgic chop suey houses. Now it has a Sichuanese restaurant and more upscale Cantonese ones.

Freeways in the 1950s displaced Chinatown from the area of the old city market in downtown Los Angeles to "New Chinatown" north of the freeway knot. After the United States opened Asian immigration in the 1960s, the Chinese business world of southern California jumped a couple of freeways and rapidly spread east into Monterey Park. Thence it spread steadily northward and eastward into the San Gabriel Valley, whose main drag, Valley Boulevard, is now lined for miles with Chinese restaurants and markets.

The time-honored restaurants serving cheap, filling food to a working clientele survive in small towns, especially old railroad towns, all over the United States. They are now often operated by recent immigrants from China or Taiwan, who sometimes shake their heads in amazement at what they are expected to cook. They learn to cook it in American style, but they often have more homeland-style dishes also. One restaurant within walking distance of where I write reveals a dramatic difference between dishes that will appeal largely to Chinese (these are cooked Hong Kong style) and dishes that appeal largely to Anglos (and are basically sugar, fat, and a scrap of protein).

In short, the always-adaptable Chinese cooks and restauranteurs have learned not only to vary their models at will, but to do so within the same restaurant when that is indicated. The result is an infinity of Chinese foods and foodways. Restaurants in heavily Chinese areas like Southern California's San Gabriel Valley all try to find a signature specialty or group of specialties. They hope to have the best *xiaolongbao* or noodles or stir-fried lamb in the area. They also routinely poach each other's chefs if the latter become well known. They range from tiny hole-in-the-wall noodle stands (which often have the best food) to enormous, richly decorated establishments that have huge aquariums to hold live fish. (But the diner should not assume that the cooked fish on the table come from those tanks. They sometimes come from cold storage instead.) Many of these places are jammed on weekend late mornings, as everyone in the neighborhood comes to drink tea (*yam cha*) and eat dim sum (*tim sam*). *Tim sam* literally means "dot the heart," i.e. "hit the spot"—with reference to giving ritual life to a statue of a deity by dotting the pupils of the eyes as a final step in painting it. Dim sum snacks give life to your heart.

In a world where life is increasingly harsh and unpleasant for many, and in some ways for all of us, it is more than satisfying to see this rapid development of superb yet affordable eating.

Chinese and Italians open restaurants wherever they go, and always seem to succeed (though the failure rate is actually quite high). This is partly a function of the high value on food and cooking in those cultures, and partly a function of business traditions. Restaurants are a traditional area of investment in both cultures.

Opportunities for learning the trade and getting help starting out are abundant. Large families ensure plentiful contacts, sources of loans, and other help. In Chinese society, any and all links are drawn on: old school ties, origin from the same village or province, similar experiences in work or travel, and so on. Also, and critically important, customers from those cultures expect to pay for their food. I have studied other cultures in which restaurant owning was a hopeless line of work because firm cultural rules held that friends and relatives of the restauranteur had to be fed for free, or at least at steep discounts.

In the present book, we have a number of excellent ethnographies of particular restaurants or restaurant traditions. Most are in the United States, but we learn that similar patterns existed throughout Latin America. I well remember the Chinese restaurants of Lima, Peru, found largely near the old city market. They were known as *sifa*, presumably from Cantonese *sik faan* ("eat rice") though no one is sure. They have gone through an evolution similar to those in the north.

The chapters give a number of thorough accounts of the use of family ties, old friendships, and other links in the rise and flourishing of restaurants. We learn how mutual support and mutual aid, within relationships of trust, can defeat all comers— how Chinese restaurants can survive the racism, discrimination, economic injustice, and unfair practices that a dominant society can inflict on minorities. Of course, they do not survive undamaged, but survive they do (at least the fortunate ones), and today Chinese restaurants of all scales and types flourish increasingly.

Several of the chapters in this book remind us that the process was not easy. In a time even more racist than our own, Chinese and their food were highly suspect. Even Mark Twain, who should have known better, speculated that there might be a mouse in each Chinese sausage. The Chinese were also said to eat cats, a slur previously cast on the Germans and other immigrants; most ethnic slurs seem to be recycled for any new group that comes along, possibly because racists are not the most imaginative of humans. The authors in this book have told stories of quiet heroism and tenacity that should make us all think, and perhaps wax more than a bit emotional.

Chinese-diaspora restauranteurs, like so many other immigrant and minority people, and like so many other dedicated restaurant owners of every background, persist through indomitable courage, good will, and adaptability. Every Chinese restaurant in the western world is another triumph over hatred and bigotry, and as such deserves our admiration and support. The authors of the chapters in this book have shared in that triumphal progress. They deserve close attention and careful reading.

INDEX

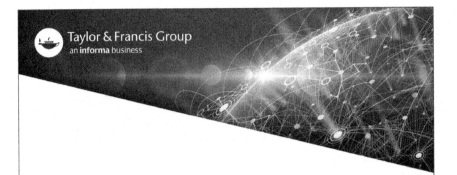

Printed in the United States
by Baker & Taylor Publisher Services